Decadence and Renewal in the Higher Learning

Decadence and Renewal in the Higher Learning

An Episodic History of American University and College since 1953

Russell Kirk

Gateway Editions, Limited
South Bend, Indiana

Manufactured in the United States of America

Library of Congress Catalog Card Number: 78-57067
International Standard Book Number: 0-89526-695-4

To T. S. Eliot, who in 1955 asked me to write such a book as this. "The communication of the dead is tongued with fire beyond the language of the living."

Acknowledgments

DR. WARREN FLEISCHAUER kindly read the first draft of this fulminatory book, and helped me to improve it, in his Johnsonian fashion. Mr. Henry Regnery, a publisher with imagination, also read the typescript and gave me valuable suggestions, as did Miss Deirdre Houchins. She and Mr. David Schock labored upon the index. Miss Teresa Hawes and Miss Kathleen Kielce did much to see this book through the press. A score of people, some of whom prefer to remain anonymous, provided me with illuminating anecdotes and pieces of mordant information. The twelve refugees who live with us at the village of Mecosta—ten Vietnamese, two Ethiopians—reminded me of how America's complacency in the higher schooling has failed us in foreign policy, as in much else.

I am grateful to The Historical Research Foundation and to The Educational Reviewer, Inc., for grants which bought me time to put this book together.

RUSSELL KIRK
Piety Hill
Mecosta, Michigan

Contents

CONTENTS

Prolegomenon: The Loss of an Object

F OR A QUARTER of a century, higher education in America has
been sinking lower. This book, of which the first part is
chronological in scheme, gives a mordant account of that decline. I have endeavored to express myself graphically, through
episode and vignette. In the latter part of the book, concerned with
renewal, I permit some cheerfulness to break in.

Since 1953, the year in which my chronicles commence, I have
written much about tendencies in American education. In my *National
Review* page, "From the Academy", I have written at least once every
month about this process. For thirteen years I touched upon it in my
syndicated newspaper column. I have discussed many textbooks in my
lengthy reviews for America's Future, Inc. My essays on colleges,
schools, and educational theories have appeared since 1943 in a congeries of periodicals, among them *The New York Times Magazine, The
Intercollegiate Review, Fortune, The Journal of General Education, Society,
Modern Age, Catholic Mind, Teachers College Record, Catholic World, Education, The Student Government Bulletin, Triumph, The Harvard Educational
Review, The Lamp, The Political Science Reviewer, Annals of the American
Academy, Law and Contemporary Problems, America, Imprimis, Social
Thought, Christianity Today, Prospect,* and *The Month*. For seventeen years
I have been editor of a small quarterly concerned with the higher
learning, *The University Bookman*. Also I have lectured upon educational subjects to more than three hundred university and college
audiences. Much of this speaking and writing has been woven into the
fabric of this book. My hope is to assist in the recovery of reason and
imagination in our higher learning.

My title has been chosen after deliberation. What does this word
"decadence" mean? My favorite definition is that by C. E. M. Joad, in
his book *Decadence: a Philosophical Inquiry* (1948). Decadence occurs, as
Joad tells us, when people have "dropped the object"—that is, when
they have abandoned the pursuit of real objects, aims, or ends—and
have settled instead for the gratifications of mere "experience." In

society, the characteristics of decadence are luxury, scepticism, weariness, superstition; also, in Joad's words, "a preoccupation with the self and its experiences, promoted by and promoting the subjectivist analysis of moral, aesthetic, metaphysical, and theological judgments." By this definition, the higher learning in America is decadent, having lost object or end—which point will be made clearer in the following chapters.

Well, then, from what has the American higher learning fallen away? What object did we drop? Strange though it may seem nowadays, time was when certain ends, classical and Christian, were acknowledged generally in American college and university. From the first, the American college prepared young people for certain professions; yet this training for a vocation was not itself the end of the higher learning. It is true that no one institution ever perfectly attained those ends, and that there has been much shoddiness on various campuses for a great while. Still, the existence of ends was recognized, once upon a time. Those ends or objects had been Plato's in the first Academy. According to Plato, the ends of education are wisdom and virtue.

Thus the higher learning, formerly, was an intellectual means to ethical objects. The disciplines of college and university were intended to develop a philosophical habit of mind, in John Henry Newman's phrase, "of which the attributes are freedom, equitableness, calmness, moderation, and wisdom."

With this high aspiration there was mingled on the American campus, from the first—and for that matter, at Oxbridge and the Scottish universities, too—a large element of professional training, for the ministry, teaching, the bar, the practice of medicine, and sometimes other vocations. But it was assumed that the ethical and intellectual disciplines must inform such professions, and that mastery of arts and sciences was not inconsonant with mastery of an occupation. The founders of American colleges and universities, and the great majority of professors, took it for granted that wisdom is objective, and that virtue is objective, and that the mission of the higher learning is to pursue these objects, whether through humane studies or through the learned professions.

It is otherwise now. I am not implying that we Americans began to neglect these ends merely a quarter of a century ago. Of course the process of falling away commenced long before 1953; my point is that we have suffered the practical consequences of dropping the object, since 1953. The old pattern was beginning to fall apart at Harvard College seven decades ago, when Irving Babbitt published his book *Literature and the American College* (1908). Babbitt's defense of academic leisure, in the final chapter of that slim book, suggests the understanding of learning's ends as they were perceived before the First World War—and as they still are perceived by some of us.

"Some of the duties that Plato assigns to his ideal ruler would seem to belong in our day to the higher institutions of learning," Babbitt wrote then. "Our colleges and universities could render no greater service than to oppose to the worship of energy and the frantic eagerness for action an atmosphere of leisure and reflection. . . . We should make large allowance in our lives for 'the eventual element of calm,' if they are not to degenerate into the furious and feverish pursuit of mechanical efficiency. . . . The tendency of an industrial democracy that took joy in work alone would be to live in a perpetual devil's sabbath of whirling machinery and call it progress. . . . The present situation especially is not one that will be saved—if it is to be saved at all—by what we have called humanitarian hustling. . . . If we ourselves ventured on an exhortation to the American people, it would be rather that of Demosthenes to the Athenians: 'In God's name, I beg of you to think.' Of action we shall have plenty in any case; but it is only by a more humane reflection that we can escape the penalties sure to be exacted from any country that tries to dispense in its national life with the principle of leisure."

By "leisure", Babbitt meant opportunity for serious thought and contemplation. On the campuses of 1978 there is plenty of opportunity for hustling or for idleness, but the claims of true academic leisure seem forgotten. Much more has been forgotten, too, especially the notion of the philosophical habit of mind. In 1952, Gordon Chalmers, then president of Kenyon College, foresaw most grave consequences to the person and to the republic, should higher education slide into technological hustling for some and into a lazy egalitarianism for others. Canon Bernard Iddings Bell, sometime president of St. Stephen's College, though dissenting from Chalmer's ideas in part, was gloomier still in his prognosis. And other voices, among them Robert Hutchins's, were raised in warning against the general drift of America's higher learning.

These vaticinations occurred about the time of our watershed year of 1953. Already university and college had been flooded with military veterans encouraged, regardless of talents, to enroll in college under the "G.I. Bill of Rights." Already, for the first time in the country's history, the number of students enrolled in state universities and colleges exceeded the number enrolled in independent institutions. That was in the green tree; now we are in the dry.

Nowadays, twenty-five years later, with campus enrollments generally static or declining, disillusion with the learning allegedly higher has become widespread—among students, among professors, among the general public. What went amiss? I set down below, tentatively, certain principal afflictions of American higher education during this past quarter of a century; I will touch upon these in some detail in later chapters.

First, purposelessness: loss of the objects of wisdom and virtue, the old ends of formal education. The place of these was usurped by confused conflicting claims and hopes: college as mere socialization and sociability ("an introduction to middle-class conviviality and middle-brow culture," Christopher Jencks puts it); college as boring means to job-certification; college as temporary sanctuary for the aimless and the neurotic; college as a huge repository of "facts" and specialized undertakings; college, presently, as refuge from military conscription; college as an alleged instrument for elevating the "culturally deprived" or "minorities"; college and university simply as an industry, employing hundreds of thousands of people at good salaries, supplying "research" services to the state or to private industry, furnishing public entertainment through quasi-professional sports and other diversions.

Second, intellectual disorder: all integration and order of knowledge in flux; the cafeteria-style curriculum, presently becoming the "open" curriculum; "discipline" reduced to a devil-term; the swelling empire of Educationism, formerly called pedagogy, with its frequent contempt for "subject matter"; the popularity of soft and often shallow "social science" degrees; the repudiation, by a growing number of professors and students, of the traditions of civility and of all concepts not born yesterday; the compartmentalizing of knowledge, leading at best to the development of elites unable to communicate one with another; the retreat of able or clever professors into "research", as distinguished from teaching; the substitution of ideological infatuation for the old philosophical habit of mind, particularly in the 'Sixties; and Joad's "preoccupation with the self and its experience", by contrast with the old concern of the higher learning for order in the soul and order in the commonwealth.

Third, gigantism in scale: the Lonely Crowd on the campus of Behemoth University. "It is not good to be educated in a crowd," wrote Lord Percy of Newcastle, rector of Durham University, about 1953—and he was thinking of English schools with a few hundred pupils. A crowd readily becomes a mob. Culturally rootless, anonymous, bewildered, bored, badly prepared for higher studies, other-directed, prey to fad and foible, presently duped by almost any unscrupulous or self-deceived ideologue, a great many of the students at Behemoth U. came to feel defrauded and lost; only the more stupid did not suspect that anything was wrong with their condition. "We don't want to be IBM numbers!" was the cry of the first wave of rioters on the Berkeley campus of the University of California, the "multiversity." Impersonal dormitories like slum tenements, blaring with television sets and hi-fis, became teen-age ghettos, the worst conceivable places for Babbitt's "atmosphere of leisure and reflection." I have touched upon these troubles in an earlier book of mine, *The Intemperate Professor* (1965); I will have more to say about them in this book. The effect of this inhumane scale upon professors and instructors, souring their tempers and frustrating their intellects, has been as disagreeable as its effect upon the rising generation—and perhaps more ominous.

Fourth, the enfeeblement of primary and secondary schooling, so that the typical freshman came to enter college wretchedly prepared for the abstractions with which college and university necessarily are concerned. The level of even functional literacy has been declining from a variety of causes, among them the triumph (now being undone, slowly) of "look—say" methods of reading-instruction over phonetic teaching, and the supplanting of books and periodicals by the boob-tube of television. An affluent society, luxurious, sceptical, weary, and superstitious, preoccupied with the self, victim of subjectivist analysis, no longer expected very much from public instruction except sociability and night basketball games.

With this drift coincided the ascendancy of the Instrumentalist theories of John Dewey and his colleagues in Educationalism, concerned chiefly with adjustment and some future egalitarian society, contemptuous both of oldfangled right reason and of prescriptive ways. The average teacher of the public-school apparatus had been badly taught himself, in high school and in teachers' college, and his pupils were automatically promoted and graduated. Despite the brummagem product of the schools of the 'Fifties, by 1953 most colleges and universities were ready enough to accept high-school graduates with a "C" average—and few questions asked; while America's general prosperity made it possible for a far larger proportion of young men and women, or their parents, to bear the increasing costs of spending some years on a campus—a phenomenon of mass enrollment in higher education never encountered anywhere before. Lest anyone be passed over for lack of money, presently governmental grants and loans were offered lavishly to practically any young person whose parents could meet, or evade, a means test.

Thus, in the prophetic rhetoric of Edmund Burke (so much reproached by Tom Paine for this), learning came to be trampled under the hooves of the swinish multitude. It is not possible to make scholars of teen-agers who have no proper foundation of school learning and who, often enough, feel understandably an aversion to classrooms, after thirteen years of compulsory attendance; it is difficult enough for a college to make of them even potentially useful employees.

Here I have chanted only some stanzas of the Iliad of our educational woes; more lamentations will be encountered in later chapters, but also some glimmerings of reinvigoration. I have suggested above some of the principal phenomena of the decadence of our higher learning. These have been proximate causes of our educational troubles; yet also they have been consequences of deep-seated misunderstandings of what the higher learning is all about. Those powerful misconceptions have not been peculiar to the United States of America: since the Second World War, they have been operating with equal force in Britain, Germany, France, and other countries. (These errors are even more saddening in Europe than in the United States, for in Europe there existed an older and more complex tradition of higher learning to break down.) I have in mind two fallacies particularly.

Fallacy I is the notion that the principal function of college and university—if not the only really justifiable function—is to promote utilitarian efficiency. The institutions of higher learning, according to this doctrine, are to be so many intellectual factories, delivering to society tolerably-trained young persons who will help to turn the great wheel of circulation, producing goods and services. For what is man but a producing and consuming animal? Modern society has a formidable burden of "welfare" cases, adult and juvenile: very well, let the colleges and universities produce more masters and doctors of "social work." Modern states require nuclear weapons of terrible power: very well, let colleges and universities produce more specialized technicians and "research scientists." Why this archaic muttering about "wisdom" and "virtue"—mere words? Who needs moral imagination? We won't buy that. Thus college and university grow more scientistic, rather than more scientific.

John Henry Newman encountered this mentality in the university before the middle of the nineteenth century. "The various busy world, spread out before our eyes, is physical, but it is more than physical," Newman said in reply to a pedant who would have expunged the spiritual and the humane from the higher learning; "and, in making its actual system identical with his scientific analysis, such a Professor as I have imagined was betraying a want of philosophical depth, and an ignorance of what a University Teaching ought to be. He was no longer a teacher of liberal knowledge, but a narrow-minded bigot." Amen to that; yet the Benthamite concept of the university has borne down most opposition.

To the masters of the modern nation-state, this utilitarian notion of the higher education is peculiarly attractive: the university and the college exist to "serve society" or "serve the people"—that is, to labor as bondservants to the political apparatus, whether in Soviet Russia or in these United States. Dante's exaltation of the university as a third authority in the world, equal to imperial power and to papacy, is forgotten except so far as it is utilized by ideologues who mean to use the university as an instrument for preparing their own path to political dominion.

Also this utilitarian notion seems congenial to the greater part of the modern public: for it promises practical success, good salaries and preferment for offspring, social mobility, the allurements of the snob-degree and the country club. Only when these promises go unfulfilled do the majority of citizens question the utilitarian hypothesis. The "service university" steadily has grown more servile for the past quarter of a century. In 1953, the president of a very large state university declared unabashedly, "There is no program to which this university will not stoop if the public seems to desire it." The more the higher learning stoops to satisfy this or that demand of commercial interest or of political expediency, the less time and money remain available for the university's genuine purposes.

Fallacy II is the notion that everybody, or practically everybody, ought to attend college. This misconception grows up from what Henry and Brooks Adams called "the degradation of the democratic dogma"—the extension of political forms to the realm of spirit and intellect. If higher education is a good thing for some folk, like lobster or air-conditioning, why isn't it a good thing for all folk? Why isn't the higher learning a natural right? Why isn't it free to all? There even have been recommendations by educationists that the higher learning, or at least two years of it (sometimes styled "the thirteenth and fourteenth grades") should be made compulsory.

This fallacy is bound up with what Ernest van den Haag calls "America's Pelagian heresy." In the fifth century, Pelagius argued that all mankind would be saved eventually, through natural goodness, without the operation of divine grace. The modern American, Professor van den Haag suggests, believes that all his countrymen will be redeemed soon, through formal schooling, without the operation of thought.

This illusion has propelled into college and university masses of young people who have very little notion of why they are there. To cope with these crowds of bored and unqualified "students", college and university must stoop very low indeed: they must make large concessions to the "counter-culture", many or most of their charges manifesting no interest in real culture. Sham courses and sham curricula are introduced, as busy-work—not very demanding busy-work—to suit the meagre aptitudes of the pseudo-students who will not study anything which challenges their intellects; for, as Aristotle wrote, true learning always is painful. Standards for admission and for graduation are lowered extravagantly, so that no one who bothers to enter a classroom occasionally will be excluded from the benefits of this learning, allegedly higher; "grade inflation" plagues even reputable old colleges and universities, for isn't one student as good as another, or maybe a little better?

The true student and the true professor are submerged in this academic barbarism, but the only escape for most of them would be to abjure the Academy altogether. Then what would they do with their lives, and how subsist? For both the political bureaucracy and the bureaucracy of business and industry demand a bachelor's degree, or a master's, or a doctor's, as prerequisite for the more satisfactory forms of regular employment.

Thus nearly half of the mass of American high-school graduates proceed to a year or more of "higher" education; nearly a quarter of the rising generation obtain, eventually, some sort of college diploma. A great many are schooled; very few are educated. And who recalls Alexander Pope's admonition that a little learning is a dangerous thing?

Fallacy I and Fallacy II, allied and intertwined, arise naturally, if banefully, from the soil of twentieth-century industrial democracy. The true higher learning is a garden plant, requiring nurture and protection. But if the Garden is not cultivated, soon we find ourselves in the parched Waste Land. This book is about the Waste Land of Academe nowadays, and about the Garden of intellect and imagination which still may be refreshed.

At this point, more than one reader may mutter, knowingly, "An Elitist!" Living as we do in an age of ideology, nearly all of us are tempted to believe that if we have clapped a quasi-political label to an expression of opinion, we have blessed or damned it; we need not examine that expression on its own merits. In educationist circles, "elitism" is a devil-tem, for isn't everybody just like everybody else, except for undeserved privilege? The degradation of the democratic dogma is fixed upon the mind.

But actually, I am an anti-elitist. I share whole-heartedly my old friend T. S. Eliot's objection to Karl Mannheim's theory of modern elites. I object especially to schemes for the governance of modern society by formally-trained specialized and technological elites. One of my principal criticisms of current tendencies in the higher learning is that, despite much cant about democratic university and college, really our educational apparatus has been raising up not a class of liberally educated young people of humane outlook, but rather a series of degree-dignified elites, an alleged "meritocracy" of confined views and dubious intellectual and moral credentials, afflicted by presumption, puffed up by that little learning which is a dangerous thing. We see such elites at their worst in "emergent" Africa, where the ignorant are oppressed by the quarter-schooled; increasingly, if less ferociously, comparable elites govern us even in America—through the political structure, through the media of communication, through the public-school empire, through the very churches. Such folk were in George Orwell's mind when he described the ruling elite of *1984*: "made up for the most part of bureaucrats, scientists, technicians, trade-union organizers, publicity experts, sociologists, teachers, journalists, and professional politicians. These people, whose origins lay in the salaried middle class and the upper grades of the working class, had been shaped and brought together by the barren world of monopoly industry and centralized government."

It is not at all my desire that university and college should train up such elites. What I am recommending in this book is a mode of higher education which can leaven the lump of modern civilization—which will give us a tolerable number of people in many walks of life who possess some share of right reason and moral imagination; who may not know the price of everything, but may know the value of something; who have been schooled in wisdom and virtue. I am suggesting that college and university ought not to be degree-mills: they ought to be centers for genuinely humane and genuinely scientific studies, attended by young people of healthy intellectual curiosity who actually have some interest in mind and conscience. I am saying that the higher learning is meant to develop order in the soul, for the human person's own sake. I am saying that the higher learning is meant to develop order in the commonwealth, for the republic's sake. I am arguing that a system of higher education which has forgotten these ends is decadent; but that decay may be arrested, and that reform and renewal still are conceivable.

The more people we have who are liberally educated and scientifically educated, the better. But the more people we have who are half-educated or quarter-educated, the worse for them and for the republic. Really educated people, rather than forming presumptuous elites, will permeate society, leavening the lump through their professions, their teaching, their preaching, their participation in commerce and industry, their public offices at every level of the commonwealth. And being educated, they will know that they do not know everything; and that there exist objects in life besides power and money and sensual gratification; they will take long views; they will look backward to ancestors and forward to posterity. For them, education will not terminate on commencement-day.

Once upon a time, said Socrates, men would accept truth even if it came from a stick or a stone; but now people ask you who you are when you presume to utter truth, and what may be your motives. So I set down here something about myself. My own adventures and misadventures in the higher learning will intrude from time to time, throughout this book, both because we ought to write about what we know and because my experiences in this domain, if not representative, at least have been variegated.

I was born almost literally in the railroad yards outside Detroit—fifty yards from the station, to be precise. My father was a locomotive fireman who had attended only primary school; my mother, who read poetry, had been graduated from high school. No one in my family, so far as I know, ever had attended a college — except for my grandfather on the distaff side, who had studied music for a few months at Valparaiso University.

The Great Depression descended upon us about the time I began reading newspapers, and it was not long before our cash resources were reduced to a twenty-dollar bill which my mother concealed in her copy of *The Light That Failed*. I attended our town's public schools, then sound. I went to college only because no gainful employment could be found for me during the Roosevelt Recession, and because, *mirabile dictu*, I won a tuition-scholarship to Michigan State College, a land-grant institution of which some account will appear in following chapters.

When I was graduated from Michigan State, hard times still lay upon the country. For lack of alternative, I proceeded to graduate study—at Duke University, which handsome institution conferred upon me a scholarship with a stipend of four hundred and fifty dollars, most of which went for tuition. I became a master of arts before America entered the Second World War; worked for a few months at the Ford Motor Company's Rouge plant; and then spent four years in the army.

While a sergeant in a desert, I wrote my first long essay about schooling. "A Conscript on Education", which was published in *The South Atlantic Quarterly* at the beginning of 1945. Glancing over this piece now, I find that I have not altered my convictions. The year 1944 was a time of what Benda called "the treason of the clerks." In America, then, their treason was against learning. The *clercs*, the intellectuals, seemed patriotic enough—super-patriotic, indeed. It was the life of the mind to which they were false. Those particular professors and writers and politicians are dead now, but they have their counterparts in this decade.

Professor George Boas, of Johns Hopkins, was very willing to sacrifice other people's educations and lives. "If training men in trigonometry and physics and chemistry, to the detriment of the humanities, will win the war, then for God's sake and our own, let us forget our Greek, our Latin, our art, our literature, our history, and get to business learning trigonometry and physics and chemistry," that professor of philosophy wrote. He was suffused with enthusiasm for one crowded hour of glorious life: "All the learning in the world", he declared of the soldier, "is not worth the experience which he will gain from his military career; and if he is killed, at least he will not have asked someone else to die for him."

The versatile and mercurial John Erskine announced then that the mechanization and technicalization of American education alarmed him very little. He did not dread the blows which the war struck at liberal learning—for, he implied, liberal learning mattered very little. Archibald MacLeish found it fashionable to declare that American intellectuals had betrayed America in her hour of need—by not being sufficiently zealous in the cause of killing Germans and Japanese. That energumen Harry Hopkins was particularly eager to crush the higher learning:

"Every college and university should be turned completely into an Army and Navy training center . . ." he wrote. "The women, too, should remain in college only while they are being trained for their part in the war effort.

"High school hours should be shortened so students will have more time to work, especially on farms. Some students should quit high school entirely. I can see no reason for wasting time on what today are non-essentials such as Chaucer and Latin. A diploma can only be framed and hung on the wall. A shell that a boy or girl helps to make can kill a lot of Japs."

Some educators looked upon this crisis and the anticipated postwar reorganization of the higher learning as a golden opportunity for federal renovation of America's educational muddle. James Bryant Conant and other university presidents viewed with rapture the munificent federal grants-in-aid proposed for veterans who might wish to attend college after Armageddon. Alexander Meikeljohn wrote in *The New Republic*, "The federal government should bargain with existing colleges for the education of young men and women in time of peace just as it is now bargaining for the education of soldiers in time of war."

Scribbling atop a sand-dune, with little lizards crawling over my pages, I replied to these gentlemen and scholars. I offered some criticisms of American education more mordant than those by these writers, but I concluded that their cure was worse than our disease.

"Is there virtue in federal money to reform a system of education?" I wrote in 1944. "Will not academic competition for public favor be supplanted only by competition for federal favor? What reason have we to suppose that the machine of state at Washington will have as much sympathy with liberal learning as have the regents of a state university or the directors of a private college? Significantly, federal grants for education thus far have been for vocational training. The more distant the source of the money expended, the more need a legislator or a director feels to justify his action as 'practical' . . .

"Can the federal organization be more discerning in education than are most of the intelligent citizens of this nation? The humanistic revival so recently gaining strength may be overwhelmed by a centralized utilitarianism. Here lies the great menace of this emergency to education of the future. Our need for speedy training of unusual numbers of men and women in technical skills for this hour of need may make us forget that man does not live by the lathe alone; and our overanxious desire to educate the discharged veteran, our blind faith in the efficacy of federal intervention, may make us forget that knowledge resides not in the state, but in the man. Regeneration of education must come from within; and it must be a training of men, not of units of manpower.

"Selfishness, pedantry, and folly in education, as in other concerns, can be remedied only by reformation of opinion, not by fiat. To institute a system of liberal learning, the man and the crowd must *believe* in a humanistic education; otherwise federal billions are of no avail. Criticism of our educational institutions by students and citizens and trustees and legislators, as individuals, can make schools worth attending and the new life worth leading. To resign the management of our educational programs to bright young men on the shores of the Potomac would be a betrayal of the intellectual trust which men of vanished ages have bequeathed to us.

"In this war, fought in the name of liberalism, very few think of liberalism of knowledge. We need an Epictetus to remind us that freedom of the mind is more important than freedom of the body. If our thoughts are not liberal, we shall not know how to rule, once we find ourselves the masters of the world's destiny. More important still, we shall find the taste of victory bitter, for the emptiness of our minds will be the more unendurable, once the hot excitement of battle has passed. The time has gone by when we were compelled to fight for our bread. Now when, at last, we have the leisure and the wealth and the power to spread knowledge and truth, we are in danger of turning to Mammon rather than to Minerva."

It seems to me that what I predicted in 1944 has come to pass nowadays. This book describes the process.

Promptly upon being discharged from the army in 1946, I was drafted into the department of the history of civilization at Michigan State College, potential instructors with masters' degrees from decent universities being then as scarce as they are now redundant. I taught classes with as many as a hundred students, while the bulldozers roared outside the classroom windows, clearing the ground for buildings to accommodate the new Lonely Crowd of Academe.

The usual pressures to obtain the doctorate being applied to us instructors at Michigan State when the flood of post-war enrollments diminished, I escaped from the empty drudgery of the usual American doctoral candidacy by going overseas to St. Andrews, the oldest of the Scottish universities. In 1952, I became a doctor of letters of St. Andrews. My second book, *The Conservative Mind* (my St. Andrews dissertation), appeared after I had returned to Michigan State. Being much published now, I might have risen in the Academy—publication, of whatever merit, being a sure road to advancement in the American university. Instead of accepting preferment, I resigned my post in 1953. My reasons for that decision are mentioned in the second chapter of this book.

Since then, I have subsisted chiefly as a man of letters, one of a dying breed: a mode of existence precarious for those not given to writing salacious novels. I have been visiting professor, over the years, at various colleges and universities, never lingering longer than three months consecutively on any campus; and I have lectured on more than four hundred campuses, I suppose, since my books began to be published. Thus I have been enabled to visit a wide diversity of institutions, and to judge them, I hope, impartially and independently. I have taught, on big campuses or on small, history, politics, literature, that vague subject "humanities", and some other subjects; I have edited two serious journals; I have been consultant to various educational foundations and publishers. Such are my principal qualifications for writing this book.

The swift passage of the years has left me rich only in doctorates *honoris causa*, wife and daughters, and friends. Having refused to run with the intellectual hounds of our time, or to ride the crest of ideological waves, I distinctly am not a member of that Establishment now so widely reviled. In educational theory and practice particularly I have been one of a forlorn and proscribed remnant—which I do not lament, being by nature a member of the Opposition. I have digressed at such length chiefly to suggest that my educational notions scarcely can be characterized as those of a Privileged Elitist or an Effete Snob. Judge them, if you will, by their independent merits or demerits.

Not long ago I spoke at a reputable liberal-arts college on the subject of the order and integration of knowledge. There came up to me after my lecture two well-spoken, well-dressed, civil graduating seniors of that college; probably they were "A" students, perhaps *summa cum laude*. They told me that until they had heard my talk, they had been unable to discover any pattern or purpose in the college education they had just endured. Late had they found me! Where might they learn more? I suggested that they turn, first of all, to C. S. Lewis' little book *The Abolition of Man*; then to Michael Polanyi's *Personal Knowledge* and to William Oliver Martin's *Order and Integration of Knowledge*. They went off in quest of wisdom and virture, of which they had heard little at their college, and I have not beheld them since. I trust that they have read those good books and have become members of that unknowable Remnant (obscure but influential as Dicey's real shapers of public opinion) which scourges the educational follies of our time.

This episodic history of mine is meant to attract more such recruits to that Remnant. There are no lost causes because there are no gained causes, T. S. Eliot wrote. Like the Seven Against Thebes, we educational renewers may be avenged by our children. In the realm of ideas, an Object that has been dropped may not be lost irrevocably.

Part One

Progressive Decadence

1

The Overthrow of Standards: 1953

A T THE NEWBERRY LIBRARY, in Chicago, during 1953, I participated in a conference of historians of universities, having
myself written a history of the university and town of St.
Andrews. One subject for discussion there was the influence of business and industry upon universities. Several participants offered
instances—mostly rather antique instances—of how captains of industry had endeavored to dictate what should be taught in universities. I suggested that nowadays the situation is somewhat different.

Whatever attempts may have occurred in the last century by "business" to control the curricula and the staffs of universities and colleges,
I said, nowadays such episodes are rare. Our trouble, instead, is that
the people who run universities, though called presidents and deans,
think of themselves as businessmen, often, and endeavor to apply
"business principles" to the higher learning. They talk of satisfying the
consumer—that is, the student, or the student's parents—and of cost
analysis; they think of the university as a species of factory, turning out
units efficiently; and their whole view is quantitative, not qualitative.

By 1953, it was clear that many university administrators were bent
upon increasing enrollments enormously, at whatever cost to academic
standards. Some of them said that they were yielding to popular
pressures. There was some truth in that, but the aggrandizing administrators helped to generate the pressures, deliberately, and cooperated
wholeheartedly in forced-draft growth of enrollments. Larger enrollments meant larger legislative appropriations, in the case of state
institutions; larger salaries for administrators; more posts available for
friends and proteges; the intoxicating consciousness of directing a Big
Business; and power, the *libido dominandi*. Bigness, they assumed, was

greatness. Also certain incidental plums fell to presidents and deans at swollen campuses: invitations to sit upon the boards of public utilities or other corporations, chances to speculate in real property most profitably as the value of land in the university's vicinity began to increase. The bigger an industrial corporation, the more successful it is, right? Then the bigger a college is, the better it must be. I do not think that I exaggerate the cast of mind of a good many educational administrators in 1953.

During the Second World War, campus enrollments had fallen greatly, what with the conscription of nearly all able-bodied young men. After victory in Europe and Asia, young veterans poured into college and university, all their costs defrayed by the Veterans' Administration. Never before, anywhere, had there been so vast or so sudden an expansion of the higher learning. But after four years or so, the majority of veterans had been graduated, and enrollments commenced to shrink again. What to do, with all the new jerry-built facilities available, and college staffs swollen? Why, go out and find boys and girls to replace the veterans—young people who ordinarily would not have gone to college: *recruit* them. Ever since, at practically every university and college in this land, the military term "recruitment" has been applied to the gathering-in of students. Time was when students entered college because they wished to learn something or other; after 1950, they must be dragooned; and if their talents were not suited to oldfangled collegiate studies—why, the college would mend its ways and alter its curricula and reduce its standards to suit the tastes of the recruits. Competition for "students" with little taste for study has been a principal cause of the present academic decadence; even the better universities and colleges were forced into this degrading search for warm young bodies, whatever the quality of the minds in those bodies.

The jamming of colleges with veterans provided an initial excuse for waiving requirements of aptitude and preparation among freshmen. Then, some college and university administrators indulging a latent passion for confounding quantity with quality, many colleges endeavored to maintain enrollments at their 1946–1950 peak by giving permanence to the standards of emergency—thus admitting a crowd of young people of the sort that would not have been admitted before 1942. In the beginning, this affection for swollen enrollments was confirmed to administrators; the true professors, overworked and exasperated by the apathy or the incompetence of the new student body, would have been happy to have returned to the quieter days of 1930 or 1940. But gradually the administrators won over to the cause of aggrandizement a large number of the professors. Salaries, they insisted, would not rise until enrollments rose; nor would promotions be frequent; and, after all, what did it matter? If the president and the deans were willing to break with tradition, how could a mere inefficient professor presume to object?

By 1953, at possibly the majority of American institutions of higher learning, the process of lowering standards was well advanced. The degradation was elevated by its apologists to the dignity of a principle. The authors of *Higher Education for American Democracy* (1947), a turgid document more generally known as the "Report of the President's Commission on Higher Education", had urged educators to admit a vastly larger proportion of young people, at whatever cost, in the name of "democratic living."

Here and there, a college courageously defied this tendency; now and then, the head of an institution—President Dodds of Princeton, or President Chalmers of Kenyon—analyzed the fallacies of this growthmanship; and at every university or college, no matter how far advanced this disease of adulterated learning, there remained at least a few professors of liberal learning or scientific knowledge who strove to arrest this manifestation of Progress. Their situation, on some campuses, became increasingly difficult. Were they fighting a rear-guard action? they began to ask themselves. Or were they, in reality, already prisoners in the academic concentration camp, mocked by administrators and educationists and most of the students? If their own consciences were not trouble enough, presently the hierarchy of the university itself often began to scowl upon them because they had not yet surrendered themselves to the wave of the future—because they clung obdurately to some tattered notions of academic dignity and decency.

Such was my situation at Michigan State College, in 1953, I being then a member of the staff of a "general education" scheme called the Basic College, within MSC. Having been an undergraduate at Michigan State for four years, I entertained no high-flying notions of what academic standards there had been or could be. It was a representative land-grant college, originally of "Agriculture and Applied Science", rightly overshadowed by the University of Michigan at Ann Arbor. In my student years, MSU was a dull campus, but genuine enough in its way. When I was a senior, in 1940, there had been six thousand students; by 1953, there were some fifteen thousand. An institution of even six thousand students cannot well be a real academic community; yet until 1940 the place had been pleasant enough, if somewhat stupid. Most of the students, except for those who had dropped out during the freshman year, had some sort of scholastic or vocational interest, and pursued those with tolerable diligence. Upon the College's faculty were some men of ability: I learned much from one of them, John Clark, in the department of English, who now lies in an unmarked grave at Cameron, Missouri. He taught courses in the history of criticism and in critical writing, and—what was very rare among the professors of MSC—his work was published in national magazines. I associated principally with him and with some other members of the staff; such personal relationships between professor and student, though virtually impossible nowadays on the mass campus, being not altogether unusual in the 'Thirties. In those years, we undergraduates had not been assigned IBM numbers.

Michigan State then suffered from the deficiencies of intellect and tone described in such memoirs of state universities and colleges as Thomas Griffith's *The Waist-High Culture* (1959) and Simon O'Toole's *Confessions of an American Scholar* (1970). Still, standards and traditions of a sort existed. These slid down to dusty death with the flood of enrollments after the Second World War.

MSC's Basic College had been established to cope with those swollen enrollments. Its purpose being to educate the ineducable, it labored from the first under grave difficulties. Here I describe its failure, and my own ineffectual resistance to the degradation of it, not because the Basic College *per se* was of any importance, but only because the Basic College of MSC was sufficiently typical of the collapse of standards about 1953.

This college within a college was supposed to provide a system of general education for all students enrolling at MSC, regardless of what school—arts and sciences, engineering, business, agriculture, and the rest—they might intend to enter presently. Initially, six departments made up this undertaking: history of civilization, written and spoken English, literature and fine arts, physical science, natural science, effective living (!), and a board of examiners. In fact, this "general education" was not much more general than education had been earlier at Michigan State, because all students always had been required to enroll in certain courses in English, history, and the sciences—as well as foreign languages, a branch of learning omitted from the new program. The champions of the Basic College declared, however, that these new course would give a broader view of each discipline; and the system was put into operation over the protests of the professors of languages, mathematics, and of other fields who believed that this Basic College was part of a cheapening process, spreading knowledge perilously thin.

From its beginnings, the Basic College suffered from certain serious defects of organization and method, which can be touched upon here only briefly. Most departments attempted to do too much and succeeded in doing little; this, however, possibly might have been remedied with experience. There was a tendency to substitute facile generalizations for the imparting of a genuine body of knowledge. More serious still was the influence of the board of examiners, a body of educationists who made up the "comprehensive" or term-end examinations almost independently of the several departments concerned, and who were dedicated to "objective" tests—that is, standardized multiple-choice questions, put to students in great numbers in a short space of time, and calculated to encourage the conditioned response of the indoctrinated mediocre student rather than the considered judgment of the earnest student. As it became apparent to the students that they were not expected to write, and scarcely to read, but only to attend lectures and set down check-marks to indicate the doctrines preached by their instructors, a subtle feeling spread among them: the conviction that the Basic College was merely a boondoggle or racket, to be endured if one must, to be escaped so soon as one might; and their performance fell far short of their abilities, limited though those abilities often were.

Yet the Basic College—which paid relatively good salaries—had on its staff some people of principle, and these contended against the degradation of the democratic dogma, hoping that in time they might be able to improve the methods of the College.

But no improvement occurred—*au contraire*. Early in 1952 a reorganization was carried out; yet this was a reorganization which intensified existing faults. My own department, for instance, formerly styled "history of civilization", was renamed "humanities", with a syllabus commencing, "Humanities is . . ." The new dean of the Basic College, formerly a professor of education, imposed upon the staff an iron-bound system of grading, under which the final examination for each term was prepared by a board of examiners; and under which the individual instructor was required to make half of his tests "objective" and to give the grade of "A" to at least seven per cent of his students, and that of "F" to not more than five per cent, with other grades similarly fixed. The several departments were compelled to draw up classroom programs that would provide for every instructor saying substantially the same thing as his fellows on the same day, lest they "teach different courses."

In March, 1953, many of us were startled to learn that a further lowering of standards was intended. Although Michigan State then boasted an enrollment scarcely less than its post-war peak, the administrators clearly were eager to expand at a great pace, so that the College would be ready for more than seventeen thousand students by 1960, twenty-five thousand by 1965, and more than thirty thousand by 1970.

A range of immense flat-roofed dormitories was built at the western end of the campus, very like so many cell-blocks. Now how were young people to be persuaded to fill these dormitories? One way for a college to solve this "recruitment" problem is to make studies easier and more entertaining and less demanding, so that more young people will wish to enter and fewer will have to depart because they cannot read.

Those of us who believed in some standards in American education were sure that this fresh proposal to lower the system of grading was calculated to fill these new dormitories. This was denied by the dean with such heat that we were more convinced than ever. At a staff meeting of the Basic College, the administrators brought forth a mass of statistics, calculated to demonstrate that the standards of the Basic College already were higher than those of some other state universities in the Middle West, and higher than those of the upper schools at Michigan State—and that, therefore, the standards of the Basic College ought to be reduced.

In point of fact, these statistics were erroneous, and the interpretations placed upon them inconsistent. But the shocking thing, to those of us who still believed that a state college has a duty toward the state and ought not to squander public funds, was that deans and heads of departments actually could propose to lower standards in order to "keep in step" (their phrase). Their constant apology was that somehow the Basic College, too toplofty for its own good, had got "out of step" and must now conform to the allegedly general (and therefore commendable) lowering of standards of educational performance in America.

Most of the staff engaged in teaching knew but too well that real standards in the Basic College, whatever they might be relatively, in any absolute sense were dismally low. And in private, certain responsible persons with a voice in the administration—the head of my own department among them—conceded that there had occurred a sad decline in students' work during the few years since I had been an undergraduate myself. In open meeting, the opposition to the de-grading proposal was candid. A cynical colleague of mine, nevertheless, as each opponent of the scheme rose to speak, whispered, "He's a full professor" or "He's a single man." With but one exception, the outspoken critics fell into one or the other of these categories; and the displeasure of the administrators at such opposition was unmistakable.

"Do you feel better now that you've made your Patrick Henry speech?" inquired the dean, patronizingly, of one of the more able critics.

Yet the administration contrived to persuade the members of the staff, at departmental meetings during subsequent months, to accept the changes. American professors, never an heroic crew, are susceptible to small pressures. At the general meeting in spring term, the reduction of grading standards was accepted. All instructors thereby were required to give ten to fifteen per cent A's, twenty-five to thirty per cent B's, forty to fifty per cent C's, ten to fifteen per cent D's, and zero to five per cent F's. Anyone who had known what previous standards had been in the Basic College now became aware that it had been made next to impossible for a student to fail to obtain credit in a course, if only he would condescend to put in a classroom appearance at intervals; and any small sign of moderate talent would be rewarded with the grade of A, a procedure admirably calculated to lead small talents into imagining themselves large ones.

During that summer, I had opportunity to consider what decent course of action was open to me; and, having decided that I could do more for the forlorn cause of American education by opposing this movement from without than by compromising with it at Michigan State College, I sent my resignation to the head of my department. It was answered by a civil note from him, in which he observed that this was "the logical, and, indeed, the honorable thing for you to do," in view of my lack of sympathy with the Basic College's tendencies. I had stated in my letter that the students, because of the enforcement of educational fallacies, were verging upon illiteracy; that the instructors more and more were being treated as base mechanicals, mere operators of slide-projectors and givers of standardized tests; that the influence of the board of examiners, divorced from real acquaintance with the difficulties of schooling young people in any sound discipline, was baneful. This letter of resignation was not answered by the dean or any other official of the College, except my departmental head; an embarrassed silence prevailed for some weeks.

When my resignation was accepted officially by MSU's governing board, in October, a reporter from the student newspaper came to inquire my reasons for resigning, which I gave to him, though in a statement milder in tone than had been my letter of resignation. The public-relations director had informed journalists that I had quitted my post to "pursue a literary career." At that time, a representative of *Time* magazine was visiting campuses with a view to writing a feature about the alleged intellectual progress of "cow colleges" that had successful football teams. *Time* having recently devoted the whole of its book-review section to a book of mine, this journalist asked to be introduced to me, but was told that no one knew where I might be found (the writer being unaware that I had resigned), and was urged to converse with the head football coach instead.

When my real reasons for resigning appeared in the student paper, the administrators professed to be surprised—though my letter of resignation had been in their hands for some weeks—and employed their public-relations apparatus to end their silence with a wave of vituperation, somewhat amusing. One administrator declared that I had "got in with an aristocratic crowd"—a notion deserving a carica-ture by Max Beerbohm; he went on to direct me to go lecture at some small college, "and teach a handful of rich men's sons, but it is our duty to educate every one we can. That's what the people of Michigan want."

Across the alley from my rooms in a decayed house, as I read this, I noticed a line of sleek convertibles belonging to students, presumably the proletarians whom Michigan State was redeeming. The ugly fact remained that standards *had* been lowered deliberately—a nasty topic conspicuously ignored by the administrators in their angry replies to me.

Thomas Griffith, in *The Waist-High Culture*, writes that "any univer-sity whose president and regents make the simple, radical resolve to seek quality, and who resist all efforts from any quarter to debase it" may approach the achievement of Harvard: "For it is in providing college education that is less than it might be and poorer than it need be that the indulgent curse of mediocrity in American life begins. . . . Is it really sound democratic dogma that everyone shall have a higher education, even if quality suffers and in the process the most gifted are stunted because their best is not required of them? We deceive our-selves if we think we do not diminish what we provide. Never in the history of the world have so many people had a college education, and never perhaps has there been such a proliferation of the second-rate. The trouble in education was once that too few could enjoy it; but such a hardship may in time prove less disastrous to society than to have a people educated to the belief that they are not ignorant, and too complacent to know—as the ignorant once knew—that they are miss-ing something."

Such a judgment probably would have been incomprehensible to Dr. John Hannah, president of Michigan State College in 1953—indeed, president of Michigan State from 1941 to 1969. Hannah's doctorate was honorary, conferred upon him by Michigan State when he as-sumed that institution's presidency; his earned degree was that of bachelor of science in poultry husbandry, from the same institution. But he had married the daughter of the preceding president of MSC, had been elevated to the dignity of secretary to the College's governing board, and had succeeded to his father-in-law's majesty. Hannah travelled over the face of the United States, and later of the world, urging young persons to enroll at Michigan State because a college graduate earns more money than do those unfortunates who don't enter college—a dangerous half-truth. John Hannah will appear later in these pages, though not because of his learning (once, in a public address, he referred to the female novelist George Eliot as "that great man") nor yet because of his standing with other university presidents—though he had his emulators. Rather, the face of John Hannah will reappear because he represented the educational spirit of the age—materialistic, self-seeking, woefully deficient in imagination, confounding quantity with quality.

The chapters which follow this one are vignettes of a quarter-century of blundering—although here and there men of learning and principle have survived as university and college presidents. The days of indiscriminate "educational" expansion seem to be passing away now. What may be salvaged from the debris of the higher learning—why, that question will be examined in the second part of this book.

2

Academic Freedom: 1954

N EARLY EVERY CAMPUS in America, at the time I departed from Michigan State College for my ancestral house a hundred miles to the north, was resounding with disputes about "academic freedom." Those were the times when Senator Joseph McCarthy was something of a power in the land, and the loud fuss as to whether there were Communists on the campus—and, if there were, whether they should be permitted to teach—obscured other questions of academic freedom, particularly the relationship between academic standards and the liberties of the academy.

For five years I wrote annual lengthy articles on the subject of academic freedom for *Collier's Year Book*, and in 1955 I would publish my book *Academic Freedom: an Essay in Definition*. Whatever the relative merits of arguments on either side of these heated controversies, it seems to me that these struggles, with their verbal ferocity or hysteria, were evidence that the higher learning in America decayed. Increasingly politicized, the academic community was sinking into academic collectivism.

A few days after my resignation from MSC had been announced, the local chapter of the American Association of University Professors met. A well-known colleague of mine arose to ask that the chapter take some action concerning, or at least investigate, the conduct of MSC's administration toward Russell Kirk. But a young professor of social sciences objected, "This isn't important. Let's get back to talking about the right of Communists to teach." So they did. Probably there were then no Communist members of the faculty at Michigan State

College—which made this discussion perfectly abstract, perfectly safe, and yet an opportunity to display one's devotion to the cause of absolute freedom.

Throughout the country, much of the excitement about academic freedom had no closer relationship to reality. During 1954, the national committee on Freedom and Tenure of the American Association of University Professors dealt with 165 cases of alleged violations of academic freedom—which, after all, was no vast increase over the 122 cases which had been taken up by that committee during 1945, well before anybody had heard of Joseph McCarthy. Almost all of these 1954 cases were concerned with political opinion—generally with charges of membership in the Communist party, or of affiliation with other radical or subversive organizations, or of refusal to cooperate with legislative investigators looking into such concerns. It is worth noting that in 1954 and 1955, however, the AAUP did not formally censure any university or college for disregard of academic freedom—and had not so censured any institution since 1949.

The outcry about Senator McCarthy's inquisitorial methods drowned out most discussion of the freedom of the professor as related to the decline of academic standards. Yet the degree of academic freedom which any educational system can maintain depends upon the general soundness of that educational structure. If the professor is a half-educated man, intoxicated by his small share of learning and convinced that he has the duty of imposing his private convictions upon his students; if the student, ill-grounded and unable even to read and write with accuracy, is open to every wind of doctrine—why, then free exchange between senior scholars and junior scholars does not function well. The professor, the presumptuous "intellectual", becomes the secular indoctrinator, and the student becomes his dupe.

This question of the links between academic standards and academic freedom is connected with what Professor Harold Clapp called "the stranglehold on education." By that phrase, he meant the domination of American schooling by the doctrinaires of "education for democracy", folk much influenced by the ideas of John Dewey (who also had been the chief founder of the American Association of University Professors). In general, these disciples of Dewey, especially powerful in departments of education, were advocating in 1954 and thereafter a massive quantitative expansion of institutions of higher learning, with small respect for long-established intellectual disciplines or for the schooling of the more able young people.

These egalitarian concepts, opposed both by the defenders of traditional liberal learning and by others who believed that democracy would be weakened, rather than strengthened, by a lowering of standards, provoked bitter disputes. The AAUP and similar bodies, nevertheless, were reluctant to take up such subjects. Nor did such questions come to the attention of the public nearly so often as did political disagreements within university and college. No well-organized group sustained the protesters against educational aggrandizement.

During 1954, the only case of academic freedom as related to academic standards to receive much attention was that of Dr. Frank Richardson, at the University of Nevada. In 1953, President Minard Stout of that university had dismissed Professor Richardson, tenure or no tenure, because of his opposition to the lowering of entrance requirements and to abrupt expansion of the university's campuses. President Stout had been sustained unanimously by the regents of the University, who concurred in Stout's vexation at Richardson's having distributed to other faculty members copies of an article entitled "Aimlessness in Education", by Professor Arthur Bestor of the University of Illinois. Incidentally, Stout had been principal of a high school before ascending to his throne at Reno, and the subject of his doctoral dissertation (in education) had been "The Administration of the Extra-Class Activity Finances in Iowa High Schools during the School Year of 1941-42."

This story had a happy ending in 1954. Unanimously, the Nevada Supreme Court ruled that the University's regents had exceeded their authority and violated their own tenure-policies by expelling Dr. Richardson on such grounds. Returning from Hawaii, Professor Richardson resumed his duties in the department of biology. Later the Nevada legislature investigated Stout's conduct of university affairs, and Stout was compelled to resign his presidency. He soon obtained a post in federal educational administration.

This was a signal victory, but such triumphs for the champions of decent educational standards were few indeed during the 'Fifties. All passion was spent upon the alleged "reign of terror" ushered in by Senator McCarthy.

Speakers at the national convention of the National Education Association, during the summer of 1954, asserted that disapproval of "controversial subjects" was tending toward a "sterile education", that "the American teacher has voluntarily censored herself" out of fear of reprisals, and that "it's not bad to be afraid, but to accept it as normal is dangerous." Dr. Robert M. Hutchins, writing in *Look*, declared that American teachers were afraid to teach. President Harold Taylor of Sarah Lawrence College insisted that attacks on intellectual freedom were becoming more frequent and more successful, producing a timid-

caused fear
in teaching

ity, or even a paralysis, "in social thought and creative work." Professor Henry Steele Commager, in his *Freedom, Loyalty, Dissent*, denounced anyone who should insist on absolutes in education, and argued that the people of the United States were being subjected to a stifling orthodoxy.

But there were other voices. Professor Sidney Hook, in much a disciple of John Dewey, in his *Heresy, Yes; Conspiracy, No*, published late in 1953, denied forthrightly that any such general atmosphere of repression had developed in consequence of the disapproval of Communists in educational institutions. A close examination of the principal dismissals of Communist sympathizers and of professors who had taken refuge behind the Fifth Amendment, in 1954, bears out Dr. Hook. My own close study at the time persuaded me that few scholars and teachers worthy of their calling were overawed by administrators or legislators in the dispute about subversion and radicalism.

Robert E. Fitch, dean of the Pacific School of Religion, writing in *Commentary* (October, 1954), agreed with Professor Hook that most of the fervent professions of alarm at a "reign of terror" on campuses were no better than hysteria. "Those who are frightened are always a mysterious 'they'—a certain professor, a particular journalist, an actor, a preacher, a research scholar, a librarian. Certainly it is not Harold Taylor who is afraid, nor Henry Steele Commager, nor Robert Hutchins, nor Professor Lehmann, nor any other of the spokesmen listed." This continual twittering about being bullied and spied upon, he continued, seems to be the mark of a bad conscience, in many cases: a device to quiet or shout down one's own misgivings over flirtations with collectivism not very long ago.

"One may acknowledge in secret that one has been in error," Dr. Fitch went on, "and one may have actually moved on to new ways that are clear and clean. But it is impossible publicly to confess to error, then or now, so the intelligentsia believe, rightly or wrongly. So they take another course: any criticism of one's conduct, any allegation of grave mistakes of judgment, is to be met with outraged cries about the violation of civil liberties and the attack on integrity of conscience. This shabby kind of performance we have surely witnessed more than once. It springs from a deep instinct of self-preservation within the breasts of the intelligentsia. For there is one sin to which the professionally intelligent person may not confess without losing caste, without shearing off his own self-respect and the respect due him from others—stupidity!"

What really ails the liberal intellectuals, Dean Fitch suggested, is that, for all their clamorous insistence upon being allowed to pursue the truth as they like, actually they have ceased to be acquainted with truth. Corrupted by a pervasive relativism, they have asked, with Pilate, "What is truth?" — and have not stayed for an answer. "Could it be," Fitch asked, "that, if they lack the courage of their convictions, it is because they no longer have any great convictions?"

Aye, the loss of an object: that deficiency lay beneath the timorousness and the shrill complaint "Look, I am afraid to speak out!" so painfully common among liberal professors in the 'Fifties. Academic freedom is a peculiar privilege, possessed by the scholar and the teacher because they are presumed to be dedicated men, members of what Coleridge called "the clerisy", men who believe that there exist abiding truths superior to the ephemeral quarrels of the hour. When the scholar and the teacher lose that conviction or vocation, then the crowd will not consent much longer to confirm them in their old freedom. The debate over academic freedom in 1954 suggested, among other things, that a number of eminent professors conceived of academic freedom as merely license to say whatever they pleased to whomever they pleased; to conduct a perpetual debate without ever aspiring to ascertain any values, after the manner of the old Sophists. This was no good omen for the future of the Academy. It was as much a symptom of decadence as were the swollen enrollments. Permit me to expatiate.

The disease of our time, Edmund Burke said of his own era, is an intemperance of intellect. That is quite as true in the modern time of troubles. An intemperance of intellect, which Burke called "the cause of all our other diseases", provokes extreme views about academic freedom. Ideologues of various persuasions have been attempting to convert the higher learning into an instrument for "social reconstruction" or for "remaking human nature" or for "realizing the American Dream." These endeavors are inspired by an intemperance of intellect—the intoxication of trying to transmute wisdom into power. The freedom of the Academy, so far as that freedom is endangered today, can be preserved only if we hold fast to the principle that the ends of education are wisdom and virtue; or, to put it another way, that the higher learning is intended to work upon the individual human reason and imagination, for the person's own sake. The Academy gained its peculiar freedom because the Academy was temperate. If the Academy is blown about by every wind of doctrine, filled with professors who are intent upon power rather than upon wisdom, eager to adore the gods of the market place—why, then the Academy will have lost its principle of temperance; and, temperance wanting, will lose its freedom.

Every right is married to a duty. That duty which corresponds to the right of academic freedom is that the scholar must be dedicated to the conservation and the advancement of the truth. He must be the guardian who reconciles permanence and change, and the active thinker who remembers the wisdom of our ancestors. If, failing to fulfill these responsibilities, he becomes a secular propagandist, an ideological indoctrinator, a man in love with power, then he falls derelict in his duty, and he loses his sanction for his peculiar freedom. He must be a temperate man of intellect, in short; and though he ought to hold steadfastly by his principles and ought not to be a mere trimmer to the breezes of the hour, still he ought to remember that, by his vocation, he has forsworn the lust after power. If he wishes to be an ideologue or a sophist, he should take himself out of the academy into the market place.

A gentleman with much experience in our universities observed to me that a good many professors really are not interested in academic freedom, however great an outcry they may set up concerning an alleged threat to their right of free expression. What such professors mean, when they say "academic freedom", is academic power. What they desire, in their heart of hearts, is to obtain the power to bend their colleagues and their students to their own will. We are all of us, or almost all, too fond of power. But the scholar is a man who professes to have given up the claim to power over men in favor of the service of the truth.

This is an old problem in academic freedom, and we never will see the end of it. In recent decades, the form which this intoxication with power assumed, in America and western Europe and elsewhere, was the infatuation of some professors with Marxism, or at least with some form of collectivistic ideology. I think that, despite its occasional recrudescence on this campus or that, the Marxist fad will wane in the Academy; it cannot survive the testimony of men like Solzhenitsyn.

Yet this does not mean that the friends of academic freedom can ignore the menace to freedom presented by Leninism or Maoism. We live in a time when the fountains of the great deep are broken up, and freedom is a garden plant, easily inundated. Therefore the Academy especially should remain upon its guard against the energumen who would use his position in the Academy to subvert the moral and social order which gives him and his colleagues the freedom to speak their minds.

I believe that academic freedom should extend to the furthest limits consonant with the preservation of human dignity and all the benefits of the civil social order. But when certain persons in the Academy abuse their power and proceed to sneer at human dignity and the whole fabric of order and justice and freedom, then the license of those persons justly may be curtailed. The question is one of prudence. If the academic violators of academic freedom are numerous, or subtle and strong in influence, or successful in conspiring against the Academy itself, then we ought to restrain these violators and restore the Academy to its true guardians. If the Academy fails in this, then society at large, in self-defense, may invade the Academy and conduct the cleansing—which would become a hasty and indiscriminate cleansing.

Although the theory of academic freedom prescribes no especial form of politics, still it enjoins a decent respect for the institutions of the society in which the Academy flourishes. And Communism does not hold that decent respect, any more than did Nazism, or than do various ferocious forms of nationalism. I do not mean that we should remain ignorant of Marxism or of other modes of social totalism; in this era, ignorance is a feeble protection. Yet it does not follow that the friends of academic freedom can know Marxism only by securing academic tenure for Communists, any more than we can understand Nazi ideology only if we appoint Nazis to endowed chairs. Because church-related colleges teach Christian brotherhood, it does not follow that in deference to academic freedom they should appoint a Jew-baiter or a Black Panther to teach racial hatred, that we may be "fair to both sides."

When, in 1956, a special committee of the AAUP declared that Communist professors ought to be tolerated on campuses, "so that they may be checked by open discussion," there replied, in the pages of *Commentary*, Professor Paul R. Hays, vice-chairman of New York's Liberal party. He mentioned that some professors had been stampeded by cries of "McCarthyism" into "grotesque misrepresentations of the contemporary status of academic freedom." Of the special committee's argument that Communists ought not to be excluded from campuses, he wrote, "It seems scarcely necessary to point out the absurdity of the notion that you have to have Communists teach the nature of Communism, since this 'Relevant General Principle' is unlikely to fool many of the professors or to lead to widespread demand for Egyptians to teach Egyptology or homosexuals to teach homosexuality."

Aye, the Academy, if it is to enjoy rights, must acknowledge some principles of truth, and not constitute itself as a mere sophistical debating-society, doubting everything, sneering at all old convictions. The Academy sins if the Academy places falsehood on the same platform with truth. And when college or university offers instruction in a subject, this implies that some truth may be found in the discipline. If the rising generation already could perceive every difference between truth and falsehood, the rising generation would not need to enter the Academy at all. By treating Communism, or some other fanatic ideology, as entitled to have its ferocious say, the Academy would give political madness implicit sanction.

Many aspects of the sound and fury about academic freedom, in 1954, were disheartening. But the most saddening was the spectacle of certain professors, with tenure, good salaries, and all the benefits of a constitutional order, implying that Communism was quite as worthwhile as any other form of social organization. Let us not discriminate against the votaries of Lenin and Stalin; "let's not be beastly to the Hun." That is what Burke called a licentious toleration. The objects of a decent society have been known for a great while, within and without the Academy: they are order and justice and freedom. But the persons whom Sidney Hook called "ritualistic liberals" had dropped those objects, and so were decadent, and involved the Academy in their decay of reason.

3

Behold Behemoth: 1955

"THE PROBLEM OF THE AGE," John Henry Newman had written in 1841, "is the education of the masses, and literature and science cannot give the answer." That still was the problem of the age in 1955. Religious understanding, Newman had known, lics at the heart of education. At Behemoth State U., in 1955, religious knowledge was thrust into a cubbyhole, when tolerated at all. For that matter, humane letters and theoretical science, so much trusted by Newman's adversary Sir Robert Peel, languished in a sunken state at Behemoth State.

Yet Behemoth State U. claimed to be educating the masses. Great expectations, greater snobbery, and the florid exhortations of academic empire-builders were luring or thrusting a large part of the American population into college and university. As yet the baby-boom from the swollen birth-rate of the Second World War period had not reached the colleges, but the bulldozers were paving the way for that wave of boys and girls.

Approximately two million, eight hundred and thirty-nine thousand students enrolled at universities, colleges, and "higher" schools of one sort or another, in the autumn of 1955—an increase of more than a hundred thousand over the preceding year's enrollment. This was about one-third of the total number of people in the United States between the ages of eighteen and twenty-one: a proportion higher by far than that in any other country, ever, to proceed beyond secondary schooling. The federal Office of Education predicted a further increase amounting to thirty-six per cent of all young people during the next decade—which would mean an enrollment of more than three and a half million by 1965. Approximately fifty-five per cent of the

1955 enrollment was in state or other public institutions, and forty-five per cent in independent or "private" institutions; the public colleges had increased more rapidly since the Second World War. Indeed, the independent institutions actually had declined in number, although not in total enrollments. Some educational administrators predicted that as many as one-third of the independent colleges would have vanished by 1965; these prophets generally were officials of state universities and colleges. President Coons of Occidental College rebuked them: "Some public university spokesmen speak as if they were supremely confident of the outcome in their favor. They should be warned against arrogance and pride." Dr. Coons was more nearly right than were his adversaries, as matters turned out; but nevertheless many independent colleges would shut their doors during the following decade.

The costs of an American college education, although rising steadily since 1900 in a moderate curve, had not increased in proportion to the increase of incomes in the country. From 1940 to 1955, average family income increased by a hundred and fifty per cent; while cost of attending college increased by only seventy-five per cent. (This would be atoned for later.) Much of this relative reduction in costs had been achieved by sacrificing the interest of the college teacher, and also often sacrificing the quality—or at least the individuality—of instruction. The average college instructor of 1955 had far more students than his counterpart had faced a generation or two earlier; while the instructor's income, it was said, had increased only one-sixth as much as that of the average American. (In part, this balance would be redressed later, too.) The increased work-load and the relatively-decreased income—this in a century which had seen the working-hours of manual laborers decreased by as much as fifty per cent—of the college instructor doubtless was one reason for the shrill bitterness which lay behind the academic-freedom controversies discussed in my preceding chapter.

These statistics suggest that the quantitative growth of higher education had been achieved at the expense of quality. And even the statistics of quantitative growth do not serve as accurate measurements of accomplishment. Of the one thousand, eight hundred and forty-seven "institutions of higher learning" listed by the Office of Education, only some six hundred and fifty were "senior" colleges or universities. More than eighty per cent of all students in 1955 attended institutions with an enrollment exceeding a thousand—with some consequent loss of the community and companionship of the oldfangled liberal-arts college. The greatest increases in enrollment had been enjoyed by the junior colleges, teachers' colleges, and technical institutes, rather than by universities and liberal-arts colleges. And among the latter, standards varied immensely, from the sober intellectual disciplines of the University of Chicago to institutions comparable to the "people's universities" of Sweden.

It did not follow that all the good professors were in the reputable universities, and all the incompetent ones at institutions of small repute. Some famous universities had their backs against the wall, financially, in 1955, so that an instructor who might have preferred to teach at a Jesuit university, say, found himself far better paid at one of the mushrooming community colleges. The educational world was turning upside down.

American higher education in 1955 was experiencing what some educators called "the rising tide" of expectations, a tide submerging long-established disciplines and patterns. That tide would continue to rise, in most of the country, for fifteen to twenty years longer.

The liberal-arts colleges suffered most in this topsy-turvy era. Liberal education, for Newman and many another, had meant the examined life, the rearing of free men, the ethical preparation for leadership, the development of a philosophical habit of mind. The American liberal-arts colleges, whatever their shortcomings, had retained some bond with the old disciplines which taught what it is to be fully human. They had retained some idea of the primacy of the idea of Justice—as Josef Pieper put it, "that the educative efforts of a people should primarily aim at forming the young generation, especially those called to leadership, into just men."

But by 1955, there was reason for suspecting that most colleges were doing less to teach young men and women to examine their own lives, or to participate in the wisdom of their ancestors—over which our present preening rationality is no better than a film upon a deep well. There were financial causes for this, but also intellectual and moral causes. For any institution to endure, there must be faith and purpose in it. Whether a good many of American colleges still professed any faith or acknowledged any purpose was open to question in 1955. It is still more open to question nowadays.

To some people, prescriptive faith and purpose are repugnant. Growth for growth's sake; progress, even though no one knows toward what—these ought to be the aims of an educational establishment, according to these neoterists. In this vein, Herold C. Hunt, Undersecretary of Health, Education, and Welfare, proposed to address the annual meeting of the Association of American Colleges in 1955. As chance or providence had it, Mr. Hunt was unable to attend; but copies of his prepared talk were distributed, and the Lord delivered one into my hand.

"The Liberal Arts: the Years Ahead" was the title of Hunt's address. One is familiar with the patter of the evangels of Progress: "In this modern world of incessant change," etc., etc. The Undersecretary indulged in some of this patter.

Are our colleges, he asked, "to stand steadfastly resisting change? Or are they to respond to the massive pressure of the cultural shift?" Whether that shift was good or bad, or in what it consisted, Hunt did not vouchsafe to say. All we ought to try to preserve, he went on, is the *essence* of liberal training, "liberality", not the "unimaginative worship of a traditional concept." He was amused by an extract from the Cincinnati *Western Review*, 1820, and quoted it:

"Should the time ever come when Latin and Greek should be banished from our universities and the study of Cicero and Demosthenes, of Homer and Virgil, should be considered as unnecessary for the formation of a scholar, we should regard mankind as fast sinking into an absolute barbarism, and the gloom of mental darkness is likely to increase until it should become universal."

Now I was less amused than was Herold Hunt by these vaticinations of 1820. Although the names of Cicero, Demosthenes, Homer, and Virgil might mean little to the Undersecretary, they did mean something to me: they meant, in part, justice, liberty, order, piety. Are we so much cleverer than the men of 1820—let alone the Ancients? Has not much of the world indeed sunk into barbarism or savagery, the decay of tradition playing its malign part in this decline? And if we are to substitute something novel and progressive for the classics, or for the literary and historical studies which remain the core of the liberal-arts curriculum, just what is this brave new program to include? Perhaps it will emphasize "Non-Western Studies", an omnium-gatherum boondoggle coming into vogue about 1955. Undersecretary Hunt gave no clue, however, except to murmur faintly some phrases about training for leisure time and to quote General Sarnoff on the "amazing changes" in electronics and atomics.

Now I am convinced that by 1955 the American college had been drifting for a long while toward a vague desire to make young people (in the Undersecretary's phrase) "creators of a better world rather than precision parts in an existing world." Moreover, this amorphous humanitarianism, though it had badly damaged the old disciplines, had created no decent curricula to replace them. The unpleasant insecurity of many colleges by 1955 was produced, in part, by this very lack of form and purpose.

The dean of Columbia University Law School, in his report at the end of 1955 to the president of Columbia, suggested that many of our liberal-arts colleges seemed to be teaching next to nothing. They were devoted neither to the Undersecretary's detested "unimaginative worship of a traditional concept" nor yet to creating bright new things bent upon making a perfect world. (Just how it is possible to create a brave new world without knowledge of the past, I never have learned.) Their program of studies, the dean implied, was principally slush. Their graduates often were ignorant not merely of classical literature, but of American history, government, political economy; they could not read swiftly or comprehendingly; many of them did not even know how to use a dictionary. They were thoroughly unfit to begin the study of law (which study then was joined to the hard realities of Herold C. Hunt's deplored "existing world", rather than to dreams of Cloud Cuckoo-Land.) Seventy per cent of an entering class in the Law School had not studied English history. (We are discussing, mark you, a well-reputed graduate school of law, not tyros of engineering or home economics at Dismal Swamp A. & M.) Less than half of this law-school class had enrolled in any course in American history above the freshman level.

Undersecretaries of HEW notwithstanding, I venture to suggest that through a vague desire to "adjust to perpetual change", our colleges, or many of them, have made it most difficult for us to reconcile the permanent things with the demands of the fleeting moment; they have made it most difficult to maintain our existing civilization. For the function of truly liberal and scientific education has been to leaven the lump of the civil social order with persons of disciplined intellect and ethical understanding, acquainted with the best that has been said and done in the past. In the name of an ineffable "new liberality", we have been condemning the better minds and hearts of the rising generation to feed upon a mess of pottage, very thin gruel.

There was pottage aplenty at Michigan State, East Lansing—by 1955 converted into a *university* through act of legislature. (Thus commenced the national process of restyling land-grant colleges or agricultural colleges "universities", often virtually duplicating the names of the old state universities, and provoking bitter competition for funds and students between the once-ascendant state universities and the newly-dignified agricultural and normal schools. With all this there came waste of money and duplication of programs—and competitive lowering of standards, to secure the larger enrollments.)

Michigan State had a handsome campus, wooded until it became covered with new buildings—first "modified collegiate Gothic", then international, or featureless, style. By 1955, MSU's enrollment stood at some sixteen thousand students—the eighth largest establishment of higher education in America, then, and the oldest and biggest of the land-grant colleges subsidized by the Morrill Act of 1862. Some fifty million dollars were expended on buildings during the decade after the Second World War, and an equal sum was to be spent during the five or six years after 1955.

This increase in numbers and wealth—Michigan State being one of hundreds of agricultural schools, teachers' colleges, and technical institutes then turning into something different from what their founders had meant them to be — brought with it severe problems. Does such an institution, on assuming the name of university, take on the traditional responsibilities of university education? Michigan State had no schools of medicine or law, and a graduate program feeble generally. The tendency of most of these newly-expanded institutions was to emphasize "service to all", rather than liberal and professional disciplines. The very scale of such places, originally designed to be simple, easily-administered units, has tended to hamper intellectual growth.

At MSU, in 1955, one dormitory-complex under construction would lodge four thousand students when completed: a teen-age ghetto. The vast dining-halls were a far cry from the oldfangled college dormitory, but in effect they wiped out the little eating-houses of East Lansing's commercial district, previously places where professors and students could gather to talk. At either end of the vast dormitory-lounges, television sets kept the students from the need of ever again being alone in the chilly realm of intellect. Business-machine methods of registration, testing, and grading vitiated the old professor-student relationship. Students' numbered identity-cards were replacing even proper names. And the intelligent professor at such institutions, as Gilbert Highet has remarked, often finds himself a prisoner, not a philosopher.

When a lowering of degree-requirements had been pushed through the graduate school of MSU in 1954, the dean had found it necessary to reply to charges of debasement of standards. "Don't use that word!" he had entreated. "Say we are extending the opportunity!" The opinions of some members of the faculty were expressed by one of the better-known professors, commenting on President Hannah's first talk to the faculty in fall term, 1955: "The President gave a prodigious prognosis in his talk of all the buildings we're going to have. He wants to get the best brains he can to supervise the buildings and blueprints. He also told us to plug for a unified sewage system for East Lansing. After an hour and a half of this, he said in the last thirty seconds, 'We are interested in good scholarship here.' "

Already MSU boasted of courses in fly-casting and curricula in packaging, but progress would not end there. The annual Report of Progress at the University declared, "The literal-minded may ask us to be specific—to define the tasks, to describe the boundaries of this dedication. To them, we must reply that by its very nature, a university cannot set a limit on its mission, or define its objectives exactly . . . . We cannot rest content with the past or present, but must forever press forward . . ."

Or, in other words, the object had been dropped.

Some people were so obdurate as to question this meliorism. A professor of English at the University of Detroit wrote to me that year, "Did you see the glad announcement that Michigan State will offer in February a course for five *graduate* credits in how to drive a car safely? The descriptive blurb has much jargon about highway problems and the modern age of wheels and gears; but nothing could disguise the complete intellectual bankruptcy of this flourishing Benthamite colossus." When this letter reached me, MSU's lobbyists were at work beseeching the legislature for more bricks and mortar: a new College of Education, a new College of Engineering, a new College of Business and Public Service, a new Basic College.

After the Second World War, the oldfangled university president gave way to a new species of academic energumen. The oldfangled president often had been a scholar of sorts. The newfangled president, at many universities and colleges, was a high-powered administrator, "a good businessman." His public-relations people called this sort of president a good businessman, anyway, though often he had no real experience in commerce or industry, and they did not explain why he preferred the Academy to the Market Place. Several remarkable specimens of this new class were present at the sixty-ninth meeting of the Association of Land-Grant Colleges and Universities, convening at Michigan State University in November, 1955.

The president of Michigan State University was himself a notably successful "businessman" president, though experienced in the business of bureaucracy. He had been a member of the international advisory board for President Truman's Point Four program, and for some months, in the Eisenhower administration, had been assistant secretary of defense for manpower. (These "manpower" people have done considerable mischief to the higher learning, on either side of the Atlantic.) Soon he would become chairman of the United States section of the permanent joint board on the defense of the United States and Canada, supposed to provide for our Arctic outposts. Later, for a dozen years, he would be chairman of the United States Commission on the Civil Rights—though for the first ten years of his presidency at Michigan State, literally the only "black" employed on the campus had been a pleasant and deferential middle-aged colored man who was President Hannah's errand-boy, carrying mail from office to office.

As university president, Hannah was an Eisenhower type—Dwight or Milton, either. I never met him. During his interim as president of Columbia University, while waiting to become Great White Father, General-President Dwight D. Eisenhower had ruled the university by chain of command (like Minard Stout, at the University of Nevada), and was not to be approached by mere professors. Once the Metropolitan Museum, being unable to get in touch with President Eisenhower of Columbia, besought one of the more distinguished of Columbia's professors, Dr. Carleton Hayes, diplomat and historian, to approach the General on the Museum's behalf. Professor Hayes was repulsed at the outer defenses: he was told, after some inquiry into his credentials, that he might have an appointment with President Eisenhower, as a special favor, some months in the future. "No, thank you," said Dr. Hayes, and departed.

Such was the grandeur of the post-war breed of university president. Successful though he became, John Hannah was not the best-known of the breed. President Harold Stassen, at the University of Pennsylvania from 1948 to 1953, was a more eminent specimen of this class, sliding easily from public office into the Academy and back again to public office, ready to occupy the White House whenever the sovereign people might summon him. Hannah's ambitions did not range quite so high, although more than once he flirted with suggestions that he become a governor or a United States senator.

Dr. Milton Eisenhower, brother of General Eisenhower, and president of Pennsylvania State University in 1955 (in such moments as he might spare from advising his brother, president of the United States, who was reported to murmur devoutly, "Thank God for Milton!"), attended this meeting of the Land Grant grandees at Michigan State. He was then thinking it his duty, rumor said, to succeed his brother in the Executive Mansion. If not more intelligent than Hannah or Stas-

producing service

sen, still he stood far closer to the seats of the mighty. His remarks at East Lansing, in 1955, afforded an interesting glimpse into the mentality of this new caste of academic administrators.

For Dr. Milton Eisenhower, universities fulfilled consumers' demands, by producing services. He was more nearly a factory-manager president than a businessman president. To him, a university was an efficient plant which turned out as many degree-holders as possible: literally a degree-mill. Unlike an earlier Milton, he did not fret about hungry sheep looking up and not being fed. As certain educationists have declared that "intelligence is what our intelligence-tests test", so to Dr. Milton Eisenhower a university education was simply whatever young people with degrees had happened to obtain. What is the object of a university education? Why, to get a degree so swiftly as possible. Those who have passed through the mill are, by definition, educated people.

The only thing wrong with the higher learning in America, if one accepted Dr. Eisenhower's remarks at the Land Grant conference, was that it just wasn't yet sufficiently standardized and depersonalized. "The instructor's productivity must be increased," he declared. Incidentally, at the beginning of this century the typical college instructor had eight students; by 1955, the typical instructor had to cope with more than forty alleged collegians; but that was not enough to satisfy Dr. Eisenhower.

The president of Pennsylvania State referred in his address to the swelling state universities, approvingly, as "academic supermarkets." This educational supermarket ought to be built in high-rise style, making learning as businesslike as possible. He had thought of a way to escape from that archaic notion of Professor Mark Hopkins on one end of a log and a student on the other end: "canned" lectures on closed-circuit television, "stocked by the academic supermarket", so that a Big Brother professor can sit in remote majesty and behold his disciples through relayed images—and *vice versa*. This notion pleased Dr. Eisenhower inordinately, for it was progressive. What a pity, one may add, that Socrates and Jesus did not have modern technology at their service! The television camera is ever so much better than a mere inefficient, absent-minded old scholar pottering about the classroom. "Honors systems and examination proctors will be made unnecessary," the wire-services summarized Dr. Eisenhower's prophecies on this subject, "with half a dozen cameras scanning as many rooms and transmitting what they see to the professor and his monitors."

It is all very like Jeremy Bentham's model Panopticon—which, happily, never was completed. The Panopticon was designed for hardened criminals, of course, and Dr. Eisenhower's university is designed for the intellectual leaders of the nation. But that's a small difference. One doesn't have to worry about Honor in either institution: the TV stoolie takes care of that vexatious little outworn notion.

There occur times when words fail even a man who, like your servant, takes *nil admirari* for his motto. So I content myself here by quoting again from Irving Babbitt's *Literature and the American College*. As Babbitt suggests, the barbarisms of Dr. Eisenhower were planted a century ago. Professor Babbitt would have fancied Dr. Milton Eisenhower of Pennsylvania State even less than he fancied Dr. Charles Eliot, president of his own Harvard. Eliot, for all his misconceptions, was not a businessman-politician-turnkey president of a university:

"The firmness of the American's faith in the blessings of education is equaled only by the vagueness of his ideas as to the kind of education to which these blessings are annexed. One can hardly consider the tremendous stir we have been making for the past thirty years or more about education, the time and energy and enthusiasm we are ready to lavish on educational undertakings, the libraries and endowments, without being reminded of the words of Sir Joshua Reynolds: 'A provision of endless apparatus, a bustle of infinite inquiry and research, may be employed to evade and shuffle off real labor—the real labor of thinking.' "

4

Rejecting Tradition: 1956

WE MODERNS, the medieval Schoolmen used to say, are dwarfs mounted upon the shoulders of giants, able to see so far only because we perch upon the immense bulk of our ancestors the ancients. But it had become the fashion, by 1956, to talk of how we lived in unique times, and must solve our present problems in their own terms, and ought to consign traditional learning and traditional morality to the rubbish-heap.

I argue that the higher learning necessarily is traditional. With G. K. Chesterton, I believe in "the democracy of the dead", the filtered wisdom of men in many ages, immemorial consensus, which comes down to us in Tradition.

The tradition which our universities and colleges used to carry on was both intellectual and moral. It was assumed, until recent years, that the professor was a man steeped in the traditions of learning. It was taken for granted that collegiate studies contained a large element of tradition, and of this moral tradition was a part. But a vulgarized utilitarianism has been at work in the Academy for a long while, so that no longer may one be sure that the traditions of moral worth, or of civility, or even of reasoned discourse, form a vital element in a college.

In 1956, I came upon an admirable essay which few others have read, because it lies buried in the old numbers of a law review. It is entitled "Considerations on the Determination of Good Moral Character", and its author was the late John R. Starrs, a Michigan lawyer; it can be found in *The University of Detroit Law Journal*, March, 1955. It touches upon tradition as the source of virtue.

Starrs begins with a dialogue from an interview conducted by a

Character and Fitness Subcommittee of the State Bar of Michigan.

"Committeeman: Why did you rape her?

"Applicant: Well, the opportunity presented itself, and I took it."

And Starrs inquires, "Ought a Subcommittee be divided on the problem presented by the case of the confessed rapist? Is it reasonable to say that 'old-fashioned notions of sexual morality ought to go by the board' and therefore the applicant should be approved? Or is it more sensible to conclude that what the applicant did to the girl he might well do with his client's money or reputation, and therefore the applicant ought to be disapproved?"

Such decisions are closely related to the question of what sort of education a lawyer, or anyone else who enters the Academy, needs to have. Is pure intellectuality divorced from tradition and reverence sufficient unto our time? I think that we are going to answer some of these questions in our generation. If tradition is anti-intellectual, the world may not long tolerate new-model intellectualism. Formerly the assumption was that an educated man should aspire to understand tradition and participate in it; only the booby thought himself superior to inherited precept and custom.

John Starrs goes on to inquire into the nature of virtue. What is a good man? The most nearly adequate answer, he suggests, is that of Horace: *Qui consulta patrum, qui leges iuraque servat*. Starrs' interpretation of this phrase from the *Epistles* is that "a good man is a law-abiding traditionalist." Not all good men are law-abiding traditionalists, Starrs remarks; but it scarcely is conceivable that a law-abiding traditionalist should not be a good man. Our law schools, and our liberal-arts colleges, in the past turned out graduates who, whatever their deficiencies, were in some measure law-abiding traditionalists.

All this is changing, it seems; yet I doubt whether we have succeeded in inventing any new morality to usher in our Brave New World, or in devising any new program to improve upon the ethical and literary and historical disciplines which used to be the mark of an educated American.

In education, as in other concerns, often we find it prudent to row toward our destination with muffled oars. We do not make our educated people law-abiding traditionalists by giving them three terms of Survey of Law-Abiding Traditionalism; we achieve our end by indirection. The study of great literature, of ancient and modern history, and of scientific theory are in themselves conservative disciplines, highly traditional. When theological and ethical studies had a high place in the curriculum, an aspirant to the bar may have worked his will upon a girl now and then; but he did not endeavor to justify his action by the reasoning of dime-store pragmatism. The most bigoted anti-intellectual, I suggest, may be the most newfangled enemy of tradition.

Any society depends upon the mere mechanics of its functioning, if for nothing more, upon the maintenance of a certain level of integrity among the men and women who make decisions. Justice cannot be administered if the lawyer is ignorant of all moral principle, and the judge quite as ignorant; or if judge and lawyer are close to illiteracy, as the dean of Columbia Law School suggested many law-students are. If the ethical function of the higher learning is ignored, the framework of that educational structure soon will be imperiled. And any society depends for the mere foundation and scaffolding of its intellectual life, if for nothing more, upon the accumulated wisdom of the race, which we call Tradition. It may tickle an educationist's vanity to pose as an omniscient reformer of politics, morals, and philosophy, administering a swift kick to the stodgy old giant under his feet. But I should not like to stand beside the reformer if the giant shrugs his shoulders; nor should I like to be strolling in the ditch if the giant, startled, takes a tumble.

These considerations were in my mind when the Association of American Colleges held at St. Louis, in January, 1956, its annual meeting. The first address at the opening session of this convention was given by Dr. Goodrich C. White, then president of Emory University; the second address was mine.

President White talked about "Do We Believe in Education?" He did; but he doubted whether many of our professional educationists believe in it. The vague list of "aims of education" drawn up at the White House Conference on Education, late in 1955, was demolished in a sentence or two by Dr. White. The end of liberal education, he said in substance, is the development of the reason, for the reason's own sake; learning is an end in itself; and the amorphous sociological objectives so much in the mouths of the aggrandizing university president have nothing at all to do with truly liberal education.

And President White had some sharp things to say about "character-building" in higher education. A man acquires his character through his performance of duties in life, not through classroom processes of college instruction. The university is a place for the training of the mind, not for creating an artificial regimen of moral discipline.

Now I spend a good deal of my time lamenting the lack of intellectual content in American schooling, and so I was heartened by President White's words. Yet I suggested that evening the danger of divorcing intellectuality from moral worth in formal education, and that the aim of liberal education is ethical. A principal purpose of the American liberal-arts college, at least in past times, was the inculcation of the concept of moral worth. One of our present troubles is that many universities and colleges make little attempt either to discipline the intellect or to impart an appreciation of moral worth.

The truly good man still is the law-abiding traditionalist, who understands, with Socrates, that virtue and wisdom, at their core, are one. I think that Dr. Robert Hutchins did the higher learning a disservice when he argued that the university ought to "relax its desire to train [students] in moral virtues." President White implied, rightly, that we cannot make men and women better simply by compelling them to enroll in Moral Worth 101. A college, however diligent, cannot turn a young man of bad inclination and habits into a child of light. Yet if it ignores the ethical end of learning, a college may so separate intellectuality from virtue that it graduates men and women whose light is darkness. "I want the same roof to contain both intellectual and moral discipline," Newman wrote once. This was the purpose of the founders of American colleges. Nowadays, by offering so little for the mind, many of our swollen campuses steadily reduce the domain of conscience.

You shall have an illustration. In 1956, the public-relations apparatus of Michigan State University released to the newspapers a tidbit of news, and my eye fell upon it. Here it is:

"Many high schools across the nation show an interest in adding flycasting, fishing, and hunting to their educational programs, a Michigan State University professor said today. Associate Professor Julian W. Smith, of the outdoor education department, said a survey of 28,000 secondary schools indicated more than 50 per cent were interested in developing such courses. Discussions on the subject will be held this week at the MSU W. K. Kellogg Gull Lake Biological station at Hickory Corners, Thursday through Saturday."

Let me interject here that I have not the faintest objection to walking by the banks of the Ilyssus with Socrates, or to casting a fly with Isaac Walton, or even in company with Julian W. Smith. Outdoor education, so long as it *is* education, has no enemy in me; I have walked my forty miles a day in the Scottish highlands, with good talk along the way. And flycasting is quite all right with me, so long as it does not pretend to be something other than flycasting. But the higher learning and flycasting, like art and sex, don't mix well. Cast not your flies in Heraclitus' river of change, nor crown Nimrod with the wild olive of the Grove of Academe. The old Greeks believed in the combination of a sound mind with a sound body, but they never confounded the separate disciplines which produce these two.

I do not mean to crush a butterfly upon the wheel. The follies in the Academy for which this "outdoor education" stands as a specimen might be tolerated if college and university otherwise were doing their work well. We might then only smile wryly at the waste of public funds upon fripperies; at paying an associate professor of outdoor education (as at MSU) twice the salary of a professor of philosophy; at luring the country's high schools into recreation as a substitute for knowledge. But in our time of troubles, foreign and domestic, pressing upon us — why, cannot flycasting be left simply to vacationers, rather than converted into a solemn academic discipline at public expense? Cannot even Behemoth University pay more attention to right reason and moral worth?

Of course there are graver symptoms of decadence than an infatuation with the casting of flies. One of those graver indices is the contrast of the curricula of yesteryear with the curricula of 1956, or of 1978. I have described briefly the course of study in Michigan State's Basic College, which has been paralleled at many other institutions, large or small, under some other label: the dull shallowness of the typical survey-course, offering a little information about everything under the sun to freshmen who couldn't care less. One thinks of Eliot's lines in his first chorus to *The Rock*—

> "Where is the Life we have lost in living?
> "Where is the wisdom we have lost in knowledge?
> "Where is the knowledge we have lost in information?"

Now contrast with such a program of study the serious work required of freshmen at the better colleges a century ago. Henry Churchill King, later president of Oberlin College, entered Oberlin as a freshman in 1877. Oberlin scarcely was, or is, a bastion of tradition. Twenty years earlier, Artemus Ward had visited Oberlin, and his impression of that college is sufficiently suggested by one sentence from his episode "Oberlin": "The College opens with a prayer and then the New York *Tribune* is read." Oberlin was a center for political and educational radicalism. Yet this is the curriculum required there, in his first year, of Henry Churchill King and his classmates:

First term: Livy; Xenophon's *Memorabilia*; Greek prose composition; algebra.

Second term: Horace; Lysias; Greek prose composition; solid and spherical geometry.

Third term: Cicero's *De Senectute*; Herodotus; German; plane and spherical geometry.

Doubtless some Oberlin students of 1877 cast flies, but not for academic credit. Oberlin was not afraid to emphasize moral worth; if anything, Oberlin was too muscular in its moralizing; but Oberlin knew that the ethical end is attained through an intellectual means. Oberlin offered education, and Behemoth State U. offers diversion and dating. Yet the choices which Americans must make in 1978 are harder far than the choices which educated Americans had to make in 1877. Where did that object go?

It may be objected that the undergraduates of our day simply won't be bothered with Tradition—either the traditions of civility or the traditions of right reason; it would be love's labor lost to offer them a more demanding program of study than that survey-soporific against which they already rebel. Yet I wonder: unless one maintains that television and "Instrumentalist" schooling have damaged the genetic strain of the rising generation of Americans, presumably the native intelligence of the students of 1978 is not inferior to the native intelligence of their ancestors. And there are sentiments deeply rooted in our nature.

I think of how my friend Paul Roche, the English poet and translator from the classics, appeared in 1956 before a large student audience at a Midwestern teachers' college; and of how he conquered by reading his translation of *Antigone*, in full.

Anyone familiar with the climate of opinion in teachers' colleges will appreciate the incongruity of this situation. The classics, if taught at all in such colleges, are taught only with an eye to preparation for "Latin I" courses in such few high-schools as still offer beginning Latin. Although there has been improvement at such institutions during recent years, few of the administrators and professors at teachers' colleges thirst after Ancient Greats. How did Antigone slip past these sentinels by the unburied corpse of the higher learning?

Yet nine hundred students and staff-members turned out for the occasion, and they sat rapt through the poet's reading. President, deans, and some department-heads shifted in their chairs, but the students drank in *Antigone*. A departmental chairman introduced the poet at considerable length, during which time he misrepresented every important fact in the poet's life. Thus Paul Roche began with a handicap, his audience's patience already having been tried, and it took him more than an hour to read his translation. No one snickered; no one went to sleep; no one left.

In a generation like ours, which has forgotten the natural law and has knelt to Leviathan, *Antigone* takes on a meaning little understood during the nineteenth century. This pertinence must have touched the students when they heard such passages as Antigone's reply to Creon:

> "I never thought your edicts had
> "Such force they nullified the laws of heaven,
> "Which, unwritten, not proclaimed, can boast
> "A currency that everlastingly is valid;
> "An origin beyond the birth of man.
> "And I, whom no man's frown can frighten, am
> "Far from risking heaven's frown by flouting these."

The students applauded vigorously, somewhat to the surprise of the college's administrative hierarchy. It was explained to the poet that ordinarily these undergraduates were disorderly at assemblies, asserting their personalities by scuffling, whispering, and even jeering. August visting professors from Teachers College, Columbia, had not been proof against these incivilities—to the chagrin of the college's president, who felt, with Creon,

> "How can I, if I nurse
> "Sedition in my house, not foster it
> "Outside: And if a man can keep his home
> "In hand, he proves his competence to keep
> "The state."

"I never saw the students so quiet," the president remarked, almost belligerently, to the professor who had arranged the program. "You must have beaten it into their heads that they were supposed to be on their good behavior."

Being, in education as in politics, what David Riesman calls a "moralizer", I append to this brief relation a humble moral. There exist in human nature, common to the Greeks of the fifth century and to us, certain constant qualities. Of these qualities, among the rising talents of every generation, are a longing for poetic imagery; a dim participating in the tragic view of life; and an aspiration after ethical insights. *Antigone* is a great drama because it is humane in the highest sense: that is, *Antigone* exemplifies the educational discipline called *humanitas*, the training of the ethical faculty through the understanding of powerful literature.

Despite all the muddled positivism and pragmatism to which college students have been subjected since the age of five or six years, truth will demand a hearing now and again. The ancient hungers of the imagination are hard to deny; and though the works of Sophocles may be forgotten when the works of William Heard Kilpatrick have become Holy Writ, they will not be forgotten until that bathetic apotheosis.

5

Academic Intolerance: 1957

A T A FAMOUS independent university in the Midwest, the faculty committee for public lectures was deliberating as to what scholars should be invited to speak at their university during 1957. Someone suggested Professor Sidney Hook, of New York University. "What!" cried a dean, "that Fascist reactionary?" Dr. Hook was not invited.

Now Sidney Hook, as everybody in Academe ought to know, is a democratic socialist—strongly influenced by Marx—in theoretical politics, and a disciple of John Dewey in many other things. He also is a liberal democrat, an untiring opponent of Soviet Communism, and an able scholar. He is a practiced speaker and a clever writer. But he has the misfortune to be opposed to Communists, at home and abroad; so the Midwestern university did not hear him.

I do not suppose that Professor Hook knew of this particular incident. But he did know of similar incidents, related in his book *Heresy, Yes; Conspiracy, No*. One New York professor, for instance, informed his students that Burke was a Fascist; and according to another professor there, Hook was a Fascist, too.

Perhaps the New York zealots were Communists, but the Midwestern dean was no Communist—merely one of the breed that Sidney Hook calls "ritualistic liberals." The Midwestern dean would not go so far as to say that the Communists were in the right; he would say only that anyone who opposes Communists must be a Fascist. There's the *via media* for us.

Another tidbit: at a state college in northern Michigan, a German-born instructor was summarily dismissed because someone had alleged that he once had been a member of the Nazi party. Whether actually he had been such, I do not know; and apparently no one bothered to inquire deeply, the label sufficing. A week or two later, at a large university in Michigan, a solemn faculty group was deliberating upon the inviolable right of any scholar to teach anything anywhere, regardless of his political opinions and associations. "Now what about that fellow up north, that German?" some innocent at the meeting inquired. Up rose a female professor, ingenuous and determined. "We certainly aren't going to defend him," she declared. "He's a Nazi." Embarrassed silence; awkward cough from chairman; discussion steered to another topic. This was 1957, long after the Nazi domination in Europe was crushed.

And yet more. A young and successful lawyer decided to take up graduate work in history, for his heart's case. He began looking about for universities at which to study, and presently stopped at Harvard, where he was interviewed by a Young Lion of the history department. The lawyer made it fairly clear that he inclined toward certain conservative views of society and history. "Why did you think of Harvard?" the Young Lion coldly inquired. The lawyer said that he had admired the work of Professor Crane Brinton, and had thought he might study under his supervision. "Not all of us here think highly of Mr. Brinton," the Young Lion pronounced. He added that the lawyer had best apply to some other graduate school.

Professor Brinton was a famous and moderate historical scholar, the author of several influential books. His reputation was not sufficient to save him from the calumny of his colleague, for Dr. Brinton did not have the prudence to look always Leftward. Let him be anathema. Yet American professors, in 1957, were less intolerant and less intemperate than the professors of Europe, generally speaking; nor did so many of them murmur, *sotto voce*, "No enemies to the Left."

When the Academy is badly politicized, divided into intemperate political factions, and dominated much of the time by one of those factions, the Academy is decadent: it has lost an object, the object of "objectivity", if you will. For the Academy is meant to be a place, and sometimes *the* place, for reasoned and civil discussion of matters of enduring value. It is supposed to be an assembly of philosophers, but often it sinks to an assembly of sophists. Professors who wish to exclude or to harass colleagues of differing political views—provided those views are not ruinous to the Academy itself—have forgotten the end or aim of a community of scholars.

In 1957, or perhaps in any year, the best book on this subject to be published was Raymond Aron's *The Opium of the Intellectuals* (translated by Terence Kilmartin). Aron, a French sociologist, dealt chiefly with

the attitudes of Parisian professors and intellectuals, but also had a good deal to say about their American counterparts, at least by implication.

In our time, intolerant and intemperate professors generally are the votaries and the victims of ideology. "Ideology" does not signify political theory or principle, although newspapermen commonly employ the word in that sense. Ideology really means political fanaticism: and more precisely the belief that this world of ours, here below, may be converted into the Terrestrial Paradise through the operation of positive law and positive planning. The ideologue, of whatever affiliation, maintains that human nature and society may be perfected by mundane, secular means. The ideologue immanentizes religious symbols and religious doctrine.

What Christianity promises to the faithful in a realm beyond time and space, ideology promises to everyone—except those who have been liquidated in the process — in this temporal valley of tears. "When the intellectual feels no longer attached either to the community or the religion of his forebears," Aron writes, "he looks to progressive ideology to fill the vacuum. The main difference between the progressivism of the disciple of Harold Laski or Bertrand Russell and the Communism of the disciple of Lenin concerns not so much the *content* as the *style* of the ideologies and the allegiance they demand."

Real thinking is a painful undertaking; and the ideologue resorts to the anaesthetic of social utopianism, escaping the tragedy and the grandeur of human existence by giving his adherence to a perfect dream-world of the future. Reality he stretches or chops away to conform to his dream-pattern of human nature or society. For the concepts of salvation and damnation, he substitutes abstractly virtuous "progressives" and abstractly vicious "reactionaries."

Robespierre was the ideologue incarnate. Like Robespierre, the twentieth-century ideologue thinks that his secular dogmas are sustained by the Goddess Reason; he prides himself inordinately upon being "scientific" and "rational"; and he is convinced that all opposition to his particular wave of the future is mere obscurantism, when it is not direct selfish vested interest.

Until well into this century, French thought tended to dominate the philosophy and the politics of the Western world. The prestige of French intellectuality has had much to do with the power of ideological illusions in our time of troubles. Aron describes in detail three political myths by which the French intellectuals have been seduced from right reason: the myth of the Left, the myth of the Revolution, and the myth of the Proletariat.

The myth of the Left is sufficiently expressed in the unreasoning cry of French radical politicians, "No enemies to the Left!" Whatever party lays claim to a more thoroughgoing subversion of prescription and establishment thus is entitled to the sympathy and admiration of the intellectuals; and so they are led to the ultimate subversion, Communism. Arthur Koestler has described this species of intellectual.

The myth of the Revolution is the illusion that all revolutions, everywhere, *per se*, are Good Things. The French Revolution, for these intellectuals, remains a perfect model for rebellion, perpetual upheaval, against the civil social order. An intellectual's vocation is that preached by Marx, to gnaw incessantly at the foundations of society. To dismiss this logic as childish, Aron observes, becomes tempting; but doing so would not repel the pressing danger of ideology.

The myth of the Proletariat is the malignant notion that a mystical virtue reposes in the masses; that the Proletariat will be the collective redeemer of suffering humanity; that any act of injustice or violence is excusable in the interest of the working classes. The more remote the intellectuals are from the actual working people, the more firmly do they cling to this myth. It has a strange power: Aron has several interesting paragraphs on how this myth captured the worker-priests and "Progressive Christians" in France, and he shows how belief in this illusion must lead to a falling away from Christianity.

One of the worker-priests, quoted by Aron, makes this revealing admission: "If a worker came to us one day to talk about religion, or even to solicit baptism, we should begin, I think, by asking him if he had thought about the causes of working-class misery and if he took part in the struggle carried on by his comrades for the good of all." Thus the "Progressive" Christians were Marxianized almost without knowing it.

Now how can the intellectual persuade himself to adhere to these myths? The writer and the scholar have not always thought it their duty to gnaw at the foundations of society; and one might expect that the dreadful experiences of our century, at least, would have suggested to intellectuals that they have been straying after a corpse-candle. How have the intellectuals become slaves to deterministic theories of history and to secular messiahs? By nature and interest, writer and scholar are not levellers: John Adams, near the end of the eighteenth century, wrote that "democracy, simple democracy, never had a patron among men of letters." But matters have altered.

Aron knows that the impulse behind the radicalism of the intellectual is not economic or egoistic merely. The intellectual has lost religious faith; and he is seeking a substitute for religion, since man cannot rest content without belief. Though the intellectual may talk much about higher standards of living and social justice, he is not truly interested in these matters; they are but part of his patter. At heart, it is not the economic inequality of modern life which vexes him, but rather the crassness and ugliness of much of modern civilization. He turns to ideology, and especially to Communism, to assuage those ancient human longings for which the old satisfaction was religious consolation.

"The ideologies of the Right and of the Left, Fascism as well as Communism, are inspired by the modern philosophy of immanence," Aron says. "They are atheist, even when they do not deny the existence of God, to the extent that they conceive the human world without reference to the transcendental."

Although, as Aron knows, the American intellectuals have their difficulties and illusions, these are not identical with those of the French. "The 'American way of life,' " Aron writes, "is the negation of what the European intellectual means by the word ideology. Americanism does not formulate itself as a system of concepts or propositions; it knows nothing of the 'collective savior,' the end of history, the determining cause of historical 'becoming,' or the dogmatic negation of religion; it combines respect for the constructive, homage for individual initiative, a humanitarianism inspired by strong but vague beliefs which are fairly indifferent to the rivalries between the churches (only Catholic 'totalitarianism' is considered disquieting), the worship of science and efficiency. It does not involve any detailed orthodoxy or official doctrine. It is learned at school, and society enforces it. Conformism if you like, but a conformism which is rarely felt to be tyrannical, since it does not forbid free discussion in matters of religion, economics, or politics."

Most Americans, nearly all of them, were attached, that is, to the politics of prescription—even if very few of them were familiar with that phrase. Even during the Great Depression, Communism, although for a time it contrived to entrench itself in some high places among American intellectuals, never attracted anything like the proportion of them who went over to Marxism in France or Germany or Italy or even Britain; while Fascism took no root here at all.

Something called Liberalism, nevertheless, became nearly a secular orthodoxy among American writers and professors. No one was quite sure what Liberalism amounted to — which kept it from growing into a full-blown ideology. To some, Liberalism meant anti-religious opinions; to others, socialism or a managed economy; to another set, absolute liberty of private conduct, untrammeled by law or tradition; to a fourth group, perpetual doubt for the sake of doubting; for yet a different clique, oldfangled Benthamism; for very "advanced" liberals, "humane" Marxism.

This groping for a liberal secular orthodoxy remained strong, if somewhat chastened, in the Academy of 1957. One firm article in the creed of academic liberals still was "impartiality" or "objectivity." In plain fact, often the liberals had been excessively passionate in the cause of dispassionateness; but they had not been aware of their inconsistency. To be ardently devoted to the principle of noncommitment, but simultaneously to be unaware of one's own actual commitments, is an unhealthy state of mind.

Aron does not desire that the intellectual evade commitments. He expresses contempt for the sort of intellectual who signs petitions "against every crime committed on the face of the earth . . . a ludicrous caricature of 'clerkly' behavior"—and yet who takes no action that would require real risk or sacrifice. The conscientious intellectual, Aron continues, "will not refuse to become involved, and when he participates in action he will accept its consequences, however harsh. But he must try never to forget the arguments of the adversary, or the uncertainty of the future, or the faults of his own side, or the underlying fraternity of ordinary men everywhere."

The academic liberals' pretended "objectivity" would become a feeble reed a few years later. The destructive force of ideology would ravage American campuses in the 'Sixties; and, given a catalyst, it may rise up again.

6

Universities for Defense and Matrimony: 1958

ALARMED BY THE SUCCESS of Soviet Russia in putting into orbit a manned satellite, during 1957, the Eisenhower administration and the Congress adopted the first massive federal program for influencing American higher education: the National Defense Education Act of 1958. Universities and colleges were encouraged to expand physically by the great sums of bricks and-mortar money which this act made readily available; they were persuaded to adapt their programs of study to "defense" needs by a wide variety of federally-subsidized educational undertakings, among them abundant scholarships for teacher-training and big grants for language institutes (which latter tended to corrupt language-study into a kind of hurry-up Berlitz conversational-Urdu boondoggle.) All this federal money injected into the Academy a new motive for quantitative expansion, in a year when otherwise college enrollments were tending to drop off.

Although many of the chief people in the public-school apparatus were uncritically enthusiastic for this federal largesse, some university and college presidents dreaded the prospect of federal political direction of the higher learning. To soothe the latter, there was inserted in the NDEA section 102: "Nothing contained in this Act shall be construed to authorize any department, agency, officer, or employee of the United States to exercise any direction, supervision, or control over the curriculum, program of instruction, administration, or personnel of any educational institution or school system." Such guarantees, as in later years the federal government pushed farther into every aspect of education, would not endure.

This Act of 1958 favored applied science and technology at the expense of humane and social studies, with a consequent tendency to warp the curricula of universities and colleges in that direction. Also, in its lavish provisions for encouraging the study of languages, the NDEA discriminated against "private" or independent educational institutions. Public-school teachers who enrolled in the language programs were granted free tuition and stipends for themselves and for all their dependents; teachers from independent schools had to be content with less. Such preferential treatment was ominous for the future, but few educators objected. A long-run consequence of NDEA, moreover, would be the close linking of large universities with the famous "military-industrial complex" through tremendous governmental grants for "defense" research. This tended to divert those universities both from teaching and from non-technological programs, and in time would become the cause of one of the more frenzied denunciations of the American universities by radical students.

In 1958, however, there were next to no undergraduate "activists." The indolent mob of students on the campuses was a by-product of American affluence: these young people came from the "Eisenhower suburbs", prosperous, smug, unaccustomed to work or discipline. What might be done with one's children in their late 'teens? Few of them had been brought up in any skill or with any bent toward accomplishment; the great majority of them had been poorly, if expensively, schooled in the permissive schools of these new suburbs; they lacked norms or aims. What could be done with them before they reached the magical age of twenty-one and were cast to the world, the flesh, and the devil? Send them to college!

Despite rising costs, college remained a bargain in 1958, the state-supported colleges and universities in particular. The price of tuition, so low as to be nominal at most state institutions, in effect was a subsidy to well-to-do families, rather than a ladder up which the aspiring offspring of the poor might rise. Beardsley Ruml, commenting upon the second report (1957) of the President's Committee on Education beyond High School, had taken note of the effect of these low tuition-charges upon independent institutions:

"The tuition policy of our state institutions of higher education requires revision. These tuitions are so very low, so far below even the direct costs of instruction, that they constitute in fact a substantial scholarship to every student whether he requires one or not. The publicly-supported college or university is placed advantageously in a competitive position against the private institution which was unintended and is beginning a work of destruction to private higher education that must be reversed."

Some state legislatures commenced to groan at the price of Behemoth State University to the taxpaying public. Having no direct control over the management of Behemoth, all the legislatures could do was to impose general indiscriminate reductions. In the spring of 1958, much to the chagrin of the academic empire-builders at the University of Michigan (Ann Arbor) and Michigan State University (East Lansing), the Michigan legislature reduced the annual appropriations for these vast institutions by approximately a million dollars each.

From UM and MSU came anguished cries of "Whatever are we to do about the rising tide of enrollments?" Such was their agony that their administrators actually hinted, after this blow, that they might raise entrance-standards as a means of reducing general costs. Wouldn't that be dreadful? Yet no single action could have done more for decency in the higher learning than some improvement in standards of admission.

What educationists called "the rising tide of enrollments" had been caused, in some degree, by the increase of American population. But in large part this "rising tide" was an induced phenomenon. The state institutions welcomed and stimulated it. In my state, the best college was Kalamazoo; its president, Dr. Werner Hicks, remarked in 1957 that the state institutions were frenziedly recruiting students wherever they might obtain them, and whatever their state of preparation. From the University of Michigan and Michigan State University, he said, "Teams of recruiters armed with carloads of pamphlets annually descend on state high schools, where they sell their institutions, rather than education, to prospective students." For those young people simply not interested in the works of the mind, new curricula were invented.

Consider an innovation at Michigan State. In 1958, MSU offered a "Curriculum in Food Distribution", granting the bachelor's and the master's degree. Chain groceries and wholesalers had given MSU some money for this purpose; but, as in all such schemes, in the long run most of the cost had to be met by the people of Michigan. It had become clear that many of the big universities and colleges would descend to any depth of fraudulent vocationalism in order to attract those boys and girls who had absorbed in high school, sullenly, all the culture they meant to take.

That there was plenty of room, actually, in American colleges for intelligent applicants was pointed out in 1958 by the vice-president of Rensselaer Polytechnic Institute, John F. Morse. Not more than a few hundred applicants even tolerably qualified, in the entire country, would fail to find places in college during the year, he observed. "Most colleges in this country are still wondering how to fill to capacity their freshman classes."

It was true that some of the long-established universities and colleges received several times as many applications as they had places for freshmen. But this was merely because it had become fashionable for young people to apply for admission to a half-dozen institutions, to be sure of getting in somewhere—and then to pick and choose as letters of acceptance arrived. When the whole shuffle was over in September—a shuffle extremely expensive to college administrations, in waste of time and postage—just about everyone who ever dreamed of entering a college, no matter how wretchedly he may have been prepared for the higher learning, had been accepted somewhere.

Many of the really good liberal-arts colleges found it difficult to attract enough young people to fill up a freshman class of two hundred or less. The better the college—unless it had Ivy-League prestige—the more difficulty it found in attracting freshman candidates. For most applicants, like their parents, sought in a college such advantages as social adjustment, the snob-prestige of a degree, and prospects (often delusory) of vocational training and economic advancement. If the student, or his parents, should pay the price of four years of sham-education—well, for those who like that sort of thing, that is the sort of thing they like. But why should public funds be expended in lavish pandering to such pseudo-educational desires?

With fond parents, the most popular feature of the state colleges was their matrimonial market: a way of shuffling off the daughters, especially. This was equally popular with the rising generation. One met so many wonderful young people, and could choose. What was less agreeable to parents, whatever might be said of their offspring, also it was easy to find what Alfred Kinsey had delighted to call "sexual partners." A decade later, some parents would have discovered that so far as wisdom and virtue went, they might have done better to have sent Barbie to Montmartre than to Brummagem U.

By 1958, some good junior colleges flourished in America, though not many. But the number of "community colleges"—the term supplanting the old "junior"—was increasing speedily, most of all in California. At one time, the purpose of such institutions had been to give students their first two years of college on a humane scale, usually close to their homes, at modest cost; then, presumably, many of the students could have proceeded to "senior" colleges. Some people entertained high hopes of this development, at least as a safety-valve: Dr.

Robert Hutchins, just before America entered the Second World War, proposed that the number of such junior colleges be immensely increased, to drain off from the solid universities and senior colleges a multitude of prospective undergraduates unqualified for serious studies.

Yet somehow the community-college movement did not quite catch on until the 'Fifties. Until then, most junior colleges were situated near a public high school, and sometimes in the high-school building itself. The college-campus atmosphere was lacking, and the college prestige. During the 'Fifties, however, educationists in many states grew eager for the establishment of community colleges "to serve the community", chiefly through vocational arts, business courses, adult education, and popular diversions.

Of course it would be possible to found a really good community college, with a decent curriculum. But rarely was that what the educationists or the community-college boosters desired. Basketweaving, ballroom dancing, and courses in salesmanship do not require painful meditation. It is pleasant to spend other people's money on such activities.

In 1958, a friend of mine visited Flint Community College, in Michigan. The corridors were jammed with students, in couples—the species of student interested in mating or matrimony, and engaged in suitable preliminaries. Some of these amorous pairs had settled down in the library, too, amid a few students who perversely desired to read books. Presently there strode into the library-room a young fellow in a leather jacket, swaggering and humming. Through the open door came a tremendous babble from the loiterers in the corridor. A few bookworms ventured to frown in displeasure. "Don't blame me!" roared the scholar in the leather jacket, jerking his thumb over his shoulder toward the mob in the corridor, and swaggering on past the tables.

Flint Community College recently had discharged two members of its faculty. These did not have the good fortune to be Communists, so it was no go their trying to raise the question of academic freedom. Their offense was that they were not "integrated with the social life of the college." They possessed all the academic qualifications—one of them boasted two doctoral degrees—but they had failed to turn up at the athletic events, and they had lacked enthusiasm when expected to participate in interminable staff conferences. They were interested in teaching and scholarship, poor old fogies. They were good professors, as good professors go; and as good professors go, they went.

In many states, community-college instructors were glorified high-school superintendents, faithful to all articles in the creed of Holy

Educationism, and rewarded according to their deserts. Need I add that frequently these very administrators professed their distress at McCarthyism and our dreadful pressures toward conformity?

Any society, even the richest, can expend only a certain proportion of its national income upon formal instruction. The more of that proportion which is used for pseudo-educational purposes, the less can be spent upon genuine education. Americans pay a greater share of national income toward formal schooling than have any other people in history—and get little enough for their dollars. It remained true in 1958 that in some respects Americans spent too little. Many of the decent independent colleges were short of operating cash, let alone endowments. Real professors at real universities and colleges sometimes were underpaid. Many college libraries were inadequate. There were limited funds for sabbatical years, or theme-readers to assist leisureless professors, or certain types of unpopular study and research.

But also there was and is tremendous waste: squandering of funds that could have been used for truly educational undertakings. Much of this money was wasted in attracting to college those students who have not the feeblest interest in the learning actually higher; some in pseudo-vocational and "social adjustment" curricula at universities; some in elaborate, if ugly, "plant." A community college can be useful; some are. But I can think of no more conspicuous educational waste than that in the budget of the average community college, which too often is engaged principally in three activities: first, doing what the local high school ought to have done already; second, providing two years of idleness for young persons unable to obtain entrance to any genuine college, even in a time of conspicuously decayed standards; third, furnishing public amusements out of funds nominally raised for education.

Despite such failings, community colleges would continue to proliferate during the next two decades. For parents, they offered the advantages of low cost, keeping offspring away from the increasing disorder of Behemoth U., and preserving direct community influence upon the notions promulgated by the staff. In California, often the architecture of these colleges was pleasant. Something may yet be done with them, and already they have done a commendable work in adult education, often.

It is possible for an institution of higher learning to be something better than a matrimonial bureau, and to operate with reasonable efficiency and economy, and yet to be intellectually vigorous. During 1958 I lectured at one such establishment, the New School for Social Research, in Manhattan.

The New School's reputation for radicalism still lingered then. Founded by Charles A. Beard that his own disciples might gather round him, the New School experienced intellectual and financial vicissitudes, but was on a sound footing in 1958, when Dr. Hans Simons presided over it—a humorous sociologist, educated, like most of the School's senior professors, in Europe.

The New School was, and is, unique in America. Rationalism and positivism were strong there from the start; but they never went un-challenged, and by 1958 the New School—dedicated to variety and exploration—extended a welcome to points of view of another charac-ter. To the School's neat building on the edge of Greenwich Village Dr. Simons brought Dr. Reinhold Niebuhr and Dr. Paul Tillich, believing that they ought to be heard in what had been a stronghold of sec-ularism. At first, either of them had only ten auditors; but their follow-ing increased greatly. New School students were willing to listen to unorthodox teachers, even if they taught orthodoxy; and that was more than could be said of students at most universities. There are few colleges and universities in America at which students ever learn to ask the important questions.

Whatever the oddities of its undergraduate programs, the upper division of the New School offered much for the mind. The tone and temper of the place were such that no perfectly stupid student would have thought of enrolling. No one was seeking a snob-degree from the New School, nor expected that institution to find him a soft job with industry upon his graduation. Out of New School lectures came some important books—Albert Salomon's *Tyranny of Progress*, for one. At most American institutions of the learning allegedly higher, one could no more make a decent book out of one's lectures than a guided missile could be composed of shotgun shells; for the lectures, at many places, are themselves cribbed from superficial textbooks.

Another peculiar thing about the New School was its economy. It was literally the only free-enterprise institution of higher learning in the United States. For the occasional lecturers and the instructors received no fixed stipends (though the senior professors were paid salaries): instead, they took a share of the fees paid by their students. The New School had become the best adult-education project in the land.

The New School was tolerant—even of ideas that were not born yesterday. It was not afraid of "highly controversial speakers" such as disciples of St. Augustine or of Cicero, when a good many long-established liberal-arts colleges were terrified of admitting any opinions disapproved by the Conformists of Noncomformity. It was significant of the state of the American intellect that nowhere in America had the New School any imitators or emulators.

The New School was a far cry from Behemoth State University, job-certification center and matrimonial bureau. I could criticize Behemoth State with a certain aloofness because I had spent some years at a center of learning that was a still farther cry distant—St. Andrews, in Scotland.

This is one of the smaller British universities, though the oldest in Scotland, and the least altered by modern circumstances. The undergraduates in their scarlet gowns stroll among massive ruins: the smashed hulk of the Gothic cathedral; the brown wreck of the castle where Cardinal Beaton was dirked and pickled; the mile-long fortified walls of the vanished priory; the derelict little houses (most of them restored since my years there) near the derelict harbor. The world was not too much with one at St. Andrews; and, as Samuel Johnson said, visiting the place, it was admirably suited for study.

The silence, and the sense of the vanity of human wishes that brooded over university and town, helped in this; and then, too, St. Andrews was wondrously inexpensive. There is no necessary opposition between aristocratic principles and student poverty. Tocqueville observed that the aristocrat is indifferent to his own material condition, when he finds himself poor, because his opinion of other people and of himself is not determined by creature-comforts. At St. Andrews, in my time, the chancellor was the premier duke in Scotland, the rector the premier earl; but most of the students subsisted upon rather slim scholarships or local-authority grants, and many of the others were happily and unabashedly shabby beneath their red gowns. In Scotland, a thirst for real education long marked all classes, and once upon a time there were farm laborers in Fife who held St. Andrews degrees. But these, like the bookish farmers of old New England, have passed away, and the grants of the welfare state will not resurrect them.

Samuel Johnson's remarks on poverty notwithstanding, penury does have its pleasures. The garret-student at St. Andrews—I was one, eating very little — not only had better opportunities for study than has any student in the tremendous air-conditioned-nightmare dormitory complexes at Behemoth U., but he also leads a more varied, interesting, and character-toughening life. It is good for a student to be poor. Getting and spending, the typical American college student lays waste his powers. Work and contemplation don't mix, and university days ought to be days of contemplation. Fasting and reading, a student may see visions and be, in C. S. Lewis' phrase, "surprised by joy." The corruption of many American colleges and universities into training-institutes for material success has alienated hundreds of thousands of the better minds among our rising generation from even the awareness that a university education is supposed to be a contemplative process, not a mere hurried business of bluffing and cheating one's way through innumerable courses, crowned by a sham degree. So some such turn to "transcendental meditation", taught by a guru instead of a professor.

For St. Andrews students, in my time, vacation was the opportunity for long and serious reading in a remote cottage, or perhaps for cheap and independent roving about the Continent. The St. Andrews student knew that he was going to have to serve Mammon soon enough, without wasting his university years in washing cars or waiting on table. And then, too, the Scottish universities still expected their students to pass exacting examinations. At St. Andrews, one year in my time, the professor of moral philosophy gave every one of his students the grade of failure. They came back at the end of summer, after intensive study, to re-sit the examination; and he flunked them all again. At Behemoth U., such a professor would be got rid of, if possible; at St. Andrews, he was advanced to vice-chancellor and principal.

Little St. Andrews still nurtured graduates of some intellectual power; while Behemoth University, with few exceptions, turned out the adolescent with the sheepskin, filled only with that smattering of knowledge which is perilous to himself and his society. To renew my spirit after looking upon the spectacle of the higher learning in America, in 1958 and in other years I returned to St. Andrews for some months. Most American undergraduates nowadays never have beheld a city that was not hideous and dangerous; the cities I knew as a young man have been "renewed" by bulldozer into urban deserts and urban jungles. Similarly, few American undergraduates, except those whose lines are cast in such pleasant places as Dartmouth or Washington and Lee or the Claremont colleges or the University of the South, can understand how a college or a university ought to be loved, because it is lovely.

During the 'Sixties, it would become abundantly clear that a great many students in America and Europe (although not at St. Andrews), had come to hate the university. Inhumane scale and, in many cases, ugliness of the campus, had some part in this hatred. When such hatred prevails, obviously something is amiss either with the university or with the students—or with both.

7

Boondoggles of the Ivory Tower: 1959

T O ELEANOR ROOSEVELT we owe the useful word "boondoggle." Sometimes it appears to me that most of what occurs in today's higher learning amounts to boondoggle; and that the word may be more justly applied to follies and frauds of the Academy than ever it was to certain blunders of the Works Progress Administration. During 1959 I amused myself by collecting accounts of a number of Ivory Tower boondoggles, of which I offer only a few specimens here.

"It is the American custom never to acknowledge a lowering of standards in service or product," Thomas Griffith writes, "but to deny stoutly that anything has been lost along with what has been gained." If we have succeeded in conferring degrees upon a great many people, but in offering an education to almost no one, what does it profit us to deny the consequences of intellectual levelling? My instances of academic boondoggles in 1959 are pallid by the side of wasteful academic sillinesses in 1978—as described, for instance, in Geoffrey Wagner's recent book *The End of Education*.

Once Clinton Rossiter and I discussed the failings of American education. Professor Rossiter suggested that we ought not to lament much; because, after all, somehow the better intellects contrive to assert themselves in the long run—overcoming the handicaps which yoke them to the pace of dull or indifferent classmates. It is a matter of marking time, Rossiter said. My reply was this: it seems a poor apology for an educational system that some people, by remarkable personal endeavors, *eventually* may contrive to learn and to accomplish something in despite of the system. Tocqueville observes that democracies, jealous of strong minds and unusual talents, endeavor to delay able people by tedious routine requirements, so keeping the energetic at the pace of the slack until, worn down and disheartened and advanced in years, they present no threat to democratic mediocrity.

That egalitarian envy, never clearly expressed in statute but underlying much public policy, is one reason why educational administrators do not confess publicly that something has been lost by intellectual levelling. Those outside the Academy are more candid. Consider these sentences by Thomas Griffith, an able journalist, in *The Waist-High Culture*. He describes his own schooling at the University of Washington, not long after the first huge wave of expansion struck the state universities, and concludes thus:

"To suggest that not every boy or girl who escaped out the front door of a high school had a constitutional right to go to college was to speak the unthinkable, and to show oneself undemocratic. What's the matter, don't you think people are equal? Just who do you think you are? So everybody went to college, and the instruction sank to the level of the laggards, but it called itself a college education and conferred degrees to prove it."

Yet administrators and professors whose interests are bound up with this educational degradation of the democratic dogma endeavor to persuade themselves that if something has been lost, still something has been gained by fetching to the campus everybody who can be enticed there. When I studied at Michigan State, I learned much from a professor of history, at that time contemptuous of the cant and hypocrisy of the educationalist levellers and imperialists. His opinions then, indeed, helped to form my present ones.

Later this professor became a college administrator, and sang a different tune—especially after he ceased to teach classes altogether, and so did not have to splash in the sea of ignorance and apathy which stretched before mere classroom lecturers. At his administrative desk, sometimes he would concede that the average undergraduate might seem a dull tool, at matriculation and at graduation. Yet, he argued, somehow a bit of polish did rub off upon the bored and bewildered students, so that years after graduation they might display a veneer of culture. This made them happier, he thought, and improved the tone of American society. In public pronouncements, this administrator-professor was enthusiastic over the promise and fulfillment of "mass education." After all, mass education had conferred upon him a good salary and some authority.

I could not agree with him. As an unschooled man often is the moral superior of a man badly schooled, so is the unschooled man sometimes actually the intellectual superior of the possessor of a pseudo-degree:

the former has not wasted his time in boondoggles. I think it better to be suckled in a creed outworn than to boast of a learning which reaches only to the waist.

Of the many boondoggles afflicting our higher learning, perhaps the most general and baneful is the survey-course boondoggle. Having been an instructor in such monstrosities, I know whereof I write.

In the first chapter of Aldous Huxley's *Antic Hay*, an unfortunate master at a boarding-school sets his charges to write an essay on this subject: "Give a brief account of the character and career of Pope Pius IX, *with dates wherever possible*." All the boys know about Pio Nono is what they have gathered from a typical progressivist modern-history textbook. Their papers are dreary regurgitations of the textbook-author's prejudices. One essay declares boldly, "Pius IX was a bad man, who said that he was infallible, which showed he had a less than average intelligence." Upon reading such lines, Huxley's history-master resigns and turns to selling pneumatic trousers.

It must be said for Huxley's schoolboys, however, that they could write simple declarative sentences, and they knew that Pius IX had lived in the nineteenth century; and, after all, they were not university students. Their performance was distinctly superior to that of most students in American college survey-courses. My colleagues and I used to get such results as these:

Question: Describe St. Augustine and discuss his works at some length.

Answer (in full): St. Augustine was a man who had a Christian mother and a pagan father.

Question: Who was Martin Luther, and what doctrines did he teach?

Answer (in full): Martin Luther was a boy who had a vision when he was going home from college on the train.

Question: Describe Egyptian sculpture.

Answer (in full): Egyptian sculpture was mostly horizontal. They all had that oriental look.

The respondents to these learned inquiries now are university graduates; some may be teachers in secondary schools.

"Drink deep, or taste not the Pierian spring." The policy of most American universities and colleges nowadays is to compel their students to lap hurriedly at a shallow and muddy Serbonian bog of generalization. Usually this process is called "general education", and the terms "core curriculum" and "interdisciplinary studies" are much employed. Integration of the several major intellectual disciplines is much to be desired in a university. But students obtain no real integration from being exposed, three hours each week, for one academic year, to an omnium-gatherum called "humanities" or "history of civilization" or "general science" or "social studies."

An intelligent young woman, now a teacher of English literature, told me in 1958 that she knew nothing of history, and could not abide the thought of undertaking historical studies. The cause of this aversion, she suspected, was that in secondary school and in college she was exposed repeatedly to an amorphous series of lectures: the same rubbish, at various levels, under varying labels—"world history", "history of civilization", "general history", and the like. These courses consisted of a cut-rate Cook's tour from the Pyramids to the United Nations Building, roughly chronological; and out of the dust sent up by scurrying teacher and scurrying students there peered, at intervals, the vague faces of Good Men and Bad Men. All the color and drama of history was lost in their bewildered dash from Athens to Rome to the Dark Ages to the Renaissance to the Enlightenment to the First World War to the Brave New World.

These comprehensive surveys of history will sicken students; or such surveys of literature, or of politics, or of scientific disciplines. Also they will sicken teachers — and drive out of schools and colleges people who possess some aptitude for teaching genuine bodies of knowledge. For the instructor, like the student, begins to suspect that the whole muddled business is a boondoggle. Schooling in the humane disciplines is a difficult thing; so many educational administrators prefer the easy path of Comprehensive Survey, which leads to an intellectual Avernus.

From the historical kind of survey, for instance, the student learns only to agree with Hegel that "we learn from history that we learn nothing from history"—although he doesn't know that Hegel wrote this, and he doesn't catch Hegel's irony. Of one thing he is convinced: that, having been exposed to the Whole Truth of History, he need never again open an historical work.

And the teacher of such sham history, or sociology, or science, becomes a shallow indoctrinator. For lack of time, he must traffic in facile generalities and Olympian judgments. If he touches upon fifth-century Greece, he must eliminate all complexities—and with them, all real insights. He must talk about the Good Democratic Athenians and the Bad Autocratic Spartans; Thucydides goes down the drain. That Athenian imperialism was the proximate cause of the Peloponnesian War, alas, would require at least five more minutes to mention, and he hasn't five more minutes, not in such a survey-course. Besides, how would that truth help young persons to Adjust to Democratic Living?

I am not saying that responsibility for these useless survey-courses lies wholly with our universities and colleges. Often such courses are offered simply because the entering freshmen are ignorant of any true intellectual discipline, and the surveys are ineffectual endeavors to fill the vacuum. Probably the greater part of the guilt ought to be assigned to our public schools. Yet some administrators of colleges pretend that no guilt exists.

All that colleges and universities can do is to teach, within limits, some genuine body of learning—not promulgate grandiose schemes of omniscience on the cheap. They cannot teach Civilization, but they can teach the history of modern England. They cannot teach General Science, but they can teach botany or physics. They cannot teach Social Science, but they can teach American constitutional law or classical political theory. If they wish, they can do a few things well—and so leave the graduating senior with respect for books and some intellectual curiosity.

We may as well laugh as cry. In 1959, the absurdity of our higher learning provided me with some jolly hours. I enjoyed particularly the news from Hawaii.

Among the hymns of thanksgiving rising to Heaven since Hawaii became a state had been a joyous cry that Hawaii, with its university, would be the intellectual meeting-ground of East and West, refuting Kipling; and that students from the Gorgeous East would be edified there by American culture. Possibly so. In 1959, the University of Hawaii prepared for her glorious role as culture-blender by becoming the first institution of higher learning, anywhere in the world, to offer for credit a course in surfboard riding (HPE 119, University of Hawaii Catalogue).

Mr. Bob Krauss, of the Honolulu *Advertiser*, attended the first class session, at the University's summer school, along with "over two hundred students, mostly co-eds in pony tails and beach sandals." Only thirty of these were enrolled for credit, because "surfing instruction on the college level is still in the experimental stage." The instructor, Mr. Don Gustason, promised that "next year we'll add more sections. Meanwhile, those of you who aren't in the class can take private lessons at a discount." The first week of the course was devoted to paddling in the University's swimming pool, in preparation for the ocean. Then successive weeks were spent in learning how to surf, catching a wave, standing on the board, and surfing tandem. Class work was graded thus: fifty points for achievement in actual surfing, ten for term paper, twenty for examinations, and twenty for attitude, effort, and attendance. Oxbridge never was like this, nor the Sorbonne. We Americans have the know-how.

A crew of Waikiki beach boys—rejoicing in such names as Panama, Rabbit, and Blackout—were appointed assistant instructors, at $1.50 per hour. (Why doesn't our anti-intellectual society pay its university instructors better?) The beach boys were examined, before entering the faculty, for "competence, good morals, and teaching ability." No such Draconian code was imposed upon the students of HPE 119.

The Russians may have had their missiles, but the USA had its aquaculture. Hawaii called, and the satrapy of Harry Bridges splashed happily into the atomic age. Put up your hair in a pony tail, little Hindu or Chinee, and buy yourself a pair of tabis: you're about to be assimilated to American culture.

Also in 1959 there occurred demands at the fiftieth convention of the American Home Economics Association that all boys in high school be required to complete a year's study of home economics. And the Bureau of School Services of the University of Michigan threatened to disaccredit, so far as entrance of their graduates to the U of M went, those high schools which did not offer curricula in homemaking. America prepared to confront the Soviets on the surfboards and in the kitchens.

Still, surfing is no more frivolous than certain studies which many universities older and bigger than that of Hawaii offer for substantial credits. In 1959 I examined the catalogue of Michigan State University. Since I had been student and professor there, a very few courses taught in my time had been eliminated—among them one in "critical writing", department of English, now supplanted by "book reviewing", department of journalism. But these few deletions were atoned for by an immense proliferation of new courses—indeed, of new departments and schools.

I found forty-four courses in hotel and restaurant management; one hundred and six courses in sociology and social work; one hundred and sixty-three courses in home economics (eight of these in "nursery schools"); one hundred and fourteen courses in speech; and three hundred and thirty-three courses in education. (If one were to have enrolled in all the courses in education, but in no other courses, it would have taken him two decades to get through this university.) Among the offerings of the College of Education were "Personnel Work in Residence Halls"; "Fly and Bait Casting"; "Square Dance and

Square Dancing"; "Organization and Conduct of Large Scale Activities"; "Philosophy of Physical Education"; "Analysis of Problems of Dance Education"; "Outdoor Programs in Recreation." A student could enroll in a four-year curriculum in Packaging, or in Agricultural Journalism. There was one small department: Religion, with a mere twenty-four courses.

If one cannot contrive to pass the courses of a genuine institution of learning, in short, Michigan State—or many other large institutions — will invent curricula that anybody can master. Name your boondoggle, and we'll institutionalize it.

In 1959, Dr. Jacques Barzun, then provost of Columbia University, published a strong book, *The House of Intellect*. In "Instruction without Authority", his most moving chapter, he wrote, "Is the school a place of teaching or of psychologizing? Is it to prolong vicariously the parents' love of innocence and act out their dream of good society, or is it to impart literacy? . . . To encompass such ends the school must know what it wants, not in the form of vague private or public virtues, but in the form of intellectual powers. It must stop blathering about sensitivity to the needs of others, and increasing responsibility for bringing about one world, and say instead: 'I want a pupil who can read Burke's *Speech on Conciliation* and solve problems in trigonometry.' "

What an archaist! My mother studied Burke's *Conciliation* in school, and I have her copy, but that model of rhetoric had been abandoned before my time. How many graduating seniors nowadays have read that speech, in college, or could?

Barzun was merciless toward the teachers' colleges, dominated by the heirs of Dewey and Kilpatrick. What, essentially, was wrong with the teachers' college professors? Why, they were philanthropists, not scholars:

"This is the wickedness of the philanthropists, that they invoke the force of the group, on top of their own, to achieve something that no one has given them license to attempt. One may say that their tampering with the child's personality is saved from guilt because their goal remains vague and their effort largely unsuccessful. But imagine an explicit program, political or religious, and a corps of teachers more than gushingly dedicated to it, and you would have an irresistible machine for warping both mind and character.

"It would of course take genuine intellectuals to organize for work while concealing their hand. At present, our 'liberal' teachers' college products show but the bare makings of a totalitarian force—the zeal for inducing 'the right attitude'; a thick-skinned intolerance toward all who doubt or criticize so much goodness; and a special language, a flatulent Newspeak, which combines self-righteousness with a permanent fog, so that its users are invulnerable—others abide our questions, they are free.

"The politics of the adjustment curriculum, at any rate, are clear; it is manipulation by sentiment and dubious authority, exercised by the least educated and most vapid minds of the nation."

In the books of the National Education Association, the name of Barzun now is writ large as a Fascist and an Enemy of the Public Schools: this despite the fact, of course, that Barzun was inveighing against the totalist, intolerant—Fascist, if you will—domination of our public schools by these dreary folk. It is these people who have mis-educated American teachers; it is they who give our universities and colleges the present crop of young persons who must be diverted by academic boondoggles.

In our time, Barzun wrote, three great forces of will and mind have become enemies of Intellect: these are Art, Science, and Philanthropy. His discussion of the anti-intellectualism of Philanthropy was particularly telling. The "philanthropic gestures" of our century, he suggested, are symptoms of decadence. "The signs of these effusions are unmistakable—easy indignation, the throb of pity, portentous promises, and still more generally: vague words, loose thoughts." He tore to ribbons that Museum of Modern Art publication which had so delighted enthusiasts for One World, *The Family of Man*: "The theme of copulation is frequently repeated, notably as a restorative after the half-dozen pages devoted to schoolwork."

And—heresy of heresies—Provost Barzun was both amused and annoyed at Soviet-American cultural exchanges, the doctrines of Togetherness, United Nations Day, and People-to-People projects, upon which the tax-exempt foundations delighted in lavishing their funds. "Art is now an instrument of national policy in the ideological war. Though the Russians launched a durable satellite before us, we retaliated with the pianistic prowess of Mr. Van Cliburn. . . . The descent from world conferences through subsidized art to the wordless communion of hockey and dancing suggests the next step, which is sexual congress. It is not new and needs no subsidy, but it shows—since it is an ancient people-to-people device—that world peace is not to be attained even by ecstatic effusions of good will."

To the Lonely Crowd on the campus of Behemoth U., the philan-thropists of education presented every manner of boondoggle. Sexual congress, true, would not come for a few years—with the sexually integrated dormitories. For young people hostile toward intellectuality, other pursuits were created—with full credit. If not all can think, all can feel, in an indiscriminate academic Togetherness.

8

Secularism Militant: 1960

ALL THE EARLY AMERICAN colleges were church-related, Christian of one confession or another. When state universities began to appear, they were neutral on religious questions, generally, although often their founders and early presidents were ardent Christians or even clergymen—for instance, Father Gabriel Richard, the Catholic priest who did more than anyone else to create the University of Michigan. The University of Virginia set the example, with no department of theology or any university subscription to a creed—although Thomas Jefferson, on whose plan the University was established, had expected that the several Christian denominations would build their own colleges or seminaries in the immediate vicinity of the first state university.

In the American democracy, with more than half of the population professing Christian belief and most of the remainder at least vestigially Christian today, state universities and colleges generally have endeavored to avoid giving offense to Christian communicants. In recent decades, the number of departments of religion on state campuses has increased—without their falling into the bad graces of the Supreme Court of the United States, since such departments profess no especial creed and usually include on their staffs representatives of various religious bodies.

Yet, as Cardinal Manning said, at bottom all differences of opinion are theological. A university or college which professes no religious commitment tends to attract professors of no religious convictions, or perhaps hostile toward religious belief—militant secularists; while scholars strongly moved by religious doctrines tend to gravitate toward church-related universities and colleges. Thus as the proportion of students enrolled in independent colleges steadily diminished after the Second World War, relative to the proportion enrolled in state institutions—why, the Christian character of the higher learning in America diminished also.

Universities and colleges scarcely were affected by the Supreme Court's several decisions, during this period, on classroom prayers, public Bible-reading in public schools, and the like. As federal grants to universities and colleges grew in number and scope, a good many church-related institutions would relax somewhat their confessional attachments and perhaps remove religious symbols from their buildings—but that, in 1960, was chiefly in the future. From other motives, many of the colleges connected with Protestant denominations already had almost severed their church ties. Thus, although political authorities made no concerted endeavor to interfere with religion in the higher learning, the influence of religious doctrine upon the higher learning has declined in this century.

Powerful influences within the American educational establishment have not been content with the mere gradual decline of the religious element in the higher learning. Some educationists there are who would like to have the first clause of the first amendment to the federal Constitution interpreted not as a declaration of neutrality among creeds, but rather as a declaration of disapproval of religious faith by the state. The followers of John Dewey, if they understand their master, are committed to a rather aggressive secularism. (Dewey's "Religious Humanist Manifesto" was neither religious nor humanistic.) By 1960, this hostility toward the survival of religion on state or municipal campuses was discernible in a number of instances. I offer three here.

The first of these occurred on one of the campuses of the University of California. In 1959, on that campus, a chapter of the Inter-Varsity Christian Fellowship was formed. The Inter-Varsity Christian Fellowship is a highly reputable national association of evangelical Christian faculty people and students, with branches on many campuses throughout the country. This particular campus chapter was startled to be informed by an officious dean of women that female students, thereafter, would be forbidden to join the group.

Discussion of religion upset girls, she said, and made them neurotic. (The Inter-Varsity Christian Fellowship, far from manifesting the symptoms of the more extreme varieties of religious experience, is a sober association of some intellectual attainments and a serious press of its own.) Apparently the dean of women believed that co-eds should be confined to normal socially-approved activities, like smooching.

Student members of the local Fellowship appealed to the dean of students—who sustained his subordinate the dean of women. "But is it permitted for students to read on this campus?" a student remonstrated. Yes, the dean said warily, it was. "And is it permitted to hold discussions on this campus?" The dean conceded that. "And would it be all right to conduct a Marxist discussion group on this campus?" The dean frowned, but said it would be. "Then why can't we have a Christian discussion group?"

"You're missing the point," the dean protested. "You have more than three people in your group, and that makes it a public meeting, and you have to get the University's permission for that."

Yet, what with the protests of people on the faculty and professors at other universities, the dean was compelled to give way. The dean of women still tried to enforce her ban upon female participation, but at last was compelled to permit young women to discuss the scandalous teachings of Jesus of Nazareth.

In 1960, for all that, a fresh threat to the Inter-Varsity Christian Fellowship arose—a threat also to the Newman Centers on Californian state campuses. For there went into effect a University ban against any student group which discriminated as to "race, color, or creed." It was the "creed" which might be used as a bludgeon against Protestant and Catholic societies, if administrators had a mind to establish a domination of Holy Positivism. Were a Catholic club ordered to admit Baptists, Unitarians, and Black Muslim enthusiasts; if Protestant society were expected to welcome Papists, Jews, Moslems, and votaries of Scientology—why, the organization would lose its reason for being, and quite possibly lose control over its own funds. The Californian zealots for complete equality and "togetherness" doubtless would have commanded John Wesley's "Holy Club" at Oxford, in the eighteenth century, to open its meetings to members of the Hellfire Club—and the Tractarians, in nineteenth-century Oxford, to embrace the champions of the dissidence of dissent.

As matters developed, not long after 1960, university administrations abandoned much of any attempt to regulate student groups of any sort, and in some cases federal court decisions have prevented college officials from interference with free association of students. So this Inter-Varsity Christian Fellowship case remains interesting chiefly as indication of anti-Christian prejudices not far below the surface in some universities. It has been remarked that anti-Catholicism is the anti-Semitism of the intellectuals; it may be added that the intellectuals' dislike of evangelical or "fundamentalist" Protestantism runs nearly as strong, often. I do not think that those prejudices are diminishing much.

Anti-religious prejudices among college intellectuals have run harshest in New York City. Of American professors, Dr. George N. Shuster wrote that "many have been or are sons of rabbis and ministers of the Gospel who have preferred secular learning to the lore of Scripture. These have given to the universities and colleges they have served a very special impulse to achieve innovation and even reform. Perhaps they are primarily responsible for a quality no one can dissociate from the American campus and which is virtually unknown in Europe—a characteristic to be defined on the one hand as an almost bellicose addiction to freedom and on the other as a commitment to a 'liberal position', not quite a dogma this but almost one, which assays the Devil according to the degree of his 'conservatism.' "

The city colleges (now City University) of New York, with which Dr. Shuster was intimately acquainted when he was president of Hunter College, are notorious for the quasi-religious intolerance which looks upon conservatism—and Catholicism, too—as the mark of the Beast. Queens College seems to have been the worst offender or sufferer for some years. There occurred at Queens, in the 'Fifties and 'Sixties, several instances of professors being refused tenure, or otherwise got rid of, for presuming to hold views at variance with those of the ritualistic liberals on the faculty. One case—that of Dr. Dale Fallon, a teacher of history, who had the misfortune to be both a Catholic and a conservative—received considerable attention in the press. Dr. Fallon and others both went to law and appealed to official state commissions.

In 1960, the New York State Commission against Discrimination adjudged Queens College guilty of discrimination against Catholics on the faculty. For two years Commissioner J. Edward Conway had investigated Queens. At the city colleges of New York, tenure and promotion were granted by faculty committees, rather than by presidents or departmental chairmen. For years, the Commission found, these tenure committees had been dominated, at two or three of the city colleges, by "relatively atheistic" and radical professors. One Catholic faculty-member was told, "We have cultivated a secular attitude here at Queens College, and you don't fit here." The general conclusion of the Commission against Discrimination was that the Queens College faculty committees had adhered intolerantly to "an intellectual trend in our colleges [that] is secular and liberal . . . not religious, not conservative."

The reinstatement of Dr. Fallon was directed by the Commission. But this story does not have a happy ending: Governor Nelson Rockefeller, intervening, ruled that the powers of the State Commission against Discrimination did not extend to public colleges, and so the cause was lost.

It was not only at Queens College that toleration required official enforcement. At Brooklyn College, a professor of languages—who happened to be a conservative and a Catholic, too—was a candidate for receiving tenure. He had published more than anyone else in his department, had a good record as a teacher, and was commended by his departmental chairman; but the tenure committee put every obstacle in his way. They professed to believe that he had not really written the books and articles he listed; when he produced letters from his publishers certifying that two more books of his soon were to be published, the inquisitors of the tenure committee telephoned the publisher's office to ask if the letters were forgeries. When at last they could deny his claims to authorship no longer, members of the committee argued that if he had published so much, he must have been neglecting his duties as a teacher. At length they refused point-blank to grant him tenure, because he "had an immoral influence on students"—the charge brought against Socrates.

What did the committee mean by "immoral influence"? The candidate was told that he was "against democracy." (He had been some years a prisoner in a Nazi concentration-camp.) How was he against democracy? He had said "unkind things against John Dewey."

In this case, the college president, happily for the professor in question, was Dr. Harry Gideonse, one of the ablest and most intelligent academic administrators in America. Dr. Gideonse gave the professor tenure despite the tenure-committee's findings, knowing that the professor's political principles had been the true reason for the committee's intemperance.

Although the city colleges of New York were offenders at this time, instances of this intolerance were found throughout the country—and not merely at state or municipal institutions. Nor was the intolerance confined to attacks upon Catholic professors.

The anti-religious bigot in Academe commonly is hot against "McCarthyism" and mightily alarmed at purported threats to freedom of opinion in America; he wails about "pressures toward conformity." What he seeks, however, is not liberality of opinion generally, but a conformity to his own secular and ideological orthodoxy, enforced by himself and his colleagues.

The anti-religious bigot among the educationists would like to eradicate church-related schools, colleges, and universities altogether. In this endeavor, primary and secondary schools generally are easier targets than are colleges and universities, schools being more directly within the jurisdiction of state departments of public instruction— which, in most states, continue to be strongly influenced, and indeed staffed, by what David Riesman has called "the patronage network of Teachers College, Columbia."

That famous institution, until recent years, indeed had converted the doctrines of John Dewey into an ideology, which many of the Teachers College people endeavored to enforce upon schools. Matters have changed there considerably now, with a new president and the presence on the Teachers College faculty of such well-known educators of Christian profession as Dr. Philip Phenix. But in 1960, the old doctrinaire Deweyite clique, belligerently hostile toward church-related schools, remained strong there. Here is an instance.

Near the end of 1959, there was sent to school administrators in the state of New York a Questionaire "in Connection with a Study of the Effect of Attendance in Non-Public Schools in New York State." A covering letter was signed by William P. Anderson, associate professor of education, Teachers College, Columbia University—under the Teachers College letterhead, which is calculated to make school administrators take notice.

"The attached questionnaire is one aspect of some research which we are undertaking here in the Department of Educational Administration," Anderson wrote. "You will see that it is an attempt to get some relevant data and to obtain some of your perceptions regarding the effect of non-public schools on securing money for public education. We are not at a stage in our research here where we wish to publicize it and would appreciate your keeping this inquiry confidential."

This Teachers College questionnaire seemed intended to form, rather than to ascertain, the opinions of school administrators. As with many "surveys" of the professional educationists, the questions were so phrased as to extract, if at all possible, the desired answers—or at least to make clear to school administrators the approved party line of the professors of pedagogy.

For the principal implication of this questionnaire—which extended to seventeen items—was that Catholic, Protestant, and Jewish schools took away money that ought to be levied for state-supported schools; and that citizens and school-board members with church affiliations tended to obstruct the raising of taxes and bond issues in support of public schools. I cite a few of the questions.

(Question 5) "What is the number of members on your Board of Education whose children attend or have attended non-public schools or who are otherwise identifiable as strong supporters of non-public education?"

(Question 12) "Assuming that a plan could be devised for providing teachers and facilities, do you believe that all students should be required to attend public elementary and secondary schools?"

(Question 13) "If a budget or bond issue has been defeated in your district, have the supporters of non-public schools been a major factor in this defeat?"

(Question 15) "Regardless of your previous responses to questions regarding your school system, do you think that the existence of non-public schools is a source of difficulty in the total effort of the profession to obtain adequate financial support for public education?"

It seems clear enough that the sort of democracy in favor at Teachers College was what J. L. Talmon called "totalitarian democracy"—at least among the author of this questionnaire and his circle. Although occasionally the suppression of all church-related schools is mentioned publicly at meetings of professional educationists, usually this propaganda against "non-public" schooling is carried on behind closed doors or in "confidential surveys." These advocates of total secularizing of the schools are nearly as hotly opposed to Protestant and Jewish foundations as to Catholic; but because the Catholic schools have by far the larger enrollments in most regions, they receive the bulk of the educationists' abuse, public and private.

The final inquiry in the Teachers College questionnaire was this: "Do you believe that the increasing practice of educating young people in church related schools will lead to religious group cleavages within our society that will be so strong as to result in general intolerance and unacceptance of people of different religious beliefs?"

No, Associate Professor Anderson, I do not so believe. But I believe that any society deprived of its religious convictions will become fiercely intolerant of minorities and of private opinions. And I do believe that such "cleavages"—that is, freedom of opinion and diversity of associations—are healthier than an enforced conformity to a humorless and dogmatic latter-day instrumentalism and positivism. I do not think that Anderson and his colleagues were solicitous, really, for religious toleration.

The grand tendency of our age is toward concentration of power. Once concentrated, any power tends to suppress the slightest challenge to its supremacy. And no form of monopoly is more oppressive than intolerant control over the mind and the conscience of the rising generation.

Certain recent court decisions, federal and state, appear to afford church-related schools more protection against state interference than they formerly enjoyed; yet other decisions hint at increased interference in new ways. In this book, concerned with the higher learning, I cannot go deeply into these school controversies. Yet the hostility in strong educationist circles toward church-related education at every level, notable in 1960 but present every year of the past quarter of a century, probably has not diminished. Ideas filter down from the universities to state and federal bureaucracies, to teachers' colleges and teachers' unions, to schools. Because the ultimate questions of education are religious questions, as Plato knew, any system of instruction which forbids discussion of religious concerns cannot touch upon objects and ends; and therefore is decadent. The whole dispute, raising the old controversies between state and church, almost certainly will burst out again in the next few years.

9

Withered Authority: 1961

W HY SHOULD we believe anything or do anything? On what authority? That question, although put into words by few students during 1961, lay uncomfortably just below the daily consciousness of many of them. In every generation, among every people, the young who are about to enter upon independence make some such inquiry. Ordinarily answers are given, whether or not those replies are wholly satisfactory, and the young accept the answers, if grudgingly. Authority is pointed out to them, and in general they submit.

But the liberal democratic age after the Second World War, in America and western Europe, seemed to provide no answer to the question "on what authority?"—or at least no answer that satisfied the restless and uncertain rising generation. When journalists wrote of an "authority", they meant a specialized scholar in some field or other—an expert. Among liberal social scientists, "authoritarian" had become a devil-term, confounded with "totalitarian." Once upon a time, a bishop or a famous preacher had been an authority; an eminent public man or a strong-minded general had been an authority; great books had been authorities; a university president or a confident learned professor had been an authority; a parent had been an authority. And above all these authorities, in the old culture of which American society in 1961 was a continuation, had stood the authority of God, as expressed through the Bible or the church's tradition.

But these old authorities were enfeebled by 1961, or had even repudiated themselves. The culture of the new suburbs, from which most college students came, was soft and permissive; its schooling, too, was soft, and its religion often what Will Herberg called "the ethos of sociability." The generation of the suburbs had no saints or heroes for exemplars. The arbiters of the college generation's taste had been the television masters of ceremonies, the Wise Men of the network news broadcasts, the freaks of rock music; many of the college generation had been reared on salacious magazines and pornographic films, which they took for granted. Many were precociously experienced in sexuality, or marijuana, or drink. They knew, most of them, that something was lacking in this life of theirs, they being often bored; but what was lacking, few had any notion.

They were looking for authority—if only for authority to challenge. Life without authority to oppose or support was like a game of solitaire. They needed someone to tell them the rules of the game of life, if only so that they could break the rules. But no one seemed to be in charge. Parents, teachers, clergymen, even policemen were indulgent and vague. No one ever firmly said "No!" As tiny children are said to court punishment, that they may learn definitely what is permitted and what is not, so the college generation of these years probed again and again for solidity, but encountered only flabbiness. Without vice there is no virtue; without folly there is no wisdom. The rising generation could not discover virtue or vice, wisdom or folly: only the phrase of empty consolation, "Do your own thing." Without authority, the world was meaningless.

During these years I spoke at La Jolla to a group of young men who were students of old Herbert Marcuse, the unconventional Marxist. I found them civil and interested; they informed me that Marcuse and I agreed about some things, particularly about the futility of student "Activism", as opposed to serious study. Marcuse was neither a lively man nor a lively writer. What did they see in him? What Kent discerned in Lear: authority. Marcuse's, to their eyes and ears, was the *potestas magisterii*, the authority to teach. Their friendliness suggested that they found something of that authority in me also. I suspect that it did not so much matter to them what was taught, as that it should be taught by a man who clearly believed in the truth of what he was saying, and who possessed some reputation for learning of a sort and originality of a sort. Had they come to me first, my politics of prudence, derived from Burke, would have satisfied them as well as did Marcuse's ideology, derived from Marx. "He speaks as one having authority."

Their generation encountered few such; the more intelligent of them looked up hungry, and were not fed. Everywhere authority had withered. Their rebellion against order within the university and without it, during the next few years, would be the final form of demand for authority. "We are being dangerous," the subconscious in them said.

"Has no one the courage or the authority to say us nay?" Whenever someone did reply to them in a voice of confident authority—although that was seldom enough—they ceased to be outrageous, for at last they had found that for which they had been probing. So it would be with S. I. Hayakawa at San Francisco State. "I am a Samurai," Dr. Hayakawa would say to himself—drawing, semanticist though he was, upon the authority of militant tradition. That would suffice.

In 1961, not many students had turned outrageous; they still were asking confused questions, rather than shouting non-negotiable demands. In effect, they were inquiring, "How then shall we live?" On few campuses did they find any answers in their course of studies. Nor were there mentors who spoke to them with the ring of authority. All was existential and "ambivalent." Often the campus ministry was the least likely place to turn for counsel.

I offer you an example from Wellesley College. In the spring of 1961, Charles A. Hall, dean of the chapel at Wellesley, lectured or sermonized on "the moral tone of the college", and his reflections were reported at some length in the *Wellesley College News*. He touched upon the question of authority. I suspect that Dean Hall had been influenced by a recent thoughtful book, Alexander Miller's *Faith and Learning*, though perhaps not so strongly influenced as he ought to have been. He fell into a vulgar error concerning the nature of authority.

"Denying the concept of a college as an organ for instilling values within the individual," the report of Dean Hall's remarks runs, "Mr. Hall stated that the goal of Wellesley is instead one of setting the individual free from all external authority, including her own." Inevitably, during the college years, Dean Hall continued, there must occur a period of "brokenness", a breaking with old values and prejudices. "Mr. Hall stated that if the individual learns anything during college, it is the ability to rely on the inner self, what the Christian faith calls the conscience. He pointed out that the college cannot and will not attempt to spoon-feed the individual a quantity of principles and precepts which will become the basic context of one's conscience."

Now it is true enough that colleges and universities do not exist to instill "moral values" directly — a point I have touched upon earlier in this book. As Dr. Alexander Miller suggests in his book, Christianity is concerned not with woolly abstract "values", but with realities. The word "value" implies a relativism of taste and conduct which produces, at best, a vague eclecticism. The Decalogue is not a catalogue of "values": it is a list of imperatives.

Yet also it remains true that college and university cannot remain indifferent upon grave ethical questions, or to the consequences of study upon the lives of students. College training ought to be intellectual in character, not moralistic; yet it dare not ignore its ultimate ethical end. And one reason why some American colleges may seem morally didactic in their methods is that ethical instruction has been neglected by parents, church, and school, where such moral precepts more properly belong.

Simply to break down prejudices and traditional beliefs among students, but to supply no certitudes by way of restoration, is a risky venture in a college. "Mr. Hall stressed that the answer to the problem is not known, but that it lies partially in teaching the individual to be self-reliant."

Thus we are thrown back upon "the inner self", untutored conscience, and Emersonian self-reliance. One thinks of T. S. Eliot's strictures upon the "inner voice": "The inner voice, in fact, sounds remarkably like an old principle which has been formulated by an elder critic in the now familiar phase of 'doing as one likes.' The possessors of an inner voice ride ten to a compartment to a football match at Swansea, listening to the inner voice, which breathes the eternal message of vanity, fear, and lust."

"Follow your conscience" would become the boastful admonition of the student activists during the next decade. But the Christian concept of conscience is not that of a "pipeline to God", a mere mysterious "inner self" or "inner voice" which is morally infallible. Really, "conscience" means ethical judgment in the light of certain enduring ethical principles, tempered by the cardinal virtue of prudence. Unless one recognizes and understands norms, unless one's conscience is tutored by authority, what is miscalled "conscience" becomes self-righteous prejudice, glorying in one's own rectitude. In such circumstances, what one takes for the whispers of one's "inner self" may be nothing more than what one has read in an ideologue's pamphlet, or in the pages of *Rolling Stone*. And such a conscience's dictates ordinarily do no more than reflect personal impulses of the moment, or personal advantage: it becomes infinitely easy to justify appetite or will by convincing one's self that one's conscience dictates or allows whatever one feels like doing. Some folk find conscience very indulgent on the question of filing accurate income-tax returns; others on the question of risking one's person in military service.

If the goal of Wellesley College indeed was to set the individual free from all external authority, "including her own", then the young ladies of Wellesley after 1961 must have found themselves in a peck of trouble. People who think themselves free of all external authority, and responsible only to an inner light, cannot live in community; for the civil social order requires authority. I doubt if Dean Hall's auditors became hermits. The function of a college is not to deny all validity to just authority, but rather to teach people to distinguish between authority that is legitimate and alleged authority that is actually the reign of misrule.

The sort of intellectual and theological flabbiness displayed in Dean Hall's reported lecture was the target of one of the more important books published during 1961, *Odyssey of the Self-Centered Self*, by Robert Elliot Fitch, dean of the Pacific School of Religion. Taking for his example the sentimental complacency of Ralph Waldo Trine, Dean Fitch observed, "For the Neo-Christian sentimentalists . . . it must be observed that all this has no relationship to the historic teaching of the church. It is one thing to proclaim, in the Pelagian manner, that all you have to do is look for the Christ who is already within; and that you, too, can be a God-man just as easily as Jesus managed it, if you will but give the matter your attention. It is another thing to teach with Saint Paul that you need to have the Christ enter in where he is not now, and that whatever divine sonship you may attain to on your own does not in any way obviate the necessity for redemption by him who was uniquely the Son of God. However, a sentimental Christianity, under the banner of a liberal theology, has no difficulty at all in appropriating the revisionist rendering of Saint Paul as expounded by Emerson-Whitman-Trine."

The contempt for authority which seemed implicit in Dean Hall's sermon was dealt with shrewdly in another good book of 1961—Denis Baly's *Academic Illusion*, which had to do with Christian teaching in colleges. If just authority is lacking, as Baly pointed out, freedom is not possible; and this is as true morally as it is politically. Conscience, indeed, is an authority of sorts; but it cannot do duty for every source of authoritative knowledge. John Henry Newman gives this description of authority: "Conscience is an authority; the Bible is an authority; such is Antiquity; such are the words of the wise; such are hereditary lessons; such are ethical truths; such are historical memories; such are legal saws and state maxims; such are proverbs; such are sentiments, presages, and prepossessions." Yet the "activists" of the 'Sixties had been encouraged to recognize no source of authority but the first of these—and that in a secularized and corrupted aspect.

If, indeed, one could dispense with any authority but that of private judgment, why bother with a liberal education at all? One can experience "brokenness", for what it is worth, less expensively by getting a job at Woolworth's. Formal education necessarily consists, mostly, of imparting a body of ascertained knowledge and a body of received opinions. "All the college can do is to try to teach each student how to discriminate for herself," Dean Hall proclaimed. Yet how does one discriminate without ascertainable standards? Protagoras, rather than Socrates, seems to have been in vogue at Wellesley and many other colleges in 1961; and Walt Whitman, rather than Saint Paul.

Yet cheerfulness would keep breaking in. For decades, John Dewey's educational theories, from their fortress at Teachers College, Columbia, had been breaking down old educational authorities. And yet by 1961, Teachers College had begun to alter its direction and even appeared to be shifting toward a fuller concept of authority. Its new president, Dr. Fischer, was emphatic that the purpose of schooling is the *intellectual* cultivation of the person; that the school exists not to "develop the whole person", not to serve as a community center, but to do something for the mind.

Although it would take a great while for the amended doctrines of Teachers College to penetrate to the School of Education at Dismal Swamp A. & M., these new or revived theories of education were beginning to leaven the lump in 1961. The most heartening production of the Teachers College professors was Dr. Philip Phenix's book *Education and the Common Good: a Moral Philosophy of the Curriculum*. It was a book suffused with veneration. Dr. Phenix desired to restore "values and ideals"—I would have preferred the word "norms"—to the curriculum. His values and norms were religious. Practically speaking, Christian love, rather than the ego, should be the moral foundation of learning. The public schools, Professor Phenix was bold enough to say, can and must return to this normative task; they must not fear to teach religious truths:

"The state and its agencies, including the public schools and colleges, can be true to the principle of religious liberty without giving up their primary obligation to promote the religious life, in the fundamental sense of reverent devotion. Freedom of religion is itself a religious principle, since it rests on the conviction that no man, group of men, or institution can claim final and authoritative knowledge, perfection, or righteousness. If a wall of separation is erected between religion and the state (and its schools), that will prove to be a tomb in which church, state, and schools will decay with a civilization that has lost its soul. Schools that are purged of all religious concerns become agencies for the propagation of irreligion or idolatry—for the feeding of selfish ambitions or training for subservience to secular utopias. If religion is understood in its elemental sense, and not merely in its sectarian expressions, it is entirely practicable for the public schools to educate religiously without violating any ideals of religious freedom, without partisanship for any historical tradition, and without transgressing the principle of persuasion, not compulsion, in all matters of faith."

As Professor Phenix went on to argue, first it will be necessary to instruct teachers in the major religious traditions of mankind, and to secure as teachers people who are reverent. To develop intelligence, to encourage creativity, to inculcate reverence—these, Dr. Phenix wrote, are the ends of education. And to accomplish these aims, all studies at all levels, both humane and scientific disciplines, must recognize the primacy of religious insights. Professor Phenix urged Americans to emancipate themselves from the concept of social engineering, with its "mechanistic attitude toward human beings."

The disciples of Ayn Rand, then not infrequently encountered on campuses,would have profited from reading Professor Phenix's passage on irreligion: "*Irreligion* stands in diametric opposition to religion. It consists in self-seeking orientation. It is the denial of any object of supreme worth beyond the self. It is founded upon the conviction that man himself is the source of values, that human beings do not discover the worthful but themselves create and decide whatever is to be counted as good. . . . It is founded on the premise that the proper end of man is to become independent and autonomous." With the delusion of "autonomy", whether the variant of David Riesman or that of Ayn Rand, Phenix would have no truck.

Perhaps the fundamental error of John Dewey was this: the notion that society itself, *en masse*, somehow provides objects or ends, and that the individual need merely adjust to such democratic goodness. But Professor Phenix takes us beyond both egoism and collectivism to that wise Love which moves the sun and all the stars.

It was not Philip Phenix that the more restless spirits had begun to read, when they read anything; nor yet John Dewey. They, especially the teaching assistants on the campus of Behemoth State University, were reading C. Wright Mills, Herbert Marcuse, Norman O. Brown. They were "oppressed", they began to say: and all authority must come down.

10

Neurosis, Ideology, and Indifference: 1962

A GOOD MANY BOOKS have been written about the radicalism of college students during the 'Sixties, but probably American historians, a few years from now, will say little about those campus disorders. Those troubles interest me chiefly as evidence of the unsoundness of American higher education, and my chapters on the subject are drawn from my personal experiences, in part, during the 'Sixties. To those who desire a systematic and perceptive study of the radical movements, I commend Dr. Edward Ericson's *Radicals in the University* (1975).

So far as the higher learning was concerned, the students' riots accomplished nothing but a further lowering of intellectual standards. In practical politics, the radicalized students did contribute toward the altering of American policy in southeastern Asia; yet the American government presumably would not have much prolonged its military operations in Vietnam, anyway, the whole military design of the Johnson administration in that quarter of the world having been ruinously impracticable from the first.

One reason why the student activism of the 'Sixties achieved little of substance was that its rhetoric sounded either detestable or incomprehensible to the general public; another was that the general public of that time yearned for stability and security, within a constitutional framework, while the young activists shouted emptily of destruction. Had the students risen in revolt thirty years earlier, during the Great Depression, they might have been formidable, for then they could have allied themselves with the labor unions and the radical political movements of that period. But that is a silly speculation, for in the 'Thirties the mass of the college students had been Tory, especially on the big campuses; I had been one of the Michigan State students who repulsed the goon-squads of the United Automobile Workers, at East Lansing, when the UAW seized control of Michigan's capital for a day in the autumn of 1936. Most of us students were straited in our means then. By 1962, the ideological spectacle of the children of affluence proclaiming their solidarity with "the oppressed working masses" was merely comical, while students' adulation of Fidel Castro and Mao Tse-tung made it certain that they must alienate the immense majority of the American public.

At the University of Michigan, a few days after the Kennedy-sponsored landing of Cuban exiles at the Bay of Pigs, I was debating Senator Hubert Humphrey on questions of American foreign-aid policies. In the front rows of Hill Auditorium sat bearded students wearing Cuban-style fatigue caps. Once the question-period had commenced, these ideologues asked the liberal Senator what they might do to assist Dr. Castro in his hour of need. Humphrey replied, in effect, that they might hang Fidel Castro to a sour-apple tree. Thereafter the controversy was between Humphrey and the radical students, rather than between him and me.

Politically, the hostilities on the campus during the 'Sixties were between liberals and radicals, for the most part. From time to time, on this campus or that, I found myself debating against William Kunstler or Saul Alinsky or Dick Gregory or Leonard Weinglass; but the radicals' wrath was directed more against the Kennedy and Johnson liberals than against conservative spokesmen like myself. I was even applauded by chapters of Students for a Democratic Society, as a sardonic critic of affairs at Behemoth U. I talked with a good many of the student radicals, and often found that their discontents were not political in origin, though their protests took a political form.

The radical student movements commenced with involvement in the "civil rights" struggles that went back into the Eisenhower years. By 1962, the Congress of Racial Equality and SANE, the nuclear-disarmament outfit, were the most flourishing of the activist groups. When I spoke at the University of Chicago, that year, it was rumored that the local chapter of CORE would picket my lecture; but they did not, perhaps because they were busy vexing the university's chancellor by occupying the chairs in his office. They definitely had considered picketing, the previous night, a lecture by Professor Lionel Trilling, critic and novelist, on the general principle that somehow this might call attention to the Simon Legrees of Mississippi. Any pretext for "activism" would do. I suggested then at Chicago that if students yearn to picket and sit, they might picket the ideologue professor, the dull professor, the lazy professor. As for sit-ins, such professors already had the students sleeping in their chairs.

The student activists of 1962 were a dull lot themselves; even their well-wishers confessed that the radical students were not thinkers. Picketing often was one means for evading thought and even for evading the tasks of efficiently organizing their own groups. Measured by college grades, most of the CORE and SANE zealots ranked well toward the bottom of their classes. They lacked what student radicals (few in number) of my own college days had possessed: Marxist resolution and Marxist logic. More neurotic than idological, they and their type could not have made much impression, had it not been for the failure, later, of the American military endeavor in Vietnam, and for the American draft. Those, particularly the latter, became issues which attracted a large and vigorous following to the radical associations.

The National Student Association began to shift from liberalism to radicalism in 1962. For several years I had been one of the six national advisors to NSA, speaking more than once at their national conventions. The 1962 Congress of NSA resulted in a document called "Codification of Policy", which remained temperate enough. It put the matter thus: "While recognizing that the student must devote primary attention to his academic program, the USNSA urges student participation in legitimate social and political activities." The Codification contained one page concerned with "The Aims of Education", with two very sound paragraphs:

"Atmosphere: American colleges lack devotion to the intellect, a sense of dedication, and a profound respect for the education which the student should be pursuing. The loss of the proper intellectual climate has been accompanied by a misdirection of extracurricular activities through an overemphasis on social, athletic, and governmental activities for their own sake rather than for the sake of the overall educational process.

"The Individual: USNSA has observed that in the haste to bring more education to more people, and as a result of the change in the emphasis of education from academic achievement to social adjustment, the individual—the center of the educational process—has been forgotten. The aim of education is individual development—not social adjustment."

It was well said, and something that intelligent students urgently needed to examine. Most of the NSA's Codification, however, was concerned not with the life of intellect, but rather with political and social pronunciamentos, sometimes of a character extremely naïve, yet uttered *ex cathedra*. More than a page of this document was devoted to "Africa under Portuguese Domination", and two pages were allotted to denunciation of South Africa.

The politicizing of the USNSA was carried much farther not long later, in 1962, when the national headquarters of the organization mailed to student leaders throughout the country a lengthy mimeographed document, cloaked in sociological jargon, the authors of which argued, in effect, that students ought to spend their time perfecting society—and to let learning go hang. Already some of the bulletins from the NSA offices might have led the uninitiated to conclude that NSA was a branch of the Congress of Racial Equality. Thereafter the National Student Association was swept into the radical mill-race.

Other student groups also shifted from liberalism, or from moderate radicalism, into extreme courses. Chapters at various colleges of the Young Socialist League began to invite hard-line Communists to address them, from a hazy Popular Front notion of sympathy and common aims—an illusion which was anathema to knowing socialists like Norman Thomas. At the University of Arizona, in 1962, the Young Democrats distributed many copies of the Communist-line weekly *Guardian*—perhaps mistaking it for a mere pacifist sheet, when they should have known that *The Nation* was true-blue Tory, by the side of *The Guardian*.

From shallow discussion, such groups would pass to noisy and often violent demonstration, during the next few years. That shift to action is an important reason why most of the young radicals of those years are obscure and forgotten nowadays. Herbert Marcuse told his disciples to stick to their books and their discussions, that they might wield influence later in life; and I was to find that he was using the same illustration as I did to drive this point home. Suppose, I kept saying throughout the years of campus turmoil, that Karl Marx, instead of spending his days in the reading-room of the British Museum, had gone daily to Piccadilly Circus, bearing a sandwich-board with the legend, "Workers of the world, unite!"—why, would anyone recall that eccentric's name now, and would he ever have finished *Das Kapital*?

Most students of 1962 seemed interested only in eventual self-advancement, if that. So I did not mean to discourage students from sensible political activity—so long as they should remember that the Academy, by its nature, is a place for leisure, contemplation, and the acquisition of a body of knowledge. The university is a place for preparation, not a battlefield. The university is not the world. For action, graduates have abundant opportunity all the rest of their lives. But never again will they have four years among scholars and books, when they may prepare themselves for the imaginative and temperate action that is the object of the liberal and scientific disciplines.

As Lord Keynes said once, today's classroom lectures become the slogans of tomorrow's crowd—though with unideological America or Britain in mind, he might better have said, with less hyperbole, that those lectures become crowd-slogans three decades later. If the lectures and the books have taken second place to sit-ins, marches, strikes, an amorphous bumbling eagerness to ride the whirlwind and direct the storm, at the age of twenty—then the slogans of the future crowd will be someone else's slogans, perhaps the cant of demagogues and of men who cannot govern themselves, let alone govern a great nation.

Professor Harold Lasswell and his school of behaviorists, for decades, had been endeavoring to attribute all political behavior, except their own, to neuroses—mental sickness. Certainly there is much oddity in practical politics; but the neurosis-hypothesis leaves out of account the power of ideology. Far from being identical with political philosophy, "ideology" means political religion—as I have pointed out elsewhere. An ideologue may suffer from mental illness: many do, and others behave as if they had so suffered. Yet also an ideologue may be thoroughly rational, as the world judges rationality and normality, at least within the confines of his system. In revolutionary times, Tocqueville tells us, madness may be no handicap; indeed, it may help one toward a temporary success. Yet it does not follow that all revolutionaries are quite mad.

Both ideologues and neurotics made up the leadership of student radicalism in the 'Sixties. The latter were the more numerous. As the campus disturbances began to wane, Professor Bruno Bettelheim, the psychologist, said that at the core of every radical student group there could be found a tiny handful of very clever young people who knew what they were doing. These were surrounded by a much larger body of neurotic young persons with proclivities toward violence, who served as the striking-force of the inner core: precise in his use of psychological terms, Dr. Bettelheim called these latter activists paranoiacs. Then there could be turned out by the radicals, on occasion, a mob of boys and girls with no real commitment to the ideological cause, but ready enough for a varsity rag—bored, other-directed, happy to escape from campus routine, eager to be where the action was. Of such elements were the "idealist" student organizations made up; and ordinarily the activists did not exceed more than five per cent of any student body, even on the more systematically radicalized campuses. The paranoiacs among them were capable of destroying offices, damaging or even burning libraries, setting off bombs, and beating fellow-students or recalcitrant professors. The presence on a campus of a few shrewd and energetic young ideologues often sufficed to paralyze, thus, the normal functioning of a big university.

Although some ideologues are neurotics—and certainly neurotics or even men thoroughly mad provide the hysterical enthusiasts of ideological revolutions—I repeat that there subsists no necessary conjunction of ideological belief and neurotic disturbance. An ideologue may be tolerably balanced in everything but his politics. As old John Adams put it, ideology is the science of idiocy; and so a man who takes up crazy politics presently may become odd, from contagion, in other ways. The fundamental error of the ideologue is his assumption that all the ills to which flesh is heir may be remedied by swift changes in political institutions and social arrangements. He mistakes politics and economics for the whole of life; and presently political intrigue does become the whole of *his* life—which makes him less human than he might have been. But he remains skillful at manipulating other people—in playing upon their resentments and confusions for the advantage of his cause. On the campuses of the 'Sixties, human tools were ready to his hand.

Shallowly and permissively schooled and reared, with no strong interests of any sort, sometimes with too much money and too little occupation, bored and lacking in strength of will, egoistic without real self-confidence, this category of young people seemed more numerous in twentieth-century American society than ever they had been in any other society; they have been called the products of the Freudian ethic. Jacques Barzun, in *The House of Intellect*, had suggested that pampering of the young had produced meaningless resentment and rebellion, rather than happiness: it had encouraged one type of neurosis. Many such young people sought, consciously or unconsciously, to destroy the culture which had nurtured them too indulgently. A considerable proportion of these soft and muddled rebels without a cause fancied themselves intelligent, and had been thought bright by their fond parents. Barzun had described the consequent mood:

"Nowadays . . . it is assumed that all attacks on culture are equal in virtue, and that attacking society, because it is society, is the one aim and test of genius. The young therefore enlist and fight, without asking of the ugly world they have inherited whether anybody ever received it fresh, perfect, and beautiful. Their intellect does not stretch so far as to criticize, with whatever *furor adolescentium*; it condemns, vaguely yet vehemently, as one would expect from the sentimental education they have received."

Such young Americans were likened by Barzun to Smerdyakov, in *The Brothers Karamazov*. It was our Smerdyakovs who by 1962 already were filling the ranks of the various student radical organizations. They might not know where they were going or what they desired; they might be grossly ignorant of the details of the ideologies to which they subscribed; but protest for its own sake, the more violent the better (so long as they ran no great personal risk), was an outlet for their resentments and frustrations, and a veneer of ideology sufficed for them to justify their conduct to themselves.

I have said that the radical activists, ordinarily, made up not more than five per cent of the campus population: the average collegian was no Smerdyakov. Nor was the average professor a doctrinaire radical, and a good many liberal professors grew distinctly more conservative in their views as the campus disorders vexed and menaced them and their work. To be opposed to the war in Vietnam was one thing; to destroy the university library in protest against that war distinctly was something else.

So how was it that the radicals were able to dominate most campuses when they chose, to intimidate the authorities at Harvard and Yale and Columbia and Stanford and Berkeley and Cornell and Madison and Minneapolis and Ann Arbor and many other famous universities, to shut down classes and shout down opposition? Why, the demonstrators and intimidators were assisted by the timidity and the indifference of today's campus.

With a few honorable exceptions, university and college presidents then were smug and unaccustomed to violent opposition; they had been sheltered by serried ranks of vice-presidents and deans, by the collegiate bureaucracy, by money and by a sense of their own importance; when the troubles came, they were taken aback—and some of them gave way cravenly. As for professors, as a class they are not notable for physical valor, and they had long been enervated, most or many of them, by the prevalent climate of permissive liberalism: as a body, they had not expected to have to fight for anything, and they had doubted whether there remained anything worth fighting for. Only a minority of them resisted intimidation successfully. As a waggish friend of mine once said of the town in which Michigan State University is situated, "East Lansing is a town of brave dogs and timid men."

But what of the large majority of the students, whose intellectual pursuits, if any, were interrupted by these disorders? Why did they tolerate this brutal silliness for years? Some, indeed, fought back, but usually the majority were quiescent. It would have been otherwise in my undergraduate days.

The bulk of the students, not radicals nor ideologues nor paranoiacs nor even reckless varsity-rag types, did not stir on behalf of *alma mater* because they were indifferent. They had no real love for their college or university; they were on the campus only because going to college had become the conventional thing to do, or because they had to go through the unpleasant process of job-certification. Nobody had told them that the ends of the higher learning are wisdom and virtue; for all most of them could tell, college and university existed chiefly for the advantage of administrators and professors—of whom, on the big campuses, the individual student was acquainted personally with few if any. Even famous universities like Yale and Harvard, though small in enrollments if contrasted with Behemoth State, had ceased to be academic communities; they were academic collectives. Who will adventure much for an educational establishment that seems like a factory? "Factory windows are always broken."

Ought we to be surprised that few rose up to confront the radical activists in defense of banality and boredom? The students had been instructed, moreover, that there are no "absolutes"—meaning that there are no truths, no standards, nothing worth fighting for. Often disruption of the campus, in the 'Sixties, amounted to a relief from academic fraud and meaninglessness. We learn to love the little platoon we belong to in society, says Burke. The academic collectivity, unloved, without discernible objects, does not raise up martyrs and heroes. The discontents of 1962 were only the beginning.

11

Propaganda and Planning for Mediocrity: 1963

F EW ADMINISTRATORS of the big universities, in 1963, seemed
aware that the more populous a campus, the greater its poten-
tiality for resentment and riot. Despite the rumblings of students
in 1962, the academic evangels of quantitative growth pushed cheer-
fully onward toward the doubling and tripling of enrollments.

Such was the general policy of an organization called the "Joint
Office of Institutional Research", situated in the District of Columbia.
Despite its pretentious scientistic title, the "Joint Office" was a propaganda bureau for the Association of State Universities and Land
Grant Colleges, and the State Universities Association. Some of the
more respectable universities belonging to these societies must have
been embarrassed, from time to time, by the anti-intellectual tone of
the Joint Office's bulletins.

To get more money for the big state institutions—money from
anywhere, by any means, especially through new grants from the
federal treasury—was the primary aim of the Joint Office. Any
argument that might serve so glorious an end, these public-relations
people employed. One way to persuade Congress, the state legislatures, and the public of the righteousness of this cause is to advance
the demagogue's argument that everybody has a *right* to be in college.
Who are you, you old reactionary, to say that Joe Milligan, who got D's
in high school, won't become another Albert Einstein after Dismal
Swamp A. & M. has finished polishing him?

The degradation of the democratic dogma is most saddening when it
masters the Academy and there joins with the ambitions of certain
anti-intellectual college presidents, who dream of ever more professors
and students within their own imperial systems. Of the manner of

reasoning employed by these gentlemen and scholars, a bulletin of the Joint Office, released on March 2, 1963 ("For Your Information", Circular No. 32) was a sufficient specimen.

This bulletin resorted to gross misrepresentation in order to advance the contention that there should be no restrictions upon entrance into a state institution—no weeding-out of inferior applicants, absolutely none. For the authors of this bulletin wrote, "A Columbia College experiment, designed specifically to test freshman performance of students with lower than normal verbal aptitude scores at the time of admission, found they did as well or better than students with higher scores."

Had this been true, the Columbia College experiment would have been astonishing. But one had only to read the fourth page of this bulletin itself, to discover that the Joint Office propagandists either could not themselves apprehend a serious report, or else shamelessly distorted results to make a slogan. For what Columbia College actually did, as described on the fourth page (to which the average reader of the bulletin might not penetrate), was to prove that most students with inferior "verbal" skills, even if they possess "other reliable indications of outstanding promise and potential", perform *badly* in college.

Columbia admitted seventy-two freshmen who seemed to have such promise, but "whose background, environment, poor schooling, or foreign education may have hindered them", and who ranked low on verbal aptitude tests. In the Columbia courses in English A and Contemporary Civilization A, these particular students squeaked through, nearly all of them—but scarcely with flying colors. Of these seventy-two "experimental" students, fifty-three per cent ranked in the bottom quarter of their classes in these college courses, twenty-five per cent in the next-to-bottom quarter, ten per cent in the second quarter, and only six per cent in the top quarter. The average Columbia freshman received a B minus in Contemporary Civilization; the average "experimental" student in this special group, C plus.

While this experiment does suggest that a student who wishes to work and seems to have native talent may contrive to *survive* in college, even though not very good at reading and writing, it certainly does not justify the wild claim, on the first page of the Joint Office bulletin, that these "non-verbal" students "did as well or better [*sic*—non-verbal public-relations man at work] than students with higher scores." When only twenty-two per cent of this group ranked above average, and only six per cent in the top quarter, obviously the large majority did not do so well as, or better than, the average Columbia freshman.

Another distortion in this bulletin was effected through quoting a

Dr. Ernest O. Melby, "distinguished professor of education at Michigan State University." I do not mean that Dr. Melby was misquoted: on the contrary, he seemed to be even sillier and more doctrinaire than the propagandists of the Joint Office. But they quoted his misleading assertions, without any modifying criticism.

Among other foolish things uttered by him, Dr. Melby told an audience at Wayne State University that we ought to abolish "selectivity and emphasis on grades", for these create a "human scrap heap." Alas, "we admit students largely by grades and measures of verbal intelligence, yet current studies show that I. Q. students are not necessarily those most creative."

Now the "current studies" to which Melby apparently referred did not demonstrate that one potential student was as good as another. Instead they suggested that many intelligence-quotient tests do not succeed in ascertaining qualities of imagination, ingenuity, and poetic insight. I had been saying just that for more than two decades. But an exposure of the inadequacy of most "intelligence" tests is another thing than disproving the ineluctable fact that some young people are bright, and others aren't—and that the latter are no advantage to a college. Yet for fraudulent universities and colleges, why not make up fraudulent "research" findings?

In the year 1963, when (unlike the present year) the demand for doctors of philosophy exceeded the supply—that is, in a decade when campuses were bursting with students—some of America's larger educational institutions nevertheless contrived to drive able Ph.D.'s from their doors. One efficient way to go about this was to convert the professor into a machine-tender and hired hand.

Michigan State University in 1963 paid off four such hired hands, well-known scholars in their fields, members of the department of English: Doctors David Dickson, Bernard Duffey, Norman Grabo, and James Calderwood. Professor Duffey, who taught and wrote about literary criticism, was markedly critical of "Project X", a wondrous new program at Michigan State, intended to enable that behemoth institution to jam in thousands of more students from the boondocks, without putting any intellectual strain on the freshmen or engaging any additional counterparts of Professor Mark Hopkins.

According to a press report, Dr. Duffey said "there was a definite 'rift' developing between the faculty and the administration over the project [X], which suggests various means of using modern teaching methods and organization to absorb the heavy enrollments of the years ahead." And Bernard Duffey made it clear that he departed because he knew that Project X and he were incompatible, if not incompossible.

This Project X, an "operational plan" explained in a twenty-page booklet issued by MSU's administration, was intended to prepare the University for a doubling and tripling of enrollments. (All told, total enrollments in 1963 already approximated thirty thousand on MSU campuses.) The more the merrier! What's wrong with a student body of sixty thousand, or ninety thousand, on the Friendly Campus?

Where, timid reactionaries inquired, might competent professors be found to teach these unmatriculated multitudes? Intellectually speaking, must President Hannah be expected to repeat the miracle of the loaves and the fishes?

Not so: Project X (so pleasantly redolent of *1984*, that delicious title, or of C. S. Lewis' romance *That Hideous Strength*), otherwise known as the Educational Development Project, was equipped to provide the answers. Project X supplied efficient alternatives: closed-circuit television in the classroom, and teaching machines. Those obsolete high-flown scholars could turn the television dials and oil the teaching machines. After all, wouldn't Professor Mark Hopkins be just as good on a screen, with several hundred young faces staring at his simulacrum-face, as he may have been on a nasty old log, with a nasty young intellectual on the other end?

Yet one can't please all curmudgeons. Professor Duffey (whom even the dean of the college of arts and letters had confessed to be "a first-rate scholar") suspected that some of the details of Project X might result in "a throwing away of everything we have gained" at MSU. Dr. Duffey's colleagues were no less hard upon Project X as they, too, departed from the Friendly Campus. Professor Dickson gave MSU's administration the unkindest cut of all. What ingratitude! For hadn't Dr. Dickson been the first, and for long the only, Negro scholar permitted to teach at MSU? He even had been permitted to rise, after thirteen years, to the rank of associate professor—this despite the sad deficiencies, at MSU, of his having been graduated originally from a tiny hick college called Bowdoin, his being a Milton scholar, his being a professed Christian (for which sin I once heard him derided in public by an MSU psychologist), and his being a gentleman of color.

Yet Dr. David Dickson also was a man, and his manhood would not abide Project X. Most of that project, Dickson said forthrightly, "will work against a first-rate teaching situation." The MSU faculty was presented with this Grand Design from on high, "like a new gadget on a car." The potentates of the MSU administration "are going to force it through; be sure of that," he told a reporter. "Teaching machines and that claptrap" were not for David Dickson, and he went his way.

Doubtless President John Hannah, despite attrition of his English department, was happy in the prospect of ninety thousand MSU undergraduates by 1984, and nine hundred closed-circuit television sets, and IBM knows how many teaching-machines—not counting the human faculty, machine-like though they might become by that day. With the departure of the Wild Geese of the English department, nothing had been lost save honor, and learning, and academic freedom.

Yet how pervasive is envy! During 1962 and 1963, President Hannah and his empire of learning were rudely criticized by all sorts of people, from leading lights of Michigan's legislature to President Griswold of Yale and Dr. Robert Hutchins of the Center for the Study of Democratic Institutions. Without a cross, no crown. Some carpers had gone so far as to compare the Hannah administration at MSU with the recently-dissolved corrupt regime of the unlamented President "Curly" Byrd at the University of Maryland.

In reply to such *lèse majesté*, President Hannah declared that these criticisms occurred only because he had been chairman of the Civil Rights Commission, under both Eisenhower and Kennedy. (It must have surprised Dr. Griswold and Dr. Hutchins to learn that their scorn of the sort of doctorates conferred at MSU had been motivated by their detestation of civil rights.) Actually, no critic had paid any attention to Hannah's Commission post—in which he had been about as active as a wooden Indian.

Be that as it may, "earned" doctorates were being churned out by the hundreds at MSU, some of them for rather odd intellectual achievements, startling enough to attract the interest of busy administrators like Dr. Griswold and Dr. Hutchins. If not much interested in the mind, at least MSU seemed interested in the head. Any reader who possesses a file of *Dissertation Abstracts* may turn to the number for May, 1961, and find therein two fascinating specimens of the higher learning under Hannah: two brand-new, innovative doctoral dissertations completed there.

One was the product of a scholar named John Francis Alexander, upon whom MSU conferred an earned doctorate in 1960. The subject of his learned researches was this: *An Evaluation of Thirteen Brands of Football Helmets on the Basis of Certain Impact Measures*. This valuable work, in Xerox, could be bought for $6.80. "The helmets were ranked according to the lower values for each evaluating measure at each velocity and position. Graphs depicted the mean responses of acceleration, deceleration, and rate of acceleration for all velocities and positions." Welcome, Dr. Alexander, to the company of the Schoolmen!

A worthy colleague of his was one Richard Carroll Nelson, also diligent at educational studies in football. He was awarded his MSU doctorate, also in physical education, for a curiously similar contribution to the higher learning: *An Investigation of Various Measures Used in Football Helmet Evaluation*. "Thirty-nine football helmets were impacted by a pendulum striker at four velocities." Dr. Nelson even went so far in modern scholarship as to photograph the impacts with a Polaroid camera. There was something at MSU for every head—so long as one fretted only about the *physical* impact.

12

The Sensual and the Dark in the Grove:
1964

T HE NARCOTICS-PUSHER had begun to invade the campus by 1964, although that problem as yet was not so grave as it would become later in the decade. But the newspapers and popular magazines of 1964 were filled with lurid accounts of "sexual orgies" among college students; very little was printed about their pursuit of wisdom and virtue. One might discount the reports of societies for "sexual freedom", but it remained true that much silliness about the purposes and pleasures of sexual relationships prevailed then—and prevails now—among students and professors.

From a good independent university, a young professor sent to me, in 1964, some comments illustrative of the growing preoccupation with sexuality on the campus. "I must confess that popular attitudes regarding sex have changed so drastically just in my lifetime," he wrote, "that I find myself unable to adjust to, let alone accept, these sudden innovations—or, as you say, this reversion to the 'Old Immorality.' At a student discussion of such topics that I attended recently, along with other members of the faculty, the girls left me absolutely flabbergasted. They talked freely and openly about 'sleeping with our boy friends,' and were troubled by the fact that they were uncertain as to whether they intended to marry them. Many complained about 'antiquated regulations' and 'outmoded Puritan codes' which made it impossible for some and difficult for all to obtain contraceptives—thus 'thwarting the full development of our personalities.'

"All seemed to favor abortion, which in my ancient household was regarded as murder. I had the impression that I was sitting in on a rehearsal for *Brave New World*, to be put on by the local drama club. Being a minority of one, I tended to swallow my protest and was too busy catching my breath to utter a word. I continue to walk as if I were in a dream."

Of course young people between the ages of seventeen and twenty-two always have felt strong sensual appetites, most of them; and American co-education made the gratifying of those urges more easy than in earlier times. Apologies for the satisfying of sexual desires, as promptly and in as diverse ways as possible, had been virtually forced upon the rising generation by the enthusiasm with which many of their elders had received the sober-sided, if highly unscientific, "studies" in human sexuality by the taxonomist Alfred Kinsey, enamored of "sexual outlets." And the flooding of the campuses after the Second World War and the Korean War by married veterans, with their wives and children, seems to have put the notion of early sexual union into the heads of many younger students at that formerly celibate institution the American college.

The anonymity and impersonality of the mass campus, besides, and the fact that many of the students were bored with their classes and with the abstractions of the higher learning generally, led naturally enough to a yearning for intimacy with somebody or other at Behemoth U.: an affair is a temporary remedy for loneliness, as for boredom. Such liaisons, beginning with a few daring young people, presently are accepted as common enough, and then take on the force of custom. Many parents of college students, though vexed at the amorous involvements of their offspring, had offered their college-age children little sensible advice about sexuality. As the custom of such pairing began to spread upon campuses, some students in the Lonely Crowd felt impelled to conform to the new pattern by herd-instinct, rather than by any positive personal eagerness for "premarital" experiences: the convention of being unconventional. This soon would be as true of the use of marijuana and the cult of "hard" narcotics.

College authorities, their own convictions or prejudices about sexuality and drugs unnerved by a generation of American permissiveness, often did nothing effectual to discourage actions which, nevertheless, they still felt to be mistaken and mischievous. During 1964 I talked with a tolerant and witty widow who had become housemother to a fraternity at Michigan State University. She found it difficult to maintain even outward decencies in the house which she was supposed to chaperone; and, *sub rosa*, the University authorities told her to absent herself from the house whenever there might occur any prospect of general impropriety. Had she lodged a complaint with the dean's office, charging individual students with misconduct, the dean of students simply would have closed the fraternity, obliterating guilty and innocent at one blow, to preserve the University's "public image."

Thus the average collegian, male or female, virtually was unsupervised by either parents or college officials: there were far too many collegians, by that year, for *in loco parentis* to be applied effectively. This circumstance delivered the average collegian to the domination of his "peer group" arbiters of taste and morals. Most human beings, in all ages, have acquired their moral habits through emulation and deference. If students find no upright personalities to emulate, they must defer to domineering flawed personalities. So, with the swelling of campus populations, modes of sexual conduct were determined more and more by the "emancipated" natures within the student body—by the more reckless or sensual undergraduates, swaggering and bragging in the new high-rise dorms, drinking hard and smoking pot in the fraternities.

My friend the fraternity housemother remarked that of the thirty-five young men, or boys, in her house, perhaps five were actual students; the rest had come to the University for fun, or for draft-deferment, or for lack of lucrative employment. (She had not attended college herself, and her standards for scholarship were not exacting.) Most of them had plenty of money to spend, and few demanding lessons to prepare. Idle and bored, they turned to the amatory diversions readily available on the campus.

Mere exhortation would not remedy this. "The girls are worse than the boys at the 'mattress parties,' " the housemother said. With us, at the moment, was a youngish professor who once had been a military intelligence officer and was familiar with the world's ways. "How jaded those girls will be," he observed. "Life will seem to have no future."

John Keats was writing his book *The Sheepskin Psychosis* in 1963 and 1964. Increasing silliness about sexuality on the campus distressed him: "The dominant student and faculty opinion is that each student has the right to decide whether to engage in sexual intercourse, and that if a boy and girl are in love, they ought to go to bed together. On the other hand, the overwhelming opinion of college deans and psychiatrists is that most undergraduates are emotionally unready for coitus, and that they should therefore not engage in it."

Sexual license on the campus, and increased dabbling with drugs, followed naturally enough from the intellectual confusion of college and university. Academic administrators had forgotten almost wholly the ethical object of the higher learning. Many professors had sunk into a disintegrated liberalism that taught only "do as you will!" It was not surprising that Behemoth University and Brummagem University slid mindlessly into the "orgy-porgy" of *Brave New World*.

Dr. Sarah Blanding, until 1964 president of Vassar College, had as much to do with 1964's discussion of sex on the campus as did anyone. For, in a courageous and sensible statement, she had announced that she did not intend to tolerate loose living at her college. Ever since Miss Blanding took her stand, the zealots of disintegrated liberalism have been crying up the virtues of sexual license, and college authorities have found it necessary to issue pronunciamentos of one sort or another.

Time was when, at nearly all American colleges, the authorities probably were too fussy about overseeing the moral welfare of undergraduates. They carried the doctrine of *in loco parentis* farther than it was exercised in the medieval universities where it originated. Necessarily, colleges which enroll young people between the ages of sixteen and twenty-two substitute in some degree for parents; but it can become presumptuous and self-defeating to carry such supervision beyond essentials.

The latter-day disintegrated liberal attitude of some college administrators was represented in 1964 sufficiently by Dr. Sutherland Miller Jr., director of the Columbia College Student Counseling Service. This gentleman did not worry overmuch about "premarital sexual intercourse"; for some it's good, for some it isn't; live and let live. As reported in the *New York Times*, Miller believed that Columbia students were sexually immature. Few of them, alas, were "taking advantage of Columbia's new policy allowing women visitors in dormitory rooms on alternate Sunday afternoons." To quote Dr. Miller directly, "There was no great rush to use the plan once it was instituted. I felt that this was in part a reflection of the fact that a number of students are not very eager and ready for heterosexual experience."

To judge by these remarks, Columbia College did not expect dorm-visiting to be merely for Sunday afternoon tea: that Sunday session would have been splendid opportunity for heterosexual experiences. What a pity that some immature students actually seemed to prefer books or conversation!

At Harvard, in 1964, Dean John U. Munro had more of an eye for order. He was fantastically assailed in the pages of the *Harvard Crimson* for objecting to wild parties and sexual intercourse in Harvard's dormitories. A pleasant privilege of dormitory-visiting, Dean Munro pointed out, had degenerated into tasteless license; and he proposed to exert some checks.

Now much of the controversy over these questions centered round this point: is the American college meant to decree the morals and form the character of young people? As a matter of fact, the American college, in its beginnings, was meant to do precisely such—in part. A more important point than this question of *in loco parentis*, however, seems to have been ignored by many who have written about "college sex." After all, there are vessels for dishonor, and no amount of college supervision is going to prevent many young people from making fools of themselves, if they be bent upon folly. The greater point at issue is this: have college administrators a right to preserve decency on the campus?

Most students at Columbia or Harvard, at least, are decent people who have enrolled to learn something or other. They are not drunkards or satyrs. They might even enjoy a little quiet in which to read a book, or talk. Decent people, too, have their rights: particularly the right not to have to endure a nuisance and a stench. If some collegians prefer the atmosphere of a sporting-house, let them go thither—there are many shady motels—and leave the dormitories of Columbia and Harvard to those horrible prigs who actually still believe, after their reactionary fashion, that college is a place of learning and meditation.

Judge Jennie Loitman Barron, of Massachusetts, writing in the *Ladies' Home Journal* during 1964, summarized this controversy ably. Most young people, she pointed out, really want some known rules by which to live—a measure of protection, even in college. At one college, Judge Barron observed, "coeds objected to a planned cancellation of the curfew hour; it helped them to break away from their dates and the 'obligatory kissing.' "

The traditions of civility were not established by tyrants. Our word "conventions" means "general agreements freely reached", really. Conventions, including conventions of sexual conduct, are voluntary social arrangements which have grown out of long experience in society. They have arisen for our protection and our convenience. One may say of conventions what James Russell Lowell said of manners, that they keep the Bowie knife from our throats. When conventions no longer are observed, a society falls into disorder, and eventually positive law sternly enforced has to do duty for forgotten voluntary convention. That is as true of the academic community as of the general political community. But in 1964, the flouting of conventions about conduct between the sexes was only the beginning of some years of destruction of many conventions.

American Protestantism, it appears, is reviving intellectually—in the divinity schools. But among students on the average campus, Protestant Christianity was no more intellectually reputable in 1964 than it had been in my own undergraduate days. (Our Christian devotions had consisted chiefly of singing "Clementine" and "I Ain't a-Gonna Grieve My Lawd No Mo' " at YMCA parties on Friday nights.)

In 1964 there came to my hand a leaflet published quarterly by the United Campus Christian Fellowship. It was called *Campus Encounter*; and the number to which I refer consisted almost wholly of an essay entitled "Love without Fear: a Personal View of Being Physical", reprinted from *Dialogue*, which magazine in turn was published by "the service area of the Cornell United Religious Work" at Cornell University. The author of this confused and impressionistic article was a young Robert C. Buckle, who once taught in a Nigerian village, but in 1964 was working and writing in Dallas.

Buckle's thesis for campus Christians, though difficult to glimpse through his summer-school-of-creative-writing prose, in essence was this: woe, woe, we're alone in this world, and something must be done about it. Onanism doesn't satisfy, and even the most thoroughgoing affair of young people—"two very unselfconscious people, completely naked, touching each other and being glad for each other without questioning"—may be spoilt by slyness and tedium. *Vanitas vanitatum*. All this was expressed with abundant erotic imagery. "Convention is left behind," commented the admiring editors of *Campus Encounter*, "if one finds meaning in the word." They and Mr. Buckle did not find meaning in that word "convention": they were *avant-garde* religionists.

But don't be shocked, Buckle implored us: he was trying merely to improve us out of our absurd and unsatisfactory human nature. He sought a "totality of love", in which there would be no guilt, fear, dishonesty, or jealousy (and, one suspects, no fun). He pointed the way to a totality in which everybody would love everybody else they wished to love, physically. People still would marry, and they might be faithful, he hoped, but there would remain no compulsions. Buckle was candid:

"May I make it clear that I think these people would be free sexually in ways that are perhaps startling to us. Love would characterize their relationships with other people, and this love would not be some airy spiritual-intellectual phantasy that has nothing at all to do with flesh and blood; it would be a love of bodies in all their different aspects as well as a love of sensitivity and aspiration."

It is not quite clear whether Buckle meant to approve the man "who began by loving his neighbor, and ended by loving his wife", or to advocate virtual sexlessness; perhaps Buckle himself was not sure what he wanted. What a hell of a world! Without desire, no procreation; without procreation, no children; without children, no human race: the medieval Manichee is back among us.

Lord Bertrand Russell—"all who in Russell's burly frame admire/ the lineaments of gratified desire," to quote my old friend Roy Campbell—could not have put this utopian proposal more candidly, or more atheistically. Buckle wanted self-confidence, self-awareness, acceptance of oneself; he did not mention the possibility of confidence in a transcendent power, God-awareness, the acceptance of divine love. None of this airy-faerie phantasy for Mr. Buckle. "No knots would be tied; no solemn rules enacted," Buckle cried hopefully. But something deep in human nature demands that knots be tied and solemn rules enacted: we yearn to belong to some other person, and to have some other person belong to us.

Although silly, Buckle's notions were not novel—except that they were presented as Christian, in a nominally Christian publication meant for college students. If this was the best that "progressive" Protestantism could offer to undergraduates—and this leaflet was distributed in tens of thousands upon many campuses—what wonder that churches stood in disrepute? The campus cutups could have their week-end frolics without Robert C. Buckle's sanction, and would have looked upon him as some kind of nut; while any students in search of principles to live by would have been unlikely to find much satisfaction in this tapioca-pudding notion of "being physical."

The obscure Buckle and his kind endeavored to make immanent the Christian symbols; they were what Eric Voegelin called "modern Gnostics." "One doesn't know where to begin," Buckle complained, frustrated. True; but one knew where such disintegrated "Christianity" would end.

13

Killing with Kindness: 1965

DURING THE EISENHOWER and Kennedy administrations, many of the state universities and colleges, and even some of the independent institutions, had been entreating the federal government to give them a great deal of money. With the election of Lyndon Johnson to the presidency, they succeeded. In 1965, Congress passed a grandiose bill for subsidies to institutions of higher learning: its cost would be eight hundred and forty-one million dollars, twice what President Johnson had requested of the Congress.

It assisted colleges by bricks-and-mortar money (not touching their much greater expenses for salaries and general administrative costs). It assisted students by massive scholarships and loans which would enable practically anyone to attend college—regardless of aptitude or diligence. It appropriated large sums for "teacher training"—much of which went for educationist boondoggles. Added to the funds supplied to higher education through the earlier National Defense Education Act, this measure meant that thereafter the federal government would pay a large share of the expenses of universities and college—and, increasingly, call their tune.

There had been some opposition to this financial intervention by the federal apparatus—opposition from within the Academy. In 1962, when such a program had been proposed in Congress, some presidents of independent colleges had expressed their fear of such an innovating policy. Dr. John Howard, president of Rockford College, had said that "the costs of independent higher education must be met by voluntary support which requires maximum encouragement—not competition—on the part of the Federal Government. Federal subsidy reduces voluntary giving." Dr. Donald Phillips, president of Hillsdale College, had inquired, "What of the church-related college receiving tax funds and the fundamental idea of church and state? Will we then change our traditional philosophy or will all church colleges become public? Could there, for example, legally be prayer in a classroom?" Those misgivings, as matters turned out later, were not without justification.

President Howard pointed out that federal control necessarily must accompany federal charity. "Totally apart from the provisions of the laws," he wrote, "the human factors that are active in the seeking and dispensing of enormous sums of money will also bring about conformity among colleges. Any successful manufacturer tailors his product to the personal inclinations of the public which buys his product; any successful salesman shapes his sales-talk according to the known bias of his customer. In this instance, the Federal Government which proposes to underwrite a third of the cost of construction and provide substantial scholarships to students, will become in one congressional vote the largest single customer of all private colleges and a substantial customer of all public ones, a customer in the sense that the government will decide whether to buy for the nation the services of each college, with its federal grants."

Experiment and superior performance, he continued, actually would be discouraged by federal subsidies, for those grants would relieve independent colleges of the need for a healthy competition. "The continued success of a college will no longer depend on the character of its educational program to the same extent, but rather on its ability to get its share of governmental largesse."

The champions of the new massive grants had asserted that these subsidies would not bring federal influence upon higher education. Look at the land-grant colleges, they had said: to them Washington gave an endowment, but little federal direction had resulted. The trouble with this contention was that the federal grants of land to state colleges under the first Morrill Act had been outright gifts and single benefactions, rather than annual subsidies. The new program of 1965, however, commenced continuing appropriations that would be a large item in the federal budget. Congress would be derelict in its duty if, in such circumstances, the federal government did not exercise controls of some sort.

Behind the new act was the assumption that enrollments in universities and colleges should be doubled in short order, in the sacred name of Education. Yet few measures could have worked more mischief to the higher learning. Two decades earlier, Dr. Robert Hutchins had predicted the overwhelming of universities and colleges by incompetent and ineducable "students", unless restraining measures should be taken; and Dr. Seymour Harris, the economist, had foreseen the rearing up of an "intellectual proletariat", a mass of half-schooled people with college degrees for whom there could be found no employment commensurate with their exalted opinion of their own talents. A good many professors and educational administrators were still more alarmed at this prospect, by 1965; even Dr. James Bryant Conant grew uneasy. Should existing enrollments be doubled, the works of the mind might get short shrift at most institutions.

Dr. Carroll Newsom, president of New York University, had stated in 1962 that even independent institutions, if they possessed any merit, could find through ordinary channels the money needed for justifiable expansion, without begging for federal grants. In 1965, Dr. David McKenna, president of Spring Arbor College, declared that America was moving toward "a national system of higher education" in which "education for moral and spiritual values will become even more perplexing and difficult." Dr. Louis Benezet, then president of Claremont Graduate School, was still more disheartened: "We may expect to see the monumental construction of state university metropolises on the one hand and on the other the disappearance of most of the private colleges—perhaps in a state junior college system, or possibly into mental hospitals, another growing public need." Five years later, Dr. Benezet, as if providing for his own salvation against this doom, would shift to the presidency of the Albany campus of the University of the State of New York, grandest of state university metropolises.

By its nature, the new federal program favored state universities and land-grant colleges, and other tax-supported institutions, to the detriment of independent colleges and universities. Already the proportion of American students attending independent institutions had shrunken to thirty per cent, or little more. That did not dismay the state institutions.

The Association of State Universities and Land Grant Colleges, along with others who expected to profit greatly from the new federal subsidies, saw no dangers at all in prospect. President Hannah of Michigan State had said forthrightly, "Some form of outright federal aid to education is essential if we are to meet the demands upon our colleges and universities in time." Apparently this largesse of public funds would not be discriminatory: Dismal Swamp A. & M., or Limberlost Community College, in theory, would be as deserving as Princeton or Brown; the only test of need was appetite.

The more money that the Internal Revenue should take from taxpayers to pay for federal educational subsidies, the less money would be available for private benefactions to higher education. This prospect was not unpleasant to John Hannah, who once said that there was no reason why ninety-five per cent of Michigan's students should not be enrolled in public institutions, at the expense of independent colleges—with the implication that the figure of one hundred per cent would present no difficulties, either. Once Washington should begin to pay the bills for all colleges, the mediocre or inferior institutions would fare at least as well as would famous universities, per student; and the better colleges, especially the church-related ones, would know harder lines than before. In the long run, federal grants might kill with kindness.

So long as the American population was increasing, a good case could be made for increase of college enrollments. But normal expansion of facilities from normal sources of college income already was being accomplished, before the passing of the act of 1965. What the advocates of massive federal subsidies desired was the doubling or tripling of enrollments. The day might come when scarcely one hidie-hole should remain for the professor who seeks genuine academic leisure and learning; or for the sincere student who should wish to get away from the campus fun and games to read some books. Pressures for more snob-degrees and more campus playgrounds seemed irresistible in 1965.

Massive federal subsidies were approved at the very time when violent protests against the inhumane scale of higher education had become formidable. American college students had not proceeded to quite such lively measures as those employed by rioting students at Coimbatore, in Madras, where two police inspectors had been burned alive by way of objecting to the Indian government's adoption of Hindi as the official language of the land. But the malcontents on the mass campuses of America were ruffling the dove-cotes of Academe. At the Berkeley campus of the University of California, the first cry of the rioters was "We don't want to be IBM numbers!" The "Free Speech" enthusiasts at Berkeley seemed absurd, since a higher degree of free speech long had prevailed there than at nearly any other state university. Freedom of speech, actually, was not the real cause of the Berkeley demonstrators. The grievance which they felt deeply was the in-humane scale of the mass campus, Dr. Clark Kerr's "multiversity." They denounced "The Machine"—which, like Luddites, they desired to break. They did succeed in bringing down Kerr, the architect of gigantism in California's higher learning.

External disorder, as represented by the Berkeley riots, was parallelled by American students' internal disorder, as suggested by the expulsion of dozens of Air Force Academy cadets because they had cheated on their examinations. (Almost nowhere else were cheaters, however numerous, actually expelled.) At last the plague of campus dishonesty was openly discussed; only a few years before, Jerome Ellison had been removed from the faculty of Indiana University because he had the temerity to suggest, in the pages of *The Saturday Evening Post*, that many students cheated.

Rioting and cheating were the ineluctable consequences of Behemoth University's inhumane scale. Anonymous students in the campus' Lonely Crowd, knowing no true academic community and finding no norms acknowledged by a university's administrators or many of its professors, sank into cheating as the quickest way out of a pretentious educational racket—and besides, an IBM number knows no shame. The college teacher, isolated and unrecognized in such an amorphous academic empire, sometimes becamed a "sp'iled praist" or "stickit minister", an ideologue, sour and carping, inflicting upon a captive classroom audience frustrations which were disguised as "social protest."

The first step toward restoring an object to the campus and purpose to the students' life would have been the recovery of a humane scale. The campus needed genuine academic community, among scholars and among students. Community, which necessarily is voluntary and comparatively small, was a world apart from the prevalent academic collectivism of the mass campus.

Love of one's academic community might have put an end to the disorder of the Lonely Crowd; and that kind of love, being honorable, casts out fraud. Education not being an industrial process, we should have ceased to construct educational factories: for mind and conscience, and the idea of a university, only the humane scale will do.

Yet more bricks and mortar, and student populations even more swollen, were the answers of Congress and the Johnson administration to the educational ills of 1965. "Stay in school!" President Johnson exhorted the rising generation, over television. "Stay in school!" The military draft was insuring that many young men would do precisely that, so long as they could, benefiting thus from what amounted to a class-exemption. The time was not far distant, however, when President Johnson would not venture to speak on campuses—when, indeed, his public addresses would be delivered chiefly in the security of military bases.

* * *

Before the end of the 'Sixties, at this rate of expansion, American universities and colleges would require far more money than the federal subsidies voted in 1965—some seven billion to eleven billion dollars more, according to Roger Freeman, in his book *Crisis in College Finance*, published in 1965. Was there no alternative to gigantic grants from the federal treasury, with its corollary of central direction of higher education? Freeman and other specialists in this field recommended various forms of relief from federal income taxes as another method—so getting the necessary funds into colleges without filtering money through the Washington bureaucracy.

How might the public be induced to contribute more dollars to remedy college deficits—those of both state and independent institutions? By tax relief, and particularly tax credits—that is, not merely allowing a deduction from net taxable income, as the internal revenue code already permitted, but rather subtracting the amount (within rather narrow limits) of a donation to a college from the actual total of income tax which otherwise a taxpayer would surrender in full to the Internal Revenue Service. Some college presidents recommended a plan by which any taxpayer might donate as much as a hundred dollars to the college of his choice, and receive a tax credit; this, they argued, would be more efficient than federal subsidies and would not endanger academic independence.

A more widely-supported proposal, presented in a bewildering variety of forms (all of them carefully analyzed in Roger Freeman's book), was that the parents of students should be allowed a tax credit amounting to some part, or perhaps the whole, of the cost of keeping their offspring in the Grove of Academe. This measure would have helped the state-supported institutions, too, since presumably public colleges and universities, in such circumstances, would have increased their tuition charges to the level, more or less, of fees at private colleges—so putting the competitors for student enrollment on an even footing.

At that time, in 1965, prospects seemed fairly bright for the adoption of some tax-credit scheme to help colleges. A bill of that sort, with Senator Abraham Ribicoff as its chief sponsor, very nearly had been approved by the Senate the preceding year, and indeed would have passed but for intense lobbying by the White House, President Johnson believing that a large tax credit would have disturbed his budget. But such proposals were not adopted in 1965, nor did they obtain enactment later, even though Roger Freeman loomed large as an economic advisor to the President during the Nixon administration. Probably the Supreme Court of the United States still would find such means for aiding independent schools and colleges quite constitutional. But the

educational establishment has contented itself with demanding annually still larger grants from the federal treasury. With those subsidies,
as the years passed, came increasing demands from the Department of
Health, Education, and Welfare upon university and college, both
public and private. It would be demanded by HEW and other federal
agencies that educational institutions receiving federal grants submit
themselves to all sorts of requirements—opening men's physical-
education classes to women, employing more members of "minorities"
(including women) upon staffs of colleges, and universities, complying
with federal safety regulations, and the like. The paperwork resulting
from such requirements would cost Duke University alone—not one of
the bigger universities—a million dollars a year. And presidents of
famous old universities, who previously had fancied themselves rather
powerful, were to find that some obscure female clerk in HEW, by
private interpretation of acts of Congress, could give orders to college
officials as if they had been privates in an academic army. Some
Catholic colleges and universities would think it prudent, before long,
to remove crucifixes and saints' images from classrooms and corridors,
lest they be accused of breaching that alleged wall of separation between church and state, and so lose federal subsidies. Government
contracts with universities for "research", sometimes scientific, sometimes not scientific at all, further increased the dependence of the
Academy upon the Washington political apparatus. And all this was in
the green tree of the next decade.

So did the higher learning begin to be assimilated to the interests and
the power of centralized political authority, and universities to decline
even more sharply into "service institutions."

14

How to Lower the Higher Learning: 1966

WOULDN'T IT BE FUN to attend a university with two hundred and sixty thousand students? Soon one could do just that, it was revealed in 1966: no matter how low one ranked on intelligence tests, no matter how indolent one had been in high school, no matter how averse to the works of the mind one might be. Dr. Samuel B. Gould, president of the State University of New York, was waiting to welcome all comers, he having something for everybody.

The State University of New York, an educational octopus sprawling all across that state, was the creation chiefly of Governor Nelson Rockefeller's administration; when Averell Harriman had been governor, he had resisted pressures to enlarge the state apparatus of education inordinately, for the state of New York had many independent universities and colleges of high reputation. But the old order gave way under Rockefeller's appropriations, and a miscellany of state teachers' colleges, state technical institutes, and colleges formerly independent but acquired by the state, was erected into the State University, with headquarters at Albany.

By the spring of 1966, the State University of New York had some fifty-eight campuses (depending on what one counted), more than eighty-four thousand students, and nearly six thousand teachers. This, said Dr. Gould and his colleagues, was only the beginning. It became the announced goal of this new educational empire to lure *every* high-school graduate in the state to its embraces—except, of course, those reactionaries who still insisted upon enrolling in independent universities and colleges, and those young people enrolled in the City University of New York (which latter system had lowered its academic stan-

dards several years earlier, and virtually would abolish standards altogether some years later.)

Gould and Company, in 1966, planned eagerly for a quarter of a
million students by 1974—plus more multitudes later. There was even
talk of making the "higher" learning "free and compulsory" until the
age of twenty-one. (Although this system would grow by leaps, these
predictions were not fulfilled: by the spring of 1974 there were some
143,000 full-time students in the State University, and by 1977 less
than 150,000. This comparative failure was concealed after a fashion
by the University's authorities, who in 1977 would claim to have
343,000 students—a figure created by counting part-time night students, extension services, "adult education" lectures, and the like.
Enforcement of school truancy laws having become impossible, no
more was said about compelling college-age youth.)

By the autumn of 1966, student enrollments and the number of
full-time faculty members already had grown gratifyingly in the State
University. The anticipated enlargement to some two hundred and
sixty thousand students, by 1974, would require a construction-pro-
gram unparalleled in the history of higher education. (A lively doctorate in political science, or even in education, might be obtained through
writing a penetrating study of the influence of the contractors' lobbies
upon governors, state legislatures, Congress—and, of course, university presidents—in the extravagant expansion, physically, of higher
education during the past quarter of a century.) All this would be paid
for by public taxation—at the relative expense of the independent
universities and colleges, since their old sources of income would be
reduced, in effect, through increased taxation upon the patrons and
benefactors of "private" education.

So grand was the design of Dr. Gould and his allies that it seemed as if
higher education would become the principal industry of the Empire
State: practically everybody working for the State University, either
through being put upon the payroll (if not enrolled in classes, or
perhaps even so) or through laboring lustily to pay the state's taxes in
support of the State University.

Dr. Gould's administration did not worry in the least about the
problems of the Lonely Crowd on the mass campus. For the State
University had conducted a "nationwide survey" which purported to
show that the size of the campus population bore no relationship to the
quality of instruction. There had been yet other surveys allegedly
demonstrating, in erring reason's spite, that it did not matter in the
least how many students were enrolled in any particular class: so much
for Mark Hopkins and that log of his. Doubtless surveys could have

been contrived which would have proved conclusively that Dismal Swamp A. & M. was decidedly superior to Oxford University in the accomplishments of its graduates.

Where, I asked in 1966, would the boondoggle of the State University of New York end? First of all, I wrote then, most branches of the State University would sink to the level of glorified high schools, though much more costly than high schools. Public high schools, in turn, would be relieved of pressures to improve their lamentable standards, on the pretext that "you'll get all that academic stuff in college." At least half of the high-school graduates in the state of New York, in the fullness of time, would receive degrees or diplomas or certificates of some sort from the State University—documents not worth the parchment or paper on which they would be printed. These graduates would expect lucrative white-collar jobs which they would not obtain, most of them, for a university degree would have lost its scarcity-premium. Nearly all of this has come to pass by 1978.

Any person desiring a genuine education, I continued, would have to enroll at an independent university or college, as he would have had to do before the State University rose up monstrous. But it would be more difficult than before to pay the fees of independent institutions, since the higher taxes to support the state system must decrease parents' incomes and reduce sources of private benefaction. Also many good professors would be drawn away from the independent institutions into the state system, what with the increasing state salaries. And some private colleges and universities soon would go to the wall. These things, too, have come to pass by 1978.

As I visited the new campuses of the State University of New York, in the 'Sixties and 'Seventies, I was staggered by their architectural barrenness and monotony. In their high-rise sterility they were equalled only by the grim tall campuses of some state colleges of California. (The architecture of the Californian community colleges, by contrast, generally was pleasant and humane.) Clearly these academic bee-hives or ant-hills, on either coast, at Albany or at San Diego, would not warm the cockles of the heart. The real professors and the real students at such establishments would be rare birds; certification, not education, would be the object of these monstrosities; and there would be graduated from these dreary campuses a generation both sullen and ignorant. Yet from Atlantic to Pacific the depersonalizing of higher education proceeded apace. There was money in the process for plenty of people.

* * *

Already there were misgivings in California. By the end of 1966, more than seven hundred thousand young Californians were enrolled in that state's public institutions of higher learning, from community colleges to graduate schools. None of these paid tuition in 1966.

Although California had the highest proportion in the nation of high-school graduates enrolling for at least a year of college, California's drop-out rate was higher than the national average, and the percentage of students who actually obtained degrees was correspondingly lower than in the average state. In 1965, the California Coordinating Council of Higher Education had concluded that the policy of free tuition at all state institutions ought to be much altered, in one fashion or another. As Governor Ronald Reagan then put it, there is no such thing as free education; there is only costly education. It is a question of who is to pay the bills.

Against the Governor's plan to charge some tuition (only a fraction of the actual cost of instruction) for students at public colleges and universities, a ferocious outcry arose—but mostly from students. It was common in 1966 and 1967 to see, affixed to the bumpers of expensive new automobiles belonging to university students, signs demanding "No Tuition!" Actually, eleemosynary higher education was a state subsidy to the affluent classes, at general expense, for the large majority of students at the state institutions came from well-to-do parents. If students at California's public campuses—the universities and state colleges, that is—had paid three hundred dollars to four hundred dollars apiece per annum, still they would have been defraying only a fraction of the cost of their schooling. The annual expense to the state, per student, at public institutions in California, ranged from $3,051 at the state graduate schools to $540 at the community colleges. (The Reagan reforms did not establish tuition-charges at the community colleges.) These figures did not include the huge capital outlays which had been incurred during the 'Sixties for building new campuses or enlarging existent ones.

Nor were the students (or their families) unable to pay a tolerable proportion of the cost of their study. Some twenty per cent of the students at the University of California, with its nine campuses, came from households with an annual income between $14,000 and $20,000—sums which bought much more in 1966 than they do in 1978. Another eighteen per cent came from families whose income exceeded twenty thousand dollars. Only about twelve per cent of the students came from parents whose income was less than six thousand dollars. The just and economical arrangement, obviously, would have been to grant scholarships to deserving students who really were short of funds—and to require payment of at least part of the cost of instruction from those quite able to bear such costs. California was the only big state that did not charge tuition for higher education; indeed, the only other large public system of higher education which remained tuition-free in 1966 was that of the city colleges of New York. The Reagan reforms moved in that direction.

Another scheme, advocated by some in 1966 and 1967, was the "Collier Plan", by which Californian university and college graduates would have been expected to repay to the state, gradually, the cost of their education at public expense—once their income-tax returns should show them sufficiently affluent to afford repayment by the installments. Although this principle has been applied to federal and state loans for higher education, in one fashion or another, it was not adopted by the Californian legislature, and has not made headway since then in other states.

To reduce the burden of public expenditure upon higher education in California, some legislators in Sacramento supported proposals to expand the relatively economical community colleges rather than to enlarge the state system of universities and colleges. They argued that the costs per capita were much lower at the community colleges; that local control of the junior colleges (which raised more than three-fourths of their funds through local taxation) was a more democratic system, comparatively free from the ideological passions then predominant at the state institutions; that actually some of the community colleges—long-established ones, with good libraries—were more competent to instruct undergraduates than were the newer university campuses and state college campuses. Probably the best case for permitting the community colleges to become four-year degree-granting institutions—and for converting the state universities and colleges into graduate schools—was the relatively humane scale of the community colleges (though some of those, too, were swollen).

"Perhaps the most cogent argument for a complete evaluation of the tripartite system of higher education, however, is the lack of contact the parents of children feel they have with the two upper echelons and their appointed regents," an official of California's department of public instruction wrote to me then. "They all see thousands of students, their youngsters, drawn into questionable 'political action' movements by the techniques of mob psychology. They see the university and state colleges as training camps for revolutionists, not for the cultivation of the mind or the inculcation of reverence for our heritage, which is what a university is all about. Taxpayers resent the intellectual climate at these institutions, yet they feel helpless to influence the present trend. The four-year community college would provide them with a solution."

But this did not come to pass, in California or elsewhere, in 1966 or later. Behemoth State University grew ever larger and less manageable.

15

Rebellion against Boredom: 1967

L ET NO MAN expect gratitude. President Lyndon Johnson,
though he had lavished public funds upon college and university, was more bitterly unpopular with students than ever had
been any president before him. I waited upon him at the White House,
putting into his hand a copy of my book about Robert Taft, a political
adversary whom Johnson had esteemed. Taft had said that it would be
ruinous folly to send an American conscript army into Asia, but I did
not recall that declaration to President Johnson's mind.

Lyndon Johnson's great height and physical power still made him
seem formidable, and he remained an astute political manipulator,
wheeling and dealing with Senator Byrd and Senator Tydings, also
present in his office as he and I exchanged a few remarks about the first
Senator Robert Taft. Yet his weary face was thickly coated with cos-
metics, because he was about to be photographed, and it was prudent to
disguise the sickliness which had fallen upon his face. It passed
through my mind at the moment that he might have been created by
Madame Tussaud. It had been his high aspiration to win an enduring
reputation similar to that of Franklin Roosevelt—to be set down in
history as an energetic reformer and a benefactor of the American
people. Instead, he was being howled and hooted out of office. Herbert
Hoover, with whom I had conversed in his Waldorf Towers apartment
a few months before he died, had seemed confident that sober historians would vindicate his course in public affairs; Lyndon Johnson
could be confident of nothing of that sort.

President Johnson had won his big victory over Senator Goldwater
because of the public's assumption that Johnson was less "trigger-
happy" than Goldwater. The public had been mistaken. What with his

overwhelming majority in Congress, Johnson had been able to launch a massive federal program for putting people into college and subsidizing institutions of higher learning—more than two billion, six hundred and fifty-six million dollars for higher education in 1967 alone. His administration's benefactions had sent to campuses many of the students who now were hottest and most merciless against him.

It was military conscription that undid Lyndon Johnson with the rising generation. His thrusting of a half-million soldiers into Indo-China, and even his bungling of the Asiatic war, would have been tolerated by the students if the troops in Vietnam had been volunteers. But so great a force to fight campaigns in a remote land could be raised only through the draft.

This meant that the campuses were jammed with young men, many from affluent families, whose chief motive in enrolling had been deferment from conscription. Their class was privileged to escape the draft so long as they would obey Johnson's injunction to "stay in school." But they knew that they would be conscripted upon graduation or upon being cast out for failure in studies. (Many professors, hostile to the Asiatic involvement, graded students most tolerantly, so that they would not drop out of college and be conscripted—this producing a still greater reduction of academic standards.) Besides, many of those young men enjoying draft-deferments suffered from subtle emotions of guilt and misgivings of conscience: why were others being shot, and yet they, thanks to their parents' ability to pay college charges, were being cosseted on the campus? This latter state of mind was little discussed at the time, but it was a powerful motive for the students' militant demand for ending the Vietnamese war: salve our consciences by bringing the troops home.

Young ideologues could stir to rebellion, without much difficulty, those numerous undergraduates and graduate students who were resentful, bored, and uneasy in conscience. Of the campus ideologues, some were pacifists, but others saw their opportunity to advance the interests of Soviet Russia or of Communist China by working toward the defeat of America's Asiatic policy and the fall of the government of South Vietnam. They could make headway on the campus because there were so many discontented students, because the Lonely Crowd easily is converted into a mob, and because of the sheer size of campus populations, difficult to control.

Demands for "Black Power", insistence upon open admissions and open curricula, cries of "sexual freedom"—these were causes which would have gained little ground upon the campus, had it not been that a general spirit of sour unrest brooded over the typical university, and had it not been that the detestation of the military draft provided a catalyst to convert resentments into action. Some students dashed with relief into marches, demonstrations, sit-ins—and presently acts of physical destruction.

Even indignation at military conscription would have been less militant, had most students recognized any real objects in the higher learning. But many of them found college and university no better than relocation centers to lodge young people during that awkward transition from high school to adult existence.

"I'm not surprised at all that many young people—those who are naïve and searching for identity, as well as those who are quite mature and clearly motivated—'drop out' of their studies." So wrote to me, in 1967, a scholarly editor and critic, professor and sometime administrator at one of the newer state universities in Illinois. "Professor Bruno Bettelheim's recent statement before a congressional committee was entirely accurate. As you know from your own past experience, many of our faculty have good reason to be disaffected, and their common reason is similar to the reason the students are unhappy and unruly.

"One can easily lose his identity, even before he becomes aware of it. The facelessness and namelessness of the modern university are horrifying. I just heard today that the appropriate presidential commission in Washington is prepared to recommend that no universities be established and allowed to grow over a student body of ten thousand. But what about the present monstrosities?"

Just so. In the academic mob of 1967, the better students were frustrated, for general standards had been lowered beneath their interest and capacity. In this academic mob, the inferior students were bewildered and baffled, for even degraded standards were too high for them. In this mob, the scholar was deprived of influence, though he might be paid well enough. In this mob, the teaching assistant and the research assistant—many of them dull doctoral candidates who never should have been encouraged to enter graduate schools—were worked to the bone, paid a pittance, and generally induced to think of themselves as members of an intellectual proletariat. Down with the Establishment! Teaching assistants, in many of the big student riots, were the organizers of insurrection.

The temporary power of the student radicals was disproportionate to their numbers. They were unopposed, and sometimes abetted, by the mass of students from the Permissive Society. Such students did not find it unpleasant that administrators and professors should be reviled publicly; they had no strong loyalties, and had been taught to venerate nothing; so long as their own diversions were not much interrupted, they would not lift their hands in defense of academic order.

Preoccupied with sociability and vocationalism, the administrators of Behemoth University and Brummagem University were hoist by their own petards. After tremendous bricks-and-mortar expenditure, after endless empty talk about the egalitarian culture they were building, after promising an easy degree and a prosperous career to every boy and girl who might be enticed into their degree-mills—why, Chancellor Booster and President Boomer found that they had alienated both the enterprising talents and the mediocrities of the rising generation. Now the paranoiacs were smashing the computers, while the ideologues were busy abolishing the liberties of the mind.

Among the better young minds, unchastened or uninformed by the moral imagination, the development of defecated rationality had produced ideological yearnings that led to impatience—literally burning impatience—with the old imperfections of man and society. Among the inferior students, bored, ill prepared, or emotionally disturbed, there had occurred a transferring of personal discontents to the nearest symbol of authority and order—to the college or the university. The inner disorder of these pseudo-students was vented upon the liberal establishment which had set them adrift on the raft of autonomy. And their own campus was the most vulnerable outpost of that liberal establishment.

American affluence had produced a college-age population often intellectually flaccid and long insulated against the more trying aspects of the human condition—although sentimentally lachrymose whenever the "underprivileged" or "culturally deprived" were mentioned, not knowing that they themselves were culturally deprived. Roughly speaking, the higher the students' background of prosperity, the more radical their rebelliousness. On the other hand, where most students were children of hard-working parents, the radicals were rejected: when Mark Rudd, the radical hero of Columbia University, tried to shut down Brooklyn College, he promptly was ejected by the Brooklyn students, and similar resistance to ideologues and fantastics occurred at Queen's College and at City College.

It needs to be remembered that in 1967 the young people between the ages of seventeen and twenty-two had been fed the pabulum of television all their days. The TV-show producer must solve every personal or social problem within half an hour, or an hour at most; so students were indignant when the difficulties of the college, or of the nation, were not resolved with equal celerity by the possessors of authority. Man and society, they had seen, were perfectible on the flickering screen. On their television sets they watched riots on other campuses—some of them pseudo-riots, engineered by television producers. At a Californian state university, about this time, I happened to pass by while a film company was photographing such a simulated "protest", complete with bonfires and bricks being tossed; the student participants were real enough, but they had been hired as extras for that evening. Disorder became contagious. Why shouldn't students have their action at Behemoth State U., too? It would get them out of those boring classes for a week.

A few years later, at a Tulane University symposium, I shared a platform with Dr. Clark Kerr, whose mismanagement of the University of California had brought on the Berkeley riots. Now employed by the Carnegie educational apparatus, he declared complacently at Tulane that the only cause of the campus disorders had been the Vietnam war, and that Carnegie polls showed how thoroughly satisfied with the American higher learning were the vast majority of students. I replied that if this smug satisfaction actually were prevalent, it simply would demonstrate my point about the decadence of American university and college. Our student audience at Tulane laughed their approbation of my retort, uproariously; they at least did not suffer from illusions about the perfection of our higher learning.

On most campuses, the students of the sort who troubled themselves to attend symposia and formal lectures by visiting speakers were painfully aware that much was wrong with the higher education—much that had nothing to do with war or conscription. At Stanford University, hard hit by the radicals' violence, there was published a pamphlet entitled *Freshmen Voices: Student Manners and Morals*, to which all contributors were first-year students at Stanford. Most of these contributors exhibited the familiar attitudes of rebellion, for institutionalized "revolution" had become the new conformity. But in some of the contributions to this publication, one encountered a serious questioning of the postulates of liberalism and rationalism that had dominated the intellectual climate of opinion until the student protests.

"In all industrialized nations, but especially in the United States, rationalism is gradually becoming outmoded," a student named Jeffrey Harris wrote. "By this I don't mean that the amount of knowledge is decreasing, or that the average IQ is slowly dropping; if anything the opposites are true. But I do believe that rationalism, as a single directive force in daily life, is becoming less important. This change is not due solely to human reactions against the dehumanizing forces in rationalism and technology. Rationalism, having been too successful, is destroying itself."

This student had glimpsed the aridity of the Benthamite notion of education, which starves the imagination; he had sensed, with Pascal, that the heart has reasons which the reason cannot know. Another contributor, Don Farrow, discussed "Influence of the Liberals." He was not satisfied that latter-day liberalism possessed answers to present discontents:

"The protestors, by presenting the concepts most alien to us, have made us understand ideas that before would have been flatly condemned; we learn to overcome our initial prejudices, to listen to the unusual. But because we are seldom challenged by conservative arguments, and because we are detached from the influence of our parents, we sometimes hold in contempt anyone who is traditional, or patriotic, or socially popular, and we see ourselves as enlightened and our parents as ignorant. It is easy to condemn society in college, and to think yourself a liberal. There are few people who will argue back . . . .

"The liberal stance is convincing, and most of us are convinced by it, but for many there is often the feeling that we are being inundated with one point of view, that the more conservative side of each question is being hidden."

This was a canny surmise. Farrow implied that the questing intellects among the freshmen were not content to abide in the shadow-world of doubt for doubt's sake. He recognized that his generation might be conceited:

"Our morals, or lack of morals, show our increasing conviction that there is nothing absolute or dependable in this world, that nothing is real and no purpose is valid unless we make it so and believe in it. There is no God, or if there is, the code that people attribute to him is only an invention of man. There is no country in itself worthy of patriotism, unless its ideals coincide with what we personally feel is just. And since Nuremberg, we even feel that a person must decide whether the laws are good and should be followed, or bypassed because they contradict what he believes is right."

So the boasted tremendous achievement of American education had come to this: loss of all ends or objects, abandoning of all old certitudes, substitution of vague private sentiments for reasoned standards of judgment. But some students felt the lack of substance, and had begun to ask the right questions, looking for an avenue out of the Waste Land. There were students in 1967 whom administrators and professors might have consulted with profit; yet almost nowhere were the opinions of the more serious students solicited.

The student activists were demanding, on many a campus, "Student Power"—by which they meant, usually, opportunity to prescribe the curriculum, choose the professors, and supervise the finances. It was impossible to gratify such wishes. For students necessarily are probationers in the Academy. If they were already sufficiently wise to administer the principal affairs of an academic corporation, there would have been small need for them to have enrolled at all. If so talented, why not embark immediately upon the business of life—especially if an activist?

The notion that in medieval times great universities were governed collectively by the undergraduates is a fable only, even though promulgated by some people who ought to have known better, among them Robert Hutchins. Only one university, Bologna, ever was so controlled for a time; and there, what with bitter complaints from the townsfolk, it did not endure. Ordinarily the medieval schools were church foundations, subject to some ecclesiastical authority; at many of them, in the beginning, the students were acolytes, there on sufferance to gather what crumbs of learning they might from the men in holy orders who had been provided with academic leisure by pious benefactors of the infant university.

Nevertheless, it remains true that on nearly all American campuses, for a long while past, the students had been given next to no hearing in matters which seriously concerned themselves; nor had many of them sought to be heard, until the outbursts of the 'Sixties brought the famous Non-negotiable Demands. That was one aspect of the decay of academic community.

16

Continuity and Relevance: 1968

ALTHOUGH IT IS EASY to become a nihilist at the age of eighteen, for such precocious philosophers work is as painful as thought. During the riots of 1968 at the Sorbonne, some Parisian students sprayed a legend in paint above a doorway: "No work!" Like many others on either side of the Atlantic, they thought it amusing to spend one's university years in protest, not study. That is what George Orwell called "the strange, empty dream of idleness"; also one thinks of a book by a grandson of Karl Marx entitled *The Right to be Idle*.

At French, German, Italian, Spanish, and other universities during these years, the riots often were more violent than were the American demonstrations; and those in Britain were no less tumultuous than the American disorders. Clearly, the causes of unrest among students throughout the western world were something more than American intervention in Vietnam. In Europe, as in America, there had occurred a sudden and vast expansion of university enrollments, and many new universities and technical institutes had been created since the Second World War. Thus there had come into being almost everywhere in the West a swarming population of students, many of them culturally rootless, bored with the abstractions of the university, unprepared for higher study, some enrolled only to postpone or avoid the labors of adult life. Such crowds lay ready for young ideologues. For radical groups to dominate a university, it was necessary that much of the student body must be alienated from the university itself. Such conditions existed throughout the 'Sixties. Unable to master the old culture of the higher learning, many thousands of these students fell into the much-described "counter-culture" of intellectual shams, bohemian poses, narcotics, noise, and violent attitudes.

A word of power within the counter-culture was "relevance." All intellectual disciplines were to be put to the test of relevance. Relevance to what? It was rather rude to ask that question. In general, the zealots of the counter-culture implied by this word their detestation of any exacting humane or scientific studies. They implied also that whatever they might tolerate in the higher learning must be related to immediate concerns—especially to revolutionary change. For the patrimony of culture, as for established morals and manners, these children of the dawn expressed their thoroughgoing contempt.

Now it was all too true, at least in America, that much of the typical college's curriculum was relevant to nothing important, old or new. The college catalogue was crammed with academic boondoggles or purposeless specialized courses that pleased only over-specialized Ph.D.'s. In that sense, I sympathized with the call for "relevance."

When I spoke at the Berkeley campus of the University of California in 1968, a tight-knit band of students of the New Left (more civil to me than to most) protested that the modern college and university were not relevant to our need for "creating a better world." Revolutionary action, these students thought, is the object of the Academy. Lectures should be harangues meant for the propagation of a new social faith, they implied, and campuses should become staging-grounds for the overthrow of existing public authority.

A graduate student informed me that the study of foreign languages and of the sciences was irrelevant to higher education—or irrelevant, anyway, to the sort of higher education he desired. If one wishes to become merely a leader of the crowd, a demagogue, I replied, indeed these disciplines are useless luggage; for such spirits, in Yeats' line, "That lamp is from the tomb." Actually, I suspected, this graduate student was capable of something better. Like many other radical students—I encountered such at Cornell, at Valparaiso University, on many campuses other than those of state universities—this particular angry young man did not understand the need for continuity or the character of genuine relevance to wisdom; for that matter, he did not understand how universities are supposed to work beneficently upon society.

In the long run, the sort of education which most profoundly affects the civil social order is that education which lifts the student above the confusion of the hour's quarrels. The function of the college is not to gratify material hopes, but to introduce students to long views. The function of the college is not to rouse the young to revolt against the nature of things, but to acquaint them with the wisdom of their ancestors. The function of the college is not to promulgate an extravagant ideal of human perfectibility, but to teach us the joy and the tragedy of the human condition. The function of the college is not to inflame the passions, but to lead us toward right reason.

Yet many students of the 'Sixties went about like so many Cains, angry and confused, crying "Pull down! Pull down!" This pleased the ego, justified absence from classroom and library, and filled the wrathful with a warm sense of righteousness; and it made thought unnecessary. It was Theater of the Absurd.

The most truly relevant things have been discerned by men of genius in different times and lands. Prophets and poets were relevant to the personal and the public disorders of 1968; it was the demagogues and the charlatans who were irrelevant, if we were to regain the inner order of the soul and the outer order of society. The calm analysis of Tocqueville was more relevant to 1968 than was the burning of draft-cards or the Poor People's Campaign in Washington; Virgil's advocacy of *labor, pietas, fatum* had more meaning for 1968 than had the black flag waving above the Sorbonne.

To *labor*, purposeful work, the radicalized students especially needed to apply themselves. They were revolutionaries subsidized by the prosperous Establishment which they meant to destroy—the scholarship boys, the Meritocracy, the bored children of parental affluence. They wore railwaymen's overalls, though many of them never had boarded a train, having their own sports-cars; they carefully faded their blue denims to show how very proletarian they were; they affected foul speech to prove their maturity. They emulated the "working classes"—by whom they were abhorred, they soon discovered—in everything but work. No work!

"Today's youth have not learned 'to see humor in misfortune' because they have hardly known what misfortune is," my friend Julián Marías, the Spanish philosopher, wrote at the time. "They are being asked to do the opposite: they are being asked to declare a state of mourning and to make sadness and protest the rule in what must be considered—in view of the true state of the world—an incomparable example of well-being, justice, freedom, and prosperity." He was referring to American students, whose self-pity he found inexcusable. Marías, like Unamuno, possessed the tragic sense of life; the typical radicalized student had nothing of that, but only too much ego in his cosmos. I used to tell them that revolutions destroy their own children, which infuriated them; for they suspected the aphorism to be true, and they did not yearn to become martyrs. Actually, they were prisoners, slaves to time and circumstance.

Twenty years earlier, I had first stood on Morningside Heights, in Manhattan, where the stone steps lead down through Morningside Park, nowadays the predator-haunted *cordon sanitaire* that separates Columbia University from the pandemonium of Harlem, far below. How long would it be, I wondered then, before "Sansculottism, many-headed, fire-breathing," should scale these Heights?

The first wave of that uprising broke upon Columbia University, atop the Heights, early in 1968. To borrow terms from Arnold Toynbee, the "external proletariat" from the black slums joined with the "internal proletariat" of Columbia's white radical teaching-assistants and students to plunge into anarchy this famous university.

In the midst of Columbia's suffering there was published an important book by Jacques Barzun, *The American University: How It Runs, Where It Is Going*. Dr. Barzun did not actually call our higher learning decadent, but that implication ran through his pages. When I had been less than eight years old, Barzun already had been publishing essays on education. For twelve years, until the middle of 1966, he had been provost at Columbia University—leaving that office shortly before things fell apart. In his *House of Intellect* and other books, he had been one of the shrewder critics of higher education. Although his accustomed perceptivity was evident in this later book, a certain weariness seemed to afflict Jacques Barzun in 1968. At best, the American university ran creakily that year, and worse might come unto it.

Columbia's plight in 1968 was like that of the University of Chicago, also hemmed in by slums; Yale and the University of California were nearly as distressed in their situations. Yet the proximity of poverty and social disorder is not of itself fatal to a university: the University of Paris endured such conditions for centuries, and Glasgow University held out for a long time amidst urban decay. Only when the internal community of a university disintegrates can the external proletariat break in.

Professors and students are citizens of the republic of Academe. When academic ends and standards give way before the degradation of the democratic dogma, then the "internal proletariat" of an educational establishment attains dull domination, and the whole academic corporation sinks lower.

In 1945, when Barzun had published his book *Teacher in America*, Nicholas Murray Butler still had been master of Columbia University.

But even then the Second World War had been transforming Columbia, along with nearly all other American universities. Reform and reinvigoration did not come to Columbia in time. Black Power, Students for a Democratic Society, and a profound confusion at the heart of Columbia therefore did their baneful work.

At Columbia after 1945, the enfeebled liberal climate of opinion had provided neither sufficient imagination nor sufficient strength of will to bring about healthy reform—nor yet to resist effectually the ignorant democratism assailing the Academy from without and within. Grayson Kirk, Jacques Barzun, and a few others at Columbia had some understanding of what needed to be done, and so far as they could they rose superior to the general atmosphere, achieving certain administrative improvements, though not enough. One could look to Dr. Barzun for sound sense, but perhaps not for that bold affirmation which arises from a belief stronger than attachment to humane culture.

What reforms the Kirks and the Barzuns might have effected at Columbia had been delayed by the academic affliction I call President Boomer (to borrow a character from one of Stephen Leacock's spoofs). The Boomers who ran American universities, during the period from the end of the Second World War until quite recently, were interested in quantitative expansion, successful athletic teams, "higher" vocational training as related to the nexus of cash payment—and little else. Columbia's President Boomer had been General Eisenhower. A political innocent, Eisenhower also had been an educational innocent: he had been King Log in office, while discontents of staff and students had accumulated.

Such Presidents Boomer as Dwight Eisenhower and John Hannah were not mentioned in Barzun's pages. But Barzun found the decadent American university "bankrupt in mind and purse" and knew that this fallen state had been brought about by college presidents in large part.

"Relevance", Barzun said, is in the mind. When students declare that their studies are not relevant, they do touch, however confusedly, upon the central failure of the American university. By their attitude that liberal education is an impertinence, many college administrators have misled the mass of graduate students and undergraduates, for they have taught students that their needs are identical with their wants.

"It would be easy to show from history that when the cry of Relevance is heard, it is because the spirit has gone out of whatever is being taught," Barzun wrote. "And spirit in education also means *spiritedness*. . . ."

When college and university claim that they can confer worthwhile *experience*, those institutions are becoming irrelevant to the real task of education. "Because 'values,' 'creativity,' 'living and giving,' lie in the realm of experience and are good, it is supposed that they can be 'given' directly, taught as experiences, and that the college is the institution to contrive all this: have a syllabus on effective living, and then say 'I've had effective living.'" The business of the college, its relevant concern, is the development of the intellect.

Once the university or the college undertakes what is irrelevant to its purpose, its energies are diverted into social-welfare projects, parochial concerns, technological contracts, publishing enterprises, and fiscal schemes which drain away the institution's funds and obscure the primary purpose of cultivating the intellect in a community of scholars. So university and college end by accomplishing little and displeasing everybody.

What must the university do if it is to regain relevance to its central task? From long experience and much reflection, Barzun offered advice.

Simplification and austerity must govern the "revelant" university, he argued. Survey courses must be abandoned. New projects must be inspected with a suspicious eye. Less emphasis must be placed upon "research", and teaching and research must be separated. The number of courses offered must be reduced. Upon "educationally motiveless people," mere "pass degrees" must be conferred. Why not confer upon every American at birth a Ph.D. (a recommendation previously promulgated by Robert Hutchins and myself)? Or, failing that, why not diminish educational snobbery by awarding the Ph.D. immediately after oral examinations, without a dissertation?

University and college, if they would be relevant, should cease trying to be all things to all men: "If a youth feels a vocation for social work, let him either prepare for it through study or drop studies and go use his talents in the midst of life."

Also Barzun offered many practical administrative reforms within the university. He would have had the university recover respect for its own dignity. If the university is not reformed, Barzun said in his concluding paragraphs, it will cease to elevate the tone and temper of American life; and then we will sink into a decay of intellect and imagination.

"What develops then," Barzun wrote, "is a proletarian culture, by which I do not mean the culture of intelligent and cheerful working men exclusively, but one in which the prevailing tendency is to suspect *height*—standards of work and degrees of achievement, except in sports. Learning, the search for truth, and high art are then gradually discarded in favor of practical training, applied research, and consumption art. The full professor is intelligent and cheerful too: he responds to the common agitation, discontinuity, and excitement of the mass culture; he prides himself on not being an intellectual, though he enjoys 'the finer things of life,' in a widely shared attachment to 'gracious living.' "

Jacques Barzun reminded some, in 1968, that the university was intended for the quickening of the intellect, and that no task could be more relevant to the real needs of our time. His *American University* remains probably our best manual for reform; here I have merely suggested its strength and practicality.

Yet Barzun did not mention that the universities began with a bold premise: "The fear of God is the beginning of wisdom." Had Dr. Barzun and some other gentlemen and scholars of strong intellect, much experience, and good will been more ready to profess such principles, we might have been less plagued about 1968 by such preposterous figures as Tom Hayden and Mark Rudd. As it was, first the squads of Black Power zealots and then the still more barbarous white radicals seized upon Columbia University, which stood almost undefended because not loved by enough. "Relevance" tore Columbia apart for some months.

Real intellectual relevance does exist, but it cannot be found in the multiversity. Only the community of scholars can reveal that relevance to the permanent things. Columbia in 1968 was more collectivity than community.

In 1968, university and college needed more drop-outs. Those enrollees who had no interest in philosophical questions, or in pure science, or in the moral imagination, ought to have dropped out altogether; they were wasting their time and money, and the time and money of others, because the higher education is meant for those who can apprehend abstractions.

Jacques Barzun, unlike most men who had held high posts in university administration, knew such truths, and published them. His book was highly relevant to the troubles of 1968, but few of the "activists" read it. They did not read many books of any sort, although some of them did dip into Chairman Mao's *Thoughts* and Che Guevara's manual for guerrilla operations. Those works of literature seemed relevant enough—relevant to the dreadful servitude into which half the world had fallen.

*   *   *

By "relevance", even the more moderate students generally meant "relevant to current affairs." But as applied to the higher learning, the word should signify "relevant to wisdom and virtue." I offer here some reflections on what is *not* relevant to the work of college and university.

First, the exploded notion of "adjustment to society" is not relevant to the higher learning. Those who have read Evelyn Waugh's sardonic little novel *Scott-King's Modern Europe* will recall how its luckless schoolmaster hero learns through a summer's experience of modern disorder that it is infinitely wicked to teach young men to adjust to life in the modern world. To "adjust" to the power of the total state, the concentration camp, the secret police, and the triumph of violence would be adjustment to abnormity. The higher learning is not meant to inculcate conformity to the processes of the hour. It is intended to open our eyes to the norms, the enduring standards.

Second, college and university do not exist to promulgate the latest quasi-intellectual novelties; for those are not relevant to enduring truth. Some subjects which are puffed up as related directly to the moment's events are hopelessly unrealistic, and irrelevant to any enduring needs of the student. In 1968 there was a vogue for courses in Swahili, as a token of interest in African peoples. Now Swahili—a bastard tongue containing many European words—would be useful to persons like me, who occasionally travel in Africa. But it never would be employed by even one one-hundredth of one per cent of a college's graduates; and no literature exists in that language. What a notion of relevance! Similarly, the typical "current awareness" program, meant to inform students of journalism or of international affairs, is a boondoggle and irrelevant. For one can understand the events of the hour only in the perspective of history and literature and philosophy and religion—true subjects for collegiate study. The wise college confines itself to study of the permanently significant, and is not obsessed with ephemeral events.

Third, a misplaced vocationalism in the college is irrelevant to the pursuit of truth. This is especially so with attempts to prepare young people for taking a place in modern industry. The university or college which pretends to prepare a student for a particular job is the institution which condemns its graduates to servitude.

To be succinct, the truly relevant things in a college are the permanent things. They constitute the body of knowledge not undone by modern winds of doctrine or by modern technology. The truths of the fifth century before Christ, or of the first century of the Christian era, possess as much meaning today as they did many centuries ago. (I am unable to think of any "social studies" more relevant to our social perplexities today than study of the history of the age of Augustus Caesar.)

A hastily got-up course in "urban problems", for instance, is irrelevant if the students, and perhaps the professor, are ignorant of the history of urban growth, of economics, of political thought, and of the other disciplines connected with the life of the city. Yet a course in urban affairs may be highly relevant to truth, and productive of good, if it integrates, at an advanced level, genuine intellectual disciplines— and relates them to our present urban discontents.

If a formal education does not bear at all upon our personal and social concerns today, it is a snare, and worthless: in that, the students of the New Left were quite right during 1968. But no modern authors are more genuinely relevant to our present perplexities than are Plato and Augustine, say. Preoccupation with the passing pageant is merely the sort of "relevance" which the big commercial book-clubs sell for discussion at ladies' literary circles. It was not for such purposes that university and college were endowed. It is Confucius who remains relevant, not Mao; Aristotle, not Sartre.

17

Educational Luddites: 1969

FROM COLUMBIA TO BERKELEY, from Brummagem U. to Our Lady of the Sorrows, in 1969 a mob of college students embraced the ideology of Captain Ned Ludd: smash the machine! Once so beloved, the campus now was hated by many of its denizens. Yes, I do mean "denizens", as in "denizens of the jungle", or "foreigners admitted to residence."

I pitied those denizens, and sympathized with them in certain of their distresses, although not with their lynch-law attempts at obtaining redress. The heart of the matter was this: the academic community had decayed into an academic mob. Tens of thousands of young people, on big campus after big campus, had been crowded into teen-age ghettos, and of those at least half had not the foggiest notion of why they had come. Of those who did acknowledge some objective, only a remnant really desired a thorough disciplining of the intellect.

From Jacques Barzun to the wild spirits of the New Left, everybody was rushing into print to lament the failings of the higher learning—often, to my wry pleasure, in terms that I had employed for the previous dozen years. Behemoth University had become decadent, dreary, disgusting: in that judgment, if in no other, the critics concurred. The professor was alienated from it; so were the students—the better student and the inferior student both.

Yet in that rough hour, when many voices demanded some qualitative reform of the higher learning, there tripped upon the stage Dr. Clark Kerr—Multiversity Kerr, late of Berkeley, in 1969 a factotum of the Carnegie Foundation for the Advancement of Teaching—to inform us that all we needed was more of the hair of the dog that bit us. As chairman of the Carnegie Commission on Higher Education, Dr.

Kerr desired to jam practically everybody into Behemoth University and new institutions, at federal expense.

Kerr and his thirteen educationist colleagues proposed that the Nixon administration (actually, they had counted upon a Humphrey administration, but the best-laid plans . . .) should gratify the desires of the American public by making college degrees almost universal and almost gratis. According to a Gallup poll quoted by the Commission, ninety-seven per cent of American parents desired that "higher education should be available" to their offspring. *Vox populi, vox Dei.* Therefore let President Nixon and the Congress appropriate seven billion dollars for expansion of universities and colleges, and for direct grants to students (the 'disadvantaged' especially) by 1970; let Nixon and his successors enlarge this appropriation to at least thirteen billion dollars by 1976; let the federal government finance five hundred new community colleges instanter, and fifty four-year urban colleges, "which would specially concern themselves with the educational underprivileged and with a broad social spectrum." Centralize, bureaucratize, standardize: let the federal government supply thirty-two per cent of the costs of higher education, but let the states decrease their share from twenty-seven to seventeen per cent; leave the rest to the "private sector"—supposing the private sector to have any cash remaining after taxes.

Behind these schemes of the Carnegie Academy of Lagado lay the assumption that every mother's son and daughter burned with a pure, gem-like flame for the higher learning—at a time when the academic mob obviously was more interested in setting fire to the administration building. Every boy and girl alive an intellectual king or queen! Thus we would have proceeded to form an immense intellectual proletariat, presumptuous and unemployable.

Quite promptly, the Association of State Universities and Land Grant Colleges (ordinarily thirsting for more federal spending) disapproved of the Carnegie fantasia, mostly because the Carnegie enthusiasts proposed to pass out money directly from Washington to prospective students, ignoring state university administrations. And few college presidents anywhere were found to back Dr. Kerr and his crew. Kerr and company were bent upon degradation of the democratic dogma: everybody a B. A., at least, almost tomorrow. "The right to higher education would follow the path blazed by civil rights," said one friendly commentator on the Carnegie report. "There would be no discrimination."

How true! No discrimination—except for discrimination against the humane scale, the serious student, the able professor, the order and integration of knowledge, the industrious parent, the claims of reason. *Only* forty per cent of college-age Americans even entered college, Clark Kerr lamented. They were all so happy on the campus, he assured us: so why exclude the stupid, the slack, and those who (strange folly) would prefer to thrust themselves immediately into the sphere of gainful employment?

In 1969, Robert Finch, Secretary of Health, Education, and Welfare, was not favorably disposed toward this nonsense; nor was President Nixon. They had more pressing problems than this design for intellectual levelling. Nor has the Carnegie extravagance made real headway during the decade since its publication. The ungovernable academic mob which the Carnegie educationists would have herded into their academic compounds soon would have hanged Kerr and company from the college campanile. I might have tugged upon the rope myself. It came close to rope-tugging, on more than one campus, during 1969.

Yet already the reaction was upon us. Politicians, college presidents, and syndicated columnists joined in condemnation of campus violence. Yesterday's fashionable prattle about revolution was piously reproved by those very liberals who, a short while before, had beamed upon the ferment of the rising generation. Irving Howe, socialist, editor of *Dissent*, wandered over the face of the land reproaching the more vehement dissenters and reminding them of the delicious benefits of the Social Security Act. One thought of Edward Gibbon, so progressive at the commencement of the French Revolution, observing from his Swiss retreat the course of that movement; reflecting presently that revolutionaries kill people like Edward Gibbon; and then taking another tack.

For my part, I did not deliver sermons about the naughtiness of ungrateful undergraduates who fail to look forward to old-age benefits. Whatever the silliness of revolutionary slogans and methods, one could not deal with them by finger-wagging. We needed to address ourselves to the real *causes* of the upheaval in the university.

Having been for two decades a mordant critic of what was fondly called the higher learning in America, I confess that I relished somewhat, as Cassandra might have, the fulfillment of my predictions and the plight of doctrinaire educationists in 1969. I even own to having indulged a sneaking sympathy with some of the campus revolutionaries. Consider, by way of illustration, the chastening experience of John A. Hannah, president of Michigan State University, chosen to be director of the federal government's foreign-aid program under the Nixon administration.

Called to relieve the miseries of Kerala and improve the lot of Bolivia, President Hannah delivered his farewell address to the members of his faculty on February 10, 1969. In three decades as master of MSU, Hannah had built up a student body of some forty-five thousand on his main campus—with expectations (unrealized, as it would turn out) of seventy thousand before many years should expire. In the process, somehow Hannah had grown well endowed with the world's goods. Doubtless on this day of leavetaking, President Hannah felt that he deserved well of the rising generation. Certainly he knew that he had done well out of the education business.

True, he was departing from Michigan State in the nick of time. Having passed the retirement age set by himself, he stood in an awkward situation when certain trustees of the University hinted that no one is indispensable—a phrase he had employed sometimes concerning other people. The attorney-general of Michigan had investigated charges of conflict of interest against Hannah and his subordinates; and although it had not come to a court of law, some persons whose affairs had been closely plaited with Hannah's had found it prudent to retire prematurely. Moreover, some of the students were ungrateful.

As President Hannah addressed his serried ranks of professors for the last time, riot-police with gas-masks stood guard in the auditorium. Several hundred students, a discharged instructor with a bullhorn, and a number of outsiders—among them, that eminent activist Carl Oglesby, of Students for a Democratic Society—were chanting unpleasantly near the doors of the auditorium. It was found well to cancel the reception that had been scheduled to follow President Hannah's speech.

"A small coterie," the righteous Hannah told his faculty, "has declared social revolution against America. America's universities have been marked as the first fortress that must fall. We've been warned of the weapons to be used and the tactics to be employed." Having exhorted his professors to resist these enemies of culture, even unto the last bluebook, he departed from their midst, that he might do high deeds beside the Potomac.

John Hannah had been an imperialist president, erecting new buildings even more rapidly than he had lowered old standards. He had found Michigan State a tree-shaded cow college, and had left it a sprawling educational factory. Thanks to him, MSU's fat catalogue offered curricula for every taste except refined taste. Yet somehow few in East Lansing mourned his departure.

The gentry of the New Left remained unappreciative of this educational colossus. One of them, James Ridgeway, published in 1969 a book containing lively references to John Hannah: *The Closed Corporation—American Universities in Crisis.* Here we must content ourselves with one extract.

"From 1950 to 1958," Ridgeway wrote, "more than $900,000 in MSU construction contracts went to the Vandenberg Construction Company. The president of this firm was Hannah's brother-in-law, who subsequently went out of business and turned up as construction superintendent at MSU. Hannah was quoted as saying at the trustees' meeting, 'It's true that Vandenberg is my brother-in-law, but I didn't know he was employed by the university.' He also said, 'As far as I know he never did a job for this institution. I was surprised by the figure. . . . I smell what's coming on. This is an attempt to discredit the university by discrediting me.' "

Really? Or was it the Hannahs of America who had discredited the university, and so raised up a turbulent generation of students, at once ignorant and passionate, somehow sensing that Hannah's idea of a university had injured them? Having established academic collectivism, having severed the intellectual and ethical roots of the higher learning, people like John Hannah were chagrined to discover that the proles seemed restless.

No less a public figure than Joan Baez remarked in 1969 that if one desires to make a revolution, the campus is an unlikely place to commence; that she was disgusted with the antics of campus radicals; and that she would have no more to do with them. One wished that certain activist professors might have shared her wisdom. In the long run, most of them would—for revolutions devour their fathers as well as their children.

It is not in the nature of a university to nurture political fanaticism and utopian designs. Most professors are not neoterists, and one cannot expect the university to harvest every year a crop of exotic fruits. Robert Hutchins once observed, with only mild exaggeration, that few of the Great Books were written by professors. If one would be a mover and a shaker, the forum is preferable to the Grove of Academe.

In our time, the affliction of ideological wrath descended upon the campus. What the university had offered in earlier years was freedom; what zealots sought there in 1969 was power. Freedom and power stand in eternal opposition. To demand that the university dedicate itself to the *libido dominandi* is to insist that the university commit suicide.

Many freshmen told me in 1969 that they had chosen a campus "where the action is." But of action, we all have plenty in the course of life. What the university offers is academic leisure, dialogue, and reflective preparation. Few people, after entering upon the hurly-burly of the world, ever find again enough time to study and to think. The four or five or seven years of college and university life are precious.

All this said, nevertheless I apprehended the causes of the New Left mentality on the campus, and in part shared in the mood of resentment. Against the decadence of the higher learning, the confused outcries of the New Left were a reaction—wounded though those young men and women would have been, had I called them reactionaries.

Were I to indulge my taste for Jeremiads, I might succeed in outwailing the New Left people at the Ivory Tower's western wall. The demonstrating students frequently complained that they had been taught nothing about good and evil; in this they were very nearly right. They complained that they had been taught nothing about justice; so they turned to a Marxist notion of justice, even if they had read only Marx's vulgarizers.

But their enthusiasm for pulling down was another matter. "Revolution" means violent and catastrophic change. Of catastrophe we had experienced enough in this century. Political and moral and technological revolution had fallen like the tower of Siloam upon our civilization. In 1969 we had no need to flog the galloping horses of the four spectres of the Apocalypse. Reconstruction, renewal, reinvigoration—these were the true necessities of 1969.

Shortly before the major troubles of the campus had begun, Dr. Christopher Jencks had estimated that on the typical campus only one per cent of the students had desired to obtain a serious intellectual discipline; two per cent, a more general education; perhaps five per cent had sought an introduction to middle-brow culture and middle-class conviviality; twenty per cent had been after technical training; another twenty per cent, after mere certification as potential employees. That had left more than half the campus population unaccounted for; and, as Jencks had put it, those simply had not known what they desired from college, and had not lasted out four years to take degrees. There's a mob ready to hand.

Now add to the mood of loneliness and boredom the personal

grievance of most male students against military conscription; add to it the smouldering discontent of the proletariat of Academe, the exploited teaching-assistants. Add to it the resentments and bewilderment of the Black Power students, most of them unprepared for higher studies, impelled to "do their thing"—even though, as Tocqueville wrote of the French during their Revolution, "halfway down the stairs, we threw ourselves out of the window to get to the ground more quickly." With these conditions in mind, one did not marvel that an impulse to pull down was powerful upon the campuses of 1969.

Quarter-schooled people with felt grievances are the natural prey of the ideologue. The terrible simplifiers appeared, and almost any young ideologue with a tawdry set of yesteryear's anarchist or Marxist slogans could find some following on most campuses. Any set of slogans would serve. Parallels with Nazi and Fascist and Communist student movements, four decades earlier, were ignored by the more violent student activists, sure of their own virtue and vision.

Consider a leading ideologue of this stamp—Tom Hayden, principal founder of Students for a Democratic Society. I debated with him years before he became Mr. Jane Fonda. For painstaking reform he had only contempt; he appeared to have read narrowly and inattentively; he loved mysterious missions and conspiratorial poses, about which I learned later from another Ann Arbor student who had lodged in the same house with Hayden. His rhetoric, like his program, seemed drawn from Jack London's pseudo-proletarian romance *The Iron Heel*. He would organize the poor and the uprooted, meaning to lead them in righteous wrath against the capitalist rascals. As to what would happen when the revolution was consummated, Hayden remained vague. His talent was wholly for denunciation.

When, toward the beginning of the decade of disorder, I had shared a platform with him at the University of Michigan, he had been living most of the time in Newark, then a city ready to explode. In the course of my public remarks that evening, I happened to comment upon the causes and conditions of social decay in Corktown, the old Irish district of Detroit. Hayden had been editor of the *Michigan Daily*, the student paper at Ann Arbor, and had held in Michigan the first convention of Students for a Democratic Society. Yet Hayden confessed that he never had heard of Corktown, although for years he had lived less than thirty miles from that urban desert.

It is so dull to brighten the corner where you are; so pleasant to carry a secular gospel to the gentiles of distant Newark, say. But presently Newark is aflame, literally; one flees to ivied academic halls; or one flies to Hanoi, to Dar-es-Salaam, anywhere the funds of the Movement will carry one for well-publicized press-conferences. One impedes political conventions in Chicago; one taunts police; one mocks at everybody in either great political party; one utters obscenities, sneeringly, at congressional hearings. While the novelty endures, such a career is amusing for those who like that sort of thing. Tom Hayden still was riding high in 1969: the sullen perpetual adolescent, unable to dream any dreams except Londonian nightmares of violence and triumph. As leaders for reforming society, or for renewing the university, such people—but I need not labor the point.

In 1969 I admired a recent painting, rather in the manner of Daumier, by Renee Radell. It was called "Doing Their Thing." In the foreground stood two young men bearing placards and barring the way. On their signboards was no inscription at all. The young men were grinning, and their amusement was the mirth of hyaenas: they were smug and well-fed and well-dressed nihilists. They barred the way to virtue and wisdom.

Renee Radell had caught perfectly the tone and temper of a type of student activist. These two in the painting, members of a privileged class deferred from military conscription, were free to try to disrupt the society that paid their bills. Their schooling, one gathered, had been costly and bad; their suburban environment had kept them from knowledge of the world, except for the cosseted suburbanite-collegiate realm of fast cars, marijuana, and erotic escapades. Such sneering "revolutionaries" did no more than play a disagreeable game when they did their thing, and from them there could not possibly come the regeneration of the university, let alone a transformation of the social order. Their faces were imprinted on the obverse of the academic coin; on the reverse of that coin was the visage of John Hannah.

There exists a moral order, Edmund Burke wrote, to which we are bound, willingly or not—the "contract of eternal society" joining the dead, the living, and those yet unborn. There exist certain conventions and institutions that we must accept, if the civil social order is not to dissolve into the dust and power of individuality, where every man's hand would be against every other man's. For very survival, in any society, we must submit to the traditions of civility. "But if that which is only submission to necessity should be made the object of choice, the law is broken; nature is disobeyed; and the rebellious are outlawed, cast forth, and exiled, from this world of reason, and order, and peace, and virtue, and fruitful penitence, into the antagonist world of madness, discord, vice, confusion, and unavailing sorrow."

Into that antagonist world, the terrible simplifiers, the frantic ideologues, would cast us; and by revolution, they would make reform impossible. Stir the molten bronze in the cauldron, with Danton, and presently you slip, and are consumed in one agonizing moment.

Yet even if one cannot resist the temptation to stir the cauldron—even if the young revolutionary cries that one crowded hour of glorious life is worth an age without a name—still the university is a curious place to play at being the revolutionary. The perennial strutting and snarling undergraduate, the carping instructor who cries havoc from the sanctuary of the Ivory Tower, the intemperate professor who hankers after power rather than freedom—these are "revolutionaries" deserving of Joan Baez's scorn. "He that lives in a college," wrote the young Burke, "after his mind is sufficiently stocked with learning, is like a man, who having built and rigged and victualled a ship, should lock her up in a dry dock." Those who mean to direct the world must enter the world.

We were assured frequently by our comforters that the great bulk of American students did not participate, even on the most radical of campuses, in the massive demonstrations of 1969—and doubtless this was true. But apathy and indifference were no reasons for a society to congratulate itself. The passive average student did not assault his college; yet neither did he defend it.

Ideologues' pranks may injure a university permanently, though they cannot improve it. In India, in Africa, in much of Latin America, universities were unable to recover from the damage inflicted by student fanatics during the 'Sixties. Stifling free discussion, intimidating all opposition, abolishing standards of scholarship, the triumphant radical students in those countries put an end to academic freedom and academic achievement. The logical culmination of such "progress" occurred at Rangoon, in Burma, where the army used heavy artillery against the university, levelling its buildings to the ground that they might no longer shelter the Communist partisans. Because of the empirical and prescriptive character of American politics, for one thing, the assault of American students upon the university was less ferocious and more ephemeral than the capture of German, French, and Japanese universities by gangs of young fanatics. A decade after the worst of the campus disorders, nevertheless, even the better American universities and colleges have not yet wholly recovered from the fury and the folly of the 'Sixties.

The campus radicals were unable to make any impression upon the shape of American society, though a good many of them actually thought, in the 'Sixties, that they were the triumphant advance-guard of a genuine revolutionary movement which would sweep away "capitalism", old constitutional forms, private property, the old morality, the State Department, draft board offices, and practically everything else. They could inflict serious damage only upon the Academy. For the American social order, whatever its deficiencies, was broad at its base, prosperous, and supported by the overwhelming majority of its citizens. Even during an unpopular war, the American social order could not be altered, let alone overthrown, by any cabal of radical utopians.

Empty talk of revolution, and sporadic violence on the campus, could not improve the academic community, either. Only patient intellectual labor and the use of imagination can restore purpose and loyalty to the university. Frivolous "revolutionary" gestures like burning down the ROTC building had no effect other than to diminish the serious voice in a university's concerns which responsible students ought to have.

Where university reform was concerned, I did not disagree with all the notions of the New Left. Some of the radicals recommended, for instance, that the alumni of a college should exert larger influence upon a college's academic program and business affairs; and I agreed that it would be well to interest the alumni in something besides season tickets for the football games. The student activists sometimes demanded and obtained ombudsmen on the campus, but I was surprised that they did not think of setting up a kind of students' tribune, after the manner of the rector (elected by the students, as representative of their interests) at each of the Scottish universities. So much shouting, so little imagination!

To have recognized at last that something was amiss with the higher learning in America was some gain. Yet the university is not the Bastille, to be taken by storm and razed to the ground; nor ought we to massacre the *Invalides*, dull dogs though some professors may be. The university is not a prison or a fortress, but a community of scholars— and not a community of one generation only. Those who would reform the university must understand its past greatness and its surviving promise—and, to quote Joan Baez a final time (her words in the first turbulence at Berkeley), "Do it with love."

18

The Intellectual Situation: 1970

S VIOLENCE on the campus began to diminish, the federal government looked into the troubles, tardily. Late in 1970, the President's Commission on Campus Unrest—nominally headed by William Scranton, the Pennsylvania politician—submitted a report remarkable only for its lack of insight.

Consider this recommendation from the Report: "The university, and particularly the faculty, must recognize that the expansion of higher education and the emergence of the new youth culture have changed the makeup and concerns of today's student population. The university should adapt itself to these new conditions."

What a muddle of notions! Certainly vast improvement needed to be made in the "teaching programs" of the average institution of higher learning; but scarcely by adapting them to the "new youth culture", otherwise known as the counter-culture. If the university were to remain a real university, it could not convert itself into a counter-university. By nature, the university is not a center for diverting the rising generation; it is supposed to be a center for serious learning, without which no culture can endure. The new "youth culture" had arisen out of commercial television, rock records, and marijuana—or worse substances. It is difficult for an educational institution to "adapt itself" to elements so anti-intellectual. Indeed, universities never have been places for pandering to "youth." Universities are centers for the acquiring of *maturity*, rather. We do not remain young; as adults, we cannot live with a "youth culture" indefinitely. To transcend "youth culture" is a reason, presumably, why at least the better students enroll in the higher learning.

Such contradictions ran through the whole shallow Report. On the

"Scranton Commission" had been few men of talents. Such sober commentators on campus unrest as Seymour Martin Lipset, Sidney Hook, R. A. Nisbet, Jacques Barzun, Edward Levi, and S. I. Hayakawa had not been appointed to the Commission; most such authorities had not even been invited to testify before the Commission. The Report exhorted the nation to subsidize massively "black colleges and universities"; yet at the same time, to recruit black (and other minority) students, massively, to attend "formerly all-white universities." How pleasant to keep one's cake and yet eat it!

One scarcely would have guessed from this Report that the university is intended to nurture the life of the mind. There ran through the Report the assumptions of the ethos of sociability, the barbarous error that respectability would be guaranteed by the acquiring of a college sheepskin. Get everybody into college, and make life easy for everybody there, and conform the policies of the American republic to the undergraduates' mood of the moment, and compel the Great White Father in Washington to spend half his time apologizing for himself "at a series of national meetings designed to foster understanding among those who are now divided"—thus, the Commission declared, peace would be restored to the campus.

Upon the fundamental reasons for disorder in the Academy, the authors of this Report scarcely touched, except in this one sentence about alienated students: "They seek a community of companions and scholars, but find an impersonal multiversity." Just so. And would this deep resentment be cured by increasing enrollments, and thus wiping out academic community altogether? Does one restore community by new federal grants for bricks and mortar, or by devising feeble curricula sufficiently imbecile to guarantee degrees for even the illiterate "student"?

This Report of the Scranton Commission, so shallow, so illogical, so unimaginative, nevertheless was evidence of a sort: evidence of a widespread intellectual decay, extending to most public men, which we may call, as others did, The Situation. Let me examine The Situation in 1970.

Two years earlier, George Scott-Moncrieff, the Scottish man of letters, had assured me that The Situation was as wretched in Britain as in the United States. "Newcastle has produced a multiple murderess aged eleven," he had written to me, "but I suspect that the most insidious influence is purveyed by our enlightened intellectuals, whose fudging of all moral boundaries in the cause of license is staggering."

About the same time, I had encountered in the just-published final volume of Hoxie Neale Fairchild's *Religious Trends in English Poetry* a succinct description of The Situation. By "The Situation", Professor Fairchild meant the intellectual and moral condition of opinion among twentieth-century *cognoscenti* and their followers. Here is Fairchild's "pointillistic sketch of modern misery I call 'The Situation' ":

"The Modern Temper. Hollow Men eating their Naked Lunches in the Waste Land while awaiting Godot. Botched civilization. Sick world. *Untergang des Abendlandes*.

"No suprahuman Creator or Judge Redeemer or Lover or Guide. No life beyond the grave. Loss of the traditional symbols of Western culture. No integrating myths. No worship.

"No reality independent of the disintegrated observer. No objective sharable truth or truths. No scale of values. No norm of human nature. Dissociation of sensibility. Discursive and intuitive reason equally distrusted. No boundaries between rational and irrational, normal and abnormal. Pluralism liberates, but only into bewilderment. Semantic stultification: chasm between words and meaning. Solipsism. Nothing to discipline our emotions. No firm roots in domestic or civil ritual. Life patternless, purposeless, meaningless. Everything 'phony.' "

Here Fairchild was describing not his own state of mind, but rather the climate of opinion that oppressed "intellectuals" generally. It was the waste land of defeated intellectuality, this consciousness of the secularistic intellectual. And of course it was not mere "anxiety." It was what Max Picard had called "the flight from God." The Situation, or the fancied Situation, was in large part a necessary result from the latter-day liberal mentality, which had been dissolving all traditions and loyalties. And in part through the professors, awareness of The Situation was transmitted to the mass of university students, most of them already culturally deprived in their upbringing. What wonder that they behaved as nihilists, when they had been taught the impossibility of believing in anything?

John Lukacs' book *Historical Consciousness* had been published about the same time as Fairchild's last volume. A learned and lively scholar, Lukacs implied that we must liberate ourselves from the spell of the dreary intelligentsia. Through awareness of the past, we moderns still enjoy the opportunity for understanding what has happened to us, Lukacs wrote.

"There are many symptoms which suggest that the dangers of professional intellectualism are now the opposite from what people had thought," Lukacs reasoned: "instead of pedantry, sloppiness; instead of the narrow burrowing of the parochial bookworm, the sleazy super-

ficiality of the professional intellectual. Tocqueville's conservative con-
temporaries used to rail against the bookish pedants of the coming
democracy, against the epoch of the specialist who would replace the
more spacious epoch marked by the chivalry of the mind. But Tocqueville saw further: he foresaw that the successful professional intellectuals would be the prime idea-mongers. . . . The single-mindedness,
the unworldly devotion of the historian-specialist is, I am afraid, quite
out of keeping with the spirit of the second half of the twentieth
century, when professional intellectuals abound and when even professional historianship has become a lucrative occupation, attracting
many people whose principal ability consists in their exemplification of
those general ideas that are currently respectable in professional and
intellectual circles."

Among these professional intellectuals, most of them with university
sinecures, situationalism and the famous Situation Ethics had prevailed during the 'Sixties and earlier. An intellectual, Bertrand Russell
wrote once, is a person who pretends to know more than he really does
know. The university intellectuals, since the Second World War, had
pretended to know the impossibility of knowing anything. Because
genuine students yearn to know something, the prevalent climate of
opinion in the universities, though alienating them from their cultural
patrimony, had thrust them into the arms of fanatic ideology. For the
ideologue claims to have the answer to everything; with Robert Frost's
Prophet, he cries, "They say the truth will set you free/ My truth will
bind you slave to me." Thus the professional intellectual, doubting or
condemning all received convictions and all established institutions,
had delivered many of the better minds and consciences among the
rising generation to the ideological enemies of both discursive and
intuitive reason. That was not quite what the professional intellectual
had intended, and a good many of the breed paid for it through the
treatment which they received from radical students.

Awareness of The Situation no longer was confined to the intellectuals, Professor Fairchild had written. For the men in the street had
begun to feel The Situation painfully; and "it is probably that large-
scale democratized higher education will gradually spread popular
awareness of The Situation."

By 1970, that awareness had engulfed many students at such famous
universities as Harvard, Yale, and Princeton. Even though enrollments
had increased since 1953 at those institutions, of course they had not
surrendered incontinent to mass education; and most of their students
possessed reasonably high intelligence-quotients. Yet the disorders on
such venerable campuses were as rough and irrational as those at

Behemoth State U. Why so? Because Situationalism, and the consequent flight to ideology, were most marked at the more "advanced" institutions. When I spoke at Harvard about this time, a German student had his skull bashed in by robbers on the doorstep of a residence-hall, that night; the campus police rather abashedly said that once upon a time they had picked up suspicious characters prowling about Harvard o' nights, but that nowadays it was impossible to tell the thugs from the students. A fortnight before I spoke there, two of the most radical student groups had crushed a public discussion of a peace-settlement in Vietnam by shouting through bullhorns and stamping their feet so ferociously that the hall was in danger of collapse. Similar episodes, many of them, had occurred at Yale and Princeton, about the time I spoke at those universities in 1969 and 1970.

Except for President Levi at the University of Chicago, Acting President Hayakawa at San Francisco State, and a few other educational administrators, the people in nominal charge of universities, even the better ones, seemed themselves paralyzed by Situationalism: the students detected their irresolution and lack of firm belief in much of anything. For the radical students, violent if meaningless action was a release from depressing awareness of the greater meaninglessness of The Situation. Here I am referring to radicalized students with some natural endowments; the mass of student demonstrators, if only vaguely conscious of The Situation, followed the ideologues out of herd-instinct and petty grievances. For their leaders, God being dead, Whirl was king; or perhaps they accepted the new commandments of ideology, the Savage God. Even at Harvard and Yale and Princeton, for a time, indeed it seemed as if the best lacked all conviction, while the worst were full of passionate intensity.

"No vital sense of human unity"—so Fairchild's Jeremiad about The Situation ran on. "Collapse of nineteenth-century liberal hopes. No intelligent conservatism. Social and racial inequities. Political corruption. Bureaucracy. Contra-human machine-made cities. Greedy capitalism. Rat-race of the status-seeking hucksters. Totalitarianism, fascist or communist. Welfare State, a paternalism of flavorless homogenization. Vulgarity of democratized education, popular culture, mass media. Alienation of the distinguished individual from society in fear, scorn, loneliness. Despite withdrawal, no real privacy."

By such slogans and notions, some false, some true in part, the Academy had been unnerved. The intellectuals had done their best to make faith in anything old impossible, to cut away all anchors. "Nothingness—but with something loathsome at the core of it," Fairchild concluded his litany. "Sense of doom, but no tragic grandeur. *Angst*. The Absurd. Nausea. Hysterical defiance lapsing into self-pity, self-contempt. Boredom with cycle of birth, and copulation, and death. The Abyss. Worms. Rats. Merds."

To The Situation, the professional intellectuals had been opening students' eyes. But the consequences of that grand revelation could not be controlled by tenured intellectuality.

Some educationists positively rejoiced in The Situation. To break down students' "values" and prejudices; then to impose upon those students one's own value-preferences and social convictions—there's glory for you! The *libido dominandi* operating upon intellects can be more gratifying to the ego than the same lust operating upon bodies.

In 1970 there fell into my hands a memorandum entitled "What Happens to Students in College?" Its author, who not long before had published a book, *The Impact of College on Students*, was a Dr. Theodore M. Newcomb, professor of sociology and psychology at the University of Michigan, Ann Arbor. His "What Happens . . ." memorandum was prepared for the Center for Research in Learning and Teaching of the University of Michigan. This publication illustrated tolerably well the ideological *libido dominandi* among professorial behavioralists.

Professor Newcomb's own prejudices and attitudes were not uncommon among behavioralists. He equated "conservatism" with stupidity, and called adherence to norms "authoritarianism." With the impact of college upon students, he was not wholly satisfied: the colleges' destruction of "conservative" and "authoritarian" beliefs had not been proceeding fast enough.

Most conspicuous among the changes which occur to college students, Newcomb wrote, "are a decrease in conservatism and dogmatism, an increased interest in intellectual pursuits and capacities in independence, dominance, and self-confidence, and a greater readiness to express rather than to inhibit impulses." This last tendency might have been exemplified, about the time of the Newcomb tract, by the blowing up of the Mathematics Center at the University of Wisconsin, and of one of the Center's researchers, by free spirits of the New Left—my own observation, this, not Newcomb's: the militant pacifists of Madison, Wisconsin, certainly had expressed their impulses. "Generally, then," Newcomb continued, "shifts away from conservatism are the rule among mid-century American college students."

Yet, he went on, other people in the same age-group shift similarly— those who don't go to college, and those who drop out; the change to liberalism (and perhaps to high explosives, one may add) merely "is more pronounced in those who remain in college for two years, and still more in those who complete four years of college." We must not rejoice inordinately: "Even when the average changes in conservatism or authoritarianism over four years are statistically significant, as in many (but not all) studies, they are not dramatic. Relatively few students (judging from the few studies that report individuals' *degrees* of change) shift from extremely conservative to extremely liberal positions, or vice versa. Indeed, those studies commonly report a positive correlation—usually at rather high levels—between freshmen and senior scores for the same individuals."

Alas, can it be that politicizing of students—or indoctrination by professional ideologues—doesn't take as it should? With a melancholy scarcely veiled, Professor Newcomb reported that "by and large there is not much evidence that faculty members are directly responsible for whatever impacts colleges have on their students." The obdurate students most resistant to the liberalizing influence of professors were members of fraternities: upon the Greek Letter folk, there was little discernible impact of "changes in Family Independence, Social Conscience, Cultural Sophistication, and Liberalism."

Moreover, Newcomb pointed out, the mass scale and impersonality of the typical American campus have diminished the influence of professors upon students. The chief ray of light comes from RCs—not Roman Catholics, but Residential Colleges, those "newly-instituted 'living-learning complexes' " where resident sociologists and psychologists, say, can more effectively demolish outworn creeds still vestigially clutched by students.

Yet Theodore M. Newcomb did not despair of liberating the students at Behemoth U. from the superstitions of the childhood of the race; residential colleges might do it yet. "In days to come, it may be that small units of large universities will best provide those conditions." In short, get the young obscurants into the Lonely Crowd of Behemoth U., where they will be sufficiently bewildered and rootless; and then proceed to rearrange their intellects by close attention from social scientists within the confines of small residential units. Introduce them intimately to The Situation, and offer them ideological salvation—Social Conscience, and all that. What ideological convictions should be substituted for conservatism, dogmatism, and other old rubbish, Newcomb did not vouchsafe: such educationists commonly are specific as to what they would destroy, but vague even in their own minds as to what they would build upon the rubble-strewn site.

So cheerfulness will keep breaking in, even at centers for research in learning and teaching. Yet I had another vision of the collegiate future. Already, by 1970, some of those untrammeled young intellects had applied dynamite to the Center for Behavioral Studies at Stanford University. I devoutly hoped, in 1970, that the Ann Arbor Center for Research in Teaching and Learning had employed enough security guards, and that its basements were being searched nightly, in the spirit of "remember, remember, the fifth of November . . ." When professional intellectuals have taught the rising generation all about The Situation, and how to eliminate archaic limits—why, luscious liberalisms sometimes end in fractured atoms.

Is such a one as Theodore M. Newcomb—or such a one as Robert Paul Wolff, whom I will discuss in the next section of this chapter—quite at liberty to dominate the minds of students as much as he may choose, ethically speaking? This general question was touched upon nicely by Professor William Oliver Martin, during 1970, in his slim book *Realism in Education*.

The freedom to learn is more important than the freedom to teach, Dr. Martin argued. Although there is an art to teaching, the teacher is not morally entitled to act as if he were a sculptor, carving inanimate stone when he works upon students' intellects. "The student is a person who has a nature which is to be perfected in the way of knowing. The student is not just 'stuff' to be molded or shaped into an artifact according to the purposes of the teacher," Martin put it.

"If all this is denied, then a kind of knowledge is reduced to ideology; the teacher becomes a technician propagandizing for personal and/or social ideological purposes; the student becomes an object, a thing; learning becomes parroting (the teacher's or the party's 'line'); and the teaching activity is reduced from the triadic to the diadic relation, that of conditioning or determining the student in a subintellectual manner."

Martin remarked that he was uttering truisms in this book of his. True; but those truisms had been neglected so long by most within the Academy that to many a student Martin's arguments must have seemed wondrously original. Some students who happened to read this book, having believed themselves to be radicals, may have discovered that actually they had been demanding the restoration of what once had been taken for granted in every decent college.

The school exists primarily for the student, not for the teacher, Martin went on. "The student cannot effectively learn without the freedom to learn, and that freedom is not something to be tolerated in a negative manner, but rather something to be actively encouraged and developed. Is this a natural right or merely a positive right? It is primarily a natural right, and, because it is so, it is concretized through law and becomes a positive right."

But no man has a natural right to teach in a school: there exist only certain positive rights of teachers guaranteed by particular societies. Prudence must enter into the duties of the teacher.

Intellectual arrogance on the part of teachers frequently becomes immorality and injustice toward students. Professor Martin offered the real example of a professor of biology who informed his students that "to have peace there must be, of necessity, a world government; for nations are like cells in an organism, and if cells were separated from the organic whole there would be only disintegration and death, etc., etc."

Against this sort of professorial presumption, the student can and should protest, for it is a violation of the natural right to learn. "The issue," in Martin's words, "is not whether world government is desirable and is necessary to achieve peace in the world; nor is there any question about the right of the professor to know what he is talking about, and to know the limitations of his own special field. But there is a lack of justice in the classroom in such a leap from biology to international politics. . . . What the teacher is doing, then, is imposing his own ignorance on students under the guise of wisdom, and by virtue of his status he renders them rather helpless."

The student's freedom to learn, being natural, has no express duties wedded to it. "The right of the student to learn is independent of merit, but not his right to stay in school. But in the case of the teacher both his right to teach and his opportunity to teach rest on merit, on whether he fulfills his duty. To the degree that this is not recognized in practice, there is injustice . . . . It is for this reason that the persistent concern of the teaching profession with the rights of teachers, without being equally clear and concerned about their duties, is evidence either of naïveté, of ignorance, or of just plain bad faith."

Just so. The cry for "student freedom" during the 'Sixties and later often was provoked by professorial neglect of duties. Yet the student who is ignorant of those moral relationships described by William Oliver Martin may become false to the freedom to learn. The worst enemy to academic freedom in 1970 was the sort of student who shouted "freedom!" but really was servile to the ideologue-professor. That sort of student was the dupe and the victim of the professional intellectual moved by the *libido dominandi*. He was being treated as marble, not as flesh. Such a student had lost the appetite for freedom to learn; he retained only the appetite for slogan—which does not require thought. To be conditioned, in an RC, to embrace Approved Advanced Attitudes toward Social Conscience, Family Independence, Cultural Sophistication, and Liberalism—well, such a process is not true education. It is merely part and parcel of The Situation.

The year 1970 was crying out for radical reform of the higher learning—yet reform in a conservative spirit. It was somewhat heartening, therefore, to encounter in 1970 another interesting diagnosis of higher education: *The Ideal of the University*, by Robert Paul Wolff, a professor of philosophy at Columbia University. Wolff called himself a radical. He advocated some sensible, if difficult, reforms.

Indeed, Wolff called himself a utopian, too, and something of "an old-fashioned Marxist." I wished that his radicalism had gone deeper, for he treated only glancingly, or not at all, certain of the more serious afflictions of the higher learning. Except, as he wrote, for a brief and involuntary period of military service, he knew little of the world beyond the campus—a common affliction among professors; in college and university, worse still, he was acquainted with little beyond the Ivy League and Columbia, and was handicapped somewhat by the necessity of maintaining a radical pose and by a quasi-Marxism that led him to refer repeatedly to the war in Vietnam as if it were a crime unparalleled in history. Like many other youngish scholars of 1970, that is, Wolff talked much of "liberation", but had not wholly liberated himself from the clutch of ideology.

Yet Wolff endeavored honestly to go to the root of things, and sometimes succeeded. His book's title was evocative of John Henry Newman; and though a doctrinaire hostility to the Catholic mind peeked out of Wolff's pages now and again, still there survived in his arguments some suggestion of Newman's imperial intellect.

There exist four models of a university, Wolff commenced: the university as a sanctuary of scholarship, as a training camp, as a social-service station, and as an assembly line for Establishment Man. For the first model, he would have reserved some place in his ideal university, if only for the sake of the traditions of civility. For the other models, however, in general Wolff entertained a contempt shared by me. Certain aspects of the "training camp" he would have tolerated, from necessity—though he would have severed them from humane education at the college level. At the end of his book, one was chagrined to find that Wolff's utopian university remained dim in outline—but one was not really surprised, because utopians usually are vague, and because Wolff, after all, was willing to settle for the conceivably possible. The virtues of his analysis turned out to be candid criticism and hopeful particular reforms, not a grand New Model.

Three myths afflict our higher learning, Wolff declared: the myth of value-neutrality, the myth of relevance, the myth of efficiency. In this denigrating employment of word "myth", perhaps ideology crept in; for "myth" means, really, not delusion or fraud, but the symbolic expression of a truth apprehended; one might have expected a teacher of philosophy to be more careful with his terms. Yet if we substitute "delusion" for "myth" in Wolff's argument, we find Wolff perceptive.

The liberals have lived, and are expiring, in the error that the higher learning can be "value-free", or at least neutral. But truth is not neutral, or middle-of-the-road. In repudiating this notion of perfect neutrality, Wolff assisted in our emancipation from intellectual dullness and moral grayness. He tended to slip into the opposite pit of ideological "commitment", nevertheless, and was saved only by prudential considerations. The New Left students, he declared (with some courage, considering his political inclinations), offered "a grotesque misrepresentation of the character of a university," especially when they persuaded themselves that they were a suffering proletariat. The university ought not to be totally politicized, he decided, because the practical effect of such a revolution would be a counter-revolution. That is, "faculties and student bodies tend, by and large, to be conservative in their leanings; and once a university is forced to bring its policies out into the open, the majority is liable to move the direction of those policies even farther to the right." Wolff was no majoritarian; he was a faithful Marxist in recommending that the intellectual gnaw at the foundations of society, bourgeois notions of democracy notwithstanding. "For the present, therefore, I would strongly urge both students and professors to hide behind the slogans 'Lehrfreiheit' and 'Lernfreiheit,' and give up the attempt to politicize the campus." They should use the universities, rather, as so many of Mao's "protected base camps"—and develop cadres, presumably, awaiting The Day.

On relevance, Wolff set himself against the radicals of the hour, in part. He admired an interesting congeries of social critics: Kenneth Boulding, Milton Friedman, Robert Heilbroner, Herbert Marcuse, Barrington Moore, Jr., Paul Goodman, David Riesman—masters of their disciplines. Only from a thorough foundation in discipline could one criticize intelligently, Wolff remarked. He found Kant very relevant. "A student who reads books devoted to the solution of present problems will learn nothing which can help him to identify and solve future problems."

The modern university's obsession with efficiency was mostly crazy, Wolff observed. "Suppose my colleagues and I discover that fully half of next year's students are intellectually and temperamentally unsuited for careers in philosophy. If we conscientiously discourage them from continuing, thereby performing one of the most valuable and difficult of all educational tasks, we shall constrict our 'production' and lose fellowships in years to come. On the other hand, if we see the unfitted candidates through the doctorate, thereby acting in an *educationally* inefficient manner, we will be rewarded with fellowships, additional positions in our staff, and even salary raises."

In his concluding section, Wolff was fruitful in proposals. Among other reforms, he would have reduced the duration of high school to three years, have divorced college from pre-professional studies, have abolished the bachelor's degree altogether, and have replaced the doctoral degree with "a three-year professional degree designed to certify candidates as competent to teach their subjects at the college or graduate level."

Clearly *The Ideal of the University* was a bold book calculated to rouse serious discussion of important questions too long obscured by our national complacency and busy-ness. Yet Wolff did not touch at all upon what, outside the Ivy League and other "elite" institutions, was the most pressing difficulty of the higher learning: that is, the crowding of the campus by a mass of young people uninterested in, and often incapable of apprehending, those abstractions with which true college and true university necessarily are concerned. When half or more of the students are bored with the whole business, Wolff's "utopian" reforms are unattainable. "I am of course assuming," he wrote between parentheses, "that the United States is moving toward a system of guaranteed higher education for all." And guaranteed mediocrity for all? The representative student at Behemoth State U. would not be able to make head or tail of Wolff's lectures, and President Boomer would fire Professor Wolff.

Yet some of Wolff's proposed reforms would have been palliatives. Were the bachelor's degree abolished, the snob-advantage of that degree would cease to exist, and only those young people genuinely desirous of learning would persist in college with no degree-carrot held out to them. Were the degree of Ph.D. abolished, and professional certification substituted, we should be rid of a sprawling dull boondoggle; and the overworked, underpaid, resentful graduate-assistant would vanish. Once more, we might know academic community instead of academic collectivism.

That Professor Wolff could combine these suggestions with "old-fashioned Marxism" (his phrase) and imply that learned professors should bore from within, gradually, with the eventual aim of gaining total control over university and society, I found an insane conjunction. But such inconsistencies were common enough among younger faculty people in 1970. No existing Marxist regime would grant preferment to such a one as Robert Paul Wolff. Need I add that his recommendations—not so very utopian, after all—have taken on no flesh whatsoever, anywhere, during the past eight years?

19

The Intellectual Proletariat: 1971

THE TIDE OF ENROLLMENTS was turning in 1971. Except where the general population still was growing, or where new state colleges or community colleges were founded in areas previously innocent of the higher learning, the rate of increase of enrollments had slowed noticeably; some universities and colleges experienced no increase of student population at all; others began to find it hard to fill their dormitories.

There were several reasons for this. Disorder and terrorism on the campus had disillusioned many parents who previously had assumed that whatever their offspring's shortcomings, the college would pour wisdom and virtue into them. Many students or prospective students themselves were complaining that Behemoth U.'s amorphous curriculum was "irrelevant", and were dropping out to enter gainful employment or to roam the world. The "baby boom" which had followed the Second World War had diminished after some years, so that the total number of seventeen- and eighteen-year-old potential collegians was not increasing as the evangels of educational imperialism had predicted. But the greatest obstacle to further increase of enrollments was the fact that university and college already had cajoled into the classrooms as large a proportion of the rising generation as could be prevailed upon to prolong their education beyond high school. Short of positive compulsion by force of law, the remaining young people simply wouldn't go to college: twelve or thirteen years in the classroom already, for most of those, seemed enough and to spare. Scholarships and other inducements for "minority" young people remained a means of filling up vacant places, but this too became disappointing, for many such dropped out after a few weeks or months, and no "minority" contributed a college-attendance quota proportionate to its size in the general American population. Academic standards had gone down on most campuses, but costs had gone up. There were simply few more potential freshmen who could be roped in.

And already the tales of Harvard graduates who found it necessary to work as taxi-drivers, or of Berkeley graduates who had turned carpenters' helpers, were appearing in the newspapers. Prospects for posts as instructors in practically any discipline at any tolerable college were dimming. Business and industry seemed to be glutted with young people holding college diplomas. It was becoming obvious that the grandiose system of higher education had produced already a surplus of young people who had passed through the degree-mills but had not been tolerably educated; and that even those who had contrived to learn something or other must prepare to reduce their great expectations of swift material and social advancement.

After the Second World War, campus populations had commenced to swell monstrously, and those in authority, far from resisting this development, had done everything in their power to accelerate it. University presidents had gone up and down the land for a quarter of a century, urging parents and high-school pupils to aspire to college studies, because a college graduate's earning-power would be far greater than that of the poor boob who didn't enroll at Behemoth State University.

That was done in the green tree. In this dry season of 1971, the plight of many of the previous year's graduates, and the perplexity of many college seniors, gave the lie to this premise. In some states, only half of the new graduates with teaching certificates could find employment in schools; engineering graduates were said to encounter still greater difficulties; most fields of gainful employment of masters of arts and bachelors of arts were overcrowded, except for such old and exacting professions as medicine and the law—which required advanced studies. America had been preparing too many young people for "opportunities" that did not exist. And most graduates had not been well enough schooled in either the real arts or the real sciences to enable them to obtain satisfactory employment not directly related to their college "majors."

Eventually nearly all graduates would find some sort of job, somewhere. But a great many young people would not find the sort of employment or the scale of emolument they had been led to expect. They had been resentful in college, many of them; they might be resentful life-long, out of college. Whither might a charismatic ideologue lead such a disaffected class, in some time of national adversity?

O to be a new bachelor or master or even doctor in literature, now that the enrollment-boom was over! Some departments of English at rather obscure colleges reported that they had received a hundred or two hundred applications for a single vacancy—many of those applications from young Ph.D.'s who had just graduated from reputable universities. Actually, some of those fresh Ph.D.'s had no right to expect academic posts: they were dull tools whose dissertations had been incompetent (or ghost-written), and who had small promise as researchers, let alone teachers. This was quite as true of other disciplines. History was quite as bad; sociology was worse—though the immense welfare apparatus offered a good deal of steady employment in that field.

Why had American degree-mills been tolerating Ph.D. candidates of scant merit, granting them their doctorates eventually, although some of them could neither think clearly nor write decently? Why, because those unfortunates had constituted a cheap labor-pool in Academe. Teaching assistants and research assistants had to be found to instruct, after a fashion, the horde of undergraduates who had been cajoled or thrust into college. There were not enough genuine professors to go round, nor was there enough money. The pseudo-scholars of the degraded Ph.D. mill had supplied that labor, for a pittance; from their surly ranks had come many of the leaders of campus rebellion. And now, having put in their weary years of servitude to the graduate schools at Behemoth U., and having been awarded their sham doctorates if they were lucky, these young men and women found themselves unemployable in their chosen occupations. When one had expected a fat salary and tenure and no challenge in life, it is distasteful to find oneself a proletarian instead. One may detest the Establishment more than ever one did before; one may make trouble.

At many of the lesser, though sometimes bigger, universities, existed departments of graduate study that never should have been authorized; nay, whole graduate schools which never should have been created. These whited sepulchres of "scholarship" found by 1971 that they could not place their graduates anywhere.

An able young vice-president for student affairs at a state university told me in 1971 that we must find alternatives to the mob-life of the mass campus—and soon. Violent protest about the fighting in Indo-China had been only a pretext of sorts for expressing deeper resentments among the students; and when every American soldier had been withdrawn from Vietnam, some new fanatic cause might serve to focus the vague but burning discontents of the depersonalized and anti-intellectual campus.

"We don't have any radical students on our campus," this administrator told me. "We have only characterless students, calling themselves radicals; they don't even know enough about anything to go to the roots of it; they don't even know what 'character' means. They might acquire some character by pumping gas or stacking groceries, but on the campus they remain petulant adolescents, badly reared and badly schooled. We can't go on much longer herding these children into dormitories where they are frozen for four years in an eighteen-year-old mentality, led by the silliest and worst among them."

My friend the vice-president believed that we must take steps promptly to "de-campus" a large part of the present and potential student populations. If they should desire to learn, well and good: most of them could have learnt better if they had stayed off campus. Part-time "in-service training", combined with part-time academic study; use of educational television and closed-circuit television; small study-groups and classes held downtown; correspondence courses—these and other devices could suffice to prepare boys and girls adequately for an "external" degree, without a full four years at Behemoth.

At some universities, in 1971, the better students had become acutely aware that administrators' appetites for educational aggrandizement were working mischief—lowering intellectual standards and turning the grove of Academe into an unattractive educational factory. The most interesting contest of this sort arose at the University of Virginia.

There were nearly eleven thousand students at Charlottesville in 1971. Between 1960 and 1970, enrollment at the University had almost doubled. That was not nearly enough to satisfy the president of the University of Virginia, who wanted a thousand more students by 1972, fourteen thousand by 1977, and eighteen thousand by 1980. "*Sic transit gloria* Jefferson," a graduate student at Charlottesville wrote to me.

He was not alone. The student council and the student newspaper, *The Cavalier Daily*, took alarm. Over the preceding three-year period, the number of applications for admission to the University had decreased—yet the number of acceptances of freshmen had increased, this in effect lowering standards to attract a larger student body at whatever cost to quality of education.

As an editorial in *The Cavalier Daily* argued, this indiscriminate expansion at Charlottesville, unlikely to be well financed, might bring on consequences miserable for all concerned. The parking problem alone, already dreary, might suffice to provoke student disorders. "Legislators, who are so concerned with campus violence, should know that the most violent demonstration on the grounds in recent history was not the strike of last May, but rather the car riots of 1957," the editors pointed out.

The Charlottesville students suggested practical alternatives to turning the University of Virginia, with its beautiful buildings and traditions of civility, into Behemoth University. Other state educational institutions might be enlarged, for one thing. The administrators not yielding to persuasion, there came about a massive strike and demonstration, quite peaceful and good-natured, at Charlottesville, with practically all students participating. They found considerable sympathy in the legislature and in the press. In the long run, the University's president lost the battle, and went elsewhere, his place being taken by a new president less infatuated with growthmanship. By 1977, the enrollment at Charlottesville was about fifteen thousand, after all, so the expansionists had worn the students down; yet at least the protesters had discouraged what might have become an indiscriminate enlargement even greater than that projected in 1971.

What with vehement student protests against the boredom of the typical curriculum and the dreariness of existence in those teen-age ghettos called dormitories, during the academic year of 1970-71 several large universities set up "experimental colleges" of a more intimate and exploratory character. Some of these were remarkably eccentric undertakings, and most collapsed after two or three years. One such experiment was the University of Pennsylvania's.

At Philadelphia there were established Experimental Colleges I and II—groups of thirty and twenty students respectively, plus such faculty members as could be persuaded to sacrifice and contribute "in addition to the regular teaching assignments" and engage in "group education." "It will be a full-time educational and living experience where not only intellectual but emotional and communal education will be emphasized," the prospectus for Experimental College I ran. "It will try to interconnect and relate the total world around us." There was ambition: relate the total world to *what*?

Some professors at Pennsylvania took a dim view of these aspirations. They indulged reservations about the "Basic Layout: The college will consist of fifteen girls and fifteen boys located in a single residence. In addition, there will be four to eight faculty advisers (residence optional). The faculty will be equal to the students in every way except their knowledge in particular fields."

"I don't profess to understand what is involved," one University of Pennsylvania professor told me, "although the scheme looks like a combination of Free Love and Intellectual Disorganization."

Educational content at the Experimental Colleges was to be decided by the students and faculty involved, although two regular courses in the University's curriculum had to be taken by every participant, if only to "help prevent the Experimental College from being entirely isolated from the University community." There were to be seminars.

Some of these ideas were not new. The voluntary residential association of students with common interests had existed for considerable time (with segregation of the sexes, however), in the form of fraternities and sororities. Intellectual discussions at frequent intervals, in a loose "seminar" form, by a circle of reasonably earnest undergraduates, deserved encouragement; but that, too, was no startling innovation.

Such associations and discussions were valuable, and had been sadly neglected in Behemoth University during the 'Fifties and 'Sixties. Whether they could take the place of a regular intellectual discipline is another matter. If this rather misty plan should turn out, at best, to be merely a running discussion on the basis of some general reading— why, one might as well have merely joined a Great Books discussion-group, so saving tuition and lodging-expense.

I did not set my face against all experiments meant to restore a humane scale and a personal character to undergraduate life. Common residences could do much, if restricted to twenty or thirty students, in the recovery from anonymity at Behemoth State U.

Besides, on practically every campus, in 1971 as now, undergraduates have been required to enroll in too many lecture-courses and to accumulate an absurd number of formal credits. Two regular courses, earnestly undertaken, would be better than five or six courses of the usual diploma-mill sort. If residential seminars should have pattern and purpose, they might accomplish more to wake intellect and imagination than any amount of note-taking in Humanities 103 or Sociology 421.

One danger in these college communes was that students tended to become preoccupied with the current, the ephemeral, the immediately dramatic. "Improvisational drama done by people living together" was emphasized in the Pennsylvania experiments. For students genuinely in search of wisdom, and adequately prepared by their earlier schooling—that is, for a handful of students on the average campus—such experiments held promise. "The primary goal," said the prospectus for Experimental College I, "will be to prepare the individual for life-long education rather than the secondary goal of accumulating a specific body of facts—facts that may be obsolete in a few years." This was a sound principle—provided that the students involved should not settle for "getting the general idea" about some discipline or other, and then rejoicing in an indiscriminate exposure to every wind of doctrine. Such an "emotional involvement" would convert them into philodoxers, not philosophers.

The meanings to be obtained from a serious study of history, for instance, are not acquired by the mere accumulation of passing acquaintance with a number of historical events; but neither are those meanings acquired without some ordered mastery of the "facts" or events which distinguish historical knowledge from ideological fantasy. To sit through interminable shallow lectures and take countless "objective" tests is a wretched way to try to obtain an education. Yet the notion that the culture of the mind may be got through "group interaction", jolly boys and girls together, me and Mamie O'Rourke, could be more ruinous still.

In 1971, Goddard College, in the hills of Vermont, sufficiently illustrated the extreme of "group interaction." This college's brochures were handsomely printed and highly eccentric. Its elaborate "Trimester Calendar", prepared in 1971 for the next academic year, concluded with a full-page photograph of a naked young woman endowed with monstrous breasts—whether a member of staff or of student body, the reader was not informed. This document was posted to me by a school principal, with the notation, "This is the weirdest batch of literature that I've received from any college."

Goddard had grown out of the educational theories of John Dewey and William Heard Kilpatrick. It was meant to be a center for "education for real living, through the actual facing of real life problems"; it was to use the local community (a Vermont village so isolated as to be virtually defenseless against experiment) as a laboratory.

Goddard had no regular curriculum and no formal classes. It charged high fees, and got some money from the federal Office of Education and the Ford Foundation, for developing a university—without-walls program. What did one study? Well, study was something of a dirty word—perhaps the only dirty word at Goddard—and the "work program" was treated gingerly in the Goddard prospectus; but "a student's educational program at Goddard is conceived as a total experience."

There was the Bread and Puppet Theater, enjoying pride of place among Goddard's "Programs, Projects, Current Experiments." There was Design and Construction—mostly carpentry. There was ESP, Environmental Services Program, which "will combine the previous operations of the infirmary, housing office, recreation office, and environmental center." There was GIFAS, the Goddard Institute for Anthroposophical Studies, a group joining practical organic gardening to yoga exercises. There was Bill Osgood, who planned to lead Northern Studies, concerning the polar regions. There was a Radical Studies Program, the character of which was candidly described by its creators:

"Political action is harder to achieve in central Vermont. Functioning as a focus or forum for smaller groups, Radical Studies has most recently organized a local demonstration against the invasion of Laos, helped publicize the 'People's Peace Treaty' for ending the war, and won official college support for the farm workers' national boycott against non-union lettuce."

No philosophy, humane letters, mathematics, physical sciences, biological sciences, languages, and such impedimenta? No. Goddard was free, creative, unstructured. How joyous to be a subsidized academic proletarian!

To be a proletarian student (or to pose as one, more commonly) was not sufficiently startling on some campuses in 1971: the perverse was more lively. The University of Michigan did not lack for evangels of progress.

During the academic year of 1970-71, the University of Michigan's office of special services began to offer services very special indeed: aid and comfort for sodomites and lesbians within the student body. This was not psychological counseling of a remedial sort. On the contrary, the university appointed, with salaries, two advisers on homosexuality, both self-declared sexual deviates, male and female: one Jim Toy, of the Gay Liberation Front, and one Cynthia Gair, of the Radical Lesbians. (I do not believe that a Conservative Lesbian group existed at Ann Arbor.) "We see them as a liaison between the gays and the straights," said the director of the university's special services and programs.

Various University of Michigan administrators murmured that "homosexuals are merely another group emerging from repression"—like Negroes, Mexican-Americans, Indians, women, and so on. They did not trouble themselves with the nice distinction that while there was nothing immoral about being black, brown, red, or female—well, being a pervert was something else.

Cynthia Gair, Radical Lesbian, complained of "dorm oppression." "While the University permits heterosexuals to entertain members of the opposite sex in their rooms, gays still have to be covert in their love affairs." It was not that she objected to the dormitory becoming a bordello: rather, she wished it to be, of right, accessible to all the further shores of lust.

In addition to their other activities, Jim Toy and Cynthia Gair and their chums lectured to high-school students. "We don't advocate homosexuality by itself; we try to let our audience fit the situation," Toy said.

All this came to pass at the University of Michigan, once the best state university in the land. The University's first president, Henry Philip Tappan, was a scholar and a gentleman of intellectual power, pursuing an ethical end through an intellectual means. Some one hundred and thirty years later, these curious new members of the university's staff were pushing for a "gay studies program" and a "gay student center."

In 1971 the University's president was Dr. Robben Fleming, whose only resistance to "gay liberation" was his refusal to authorize a Midwest Gay Liberation convention in the Michigan Union. Only the president of Cornell University, at the time of the black riots there, exceeded President Fleming in pusillanimity. In 1969, black militants at the University of Michigan had bullied Dr. Fleming into "concessions", or rather extraordinary privileges, that would have been a disgrace to Dismal Swamp A. & M. Some of the militants had been armed. But it was unnecessary to brandish weapons to intimidate Robben Fleming; any pansy could have done it; they did.

To President Fleming, in a piece of mine published in 1971, I commended these lines by Alexander Pope:

> "Vice is a monster of so frightful mien,
> "As to be hated needs but to be seen;
> "Yet seen too oft, familiar with her face,
> "We first endure, then pity, then embrace.
> "But where th' extreme of vice, was ne'er agreed:
> "As where's the North? at York, 'tis on the Tweed;
> "In Scotland, at the Orcades; and there,
> "In Greenland, Zembia, or the Lord knows where."

Was the extreme of academic folly, not to mention vice, at Ann Arbor, in 1971? If not, the Lord knew where. Six years later, Sarah

Lawrence College, brutishly dominated by lesbian students, would deprive the University of Michigan of pride of place.

Meanwhile, amidst these forms of "alternative education", the older structure of college and university labored painfully. Many departments at the typical college had gone in for "remedial" courses—that is, programs to compensate, if possible, for the college students' yawning deficiencies. There was "Bonehead English"—to teach elements of reading and writing to the functionally illiterate who held high-school diplomas. Why bother with the illiterate? Why, because enrollments were dropping, especially in the humanities, and every tuition-paying student was precious; otherwise there might be reductions in staff. Functional illiteracy was not confined to freshmen: it could be encountered among candidates for the master's degree, or even among young persons holding that degree who aspired to be doctors of philosophy. College bookshops displayed profitably rack upon rack of paperbacked "answer books", cribs which promised to supply students with the examination-answers in various subjects so that they would not need to go to the trouble of reading assigned texts. At the same time, masses of "quality" paperbacks lay unsold in those bookstores, to be remaindered or thrown away eventually.

Narcotics-addiction was diminishing on most campuses, but alcoholism was supplanting it; responding to "youth culture", states were beginning to lower the permissible drinking-age to eighteen. "Vacation is his vocation," as Thomas Fuller had written of the "degenerous" university student in the seventeenth century.

Did no one have in mind any remedies? There did emerge from the confusion of 1971 one hopeful document: the Newman Report, prepared by Frank Newman, associate director of university relations at Stanford University, with seven colleagues. The Newman Report had to be taken seriously even by the educational establishment, for the foreword to it was written by Elliot Richardson, then secretary of the Department of Health, Education, and Welfare. Some students had done well to protest against the dreariness of "higher" studies, Secretary Richardson remarked: "There is a very substantial core of validity in their anger."

As for the Ford Foundation, some leading lights in that huge apparatus were reported to have been disheartened by the unpleasant fact that nearly all of the millions of dollars which they had contributed to educational experiments had gone down the drain. The Newman Report contained suggestions quite unlike the sort of thing which the

Ford Foundation had been subsidizing. Perhaps the Foundation contributed a paltry thirty-five thousand dollars for the Newman Report's
preparation because it was felt prudent to toss a bone to a project
commended by Robert Finch, in his year as secretary of HEW.

Prudent change is the means of our preservation. Whatever remained worth preserving in American universities and colleges could
be saved only through reform. Frank Newman and his colleagues were
aware of how deeply the American higher learning had sunk into
decadence.

"The modern academic university has, like a magnet, drawn all
institutions toward its organizational form until today the same teaching method, the same organization by disciplines, and the same professional academic training are nearly universal," the Report declared.
"The shortcomings of the academic university as a model for all other
institutions have been obscured by the dazzling success of the best-
known examples."

There ought to be institutions, the Newman Report said, which
would take into account practical experience of a sensible sort, not
classroom lectures and textbooks merely. More people of mature years
ought to be encouraged to become genuine students; and young
people showing no aptitude for college ought to be discouraged from
entering.

All the talk and action about "relevance" in the curriculum had been
irrelevant to the true reform of university and college, Newman and
his colleagues contended: for professors and students, themselves
cloistered, had little notion of an education relevant either to the
modern age or to the permanent things. What the higher learning
needed was not so much more money as it was proper employment of
its existing resources—and painful thought.

The Report suggested that university and college ought to recruit, as
professors or the equivalent, persons of professional and practical
talents, whether or not (and perhaps not) they should be certified
doctors of philosophy. Attempts should be made to decentralize the
hideously overgrown state systems of public instruction. Regional
examining universities ought to be created, of the sort that the University of the State of New York originally was meant to be—testing and
granting degrees, not holding classes. Credit ought to be granted (what
heresy!) for knowledge acquired outside the classroom; the merits of
educational television should be recognized; "informal tutors" should
be sought beyond the confines of Behemoth University.

It cannot be said that the more sensible recommendations of the
Newman Report took root at once; rather, such curious undertakings

as Goddard College might use the Newman Report as apology for their existence and instrument for their fund-raising. Yet the Report pointed its finger at many whited sepulchres of Academe.

There was evident in university and college, the Newman Report stated, "a growing rigidity and uniformity of structure that makes higher education reflect less and less the interests of society." Too true—although I trusted in 1971 that the authors of this Report did not mean to suggest that the "interests of society" should be the sole aim of the higher learning. A university ought to be something better than the mirror of immediate social concerns. Yet if Newman and his colleagues meant that American institutions of higher learning were growing positively hostile toward the real interests of society—why, they did not lack for evidence.

Intellectually atrophied, liberal or radical in rhetoric but dully conservative (in the bad sense of that abused word) in policy, hostile toward any criticism, smugly entrenched, America's institutions of higher learning in 1971 had discouraged the better students and had welcomed hordes of young people who showed neither interest in, nor aptitude for, real study. One principal recommendation of the Newman Report was that many of these young people be shifted out of university or college into some other sort of educational—or quasi-educational—institution.

A quarter of a century earlier, the most popular argument in favor of sending young people to college was that they would earn far more money, in the long run, if they should obtain diplomas. John Hannah of Michigan State had been one of the most vociferous popularizers of this doctrine. But by 1971 this salt was beginning to lose its savor.

On the surface, this put-money-in-thy-purse argument may have seemed as sound as it ever had been—which was not very sound. Among men who earned more than fifteen thousand dollars in 1971, the median level of education was 15.2 years—that is, the equivalent of more than three years of college. In sedentary occupations, with incomes of fifteen thousand dollars a year or more, the median was 16.3 years of schooling—or part of a year of study beyond the bachelor's degree. On the other hand, the most poorly-paid employed people, earning less than four thousand dollars, had an educational median of 8.7 years, or less than a year of high school.

Did not this prove that if one attended college, he would be rewarded lucratively? No, it did not. All it showed was that formerly, at least, young people of intelligence and energy tended to enroll in colleges; while young people less intelligent and less energetic tended not to enroll. If all higher studies had been abolished and nobody at all had been awarded college degrees, still the young people with intelligence and energy would have prospered materially in their mature years, and young people of limited talents would have done less well in terms of lifelong income. College studies, in short, in former years, had been the consequence, not the cause, of superior abilities.

Many Americans, by the academic year of 1971-72, had become aware that the notion of riches-by-diploma was a fallacy promulgated by empire-building educationists. The sad rosters of unemployed recent graduates had exploded this delusion. Only law schools were swollen with students, even turning away tolerable applicants—and that, in large part, because of the growth of political bureaucracy, administrative law, and central regulation of many kinds.

A study by the Opinion Research Corporation showed that only sixty-four per cent of the American public believed, in the academic year 1971-72, that public expenditure for higher education was desirable—as compared with eighty-eight per cent a decade earlier. Only thirty-five per cent of those Americans polled approved of higher expenditures through taxation for "higher education"—by comparison with sixty-four per cent a decade before. The same people were asked whether it was well for so many people to be enrolled in college—and the negative responses of 1971-72 were *six times* more numerous than they had been in the previous polling.

Belated understanding that a college diploma was no guarantee of wealth worked to diminish popular enthusiasm for higher education; and another reason for the public's decreasing support for the campuses was the collegiate follies of the 'Sixties. Many of the recent inmates of American colleges and universities had been distinctly unlike the image of the collegian which formerly had drifted through fond parents' fancies. The typical parents had thought that college would polish their offspring, improve their morals, give them a veneer of polite culture, and make them eligible for membership in some country club. (This last dream was especially influential upon parents who never had belonged to country clubs.)

But the hordes of male and female collegians who for the past two decades had been descending upon Fort Lauderdale at holiday-time did not seem quite the sort of cultured and diligent young people whom the parents had expected to emerge from college; still less did the bearded barbarous young men and the frantic unkempt young women of the campus riots seem to be future country-clubbers and pillars of Middle America. Was it for this consummation that the elder generation had paid large tuition and borne heavy taxation?

What to do with the pseudo-proletarians of the campus? The Newman Report had suggested that they be drained off to non-collegiate institutions of one sort or another. A good many parents wrote to me in 1971, inquiring as to what college they should choose for Ken or Barbie. Their children, some parents confided, had not done at all well in high school, had fallen in with bad companions, and showed no especial intellectual interests. Where should they be enrolled? Who would polish these rough diamonds?

I suggested to such parents that for their children almost *anything* might be preferable to college. No longer did the higher learning confer marked social or economic benefits—not for the mediocre graduate; certainly college, by 1971, seemed to be the last place to acquire commendable morals and manners. Emancipate Ken and Barbie, I replied: let them go to work somewhere. Apprentice them, if possible, to some decent trade; or if a little money should be available, let them travel abroad, preferably with some general object in view. Let them release their energies. But parents should not labor under the illusion that four more years of confinement to classrooms—after twelve or thirteen years of compulsory attendance already—would turn their offspring into little plaster saints. Many of the young wanted out of college, in 1971, and many of them were right.

20

Therapy and Ideology: 1972

THE CAMPUSES were fairly quiet by 1972. As cultural lag, enfeebled protests and demonstrations would linger here and there, chiefly in the backwaters of Academe—universities in the mountain states to which yesteryear's radicalism had penetrated tardily, or teachers' colleges that never heard of new notions until they had ceased to be new—but the original academic centers of radicalism had become almost decorous again.

Massive demonstrations and terrorism had been diminishing for a variety of reasons. Relatively few young men were being conscripted by 1972, and the end of the draft was in sight. To the more intelligent professors and students, it was clear enough that the Nixon administration was endeavoring to withdraw from the struggle in Asia. A good many of the campus radicals shifted their energies from academic disruption to advancement of Senator McGovern's campaign for the presidency. Most professors and students had grown weary of destruction and disruption. Educational administrators had learned how to cope with their adversaries. Prospects for the employment of college graduates were diminishing, and it seemed prudent to earn decent grades, rather than to spend a semester in shouting and marching. And the "activists" had discovered that they could not, after all, make a revolution in the United States.

Libraries, laboratories, administration buildings, and ROTC armories had been burnt during the past decade, or blown up; classroom instruction had been interrupted for long periods, repeatedly, on many campuses; administrators' offices had been occupied by rioters and plundered; some obdurate students, and even professors, had been beaten physically by the radical zealots; unfinished dissertations and professors' papers had been destroyed; university presidents and deans had been insulted and reviled; "open curriculum" and "open admissions" had been forced upon a good many universities and colleges at the radicals' demand; special programs, usually empty of real content, had been instituted for "minority students"; standards for academic achievement had been abolished, virtually, on many a campus. Yet American society at large had been scarcely touched by all this fury, except in the sense that campus "revolution" had been counterproductive so far as winning over "workers" and others to the cause of revolution was concerned. And even university and college, so far as their major failings went, had not been much altered by all the tumult. Nothing had been accomplished, it appeared, except that the students' violent protests had contributed somewhat toward gradual cessation of the unsuccessful military undertaking in Indo-China. For those campus revolutionaries who had entertained much grander designs, all this was dreadfully disheartening. Most of them, by 1972, had abandoned hope of overturning the American social order.

Now that the majority of the undergraduates had returned to their fun and games, and now that the graduate students and teaching assistants had their noses to the grindstone again, university administrators enjoyed leisure in which to wonder why they ever had submitted to such humiliations at the hands of young mountebanks improbably attired as Fuzzywuzzies, Western badmen, Skid Row derelicts, miners, comrades of Chairman Mao, Fidelistas, railway enginemen, Apaches, or Russian laborers. As a class, the academic administrators had suffered for a decade from a failure of nerve; but now they rejoiced in the prospect of President Harding's "normalcy." Pot smoking and the exasperating parking-lot problem remained to trouble them—little else, except for financial worries at the little liberal-arts colleges and some of the bigger institutions. Few administrators said much of anything in public about the deeper problems of the higher learning in America: thought being painful, they seldom inquired why it had been that great masses of students had been swept by ideological passions for ten years, or whether the objects of higher education required serious attention. They were back to business as usual, looking for more money, endeavoring to increase enrollments—or at least to prevent a shrinking of enrollments. Wisdom and virtue? Well, those words were well enough for commencement addresses, possibly. The business of the Academy was—academic business.

What of the Academy's responsibilities toward the soul and toward the intellect? It was awkward to take up such vague concerns. There was a department of psychology, wasn't there, and a department of philosophy, and a department of political science, say? Thus two curious aspects of American university and college in 1972 were not much discussed: the Academy as therapeutic community, and the Academy as staging-ground for social subversion. I propose to touch here upon half-submerged problems.

First, the "therapeutic community." At the end of the Second World War, most American universities and colleges had begun to shift—though for the most part unaware of their new direction—from intellectual activity to psychiatric activity. Behemoth State University invited all comers—the veterans, the confused children of affluence, presently the "culturally disadvantaged" minorities. Instead of disciplining their minds, which these new elements in the Lonely Crowd of the mass campus distinctly didn't desire, university and college began to minister to their feelings. But this ministry became lacking in moral imagination and grossly permissive, rather than integrating.

When the Academy concentrates upon assuaging feelings, it pays less and less attention to the works of the mind. I offer here some observations on this subject, in 1972, from a graduate student at a big undistinguished campus in Ohio, its chief boast a curriculum in Popular Culture—the study of comic books, drugstore paperbacks, rock recordings, and all that, as an analysis of American civilization.

"Your reservations concerning universities with Popular Culture programs have been affirmed and justified," this graduate student wrote to me. "The Law of the Lowest Common Denominator prevails in classrooms; professors tend to be bourgeois tenure-hunting parasites who rely on worn notes or folksy largesse instead of intellect; administrators generally are political hacks with an interest in real estate. The intellectual range of my peers (except for a few brooding, shadowy figures given to inhabiting the darkest recesses of the more remote sectors of the library, and to lonely walks in abandoned cemeteries on cloudy days) is Neanderthal to merely academic, with only occasional flashes of anything resembling art; and there is little light. I am no longer shocked by this: I accept it as 'given,' and simply circumvent the institution, as you have recommended in the past, and as I have always done."

The name of that state university, formerly a teachers' college, is Legion. But if Legion State U. and its counterparts, offering next to nothing for the mind, have failed so dismally to impart right reason, why do legislatures and private benefactors continue to lavish upon them immense sums of money? Why, for one reason, because these institutions have assumed a new, non-intellectual function: that of mental institutions of a different sort, psychiatric hospitals or rest-homes in disguise, sanctuaries for neurotic or psychotic youth.

This point was made forcefully in an article entitled "The University as Therapeutic Community", published in the June,1972, number of *Change*. The authors of this mordant piece were a political scientist and an anthropologist, Professors Carl R. Vann and Philip Singer, connected with Allport College of Human Behavior, Oakland University.

The typical campus had become something more than a day hospital for emotionally disturbed young people, Vann and Singer remarked: "It has become a therapeutic community," where the emotionally disordered endeavor to comfort or lead other emotionally disordered folk, called students. "The resident student acts out his daily existence in the same manner as that of patients confined to psychiatric hospitals."

The blind lead the blind. "It is our impression . . . that many of the academic types most involved with the era of feelings are themselves part of a dysfunctional new class," Vann and Singer wrote. "Many are first-generation college graduates themselves, children of the GI Bill or of a new parental affluence which made it possible for them to attend a university. In some cases they have become academicians rather than small businessmen, floorwalkers, merchandise buyers, or civil servants. They exhibit guilt because they are enjoying the leisure of the theory class. They possess the traditional problems of anxiety, insecurity, and identity, expressing them through an attack on rational cognition, scholarly activity, tenure, the governance of the university, and a concept of culture reflected in the traditional curriculum of the arts and sciences."

It is such "professors", professing little but muddled emotionalism, who politicize the university and reduce scholarship to "methodological trivia." Vietnam, Cambodia, the draft, and such current subjects of controversy provide excuse for escape from the works of the mind into a muddled "therapy." "In his desire to become more identified with the student," Vann and Singer continued, "the professor has increasingly divested himself of his status, his rank, his role, and his cognitive frames of reference to become, instead of 'Professor, Ph.D.,' the para-professional mental-health aide. He is no longer the professor, whose primary role is to recommend plural sources of wisdom in terms of the literature and in terms of the research being conducted in the field. . . . He has turned away even from the methodologies he is trained in, to take up instead the largely non-provable, therapeutic methodologies and techniques of advice and counsel—group therapy, T-groups, sensitivity sessions, encounter groups, etc."

Many students are worriers, certainly. Whether converting university and college into psychiatric wards can help them is most doubtful, nevertheless. "The contemporary manifestation of response behavior is catharsis through feeling outlets," Vann and Singer concluded. "This substitution of emotion and personal feeling for objective knowledge may be important in the process of therapy, but it does not provide a base for the solution of real problems in a real world."

Those students who do not desire to become the subjects of emotional therapy were, and are, in the circumstances of my Ohio correspondent of 1972. "As I have carefully nurtured such a bad disposition in classrooms," that graduate student wrote, "I am considered locally an 'elitist,' not much fun to have around, and as a consequence do not have to attend the classes for which I am registered." He went his solitary way, a sane pensioner in Bedlam.

This academic disease was not, and is not, confined to Legion State U. or Behemoth State U. or Dismal Swamp A. & M. I have encountered such "feeling" professors, and such emotional pseudo-students, in considerable numbers, at famous old universities. When will we escape from this anti-intellectual plague of neurotics? Why, perhaps when nearly all young people with a taste for reason have dropped out of Legion State, or perhaps out of any university, to seek for *veritas* elsewhere. Then Legion State and its counterparts can become mental rest-homes for the young without indulging in academic pretensions: inordinately costly rest-homes, true.

When, in 1972, I published some remarks of mine on this topic, my article attracted an interesting number of furious replies—addressed to the editor of the magazine in which my piece appeared, rather than to me. Many professors and students, finding that this shoe would fit them, had put it on. From such elements on the campus came a high proportion of the "activists" of the 'Sixties, a fact pointed out by Bruno Bettelheim and other psychologists and psychiatrists. And a vein of madness ran through many of the writings of the New Left—one aspect of the radical literary endeavors to which I turn now.

Second, the university as staging-ground for social subversion—and related considerations. Time was when the study of humane letters stood central in formal education. Public men were brought up in a literary discipline, and "rhetoric" meant more than a politician's style.

The domination of the political order by men who knew their poets and their philosophers went farthest in old China, but it existed in some degree throughout all the civilized world until the First World War. Woodrow Wilson was the last American president representing this literary culture—and he imperfectly.

In political leaders, and even among those many unknowable individuals who, each in his own circle, are the real authors of public opinion, the literary culture nurtured political understanding. To those who must make political decisions, humane letters supplied two principal supports. For one thing, the literary discipline set them in a tradition, which gave them ethical awareness and historical consciousness. For another, the literary discipline woke their imagination, so that they might approach the complexity of public concerns with broader views than a vulgarized pragmatism can give.

In such an age as ours, afflicted by what Glenn Tinder has called "the crisis of political imagination", a renewed awareness of great literature might help us toward a tolerable political order. As G. K. Chesterton said, all life is an allegory, and we can understand it only in parable. To apprehend reasonably well the nature of order and justice and freedom, we require those insights into soul and community called "poetic": the vision of Plato or Virgil or Dante. And it is not to the classics only that one may turn for this kind of penetration into the human condition. Santayana's novel *The Last Puritan* teaches us more about American character than can any number of doctoral dissertations on that theme, and Conrad's novel *Nostromo* gives us an analysis of Latin American disorder more convincing than is a shelf of behavioral studies.

In 1972, there was published a fat anthology entitled *Literature in Revolution*, edited by George Abbott White and Charles Newman. This was one of the few literate productions of the New Left, and something of a swan song. Some of the contributors to this volume were professors, some students (or former students), some "free lances" of the Greenwich Village variety. I choose this book to illustrate my point about social subversion in the higher learning because it is a superior specimen of its type.

The twenty-one contributors to *Literature and Revolution* believed that imagination rules the world; that humane literature influences politics and is affected by political circumstance. This collection was one response to a growing recognition that students of politics ought to understand something of humane letters, and that students of humane letters ought not to ignore politics—a trend which, so far, has produced one promising university curriculum in literature and politics (at the University of Dallas) and a number of snippet-textbooks meant for use in departments of English or of political science. The editors of this anthology doubtless hoped that *Literature in Revolution* might obtain college adoptions—perhaps at Harvard, where one of the editors, George Abbott White, had offered in 1969 a course in "Politics and Literature." (More than a thousand students enrolled, but soon the program was riven by New Left factionalism.)

I am not one of those who maintain that the study of literature ought to be kept pure from political contamination. When I spoke at a Michigan college on the moral imagination of T. S. Eliot, one member of the staff remarked that he did not care for poets who mingle politics with verse. But if that is so, he must dislike Plato, Virgil, Dante, Shakespeare, Milton, Dryden, Samuel Johnson, Shelley, Wordsworth, and many of the Victorian poets, as well as Eliot. The great poet, concerned with the order of the soul, finds it difficult to ignore the order of the commonwealth; and that is as true of great novelists. George Orwell wrote in 1946 that "no book is genuinely free from political bias. The opinion that art should have nothing to do with politics is itself a political attitude."

Yet recognizing that the poetic imagination often extends to politics is one thing; while chaining the poet, the dramatist, and the novelist to an ideology is something different. "Ideology", as that term has been employed by systematic writers (distinguished from newspapermen), signifies political dogmatism—what Burke called "an armed doctrine." An ideology promises salvation through politics. For the ideologue, literature and the arts must serve fixed political ends. The mastery of triumphant ideology over humane letters ends in "the captive mind", as Czeslaw Milosz put it: the poet, ceasing to be the seer, is reduced to the propagandist and is subjected to the compulsions of "Soviet realism" or to comparable literary canons.

Ideology is a terrible sickness of our time, says Irving Howe, who happens to be a socialist: "The growth of ideology, I would suggest, is closely related to the accumulation of social pressures. It is when men no longer feel that they have adequate choices in their style of life, when they conclude that there are no longer possibilities for honorable maneuver and compromise, when they decide that the time has come for 'ultimate' social loyalties and political decisions—it is then that ideology begins to flourish. Ideology reflects a hardening of commitment, the freezing of opinion into system. It speaks of a society in which men feel themselves becoming functions of large impersonal forces over which they can claim little control. It represents an effort to employ abstract ideas as a means to overcoming the abstractions of social life. It is the passion of men with their backs to the wall."

Dostoevsky, Howe remarks, "shows how ideology can cripple human impulses, blind men to simple facts, make them monsters by tempting them into that fatal habit which anthropologists call 'reifying' ideas." So Howe wrote in *Politics and the Novel* (1957).

Political theory is not identical with ideology. In their cast of mind, the editors of *Literature in Revolution* were ideological, rather than theoretical. "Some of the contributors would call themselves Marxists," Charles Newman wrote; "others would simply say that they find Marxist methodology useful." He hoped that they formed a band of brothers: "I see no evidence of the rigid ideological polarization, at least regarding the function and use of literature, which is often attributed to the Left." The editors found no need to consider other critical judgments. They did acknowledge having omitted "essays written from the black and feminist points of view," but told the reader that "it becomes very difficult to find statements which haven't already been articulated elsewhere, particularly when the major energies of the respective movements have been expended in establishing the *legitimacy* of the viewpoints in question." They took it for granted that the legitimacy of the Marxist interpretation of literature had been established.

This volume was a kind of autumnal fruit of the New Left, or "The Movement", already fading when *Literature in Revolution* came from the press. By "revolution", its contributors had in mind Marxist revolution. Charles Newman subscribed his introduction "Budapest, Hungary, December 1971"—from a country where an anti-Marxist revolution had been crushed by Soviet tanks a dozen years earlier. At Budapest, annually, there occurs a big writers' conference. But the participants from Eastern Europe do not share Newman's veneration of Marxist literary dogmas; they have had practical experience of such canons. Anthony Kerrigan, an American writer living in Ireland, was invited to one of these congresses, a year after Newman's pilgrimage to Budapest, and gave me a candid report. He found himself—although he was the translator of Unamuno, distinctly no Marxist—genuinely welcome among Hungarian writers.

"It is no mistake they invite non-Reds," Kerrigan wrote to me. "They are trying to get through to us. Not one word of propaganda at the congress; we heard the epithet Marxist twice in three weeks there, and both times in derision. . . . We were asked for nothing in return— except perhaps to think kindly of them, of Hungary, of Hungarian literature, of their (intolerable) history. I was interviewed about Ireland, over a period of two days as we were taken around and over Lake Balaton. This resulted in their printing my anti-Marxist analysis in 'Magyar Hirlap,' the government daily paper—without changing a word. This was quite unlike my experience with certain American quarterly journals."

The creative and critical writers of Hungary are dissatisfied with the "total explanation" of Marxist criticism—nearly as dissatisfied as is Alexander Solzhenitsyn. In Soviet Russia, Solzhenitsyn cannot be published at all nowadays; while in the "capitalist" United States, a thousand flowers of Marxist criticism bloom. This irony did not much distress the editors of *Literature in Revolution*.

The title *Literature in Revolution* was ambiguous. Literature *in* revolution? What revolution? Did the editors have in mind literature describing revolution, or literature in a revolutionary age, or revolutionary developments in literature itself? Charles Newman seemed to experience misgivings about his own title. He could not share "Trotsky's faith in the existence of revolutionary man," or entertain "any clear notion of the historical situation which predicates his existence." The contributors to this volume were not sure that anyone was listening to them—a melancholy change, that, since 1967: "There is a sense here not only of unease, but rather of a desperate attempt to re-establish a constituency—an audience, in a word. And as much as the collection as a whole is a lament for the consequences of radical protest of the last few years, there is very little 'repentance' here." Was this book a summons or a farewell? The best mentor its editors could find was Leon Trotsky.

In his *Literature and Revolution* (1924), Trotsky wrote of two kinds of revolutionary art—the first reflecting the [Bolshevik] Revolution, the second made up of "the works which are not connected with the Revolution in theme, but are thoroughly imbued with . . . the new consciousness arising out of the Revolution." Trotsky called for *"merciless criticism of everything that exists*—merciless criticism in the sense that it is not afraid of its findings, and just as little afraid of conflict with the existing powers." Well, no new revolution having occurred in the 1960's, the contributors to this volume had to content themselves with a "new consciousness" arising out of . . . out of . . . why, out of earlier revolutions. Certainly no new consciousness emerged from the turmoil of the 'Sixties. For such "new" consciousness, one must turn back to Trotsky's Revolution, which devoured Trotsky.

Tutelege to Trotsky, however, involves writers of today in difficulties—some of those mentioned by Newman, others not. Karl Marx had next to no interest in humane letters, except so far as the writer might be employed as a propagandist in the class struggle; but Leon Trotsky was friendlier toward literature. "He is certainly a man of first-rate intelligence," T. S. Eliot wrote of Trotsky in 1933, "expressing himself in rough and ready metaphorical style, and he utters a good deal of sound sense . . . as an antidote to the false art of revolution his treatise is admirable." Trotsky's primary shortcoming, said Eliot, was the notion that art can arise out of ideology: "If we assume for the moment that the revolution is to take place, and that the final classless society will appear, then I concede the possibility that great works of art in new forms will subsequently appear too; I disbelieve not only that the new art will be any better than the art of all the past, but that the new art will owe its life to communism. The chances for art are no better than out of any other possible development of society, and are not improved by a flood of anticipatory criticism."

Eliot denied the premise of Trotsky that art is merely the product of social environment; Eliot believed that the writer must do more than come to terms with his environment. "There are also people who, while recognizing the interest of the work of literature as a document upon the ideas and sensibility of its epoch, and recognizing even that the permanent work of literature is one which does not lack this interest, yet cannot help valuing literary work, like philosophical work, by its breaking through the categories of thought and sensibility of its age; by speaking, in the language of its time and in the imagery of its own tradition, the word which belongs to no time," Eliot continued. "Art, we feel, aspires to the condition of the timeless; and communist art, according to the sentence of those who would foretell what it is to be, is bound to the temporal."

Whether or not the contributors to *Literature in Revolution* had read these remarks of Eliot (in his editorial commentary in *The Criterion*) upon Trotsky, some of them did attempt to rise above the merely temporal. Indeed, the eagerness of certain contributors to withdraw from political activism into literary scholarship was almost embarrassing. Take Carl Oglesby, who once led the riots at the University of Wisconsin. In this volume, Oglesby gave us an essay entitled "Melville, or Water Consciousness & Its Madness." Herman Melville, he wrote, found a madness he could live with. Ahab was evil, exploiting his crew, and Moby Dick was the victim of Ahab's imperialism:

"So with a subdued Melville, I ask: Given some broad estimate of the scale, tempo and rhythm at which protoimperial systems condense out and acquire historical outline and social architecture, then swell and grow festered, finally either to hang suspended a moment before a sometimes luminously sweeping descent, or else to burst all at once and splash blood everywhere, leaving little behind besides shards, cripples and memories that everyone who survives them pants to forget: given these choices, what is the political utility of the concept *anti-imperialism*?"

Is this rich, beautiful prose, transcending the sorry time? Oglesby hoped so. But Oglesby's prose would make no revolution; it might not even make sense. He sedulously avoided any direct reference to Vietnam, as if he were writing in the Circumlocution Office, as if he would be prosecuted for so heroic a dissent. One thinks of a remark by Georges Sorel: "Our experience of the Marxian theory of value convinces me of the importance which obscurity of style may lend to a doctrine."

Oglesby departed from Marxist orthodoxy only in the final paragraph of his essay. Melville wrote that "history cannot be justified from within by historical action"—while Marx regularly argued otherwise. Carl Oglesby improved our understanding as follows: "The attempt to impart meaning to history from within history, however unchallengeable its aura of necessity, succeeds for the most part only in historicizing meaning. In other words, succeeds only in changing the creature one by one into a creature of sovereign economy. No doubt the need for this economy is great. But unless politics is more than history instead of the reverse, how can some people ever ask other people to die?"

In this fashion did Oglesby rise above that mere contemporaneity which T. S. Eliot often reproached. A similar escape from activism was accomplished by Conor Cruise O'Brien, in an essay called "Passion and Cunning: the Politics of W. B. Yeats." O'Brien had conducted the United Nations' "Operation Smash" in Katanga, but was smashed in the Congo himself. Later he accepted a professorship, endowed with public funds, in New York City, and sat down upon the steps of a draft-board office. More recently, he served in the popular house of the Irish Republic. Unlike most other Marxists, O'Brien writes well, and knows that his fellow-ideologues do not write well.

"A Marxist critique which starts from the assumption that bad politics make for bad style," he remarked in *Literature in Revolution*, "will continue 'not to succeed.' The opposite assumption, though not entirely true, would be nearer the truth. The politics of the left—any left, even a popular 'national movement'—impose, by their emphasis on collective effort and on sacrifice, a constraint on the artist which may show itself in artificialities of style, vagueness or simple carelessness.

Right-wing politics, with their emphasis on the freedom of the *elite*, impose less constraint, require less pretense, allow style to become more personal and direct."

In Ireland, nowadays, O'Brien has set his face against IRA revolutionaries. Not all the contributors to this anthology would join the latter-day O'Brien on the wrong (Right) side of the barricades. Most of them, enjoying the protection of an entrenched capitalist regime in these United States, did not have to dread personally the consequences of actual revolution. Truman Nelson, in his piece "On Creating Revolutionary Art and Going out of Print" (actually about John Brown of the Pottawatomie Massacres), lamented that "No one talks of this, but somewhere along the line our primary right has been taken from us: the right of revolution, of resistance to any government which is clearly destructive of all other inalienable rights of man." Somebody came and took away our right of revolution; won't somebody please give it back?

For Nelson, John Brown was the "Great Man", because Brown killed on principle. Nelson had discovered that Brown was indeed strictly political in his Pottawatomie slaughter, and went at the task in a scientific spirit: "As a surveyor, he did what was occupationally natural to him. He selected his victims from those residing on a survey line running directly north and south, which he could follow in the night by consulting his pocket compass. It was a tactic of great economy of action and he brought it off with complete success."

Counter-revolutionaries control our universities and publishing houses, Nelson instructed us. Among those vicious reactionaries are "the super-liberals of *The New York Review of Books*." How should we rid ourselves of these tyrants? Why, recover that inalienable right of revolution, presumably as exercised by John Brown: "It is no longer possible to circumvent them by writing revolutionary history in the form of a novel nor is it possible to attain the distribution or viability of revolutionary essays or tracts until they appear somewhere on a 'reading list.' The only sensible suggestion in this matter comes from Lenin. 'The first thing to do is deprive capital of the possibility of hiring writers, buying up publishers and buying newspapers, and to do this the capitalists and exploiters have to be overthrown and their resistance suppressed.' "

Aye, the counter-revolutionary editors of *The New York Review of Books* may rue the day they slighted Truman Nelson's fiction, when Nelson leads the proletariat down Madison Avenue. But conceivably that hour of righteous wrath, in a scientific spirit, never may arrive; for Truman Nelson is not steeled to his duty by Brown's Calvinism, with its "revolutionary cutting edge and its revolutionary righteousness."

Sol Yurick, in this anthology, also celebrated killing in Kansas—a more recent massacre, the slaughter of the Clutter family, which enriched Truman Capote through his book *In Cold Blood*. Yurick said that he was writing a "Marxist detective story"; then he ran on for fifty pages, even though his essay ("The Politics of the Imagination: the Problem of Consciousness") seemed to have been severely cut by the editors of this volume. He offered his comments on Grayson Kirk, Gross National Product, the Congress for Cultural Freedom, Capote, Heisenberg, McLuhan, *Bleak House*, *Oedipus Rex*, Freud, the Great Chain of Being, *Faust*, the conspiratorial theory of history (which he embraced), "the mind-narrowing Stalinist debacle" (which he disapproved), the Old Testament, *Moby Dick*, Norman Mailer, the Puritan Ethic, John Foster Dulles, and much else besides: all this in a fantastic tapestry. Marx would have had a crushing epithet for Yurick; Lenin would have locked him up; Stalin would have shot him.

At last one learns that in Yurick's detective novel, the killing of Clutter and his family was justified, because Clutter *"had been a county agent in his youth."* (The italics are Yurick's.) You don't follow? "Wasn't Clutter just out of an agricultural land grant college (established by the Morrill Act) a county agent; and wasn't the county agent system in the past funded by railroads and Rockefellers who endowed the General Education Board, those same Rockefellers who take an interest in the education of students at Columbia, at Cornell, at Chicago, etc.?" Obviously, Clutter was an exploiter of poor peasants, as richly deserving of a nasty end as was Krook in *Bleak House*.

So, in Yurick's Marxist detective romance, "What is it that the Marxist detective does? Recognizing the execution of the killers, Perry Smith and Dick Hickock, to be a crime, a restoration of an ongoing criminal system, he recognizes the death of the Clutters to be an execution, a revolutionary court judgment, and goes back to find where the real crime took place in order to make Smith and Hickock aware of the political motives of their act . . . an awareness that would have saved them from execution." Is all this a rather heavy-handed spoof of Marxist writing?

No: Yurick's paper was written to create "comradely struggle . . . which means responses and counter-responses." Conversion to Christianity, said Yurick, is "an act of murder." Nevertheless, he admired T. S. Eliot, even though he charged him with being "the father of the fast cut of the television commercial; he is the father of the modern bourgeois movie."

Eliot, who possessed a powerful sense of humor, would have been tickled by this—and by the many other grudging compliments paid to him by other contributors to this anthology. Eliot haunted these New Left critics—for Eliot had worked a revolution in literature, and they could not. Eliot's innovating poetry had given to the modern age the possibility of recovering moral imagination. Yet Eliot's literary revolution had been rooted in tradition; and from the first, one of Eliot's purposes had been resistance against the "low dream" of the ideologues—against the Bloody Kansas notion of revolution.

In the name of "democracy", Eliot had written in 1937, new oligarchies would be created; men of arts and letters ought to beware of leagues which purported to unite artists by some idological manifesto. "The term 'democracy' must continue to be used,' he had observed in *The Criterion*, "because it is sacred to the British mind; and it will continue to be used by people whose activities are really directed towards one kind of oligarchy or another—the kind of oligarchy you happen to prefer will always be the one which is 'democracy.' I fear that groups of 'artists' who engage in political affirmations may bring about for themselves just the opposite of what they intend: instead of influencing political directions they may merely be cutting themselves off from the world of events." He might have written that about *Literature in Revolution*.

The New Left enthusiasts had talked of liberty, but had hungered for power; they had idolized The People, but had served the ego. If one is bound for Zion, it is not well to plod round a prickly pear planted long ago by Mr. Marx of the British Museum; nor is that a good exercise for rousing the literary imagination. Nevertheless, the cactus-land of ideology was perfectly safe for an American writer in 1972, as it is now. Blessed are the academic revolutionaries, for they shall know tenure. For a good many of those professed revolutionaries of the 'Sixties, ideology had been little more than a thinly-veiled form of personal therapy. It had not cured their afflictions of soul and of intellect.

Most of them had read "Marxist literature", not Marx. Had they read Trotsky, really? If so, they had not taken to heart this sentence from Trotsky's book *The Permanent Revolution* (1930): " 'Red' professors are frequently distinguished from the old reactionary professors, not by a firmer backbone, but by a profounder illiteracy."

21

Academic Freedom and Teachers' Unions: 1973

I N THE ACADEMY during 1973, one more or less native ideology
was gaining new ground; the dull, if ominous, progressivist
ideology of Educationism, especially as represented by the national teachers' unions and their affiliates. Already this was powerful
within the public-school apparatus; in 1973, it began to invade colleges and universities, with the strong political lobbies and ample
funds of the teachers' unions to back it.

Until 1973, unionizing of college professors and instructors and
teaching assistants was negligible in the United States. The nearest
approaches to unions were the American Association of University
Professors and some independent associations on various campuses;
but these groups did not bargain collectively with college administrations, and did not look upon themselves as unions. Yet certain circumstances within the Academy, combining with the ambitions and the
resources of the National Education Association and the American
Federation of Teachers, and their state and local affiliates (made up
almost wholly of teachers in public elementary and secondary schools),
made it possible for the teachers' unions to gain a little headway in
college and university as early as 1973. With some reluctance, the
American Association of University Professors entered into this competition, its local chapters offering themselves as bargaining-agents by
way of alternative to NEA and AFT affiliates.

Given the individuality of college professors, and their presumptive
ability to bargain for themselves with college administrators, unionization seems unnatural in the Academy. Certain fears of some professors
and instructors, however, had opened the door a crack by 1973. One
influence was the circumstance of static or diminishing enroll-

ments—which might mean that a fair number of college teachers could lose their posts, not being really needed, if the trend should continue. Another influence was the inadequacy of not a few college staff-members who had been engaged during the years immediately following the Second World War: in those days, anybody with the slightest pretensions to potential membership in the Academy had been sought out to teach the flood of veterans and others that had poured into college and university. Persons privately conscious that they actually are unqualified for college posts, whether by scholarship or by talents as teachers, and whose standing with improving or economizing college administrations seems insecure, tend to seek safety in numbers—that is, to league themselves with powerful organizations that call the discharge of practically any teacher "victimization." At the same time, the great teachers' unions, having already enjoyed massive successes in establishing union shops within public schools, were looking for new worlds to conquer. Their organizers turned their talents to college and university; and though they found those nuts rather hard to crack, by 1973 there was serious concern in the Academy about the growing activities of the teachers' unions and what this might do to the freedom and the standards of university and college faculties.

"The only true freedom is freedom to work," Irving Babbitt had written in 1924. All other rights depend upon the right to work, he reasoned: for if we are prevented from doing our work, life scarcely is worth living; we must find our happiness in work, or not at all. With Aristotle, he held that the highest form of work is the work of the intellect.

Even the right to intellectual work seemed insecure by 1973. What we call "academic freedom", in essence, is a protection of the right to work with one's mind. The doctrine of academic freedom declares that teacher and scholar should be reasonably free to teach and pursue the truth. Sometimes the truth is unpopular; therefore we endeavor to secure teacher or scholar against arbitrary interference with his work. In theory, the "professor" is a person who strongly professes his belief in certain truths. Unless he is reasonably free to pursue and expound those truths, he cannot accomplish his work. Thus academic freedom is a natural right: I mean that it arises from the nature of intellectual labor.

Academic freedom never is secure. Pressures to reduce it come from different quarters at different times. In the 'Fifties, it was encroached upon by educational imperialism in the Academy. In the 'Sixties, it was much harmed by infatuation with "revolutionary" ideology. In the 'Seventies, academic freedom was menaced increasingly by the intervention of government in the affairs of the Academy, and by the tendency to induce, or compel, professors to submit to the domination of unions. Both these encroachments upon academic freedom probably will grow more difficult to resist during the next few years. In this chapter, I am concerned with what may happen to academic freedom, and to academic standards, if professors are thoroughly unionized.

At the beginning of 1973, already a fair number of American professors were aware of this peril to their profession and to their freedom of mind. In January, that year, I addressed the convention of University Professors for Academic Order, meeting at the University of Florida. The UPAO had been organized only a few years earlier, in consequence chiefly of the hard blows against academic freedom and order struck by the campus radical activists during the 'Sixties. I talked to the UPAO members on academic freedom as related to the problem of excessive numbers in the higher learning. At that convention, the UPAO adopted a resolution which expressed their resistance to pressures from both government and teachers' unions. That resolution deserves to be quoted here.

"Whereas, faculty have suffered and continue to suffer from the application of nonprofessional criteria to such essentially professional matters as promotion, retention, tenure, and salary increments;

"Whereas, applying nonprofessional criteria to professional matters creates tension, strife, suspicion, and distrust within the academic community, between the academic community and administrative personnel, and between the academic community and the general public,

"Therefore, UPAO, recalling our stand in opposition to compulsory unionization, hereby

"Affirms the right of faculty to organize in such professional ways as may be locally available;

"Affirms the right of faculty members to affiliate with such associations or not, according to their independent decision;

"Affirms that such faculty associations may not claim to operate on behalf of any unaffiliated faculty;

"Affirms the responsibility of such faculty associations to offer advice, information, and general collegial support to those faculty who allege the application to them of nonprofessional criteria;

"Affirms the responsibility of such faculty associations generally to promote academic professionalism, fair return for professional services rendered, and the study of competent evaluative methodologies applied to faculty;

"And affirms the responsibility of such faculty associations to initiate professionally acceptable, legal responses to the application of non-professional criteria, provided that appropriate administrative remedies have been exhausted and provided that the affected faculty member concurs."

By "nonprofessional criteria", the UPAO delegates meant chiefly interference by the federal government with the employment-practices of the Academy, through programs like "Affirmative Action" that, in effect, set quotas favoring women, Negroes, Mexican-Americans, and other "minority" groups; political discrimination against conservative professors by dominant radical or liberal cliques in the Academy; and the new threat of policy-making in the Academy by teachers' unions, armed with powers of compulsion. In this 1973 resolution, the members of UPAO distinguished between a voluntary association of faculty members, which can protect academic freedom; and involuntary membership in, or submission to, a nonprofessional organization which would reduce the academic freedom of those whom it professed to represent. They resented the danger that possibly they might be compelled to subordinate their own interests and convictions to the ideology of some union—thrust upon them by the action of government, which already had been granting special privileges to the officials of such unions.

The members of UPAO, and professors and teachers generally, had reason for misgiving. During the previous decade, there had occurred swift unionizing of public employees—often coercive unionization, in the sense that a temporary majority of a group of employees, sometimes by a slim margin, could bind the whole of that group. To require public employees to join some union against their will, or to pay fees to such a union that may be spent for purposes opposed to the interests and convictions of many of those who pay the money, is perilous public policy. By its nature, government is a monopoly. If the people employed in such a monopoly are subject to the will of officers in a union, under certain conditions the authority of government may be defied successfully by the men who dominate the union. The real government might become the union itself. Therefore, until the 'Seventies, the federal government and most state governments had refrained from giving to unions the power to control public employees against their wishes, even though such power was possessed by unions in the "private sector."

This is true of public instruction. The large majority of college and university students, by 1973, were enrolled in institutions supported by public funds; an even vaster majority of elementary and secondary pupils attended public schools. If effectual control of the educational apparatus were to pass from the hands of public trustees and administrators to the hands of union officers, then eventually what is taught in the system of public instruction, and what persons are employed to do the teaching, would be determined by union organizations not subject to ordinary political processes. Under such circumstances, the educational system would cease to be genuinely public, and its policies would be those of a kind of union elite, perhaps ideologically bent. And in the long run, all too probably, this would result in intellectual servility.

For the national teachers' unions, whether the National Education Association or the American Federation of Teachers, and their state and local affiliates, by 1973, had ceased to be professional associations of the sort approved by University Professors for Academic Order—if, indeed, they ever had been such. Their concern, by 1973, was not for the qualitative improvement of public instruction, but with power and money for their own union organizations. These teachers' unions also had a discernible ideological warping, hostile toward genuinely higher education and toward genuine academic freedom.

In many cases, a utopian radicalism had come to prevail among teacher-union officials. On a national level, the political hunger and anti-intellectual objectives of the National Education Association were sufficiently suggested in remarks by Mrs. Catherine Barrett, president of NEA, in the NEA's booklet "Schools for the '70's." Mrs. Barrett looked forward to the time when the NEA would become the most powerful group in America, with an immense political budget, electing and defeating political candidates at federal, state, and local levels. When that happy day should arrive, Mrs. Barrett said, "We will need to recognize that the so-called 'basic skills', which currently represent nearly the total effort in elementary schools, will be taught in one-quarter of the school day. The remaining time will be devoted to what is truly fundamental and basic."

What did President Barrett mean by these phrases? Why, she advocated a "problem-oriented curriculum" which would instill correct opinions about "war, peace, race, the economy, population, the environment"—in short, the most controversial of political issues, and these to be thrust upon grade-school children. If parents should disagree with the triumphant NEA—well, it would be somewhat tardy for them to disagree, power already having passed to a union monopoly. If professors and teachers should dissent from Mrs. Barrett and her colleagues, who would control the NEA's massive propaganda-apparatus—then perhaps they could go into some other kind of work. The system of public instruction would be captive to ideology. At best, this would be an ideology of "ritualistic liberalism" alien to the beliefs of most Americans; possibly it would be a thoroughly radical ideology. If one would control a nation totally, first obtain thorough control over the schools. Under such a domination, no room would remain for the liberties of the mind.

In a few states, in 1973—among them Hawaii, Wisconsin, Minnesota, Washington, Montana, and Michigan—compulsory unionism already was fixed upon public instruction. In nearly all states, unionism had moved upward from the schools into many community colleges, and from them it was moving into some state colleges and universities. If teachers and professors would not join these unions, still they had to submit to having the union bargain for them, fixing the terms of their employment—and a good deal else besides.

Early in July, 1970, the then-president of the National Education Association, George Fisher, had declared publicly, at San Francisco, that within a decade the NEA would be the most powerful group in America, with an annual budget of a billion dollars. "The world has never seen an organization of this magnitude," he said. By the end of the 'Seventies, he continued, the President of the United States would kowtow to the NEA, which then "will control the qualifications for entrance into the profession and for the privilege of remaining in the profession." One detects here what the officers of NEA think of the doctrine of academic freedom: to teach is a "privilege" conferred by union officials.

The NEA's boast was not idle. By 1972, in Michigan (where labor unions generally are very strong), the Michigan Education Association (affiliated with the NEA) was demanding "a statewide program to limit placement of student-teachers to a number which will meet but not exceed demands beginning in the fall of 1973." In short, the leaders of the MEA wished to reduce the supply of new teachers, because there were too many teachers already—or so the MEA thought. The MEA officials aspired to control over the number and types of new teachers who would be certified in Michigan, and later would have introduced into Michigan's legislature bills conferring upon the teachers' unions the power to certify new teachers—an intended usurping of state authority which, at this writing, has not yet been conceded to the MEA.

This aspiration was resisted by universities and colleges which trained teachers. Dr. John W. Childs, assistant dean of the College of Education at Wayne State University, spoke forthrightly against the MEA's demands of 1972. "I think there is a serious question whether the MEA has demonstrated that its main interest is in kids and the quality of teaching for those kids," he said. "Perhaps its main concern should be the protection of its members, but if so, I don't think they should be given the primary power to determine who enters the profession."

Despite an occasional reverse in practical politics during 1973, teacher-union officials continued to spend immense sums on political activity, and grew more canny in political tactics and strategy as they gained experience. Their threat to academic freedom could not be safely ignored. The American Federation of Teachers, in 1972 for the first time embracing a presidential candidate, endorsed Senator George McGovern and supplied him generously with funds. The opponents of politicizing the profession of teaching had little coordination and little money. The teachers' unions possessed full treasuries, filled in part by the involuntary contributions of teachers who would have preferred not to be represented by those unions and who often disagreed with the unions' educational and political slogans and tactics —but were compelled by law in several states to pay substantial "fees" to the unions, whether members or not. Not only could the teachers' unions pay lavishly to maintain political lobbies in Washington and in every state capital, but they could afford to sustain long litigation against teachers, school boards, and college authorities that might refuse to submit to them.

In 1973, although there were teachers' union chapters on many college and university campuses, nowhere did a union enjoy a "union shop" or "agency shop"—that is, in colleges, unlike public schools, the unions as yet could not compel members of the faculty either to join the union or, alternatively, pay to the union "fees" equivalent to union dues, as a condition of employment. But by the autumn of 1975, several universities and colleges would have submitted to the union shop—no place of any great repute among these, true. The unions would continue to push. By 1976, there would be several notorious cases, on various campuses, of professors given the choice either of paying money to a union or resigning their posts. Some would resign or retire. The power of federal and state statutes was behind the teachers' unions, and the courts would afford the non-union professors no substantial redress.

Yet was this "agency shop" or "union shop" really a menace to academic freedom? Could not the professor simply continue to teach and to research as he always had done, after paying to some union a tribute called either dues or fees? Had the professor lost anything except a slice of his salary?

Yes, he had lost something: his freedom of intellectual choice. If his continued employment became dependent upon the will of some union, he might find it necessary to conform his lectures and his writings to views approved by the masters of that union. If those masters should hold strong ideological views of one sort or another, the professor might find it necessary to be intellectually servile—or to seek another line of work.

I do not mean that the professor should be a mere hired hand, with no voice in the policies of the Academy. On the contrary, I believe that on most campuses the members of the faculty have not enjoyed sufficient influence upon educational policies. I should like to see university senates and similar bodies strengthened in their authority. Indeed, one reason why teachers' unions have gained in power has been that often members of college faculties have been treated as mere employees by college administrations, and those teachers' resentments have driven them into the arms of a union.

Yet King Stork may be worse than King Log. An ideologue of a union organizer may be more arbitrary than a dullard of a college president. Some people may suggest that perhaps professors ought to join a teachers' union and then work within to reform its policies and choose better union officials. That may be possible, but it would be a rough road. The more scholarly the professor, in general, the less likely he is to attend union meetings; he is busy with his work, and he is not fond of incessant quasi-political controversy. As with other unions, teachers' unions ordinarily are dominated by political activists or careerists who mean to maintain their own power. It is these latter who determine teachers'-union policies, and they are not conspicuous for their devotion to pure learning.

Even under the "agency shop" or "union shop", the teachers' union must submit to some restrictions upon its power: a teacher or professor is engaged by college or school, not by the union, to fill his post; and he cannot ordinarily be discharged merely at union officials' displeasure, so long as he pays his union dues or fees. But it is quite conceivable—the beginnings of this menace could be discerned in 1973—that the unions' control over the teaching profession might be extended beyond the "agency shop." There exists also the "closed shop", under which arrangement the union does the hiring and firing, and employment is wholly dependent upon the union's pleasure. By the Taft-Hartley Act, as amended, practically all employees are protected against the closed shop—except for employees of state governments and their political subdivisions. Presumably, then, professors at independent colleges and teachers at independent schools would be sheltered by the Taft-Hartley Act, supposing that the institution employing them were classified by the National Labor Relations Board as engaging in interstate commerce (this itself a dubious classification).

But professors and other employees of state and municipal colleges and universities are not sheltered by the Taft-Hartley Act. And the large majority of faculty members in this country hold posts at such public educational institutions. Therefore, potentially, state legislatures could pass acts establishing the closed shop in public education at every level—in response to the lobbying of the teachers' unions. Then strong dissent from the policies of a teachers' union could result in virtual exclusion from practicing one's profession. This is no fantasy: such arbitrary measures were being discussed by the California teachers' unions as early as 1973, and have been formally advanced since then, though as yet no state has gone so far as to pass such legislation. That might be the end of academic freedom. Also it might mean the end of any qualitative reform in education at any level, for the teachers' unions, with very few exceptions, have been interested almost exclusively in higher pay and greater job-security; often they positively have opposed plans for qualitative improvement, as disturbing to their members' peace of mind.

Academic freedom, I repeat, is freedom from ideology, freedom from obsessive political activism, freedom from centralized power over the intellect. If any class of people ought to be able to bargain for themselves, or to advance their interests through genuine professional associations (as opposed to institutions of the trade-union mentality), those people are the professors and teachers. If freedom of choice is denied to such people, there might be precious little liberty left for anybody, after the elapse of a few decades; for ideas do have consequences. The forcing of all professors into unions—organizations narrowly restricted to the fancied economic interests of their group, and often subject to ideological prejudices—would be one of the graver aspects of the decadence of the higher learning. Rarely have I heard a union officer speak of wisdom and virtue.

In 1916, the railway brotherhoods thrust upon President Wilson the Adamson Act, the arrogant demand of a labor monopoly in transportation. Irving Babbitt wrote of the Adamson Act that it had amounted to "a form of the instinct of domination so full of menace to free institutions that, rather than submit to it, a genuine statesman would have died in his tracks." Compulsory unionizing of the higher education would be an even grosser form of that instinct of domination, the enemy of the freedom of the mind.

I do not suppose that many of today's public men would die in their tracks to prevent the domination of university and college by teachers' unions. Resistance within university and college to that form of domination remains stronger than the resistance of the politicians; and so far as I know at this writing, no important university, and few well-reputed colleges, have voted themselves into servitude. There is some health in the Academy still.

22

Independent Colleges and Moral Worth:
1974

ONE KNOWLEDGEABLE GENTLEMAN of my acquaintance told me, in 1974, that by 1984 no independent colleges would exist. A score of respectable liberal-arts colleges closed their doors forever during 1974—some because they could not meet the interest on money they had borrowed from the federal treasury to erect new dormitories and classrooms. Should that decay continue, American higher education would become the monopoly of the state—as it is already in most of the world.

It seemed improbable, by 1974, that either tax credits or any form of "voucher plan" for college students would be adopted by the federal government—although only four years later, to the surprise of many college administrators, Senator D. P. Moynihan and some of his colleagues would make headway once more with such proposals. A few state governments offered such forms of relief or assistance to "private" institutions, but these bones were too lean to offer substantial nutriment.

It would not suffice to turn to charitable foundations, there not being enough foundation money to go round, even had all of it been expended on independent colleges. Besides, the big foundations, like governments, often attached disagreeable conditions to such grants as they made to church-related colleges. Should a college sell its birthright? Already many Catholic universities and colleges had stripped their halls of religious art, even the crucifix, and had altered their curricula, in hope of obtaining public or private money. Survival was not worth that price: old houses have stood long enough if they stand till they fall with honor.

No, in 1974 it appeared that the independent institutions would not be rescued by any *deus ex machina*. For the most part, they must finance themselves from endowments (more difficult than ever before, what with inflation of the dollar); from tuition fees; from contributions given by church communicants, if a college retained some church connection; and from the benefactions of alumni. Those sources would dry up, unless an independent college should vigorously reaffirm the principles upon which it had been founded. I suggest here three of the more important of those principles.

First, faith. With few exceptions, independent universities and colleges in this country were established by Christian churches or associations, in the hope that these institutions would school Christian scholars and gentlemen. Nowadays, however, the parent churches (with the honorable exception of the Southern Baptists and a few other denominations) do little to help the colleges in which once they were earnestly involved.

"Faith" does not necessarily imply faith in Christian doctrine. If a college should strongly profess its faith in any body of belief, it would attract some support. But if any independent college seems merely to be attempting on a limited budget what state institutions are undertaking more lavishly at public expense—why make sacrifices to save it? So, at least, many people inquired in 1974.

Second, high academic standards and academic community on a humane scale. To endure, the independent college must promise the student something better than he could obtain at Behemoth State. But what with their distresses, many independent colleges in 1974 would accept nearly any "student" who offered himself or was offered by his parents. And during the expansion of higher education after the Second World War, many decent private colleges took into their faculties second-rate professors and instructors, not being able to afford the better candidates. As for the humane scale, most of the independent colleges still offered that in 1974, if only because they could not find enough young people to fill those tall dormitories built with federal money (and, by 1974, often standing as so many costly white elephants, the colleges finding it almost impossible to meet even the low-rate interest payments).

Third, specialization. Here I do not mean that the independent college should convert itself into a technological institute or a business school—which foolish policy had been the resort of a hundred former liberal-arts college in recent years. No one will adventure much for the sake of a second-rate hybrid or bastard: the state would do a better job of technical training, usually, or at least a job less costly to the payer of tuition.

Rather, I mean that an independent college could remain a good liberal-arts foundation, and yet attract students and benefactors by offering some special program of instruction, not directly vocational and yet still concerned with a genuine intellectual discipline. I suggest that a college which develops a high reputation in musicology, or in political economy, or in quantum mechanics, or in ethical studies, or in imaginative literature, or in some other decent discipline, will have a better mousetrap to which interested students might beat a pathway. And not only students (and their parents) would gather that this college must be in general a sound college. In fine, the independent college that endures must excel, not underbid, in its competition with Behemoth State U.

By 1974, an increasing number of young people had become aware that it was not well for them to be lost in the Lonely Crowd of the mass campus. True, the typical high-school guidance counselor, himself a product of Behemoth U., often discouraged high-school seniors from applying to independent colleges. A Texas girl with an admirable high-school record and parents of some means told her guidance counselor that she meant to enroll at Vassar. "Why, what do you want to go to a little old place like that for?" said the counselor, indignant. "With your record, you could get into East Texas State, or maybe even the University of Texas!" Still, in 1974 the prospects of good independent colleges for attracting a sufficient number of interested students were higher than they had been in any year since the Second World War—provided that the college really did offer something more for mind and heart than did the mass campus, and could make its merits known to intending collegians and their parents.

Late in 1974, I addressed the annual meeting of the American Association of Presidents of Independent Colleges and Universities, an organization then only five years old. The members of AAPICU were a sincere and conscientious set, taking arms against a sea of troubles. Several college presidents declared that they found it difficult to concern themselves with their primary duty of educating. Their days were taken up by negotiations with federal and state bureaucracies, troubles with alienated professors and radical students, recruitment of students in a time of diminishing enrollments, and desperately urgent fund-raising.

Yet the educational advantages offered by their colleges, or by some of them, still were high. With few exceptions, these colleges retained the humane scale. They were less directly subject to winds of doctrine, educational fad and foible, or political illusions of the hour, than were the big public institutions. It was possible for them to adhere to religious doctrines, and to make some appeal to the moral imagination of students. Often they remained genuine academic communities, in which the professors of several disciplines could know one another, and in which students could participate personally. These colleges were not yet subject to Leviathan.

In no small part, the American character was formed by these institutions, from Harvard, William and Mary, and Yale to the many Catholic colleges founded in recent decades. If the independent colleges should slide into oblivion, American freedom and diversity and ethical understanding would suffer irreparably. And this is particularly true if we think of the idea and the reality of moral worth.

My general thesis is this: a principal achievement of liberal education in America has been the imparting of a sense of moral worth among the more intelligent of the rising generation. But this apprehension of moral worth, as taught by the liberal and the scientific disciplines, has been losing ground, throughout the present century, to what John Henry Newman called the "Knowledge School"—that is, to utilitarian and pragmatic theories and practices, which tend to regard moral worth—so far as they regard it at all—as merely the product of private rationality and social utility. Success, increasingly, was substituted for virtue in our curricula; facts, for wisdom; social adjustment, for strength of character. In more recent years, mere sociability and counter-culture boondoggles have driven out of college catalogues, too often, what little remained of the ethical disciplines and approaches.

The very chapels have fallen into disuse on not a few campuses: some are used for visiting speakers (the more sensational, the better—Watergate burglars and black fanatics out on bail); of some the doors never are opened. Perhaps that is just as well, considering the uses to which other chapels have been put. I think, for instance, of the magnificent chapel of Yale University—converted, at one time in the late 'Sixties, into a fortress-sanctuary by, simultaneously, black militants, homosexuals, militant pacifists, enthusiasts for mind-expanding drugs, and campus vandals.

The concept of "moral worth" has subsisted on short commons for the past decade and more, not only at Behemoth State University, but sometimes at Bruno-Servetus Evangelical College or at Our Lady of the Sorrows Catholic College for Young Women. This question of moral worth in relation to the independent college now has become a question of survival, in a dual sense: the survival of the understanding of moral worth in our age and our nation, and the survival of those colleges and universities whose especial original function it was to join right reason with the moral imagination.

Time was when parents took it for granted that their offspring would acquire at Podunk Ecumenical College considerable ethical understanding—together with a touch of the unbought grace of life, perhaps. Strange to say, some parents still labor under the illusion that the typical American campus can improve the morals and the manners of the rising generation. Yet actually a well-appointed bordello would be a residence more decorous and possibly less costly, for four years, than are the co-ed dorms of Behemoth State. Doubtless one would learn more of the art of worldly wisdom in a bordello than an undergraduate learns in the various counter-culture programs. And the company of an Athenian courtesan or a Japanese geisha might be positively elevating, by the side of discourse in one of our campus teen-age ghettos, which suffer from the cruel tyranny of the peer-group.

Even the students, or a good many of them, have grown aware that something is missing. Not a few undergraduates complain that their college offers them no first principles of morality, no ethical direction, no aspiration toward enduring truth. This complaint may seem strange enough, coming as it does sometimes from students who rejoice in their defiance of bourgeois conformity, and whose private lives distinctly are not modeled upon the precepts of Jeremy Taylor. Nevertheless, what such students say usually is true enough: the hungry sheep, or goats, have looked up on occasion, and have not been fed.

At best, what the typical college has offered its students, in recent decades, has been defecated rationality. By that term, a favorite with me, I mean a narrow rationalism or logicalism, purged of theology, moral philosophy, symbol and allegory, tradition, reverence, and the wisdom of our ancestors. This defecated rationality is the exalting of private judgment and hedonism at the expense of the inner order of the soul and the outer order of the republic. On many a campus, this defecated and desiccated logicalism is the best which is offered to the more intelligent students: as alternatives, they could embrace a program of fun and games, or a program of "social commitment" of a baneful or a silly character, wondrously unintellectual.

The consequence of this altered view of the ends of American education, it seems to me, if it is carried to its logical culmination, will be the effacing of that principle which for three centuries has breathed life into the unwieldy bulk of our educational apparatus. I do not perceive any practicable substitute for this old sustaining principle. So I recommend that we do whatever we may to restore a consciousness that the aim of American higher education is this, in part: the inculcation of a sense of moral worth, achieved Socratically through right reason. Without a proper understanding of moral worth, there is small point in talking about human dignity, or education for democracy, or adjustment to society, or training for leadership, or preparation for personal success. For what gives the person dignity, and what makes possible a democracy of elevation, and what makes any society tolerable, and what keeps the modern world from becoming *Brave New World*, and what constitutes true success in any walk of life, is moral worth.

So I suggested to the presidents of independent colleges, in 1974, that the survival of colleges' independence, and indeed of the better elements in American character, may be bound up with a resuming of old obligations. There really are good students, or potential ones, who perceive that Behemoth State U. lacks order and integration of knowledge; that it lacks concern for the Socratic relationship between wisdom and virtue. There actually are many potential benefactors who inquire after some college or university dedicated to the permanent things: an institution which pursues an end genuinely ethical through a means genuinely intellectual. In diversions, the independent college cannot compete successfully with Behemoth State; nor in the immense apparatus of specialized research; nor in an obsessive sprawling vocationalism. But the independent college can, and should, stand head and shoulders above Behemoth State University in its joining of ethical apprehension and the higher reason. Thus the path of duty may be also the path of survival.

The purpose of the traditional American college never was that of the sophist, to teach success at any cost; nor that of the utilitarian, to teach pure facts. A high old function of the American college, and of its professors, has been the chastening of American materialism and American enthusiasm by a renewal of moral awareness. The universities of other nations have been more distinguished for sheer intellectual power, or for accomplishment in the arts, or for training great gentlemen, or for dedication to pure science. The peculiar achievement of the American college, by way of contrast, has been the leavening of a democratic nation by imparting to the better minds and hearts of the rising generation a union of reason and moral worth—and so developing better human beings and a better society.

Our colleges did incalculable good, in the past, by providing a counterpoise to the besetting vice of democracies—gluttony, against which Alexis de Tocqueville warned us.

"Materialism, among all nations, is a dangerous disease of the human mind," Tocqueville wrote in the second part of *Democracy in America*;

"but it is more especially to be dreaded among a democratic people because it readily amalgamates with that vice which is most familiar to the heart under such circumstances. Democracy encourages a taste for physical gratification; this taste, if it becomes excessive, soon disposes men to believe that all is matter only; and materialism, in its turn, hurries them on with mad impatience to these same delights; such is the fatal circle within which democratic nations are driven round. It were well that they should see the danger and hold back."

Our colleges, together with our churches, often have striven to hold us back from this fatal circle. They have modified our natural egoism by reaffirming our religious and moral patrimony, and have helped us to escape from the consequences of presumption by recalling that we are only part of a great continuity and essence. As a body, in some degree they still resist the claims of defecated rationality. They have clung, however feebly, to Newman's conviction that literature and science, unaided, cannot give answers to the urgent questions of modern life. In short, our independent colleges have been conservators of moral worth.

Our colleges, or some of them, have not been afraid to defend what Burke called "the contract of eternal society." They have not altogether abdicated the claims of learning in favor of the claims of appetite. They still recognize, some of them, the vocabulary of a forlorn and dispossessed orthodoxy. They may sustain that orthodoxy, that defense of human dignity, against the triumph of mass appetites and ideological infatuation.

As George Santayana wrote once, "What irony there would be in having learned to control matter, if we thereby forgot the purposes of the soul in controlling it, and disowned the natural furniture of the mind, our senses, fancy, and pictorial knowledge!" The independent college, in 1974, had not yet surrendered altogether to that irony. In an age of consolidation and aggrandizement, some American colleges still respected the humane scale. The year of 1974 was a hard time for such colleges. Yet if they should stand true to their own principle of the primacy of moral worth in a system of higher education, I suggested to the members of AAPICU, they would win through to better days.

No longer can the independent college guarantee to its students, or to their parents, even a temporary immunity from the demands of the world, the flesh, and the devil. Yet the independent college, if it retains the courage of affirmation, still can offer us that manner of intellectual discipline which teaches us what it is to be fully human. Those of the rising generation who do obtain some understanding of moral worth may be trusted to resist the follies of the time.

Thus necessity and virtue may coincide in the course of independent college and university, during the six years that remain to us before the coming of my friend's fatal year of 1984, by which time, he predicted, all "private" institutions of higher learning will have vanished from this earth. I suspect that most colleges which have converted themselves into second-rate training centers indeed may have vanished by that year. But those colleges which retain conscience and speak to consciences still will be with us.

Those independent colleges which mean to endure will have to find professors with some glimmerings of virtue and wisdom: most such colleges have too few such at present, in part for lack of trying to find them until the last hour before the fall. They may recruit some from the intellectual proletariat of this decade, the able and humane young scholars, well qualified by degrees and temperament, but cast out by Behemoth University because they will not submit to the degradation of the democratic dogma, or self-exiled from Behemoth because they know that the unexamined life is not worth living.

For not all of the educated young men and women made superfluous by our American overproduction of doctoral degrees, this past quarter of a century, have become evangels of revolution. Among them are young scholars of a conservative bent, reduced to the circumstances of base mechanicals because we have created more doctors than were dreamt of in any other age's philosophy.

One such, a friend of mine, wrote to me from Maine in 1974. He had been dismissed from a state university post as redundant, enrollments considered—and, there is reason to suspect, because he did not ride the ideological currents of the hour. He is able, temperate, personable, with a modest dignity—and when he wrote to me, he was a mason's helper. He had decided not to seek just any random opportunity to re-enter the Academy.

"I concluded that I would be better off to take a menial position which was understood to be temporary than to take a position that might prove to be unsatisfactory and from which I would wish to flee in short order," he told me. "In the meantime I am earning a bare living as a mason's helper. It is very demanding work, and I am quite tired at the end of the day, but I am thankful for a job that permits me to keep our savings intact and at the same time is such that I can leave in good conscience should something I like come up." He has a handsome wife who writes children's stories and reads seriously, and two small children.

In the little industrial town where he was living in 1974, this scholar found the schools preferable to those in the university town he had quitted. The curriculum there had been progressive and innovative, he wrote, "and, as you might expect, very much without rigor or content. Here the schools are more traditional, and, I think, more effective." His children got on well with the local juveniles—who, however, were surprised at finding a professor's offspring among them. "The schools do not appear to be troubled with some of the evils of other areas—drugs, lack of discipline, etc. It is a nice place to raise children."

Of course this husband and this wife were "proletarians" only in outward standing, temporarily. "We continue our pursuit of the understanding of the spirit," he remarked. "My wife has joined, or I should say started, a prayer-group here. . . . I see in your columns that you find much of value in the writings of Charles Williams. I believe that these books of his have influenced me as much as anything I have read. The characters of Sybil in *The Greater Trumps* and the Archdeacon in *War in Heaven* have instructed me in ways that essays, philosophic and religious tracts, and even the Bible have not been able to do.

"One line of thought I have been turning over lately has been the opposition between political concerns and the spirit. I am gaining a glimmering of that opposition intimated or asserted by Plato, Cicero, and St. Augustine. I have lost almost all interest in practical affairs and find most of them either dreary or droll. I cannot imagine myself teaching students again the intricacies of political science. I suppose I am taking one of Plato's choices—to turn my back on the city and attempt to get my soul in order. Once my soul is in some order (with God's help), perhaps I will regain my earlier interest.

"We are comfortable and at peace with the world. I have an inner calm that I have not known for years. I have a strong belief in divine providence, and truly believe that all the minor troubles we have encountered have been for our own benefit."

With strong natures, adversity is good for the soul. Yet it's a mad world, my masters, when the hewing of wood and the drawing of water is done by such a couple as these two in Maine, while tenured mediocrity prevails on most campuses. I have known not a few colleagues in the Academy upon whose shelves the only volumes to be found were free sample copies of textbooks; meanwhile, the true enterprising talents are denied fulfillment—and may turn sour.

It is natures such as my friends' that the independent college requires, if it is to renew its old task of opening minds and hearts to the claim of moral worth. With selectivity, one could recruit from among the scholar-proletarians of this decade the whole staff of a good college, in fairly short order; of a college distinctly superior to most well-reputed colleges now existing. One of the defects of the typical professor is that he has lingered in the classroom, as pupil or teacher, all his years. The scholar-proletarians know something of the world, including the varieties of moral worth.

Were I president of an existing college, and had full authority, I would draw upon such "redundant" young scholars, contemplative but not afraid of work, to fill all sorts of posts now occupied by mere technicians. I would fill all vacancies upon the library's staff, for instance, with genuine scholars in some discipline or other; they could serve as adjunct professors, too. Why, my very buildings-and-grounds crew would be composed of stalwart Ph.D.'s, awaiting suitable preferment: intelligent people generally make the best laborers in any vineyard.

These are times in which it is some comfort to reflect that learning, like virtue, is its own reward. Read Boethius, ye well-schooled workers of the world; you have nothing to lose but your transcripts. This is a very big country, but perhaps some day things will get sorted out, and colleges which are supposed to teach an apprehension of wisdom and virtue actually will find professors to do just that, rather than leaving them to carry the hod; while students in quest of something for mind and conscience will contrive to grope their way to a college which has been trying to discover them, rather than being dispatched by the high-school guidance counsellor to the state college with the biggest indoor roller-skating rink in the world. Yet it takes time, God's own good time.

23

Central Political Power and Academic Freedom: 1975

ACADEMIC FREEDOM at last confronted in the United States, by 1975, the danger which had led to the formal establishment of statutes of academic freedom in German universities a hundred years earlier: that is, the powers of the central government to influence and direct the work of universities. Although German doctrines of academic freedom had strongly influenced John Dewey and other founders of the American Association of University Professors, those American educators did not look upon the federal government of the United States as a potential menace to the intellectual liberties of professors—except, perhaps, in time or war or of controversies over foreign policy. For in those days, the federal Office of Education, and Congress, scarcely touched at all upon the concerns of university and college; and the great majority of students then were enrolled at independent institutions which owed to the federal government nothing at all, and to the state governments nothing but their charters.

Yet a century after the German universities had given the term "academic freedom" to the higher learning, American universities and colleges were compelled to spend plenty of money and time, often in vain, to satisfy or resist the intervention of federal and state political functionaries in their most intimate concerns—among these, even dormitory arrangements and regulations. (This was one reason why, by 1975, a growing tendency could be discerned to choose lawyers as college administrators.) By 1975, federal and state "compliance officers" of one sort or another were making their rounds of the big campuses almost weekly. University officials appealed to the courts, or besought the intervention of congressmen; an adversary relationship developed between government and university. Merely to fill out federal forms and to comply with the minimum regulations of the government was a large item of cost which might unbalance the budget of even a good-sized college. The intrusion of central political power became increasingly pervasive and arbitrary.

Some professors still thought of "academic freedom" as freedom from the meddling of Vested Interests, or of religious fundamentalists, or of overzealous patriotic groups. But rarely, by 1975, was there need for repelling boarders from such a craft. It had become the civil servant who dictated to president, dean, and professor; and that civil servant knew even less about a university's ends and functioning than had the meddlers of yesteryear.

This intervention by the political power had commenced with massive federal grants and subsidies to higher education—except, of course, for the power of the purse always possessed by state legislatures over state educational institutions. (This state legislative power did not often lead to the present degree of regulation and influence by federal officials; in the 'Fifties, the president of a state college in Alabama told me that the Alabama legislature, as a body, did not much interfere with his institution; it was individual members of the legislature, asking favors for the children of constituents, who occasionally troubled him.) To the power gained over the Academy, during the Eisenhower and Johnson administrations, by massive grants, there was added presently intervention on the grounds of civil rights, occupational health and safety requirements, fairness to the handicapped, and all the other paternalistic legislation of the 'Sixties and 'Seventies; and the end had not come by 1975.

As the Second World War had drawn to a close, leaders in education generally had feared the possibility of central political interference, and had spoken out against it. In 1945, a joint statement had been issued by the American Council on Education and the National Education Association:

"The first purpose of this document is to warn the American people of an insidious and ominous trend in the control and management of education in the United States.

"For more than a quarter of a century, and especially during the last decade, education in the United States, like a ship caught in a powerful tide, has drifted ever further into the dangerous waters of federal control and domination.

"This drift has continued at an accelerated pace during the war. Present signs indicate that unless it is sharply checked by an alert citizenry, it will continue even more rapidly after the war.

"It is the deliberate and reasoned judgment of the two educational commissions who join in the appeal which this document makes that the trend toward the federalizing of education is one of the most dangerous of the current scene."

That was bold language. Yet at the time of the passage of the National Defense Education Act, thirteen years later, this opposition to federal funding and to some degree of federal direction had melted away, with only here and there the sound of warning voices in the Academy: for university and college thought that they needed a great deal of money from the federal treasury. Opposition to the benefactions of the Johnson administration had been even feebler. Thenceforward, federal largesse to university and college was expanded—despite attempts of the Nixon administration to reduce the scope of such aid—and endeavors by educational institutions to resist federal controls usually were unsuccessful.

By 1975, if a university or college failed to satisfy the Department of Health, Education, and Welfare, or some other federal agency, that it had complied fully with a particular directive—why, that institution was threatened with being deprived not only of its allocation of funds for the particular activity involved, but of all federal funding whatsoever. And by 1975 academic administrators, with few exceptions, did not see how their institutions possibly could survive without money from Washington. The piper was calling the tune almost daily, on many a campus. How much academic freedom remained? The more ground that the central government (by 1975 "federal" only in name) gained, the greater seemed its appetite for power over all higher education; exemptions from Washington directives were cancelled.

The federal government's Affirmative Action program was an unpleasant case in point. Enforced by both the Department of Justice and the Department of Health, Education, and Welfare, this scheme required practically all employers to furnish proof that they were endeavoring sedulously to employ more women, blacks, and other members of "minorities". The Academy was not exempted from this federal prodding. In effect, Affirmative Action forced quotas of the newly-privileged "minorities" upon university and college faculties, even though the enforcing agencies evasively denied that they desired employment quotas, and even though there existed reasons why more professorships had been held by men of Jewish stock than by women of American Indian stock. (Jews, of course, were not permitted to enroll themselves as a minority: they were lumped together with WASPs.)

Was this the freedom of the Academy, supposed to be founded upon performance and merit, and to be no respecter of persons?

Until 1975, although Affirmative Action was thrust rudely upon all universities and colleges which had accepted benefactions from the federal government, such few institutions of higher learning as had rejected these gifts had remained exempt from Affirmative Action rules. But in 1975, a functionary of HEW issued a ukase: beginning in 1976, all universities and colleges which accepted students who received grants, scholarships, or loans through the medium of HEW must comply with all sorts of federal regulations, and most immediately with Affirmative Action directives.

The handful of universities and colleges in question did not themselves receive gifts or loans from Washington; rather, some of their students had benefited from the federal treasury as recipients of veterans' benefits, Social Security payments, federally-guaranteed loans, and the like. Even so, the independent colleges were ordered to obey Big Brother, or Big Sister. The authority cited was Title IX of the federal Educational Amendments of 1972. An obscure provision therein was extravagantly interpreted to signify that, for a beginning, private colleges which accepted students who in turn accepted some federal largesse must comply fully with the iron regulations of Affirmative Action, and prove, if possible, their innocence of "discrimination."

To this rescript, there promptly rejoined Dr. George Roche, president of Hillsdale College. That Michigan institution had a long history of welcome to women and blacks; but Hillsdale, which had refused to accept any government subsidies, did not mean to be converted into an instrument of national political policy. Not long before, Dr. Roche had published a slim book about the follies of Affirmative Action; perhaps that was why HEW chose Hillsdale as the first specific victim of this enlargement of Title IX.

"Rather than allow such a federal takeover of our campus," Dr. Roche declared, "we are prepared to refuse compliance with the government edicts now proposed. None of us at Hillsdale underestimates the power of the federal government to harass and possibly destroy those who do not comply, but we feel the fight must be made if independent education is to endure in America." If necessary, Hillsdale would refuse to accept undergraduates who held federal scholarships, grants, loans, or other benefits, but would set up its own special scholarship fund to provide for students deprived of Washington's gifts.

Taken aback by this rebuff from a college so small and so precariously financed as Hillsdale, and by a similar declaration of non-compliance from big Brigham Young University, the officials of HEW conferred among themselves. After some months, they informed Hillsdale College that HEW, while still asserting the right to deny federally-funded student loans and other benefits to Hillsdale, nevertheless would refrain from taking action against Hillsdale College—for the time being. (It would not be until December, 1977, with a new secretary in charge at HEW, that the "Affirmative Action" zealots of HEW would proceed against Hillsdale a second time.) Hillsdale's stand against submitting to federal direction was approved by most of the national press, including some distinctly liberal publications and journalists.

Nor were the Affirmative Action directives actually enforced, for the time being, against Brigham Young University. Brigham Young had two protections: first, presumably the University would appeal to the federal courts on the ground of the first clause of the First Amendment, pleading that the University's religious principles were violated by certain federal directives; second, the Mormons had considerable political influence, and not in Utah only. Hillsdale and Brigham Young thus were reprieved.

But after some months of hesitation and planning, HEW resumed its offensive against the non-juring colleges, many of them less stiff of backbone than Hillsdale and Brigham Young. A new victim for exemplary punishment was chosen: Rockford College, in Illinois, smaller than Hillsdale. Rockford's president, John Howard, had been active for twenty-three years in the resistance to governmental encroachment upon the old immunities of the Academy. Such obduracy is resented by Washington. Early in 1977, Rockford College would be informed that because President Howard had not signed the required certificate of compliance with Affirmative Action and allied federal regulations, HEW no longer would authorize guaranteed loans to students enrolled at Rockford. This hurt, Rockford being a small college.

Having set this example, by late 1977 HEW would inform all those colleges which had not previously submitted that unless their officers should subscribe to statements of compliance, various federal benefactions would be denied to those colleges and their students. Some colleges might be unable to survive, if deprived of these various forms of assistance from public funds; many more would be strongly tempted to submit, even though they suspected this to be only a prelude to more dictation from Washington. In several particulars, HEW's directives to the colleges and universities clearly would exceed what had been the intent of Congress; perhaps only additional legislation in Congress would salvage some freedom of choice for the colleges.

The problem here was larger than the question of whether one approved or disapproved of Affirmative Action, OSHA, and the various other measures which, in the Johnson, Nixon, Ford, and Carter administrations, had piled burdens and regulations upon the state and the independent colleges alike. This problem was bigger than the question of whether one was liberal or conservative in political inclination. The real issue was whether university and college must submit, thereafter, to whatever congressional or executive mood might be in the ascendant, and to whatever caprice or prejudice might predominate in the Office of Education or the Department of Justice—on pain of extinction through being deprived of federal funds, or at least much damaged by such withdrawal of support. Both federal and state bureaucracies were enlarging their jurisdiction wherever possible: this furnished employment for their numerous personnel, seemed to justify their large powers, and gave civil servants a satisfying sense of being civil masters. Universities and colleges, which had been virtually exempt from political dictation until the Second World War, were a new world for political bureaucracy to conquer.

In 1975, the decisions as to how far federal interference with institutions of higher learning should go were almost wholly in the power of the federal agencies. Congress could not well act as a national board of education: Congress had much else to do, and notoriously had been unable to control effectively the Executive Force and the federal agencies in their administration of many other federal programs authorized by Congress. University and college presidents, who previously had fancied themselves to be molders of national policy, by 1975 were chagrined to discover that they counted for little when some federal bureau had made up its mind to chasten them. They complained, too, that the mass media paid little attention to their difficulties with the government. Was Leviathan about to swallow them?

Even the first clause of the First Amendment was no sure protection for church-related colleges, by 1975, from federal or state intervention. In many states, Catholic universities and colleges had reconstituted their boards of trustees; had abandoned requirements for the study of religion by their undergraduates; had pulled down saints' images and crucifixes; and in other ways had half secularized themselves in order to be assured of obtaining public funds.

These church-related colleges, Protestant or Catholic, sometimes had even more to dread from state governments than from the federal apparatus. At a time when their problems of enrollment and finance were acute, state governments might offer them rescue of a sort—and so seduce them into becoming secular institutions subject to regulation by political authorities.

In the state of New York, by 1975, only two Catholic colleges had refused to submit their policies and curricula to the jurisdiction of the educationist authorities of New York: Niagara University and Molloy College. Molloy's courageous president, Sister Janet Fitzgerald, had set down in her report of 1973-74 the reasons why Molloy (a girls' college, controlled by Dominican nuns) had refused to accept the Bundy Money from the state of New York.

This Bundy Money commemorated McGeorge Bundy, at the head of the Ford Foundation in 1975—educational bureaucrat, Washington bureaucrat (especially grand as an architect of fiasco in Vietnam), foundation bureaucrat. Bundy it was who had headed a commission appointed by Governor Nelson Rockefeller to work out a system of direct financial aid from the state of New York to "private" colleges, circumventing the anti-Catholic "Blaine Amendment" to the constitution of New York. New York's legislature had enacted the Bundy Aid, which paid to the participating colleges varying sums of money, per capita, in proportion to the numbers of bachelors, masters, doctors, and the like whom those church-related or independent colleges graduated.

In exchange for this scanty mess of pottage, the participating colleges were required to surrender their birthright. If church-related colleges, they must declare themselves secular colleges thereafter; if Catholic colleges, they must disavow institutionally thereafter the word and belief "Catholic." They were henceforth to be lukewarm, neutral—and perhaps spewed out of His mouth. It was very thin gruel indeed that these quondam Catholic colleges obtained from the treasury of the state of New York, but they swallowed it.

Sister Janet pointed out some of the conditions exacted by the New York commissioner of education, where "Catholic" colleges were concerned.

First, if religious studies and courses in philosophy were to be included in the core curriculum, the number of credit hours required in those two disciplines could not be disproportionate to those mandated in other fields.

Second, no student might be required to attend chapel or to enroll in any course in theology.

Third, catalogues, student and faculty handbooks, charters, and other publications by the college must be submitted for review to the state educational functionaries; such publications must not contain any suggestion that the college acknowledged religious purposes in the higher learning.

Fourth, the college's board of trustees must include lay members in the majority, and no fixed number of religious might be specified as members of the board; nor might bishops, superiors of orders, and the like be *ex officio* members of such boards.

Fifth, a team of Protestant theologians would be sent to every formerly "Catholic" college that accepted Bundy Money, to interview all members of the college's faculty who taught religion or philosophy. This Protestant team would demand full information about the background of the faculty, about the content of courses, and about all final examinations given. "The team also inspects the library to ascertain if there is a disproportionate number of Catholic books."

So Sister Janet Fitzgerald and the other Dominican sisters of Molloy College, all honor to them, rejected McGeorge Bundy's thirty pieces of silver—much though Molloy College needed funds. There is something worse than academic poverty, and that is academic servility.

It is pleasant to record that taking the king's academic shilling still involves perils. Ever since the National Defense Education Act of 1958, a great part of the federal expenditures for higher education had been squandered on educationist fads, foibles, and frauds. In 1975, the long if tardy arm of federal justice began to collar some of the educationist depredators.

In Boston, during 1975, a federal grand jury indicted two schoolmen for theft of federal funds—a professor of education at the University of Massachusetts and a Worcester public-school administrator. Other indictments were to follow, and not in Massachusetts alone. The director of investigation and security for the Department of Health, Education, and Welfare somewhat ominously mentioned that similar "incidents" of theft and fraud, at the expense of HEW's educational undertakings, had occurred at universities and colleges in Chicago, Atlanta, Dallas, and Los Angeles.

The Boston indictments were for the relatively petty purloining of some twenty-nine thousand dollars, expended in part upon a junket to Puerto Rico by these scholars and their boon companions. But the total sums stolen or squandered at the University of Massachusetts alone were vastly greater. Dr. Robert Wood, president of that university, in the beginning appeared to be about as eager to open this can of worms as President Nixon had been to seek out the Watergate burglars. But *The Daily Hampshire Gazette,* at Northampton, began publishing a series of courageous and accurate articles about the scandalous doings in the University's "innovating" School of Education. By February, 1975, President Wood was informing the university's Senate that perhaps two million, four hundred thousand dollars in federal grants might have been misused at his university, through "misfeasance, malfeasance, and nonfeasance."

The University's School of Education, headed during this corrupt era by one Dr. Dwight Allen (who later retreated to Lesotho, in southern Africa), was proud of its unparalleled range of programs nobody ever had imagined before; also proud of wheedling fifteen million dollars out of Uncle Sam. Dean Allen declared after the revelations of theft and waste, "I didn't worry when things were falling between the cracks. But obviously there were some cracks that turned out to be larger than anticipated." President Wood did not fret about cracks, either, during nearly the whole of the seven-year Allen regime: in 1971, Dr. Wood had told the University of Massachusetts faculty, "The recent advances in the School of Education are undeniably ones of superb innovation and basic wholesomeness."

Yet that School of Education, despite some honest professors within it, had been worse than a thieves' kitchen: it had been a degree-mill. During the seven years of Allen's deanship, the School granted five hundred and seventeen doctorates—twenty-six per cent of the total number of doctorates conferred by the University of Massachusetts since that state university's founding. It was not difficult to obtain a doctorate after one year of "study" and attendance at few or no classes, even though the doctoral candidate might possess only an undistinguished bachelor's degree.

Take the case of the assistant professor of education indicted for theft by that Boston grand jury: one "Doctor" Cleo H. Abraham. The indicted Abraham contrived to obtain a University of Massachusetts doctorate in fifteen months—meanwhile being paid an annual salary of twelve thousand dollars as a full-time lecturer and registering in five courses. So soon as he was elevated to the doctoral dignity, Abraham was appointed a graduate faculty member, and within twelve months was made chairman of four doctoral-dissertation committees. Two years after styling himself doctor, he was handling a full million dollars in federal grants; his salary as assistant professor was nineteen thousand dollars, but perhaps he found that niggardly, for the grand jury charged him with two counts of conspiring "to steal, purloin, and convert . . . things of value from the federal government."

A principal defender of the Allen regime at this interesting School of Education was the university's provost, Dr. Robert Gluckstern—the very gentleman appointed by the university to investigate rumors of strangeness at the School of Education. Provost Gluckstern's son Steven received a doctorate from that School without being registered in any of the School's courses, as a reward for "participating in alternative schools" as he wandered over the face of the United States; he passed directly from bachelor of arts to doctor of education. Another of the Provost's relatives obtained such a distinguished doctorate, and the Provost's spouse was paid a salary by the School of Education.

Curiouser and curiouser! I obtained reams of reports on these instructive affairs at the University of Massachusetts. They were not all bad: the School had been kind to "minority" applicants seeking doctorates—especially if these "minority" representatives were powerful and affluent.

Among the doctoral candidates at the University's Amherst campus were such grandees as Bill Cosby, comedian, and Jesse Jackson, the zealot for civil rights in Chicago. Some such were recruited "to add unusual variety." Cosby, though innocent of a bachelor's degree, was awarded plenty of credits for absentee work in television; he began to prepare his doctoral dissertation—which was to be a television program. Jackson registered in 1972 for four courses, but presently ceased to appear. It is wearisome commuting from Chicago to Amherst.

While the generous efforts to elevate the culturally deprived were in progress, at least two million, four hundred thousand dollars appear to have slipped through the cracks. Former Dean Allen said that could happen easily, because HEW money-management requirements were lax. And if one aspires to become the Napoleon of "innovative education", why fret about other people's money? Feel free, and be free with the dollars; that's one form of innovative academic freedom.

HEW's money was the root of many evils in the School of Education, clearly, and did mischief to educational quality and to professional integrity on hundreds of American campuses. And now, in 1975, having taken King HEW's shilling—or perhaps having purloined it—various administrators and professors might be flung into the hoosegow. Some seemed worthy of the chair of applied electricity.

* * *

What did the management and mismanagement of HEW and other federal and state agencies mean for academic freedom in these United States?

They meant that more and more the character and general policy of university and college would be bent to suit whatever the interests of the government might be—supposing that the enlargement of political authority over the Academy should continue. Ordinarily this control would result in utilitarian emphasis, at the expense of theory, humane learning, and diversity.

They meant that a common pattern would be imposed upon all universities and colleges, in a variety of ways; innovation and reform would be discouraged; and common standards of instruction—not very high ones—probably would be exacted. One institution of higher learning seemed as good as another institution of higher learning, in the eyes of bureaucratic centralizers, or maybe a little better.

They meant that professors would be treated more and more as civil servants, bought with a price, and that those obdurate scholars who found it dishonorable to accept such political dictation also would find it difficult to do their teaching elsewhere; for encroaching centralization would have left few or no sanctuaries where dissidents might find themselves free to teach what they believed.

They mean that independent universities and colleges might find themselves quite soon with their backs to the wall—being regulated as if they were "public" institutions, but thrown only bones from public funds. The political power—or at least the bureaucracy, national or state—tended to resent the survival of "private" institutions with their vestigial claims to autonomy and freedom. Freedom and diversity being closely intertwined, the fewer alternatives to state-directed schooling there are, the less academic freedom survives.

They meant that higher education would be almost wholly secularized, with the elimination of the church-related colleges that had been the earlier sources of the higher learning in America, or with their subjection to the secularizing insistence of the political apparatus. Freedom of religious instruction in the Academy would be one aspect of academic freedom that would receive short shrift.

They meant that the degradation of the democratic dogma would tend to prevail in the American higher learning, since central political direction compels education to conform to what the average politician, or perhaps the average voter, can apprehend and approve. Why waste time and funds upon "undemocratic" and abstract intellectual disciplines? Results would be demanded, and "impractical" studies curtailed. If the federal government should pour its appropriations—the money being raised, of course, from general taxation that would reduce private benefaction to the higher learning—into technological development, say, then the complying universities and colleges would find it necessary to spend less money and time upon humane or social studies. The professors of classics or of anthropology would be free to take up some other line of work—in a municipal junkyard, conceivably. The whole intellectual and cultural drift of America would be determined by Congress and by federal agencies. What sort of academic freedom would subsist then?

That the long-run result of such "democratic" attitudes in higher education would be unpleasant for everybody; that a people intellectually mediocre would be feeble in public policies at home and abroad, and that even the economy would suffer—those arguments would not be well understood by the typical politician, civil servant, or average citizen. The higher learning would be directed by the half-educated and the quarter-educated, through the political apparatus. Anybody who has read Tocqueville understands the dangerous tendency in democracies toward intellectual dullness, and the possibility of a well-meant but repressive "democratic despotism", fussy rather than brutal, stifling all high endeavors, keeping human beings in perpetual childhood. There would survive *some* academic freedom—the freedom for every professor to be precisely like every other professor, and for every student to be precisely like every other student.

I do not say that resistance to these centralizing and politicizing tendencies is vain; I do suggest that resistance has become increasingly difficult. To establish formal statutes defining the rights and privileges of institutions of higher learning, here in the United States, right now, would be harder than it was to do that in Germany during the last three decades of the nineteenth century. This country is much bigger and more populous than Germany was; there are far, far more universities and colleges, with differing objectives; and, the encroachments of government being more subtle in our time and our universities and colleges not being so deep-rooted as were some of those in Germany, our institutions are liable to surrender to Leviathan without much of a struggle, unconditionally. So have we drifted toward academic conformity to state policy, and the concept of the university as a "service institution" eclipses the old notion of the university as a center for intellectual freedom and for the pursuit of truth. With reference to conventional limited concepts of academic freedom, I am not suggesting that academic tenure will be abolished, any more than the civil-service tenure of agents of HEW will be abolished. One could enjoy tenure, though not freedom, in the universities of Germany under

Hitler or of Russia under Stalin. The requirement for tenure was acquiescence in state policy. That would be the requirement for tenure in a standardized, nationally-directed American system of higher education.

24

Collegiate Cacophony: 1976

ON THE OCCASION of the two-hundredth birthday of the United States of America, the most conspicuous thing about the higher learning in this land was its triviality. I refer to the college, mostly, as distinguished from the graduate school; for although sometimes the graduate schools of 1976 were grossly sobersided, and sometimes pretentious and fraudulent, "trivial" was not quite the adjective for them. I happen to think that a college should consist of more than trivia. My concerns in this chapter are musical trivia, students' intellectual trivia, and administrators' muddled trivia. These trivialities made of the campus in 1976 a marvellously disharmonious racket.

"Whirl is king, having overthrown Zeus," Aristophanes wrote of fifth-century Athens. Just as surely, Dinos reigns upon the twentieth-century campus; and merry old soul that he is, Dinos insists upon his court musicians—the jukebox, the hi-fi, and the blaring TV.

I refer to the domination of the typical campus by the ghastly "music" of a kind which, far from soothing the savage beast, obliterates conversation, reason, and even genuine emotion. Plato, who made music as important as mathematics and dialectic in his educational scheme, tells us that a people's whole character may be determined by their music. That being so, it is difficult to restrain a shudder at the cacophony of the typical campus.

Take the representative student-union building. Its coffee-shop, and probably its lounges, are devastated from opening to closing by juke-box cacophony. It had become impossible, by 1976, for students and professors simply to talk together in such places: literally, they could not hear themselves think. And the juke records were not chosen by the college students, really, but on the basis of "pop ratings" nationally ascertained. That is, the college discos ordered the recordings which were reported as selling best in record shops throughout the country. Who bought most of the records in American record shops? Why, idle children twelve or thirteen years old. The taste of urchins was imposed upon the Academy.

Why did not professors and students rise against this tyranny over their auditory nerves? Well may one ask. Twenty years earlier, Professor Robert Nisbet and I, sitting with some officers of the student council of the University of California at Riverside, had asked those lively-minded students why they didn't put more nearly tolerable records in the union jukebox. They had replied candidly that the boxes were owned, and the records supplied, by The Syndicate. Nobody ventured to meddle with such arbiters of taste.

Lines from Yeats' poem "The Leaders of the Crowd" apply with a significance more than political:

"They have loud music, hope every day renewed
"And heartier loves; that lamp is from the tomb."

The scholar's lamp flickers feebly on the mass campus; it glows uncertainly in the blast of cacophony even on the campuses of old liberal-arts colleges. A decade ago I delivered the last commencement-address at the dignified old College of Charleston—that is, in the last year of the College's independence, before it was taken over by the state of South Carolina. A concert by a naval band was part of the ceremonies. It turned out to be a rock and jazz concert, at the insistence of the petty officer who was bandmaster; he knew how to drown those eggheads' ceremonies of innocence.

A college may have a sound department of music, a good staff, a very tolerable student body—and yet submit supinely to such imposed "musical" savagery. What percentage of the student body really likes the mind-blasting cacophony? About ten per cent, at best, I estimate. The large majority of students, and all professors, merely endure this as a necessary evil, like death and taxes—one of the traditions of incivility which it would be undemocratic to challenge.

Even in rough bars it is somewhat otherwise. I know a bar where a juke-playing patron was shot to death a few years ago because he insisted on playing the "Beer-Barrel Polka" on the jukebox once too often, despite the civil remonstrances of a gun-toting drinker. And I myself, in another tavern, have asked the bartender, "Has anyone requested that tune on the radio right now?" And when he has answered nay, I have said, "Then I request that it *not* be played." But nobody has that much backbone on the typical campus—not the dean, not the president. They might offend the vice-president for fiscal affairs, who thinks that the juke adds to his revenues.

Let me record one honorable exception. At Albion College, in Michigan, there lies within the student-union building a place of refreshment known as the Kulturkeller, rather pleasantly designed. There stands a jukebox near the entrance to this subterranean coffee-shop. Yet not once have I heard this juke-box play. Dr. Bernard Lomas, Albion's president, informs me that in times past a student, a black girl of herculean frame, became so vexed at the box's cacophony that she picked it up and hurled it against a wall. It has been dumb ever since. This was one act of militancy approved by both the college president and by this writer. At Albion the students can talk with one another, or study as they sip coffee, and they like it that way. At Albion, The Syndicate does not debauch the Muses.

I had found it otherwise at Ohio State University, when I had debated against William Kunstler on the question of the insurrection at Attica prison, which had occurred a few weeks earlier. What serried ranks of student freaks in the front rows of the auditorium, screeching hysterically in approval of their hero of the moment, Kunstler, fresh from Attica—Kunstler, writhing like a serpent at the podium as he praised the inmates of another sort of state institution! After this encounter, some non-freakish students wished to talk with me at length. But the student union was closing, presumably to reduce nocturnal depredations by students. We went out to the street, lined with beer-and-juke joints, and looked for a quiet student hang-out where we might converse. There was none such—not one. We had to retreat to my hotel-room, and go coffeeless, there being no public place for conversation open then in the campus hotel, either. Here, on one of the biggest campuses of the world, there apparently was not a single public spot where a few folk could talk together: in the avenue's juke-joints, crowded by thousands of students that evening, the cacophony made communication by tongue and ear quite impossible. Why wonder at the hysteria of the Kunstler enthusiasts? They never had opportunity for rational discourse; life for them was rock, rock, rock around the clock.

Within nearly all the dormitories and fraternities of the typical American campus, cacophony triumphs insanely. Some undergraduates say they cannot study unless rock devours all lesser sounds; they have been reared that way. If their roommates are vexed by this habit—well, that's the way the cookie crumbles. Occasionally a residence hall for honors students, like Koon Hall at Hillsdale College, may be spared this affliction: if you're a superior student already, you are permitted to study. Elsewhere, when the windows are open, the frenetic sound pours all the way to the courthouse.

In considerable part, this hegemony of the mindless votaries of noise arose during the 'Sixties of student unrest. Acid rock was music to the ears of student psychopaths. In the name of "liberation", the more senseless undergraduates demanded, and generally obtained, the "right" to anarchy in the dorm: no proctors, no house-mothers, no restrictions upon drink, concupiscence, pot-smoking—and no quiet hours. Dinos rejoiced.

But that decade was past, by 1976; a licentious toleration had disgraced itself; and the students of the 'Seventies had the sins of the 'Sixties visited upon them. Probably most of the dormitory inmates would have preferred, in 1976, to have the stereos and the radios and the TVs stilled in some degree, and prohibited during late hours. Many students, strange to relate, actually had rediscovered the pleasures of conversation and reading. Yet academic authorities, still trembling at recollections of Weatherpersons, failed to restore auditory order.

I did not find, nevertheless, that college libraries had been surrendered to the tastes of undergraduates who relished girlie magazines and horror comics. I did not find, in 1976, that the counter-culture had been permitted to convert chemical laboratories into manufactories for bombs. I did not find that heroin was distributed at college expense in the gymnasia.

So I marvelled at the pusillanimity of college authorities who feared to set their faces against the horrid oligarchy of the Rockers. Juke cacophony rises out of the depths; while colleges used to aspire to the heights. Carrie Nation, thou shouldst be with us now. Who will lay the axe to the Great God Juke? We might try plugging the contraption with foreign coins, coated in epoxy glue. When decent music is played in the union of Behemoth State U., we may venture to deny the aphorism of André Siegfried: "America is the only nation to have passed from barbarism to decadence without having known civilization."

In the year of our Lord one thousand nine hundred and seventy-six, I confess, no insubstantial portion of the campus population, at the average college, was very nearly functionally illiterate: ask any English instructor. Demon TV had been the nannie of such, and they had suffered, many of them, under the look-say method of non-reading, and run, Spot, run. They hooked up with the counterculture, most of these functional illiterates aspiring to the degree of bachelor of arts or of science, and found other diversions on the campus, or nearby, to while away the time.

All the bigger campuses, in 1976, had substantial quotas of these enrolled non-students, though the proportion of young folk who looked like ruffians and trulls was less than it had been a decade earlier. The humane scale had been lost long ago at the big campuses, together with tolerable manners. The illiterate undergraduates, some even unable to profit by credit-granting courses in remedial reading, seemed sour and unhappy at precisely the time in their lives when they should have been absurd in a different fashion. Often they would have felt more secure, I reflected, and have found more moral companionship, had they strolled the streets of Palermo or Fez, rather than the campus of Behemoth U. Little true love survives in an intellectual brothel.

Speaking of bordellos, Michigan State University, East Lansing, in 1976 boasted a "porn queen", with something to offer students unprepared to read or think. She had enrolled in MSU's student body, and was maintaining a B-plus average in physical education. This talented young lady had transferred from Western Michigan University to Michigan State because she had been offered the managership of an "adult" skin-flick cinema in Lansing; she had built up the volume of its business to thirty-three thousand dollars a month. Also she was holding bargain sidewalk sales of printed pornography; and she had produced on her own, with capital from the Bahamas, a delightful film about gang rape, drawing her cast from among the undergraduates of MSU. As yet, in 1976, MSU was not granting theater-arts credit for participation in this young woman's undertakings, but I suppose that cultural lag will be remedied soon, and the porn-queen will become a professor, destined to rapid advancement through Affirmative Action.

Cinematographic rape, in 1976, was less frequent at Michigan State than was actual flesh-and-blood rape. Cheap and nasty schooling tends to produce some cheap and nasty minds. Much to the chagrin of the University's authorities, the student paper, *The Michigan State News,* was reporting and lamenting the actual rapes. Yet the streets of East Lansing were safer than those of Ann Arbor, where, in the vicinity of the venerable University of Michigan, some sixteen attacks on women (official reported cases, that is) occurred during October and November alone, in 1976. Once upon a time, students professed that their minds were ravished by learning; in 1976, bicentennial year, their bodies were ravished by learners.

A steady increase in the incidence of rape, like a steady increase in the rate of abortion, is one of the more grim and accurate indices of a civilization's decay. I did not find it surprising that the decline of intellectual standards, in 1976, was paralleled by the eroding of moral standards; or that when the inner check upon will and appetite had been neglected in schooling at every level, the outer check of the police-force could not cope with porn-queens, rapes, and abortions.

Beginning in 1973, at Michigan State University, the student health service consented to perform abortions upon pregnant female students. This had come at the insistence of an eminent member of MSU's board of trustees, Dr. Jack Stack, a physician of means, very active in Michigan's Republican party. (At state conventions of that party, which had elected him to MSU's governing board, Stack was to be seen strolling up and down the aisles, often munching popcorn compulsively from a large box, tubby, dishevelled, Michigan's Napoleon of feticide.) By 1976, however, the health-service abortions had ceased; there had been public protest against feticide as an "educational" service; and besides, Dr. Stack himself was proprietor of an abortion-clinic, Provincial House, only some two miles distant from MSU's campus; it was not very far for the girls to travel.

I had read Huxley's *Brave New World* while an undergraduate at Michigan State. In those days, there had occurred mutters in some quarters about forbidding study of Huxley's dystopia, because of the cartridge-belts stuffed with contraceptives. Orgy-porgy! Some had murmured that the book ought not to have been tolerated on the shelves of the college library, let alone discussed in literature courses. But by 1976 such censorial voices were stilled: the Olin Student Health Center had been distributing contraceptives to students for some years past, and the abortionist-trustee of the University was happy, for a fee, to terminate unwanted pregnancies. Back to your folios, Barbie! By 1976, Michigan State *was* Brave New World, and the cacophony drowned out obscurants' protests.

What, were there no good colleges in 1976? The question was put to me by that youthful beauty my wife, an ardent Thomist. She had been graduated from Molloy Catholic College for Women, in Long Island, a generation after my time—Molloy, whose Dominican nuns had cast back Bundy's thirty pieces of silver in the previous chapter of this book. Bohemian Tory that I was, I had married at the age of forty-five, having been too poor and too busy with wandering and writing even to think of marriage earlier, praise be. By 1976, Annette Yvonne Cecile and I had four lively daughters, the eldest of them aged eight years. Should our daughters enter college some day—and if so, what college?

Yes, there still were good colleges in 1976, some of them old, some of them new, some of them already mentioned in this book, some to be mentioned in later chapters, though none perfect. From time to time, in my syndicated newspaper column or in my *National Review* page, over the years, I had listed and described some of those generally commendable colleges; but on every such occasion, reproaches had been heaped upon my head. For, what with limitations of space, necessarily I had omitted some good colleges that I liked: their alumni, their presidents, their professors, their students, their public-relations directors had sent me letters burning with wrath or sorrow. So I shall not endeavor to list the good colleges here. I have visited hundreds of colleges, but some of those I suspect to be good I have not yet inspected. Some commendable colleges are very little known; while some of the colleges that once were fine, and still are famous, have sunk into decadence in one way or another. One or two good professors may be found at even the meanest college, while there are some incompetents on the staffs of even the grandest universities. The vast majority of freshmen seem to have chosen their colleges quite at random, or only because some chum was enrolling there. But I cannot bring order out of that confusion in these pages.

And besides the good colleges of 1976, there were many more colleges that could have been good, if only they had not tried so hard to be marvellous. So I conclude this chapter with some recommendations as to what a college ought *not* to try to do. They ought to drop the cacophony and resume the harmony.

First, the independent college ought to stop building more "plant." In 1976, we were confronted, as now, by the insane conjunction of erecting costly big buildings at the very time when enrollments were diminishing. I know that various benefactors who will not contribute liberally to general funds nevertheless are willing to give much money for bricks and mortar, perhaps because they rejoice in the glory of seeing graven above a college doorway the legend "Erasmus T. Chetnik Jr. Hall of Applied Business Management."

But I would say unto Mr. Erasmus T. Chetnik Jr., "Take back your fatal present!" New buildings seldom are endowed in perpetuity, and the costs of janitorial services and of repairs rise dismally today. Patch and repair your old buildings, President Boomer: many of them are handsome, all have memories clinging to them. And eschew those federal loans for classroom buildings and dormitories, for on many a hard-pressed campus Uncle Sam's benefactions of only yesterday are so many white elephants already.

Second, the independent college ought to drop out of competition in quasi-professional athletics. In this field, they stand at a hopeless disadvantage beside Behemoth State U. The rah-rah spirit of the 'Twenties or the 'Thirties may please some of the alumni, and more of what I call the "ersatz alumni"—the locals who never actually attended the college and never will contribute a plugged nickel to its endowments—but it leads to Avenus, that long-distance track. Let the athletic program be intramural, or at least inexpensive and incidental.

Third, the independent college ought not to convert itself into a vocational-training institute. A considerable proportion of the little colleges have tried just that, during the past few years; in the long run they must be disappointed, and perhaps extinguished.

The most widely prevalent form of this infatuation is to build a school of business administration. Although some of my better friends are professors of business administration, and although many well-intending parents think that such a "major" will unite the dubious prestige of a bachelor's degree with a country-club income, probably it would be a happier idea to found a School of Necromancy, perhaps the Russell Kirk School of Necromancy—which would have been more "relevant" in the year 1976, with many young Americans whoring after strange gods, and might offer superior financial rewards in the dawning age.

I declare it a very odd concept that in a time when junior executives stand by their thousands in the unemployment-compensation queues, we ought to turn out more of the breed by forced draft, at the expense of liberal learning. A business-administration degree means virtually nothing to potential employers today. If a college has helped young people to think logically, to write lucidly, and to acquire an ordered and integrated body of knowledge—why, they will not be left idle. But the average business-school graduate is a dullard, and the more able employers know that.

To acquire the genuine skills of business management—and I have known a fair number of successful men of business on a grand scale, in New York, Detroit, Chicago, and Los Angeles—it is necessary to enter upon apprenticeship or internship: business practices vary too much from year to year, or from concern to concern, for the imparting of competence in the abstract. On the other hand, if a quondam liberal-arts college offers a curriculum of typewriting, shorthand, simple accounting, and all that—why, the private proprietary commercial schools with their premises in downtown lofts do a better and cheaper and quicker job of that sort of useful training. Behemoth State U. already offers, on a tremendous scale, at lower tuition-cost and with fancier equipment, this "business administration" technique for which the independent college can claim no especial competence.

What independent colleges ought to teach is political economy—not the practical management of industry and commerce. What young person in his right senses would look to preferment in this realm by studying for four years at St. Gelasius College (enrollment 727) in Fiddletown, Oklahoma (population 1,221)?

Fourth, the independent college ought to abstain from accepting students whose achievements are so low that they cannot be accepted, even in these dog days, by Behemoth State U. Survival is not worth the price of intellectual degradation. And such strategy will fail, before many years elapse: what tolerable students remain will transfer to Behemoth in disgust, the epithet "Pinhead College" will reach the ears of foundations and affluent old ladies, and stupid alumni will be impecunious alumni.

Fifth, the independent college should not sink into the ethos of permissiveness. The better students, let alone their parents, are not enraptured of co-ed dorms, open classrooms, vandalism, perennial pseudo-political demonstrations, and all that. For the student who desires to learn something or other, or merely to rap for four years, a campus with a tolerable degree of order is a blessed sanctuary. When a college remains on a humane scale, the maintenance or recovery of order is no overwhelming problem: a salutary expulsion or two will solve it.

Sixth, the independent college should not promise to be all things to all men—or to all women. It ought to cherish its established character. A women's college should not open its doors to men; they wouldn't come, anyway. A men's college should stay masculine. A Catholic college should not pretend that it is ecumenical, or secular, or a good place to master Zen. A wide diversity of types of colleges is highly desirable, and nobody likes a mongrel. Let a college be itself, rather than a shadow of Behemoth State U. with inferior facilities and superior fees.

You object that a college which conforms to the preceding injunctions may not grow? True, quite possibly, although some colleges which have stuck by their old principles are growing nowadays despite themselves. But the "growthmanship" era in the American Academy is passing away. Growth in quality, not in quantity, is our urgent need now. It is better to school four hundred students well than to school forty thousand students wretchedly—better for the person, better for the republic. Behemoth State University is beyond reformation; yet conceivably the small independent college, granted imagination and fidelity, may enter upon a renaissance.

25

Identity, Images, and Education: 1977

D URING THE 'SEVENTIES, the rising generation had been infatuated with pseudo-religion, as during the 'Sixties the rising
generation had been infatuated with pseudo-politics, or ideology. The Jesus Freaks, the Moonies, the Children of God, the Hare
Krishna beggars, and the votaries of twenty more strange cults had
swarmed over the campuses and all the places of public concourse.
Transcendental Meditation—usually amounting to meditation upon
the self, which is unrewarding—had been especially popular in the
colleges, among boys and girls totally ignorant of metaphysics, logic, or
ethics. But by 1977, the force of this wave of sham spirituality seemed
spent, and those who would have any god but God were about ready to
drift into some other illusion. The rites of the pseudo-spiritual com-
mune had been found wanting; the "trips" of the narcotic trance had
taken their dupes nowhere. One thought of Hilaire Belloc's experi-
menting acquaintance who, in such a drug-induced trance, suddenly
had discovered the Secret of the Universe—and had written it upon a
sheet of note-paper before falling into bed. On rising in the morning,
he read what he had set down:

"Hogamus higamus, man is polygamous;
"Higamus hogamus, woman's monogamous."

So the year 1977 would have been propitious for a return to reason
upon the campus, what with this disillusion of the hour—had American college and university been prepared to offer much for mind and
conscience. But they were not so prepared. It was "back to business as
usual" on the typical campus in 1977—that is, to fun and games,
vocationalism in the "get ready for a job" sense of that word, the
educational boondoggle, the snap course, the mind-deadening survey

of something or other, the blinkered logicalism of the educationists, the dime-store positivism of social studies, the cafeteria curriculum of half-cooked intellectual fare.

One cause of the rising generation's irrationality during the 'Sixties and 'Seventies had been precisely this sort of boring and purposeless pretense of higher education, which left the intellect dull and the imagination starved. There had been other causes, too, bound up with the general afflictions of modern society and the particular blunders of life in America. But college and university had been meant to contend against mindlessness—to delineate some order in a chaotic time. They had failed to do that, in the 'Sixties and the 'Seventies; they had been altogether too deeply immersed in the vanities and trivialities of American society, "service institutions" that served only superficial wants.

Throughout the 'Seventies there had occurred endless talk about the "identity crisis"—the frustrated search for personhood, the quest for self-image; most of the discussion had been conducted in psychological and sociological jargon, ill-apprehended. Certainly many college students did not understand themselves; but few professors suggested to them that it is hard to know the self without recognizing the Other. Certainly many students were seeking for images upon which to form themselves; but the colleges and universities offering them few models for emulation, the students were thrust back upon the gross offerings of the commercial image-makers, the ideologues, and the "spiritual" charlatans.

"We should seek new ways of letting messages reach us: from our own past, from God, from the world which we may hate or think that we hate," Daniel Boorstin had written in 1961, in his book *The Image*. There is no "cure", he had said; only opportunity for discovery. "We must first awake before we can walk in the right direction. We must discover our illusions before we can even realize that we have been sleep-walking."

But the 'Sixties and 'Seventies, with their shallow ideological slogans, narcotic trips, inane cults, and delusory images, had been decades of sleep-walking for many or most of the young in America. College and university, generally speaking, had offered few vistas of discovery. When objects have been dropped, it is not surprising that many people become unsure of their own identity, and so shamble along with the rest of the Lonely Crowd. In the "therapeutic community" of Academe, the spiritually indisposed nursing other spiritually indisposed, no Object was recognized clearly, and no Other. By 1977, a good many people, among them even the pundits of television's talk-shows, had become aware that something was badly wrong with education at every level. Yet, fretting about identity and self-image, few of these half-awakened critics mentioned that identity is acquired through the performance of duty; or that to understand the self, one must dream the High Dream; or that for college and university to pursue truths, Truth must exist. Here lie mysteries; but college and university, in the 'Sixties and 'Seventies, had refused to admit the existence of mysteries; so the unsatisfied students had turned to the political mystagogue and the spiritual mystagogue, charlatans both. "Give us a sign!" Repelled by an arrogant smug rationalism, many students had recoiled into political or religious superstition. So some words of mine concerning the rediscovery of mystery, true mystery, may not be inappropriate as commentary upon the climate of opinion in 1977.

Who am I? That question troubled me when I was very young. One is fortunate if this problem enters one's head in childhood: for if one grapples with the conundrum as Hercules grappled with serpents in his cradle, he does not suffer an "identity crisis" in later years.

When a child, I used to look into a glass darkly. A recent version of the Bible translates that Pauline phrase as "Now we are looking into the riddle of a mirror." Staring fearfully at my reflection in a mirror, I used to ask myself, "Who am I?" Who is this little being to whom others have given the name "Russell Kirk"? I was conscious of my mirrored reflection: yet what is consciousness?—so the infantile metaphysician asked himself. Just who is this spark of consciousness beholding its flesh? Surely I, the beholder, was something more than flesh, I thought; for how could mere flesh ask the dread question, "Who am I?"

The awesomeness of such an inquiry by a child, I may add, is redoubled if he stands between two large looking-glasses, seeing his image reflected in both, diminished image succeeding diminished image, glass mocking glass, on to infinity, on to eternity. "Eternity, thou pleasing dreadful thought!" In heaven's name, who *am* I?

This questioned troubled the magnificent Hadrian, master of the world, and perhaps his ghost still ponders these mysteries, walking invisible the interior ramp of his tomb on the Tiber. This question perplexed the chief poet of our age, T. S. Eliot. One thinks of his Ariel poem "Animula":

"The heavy burden of the growing soul
"Perplexes and offends more, day by day:
"Week by week, offends and perplexes more

"With the imperatives of 'is and seems'
"And may and may not, desire and control.
"The pain of living and the drug of dreams
"Curl up the small soul in the window seat
"Behind the *Encyclopedia Britannica*."

These melancholy misgivings assail us all—or all of us who seem endowed with some degree of imagination and reason. Who am I? Eliot wondered that, grievously, in his early poems when his studies in Idealism led him perilously near the brink of solipsism. "I know who I am," Don Quixote de la Mancha exclaims, waking from his delusions; and as Miguel de Unamuno comments on those words, this discovery of one's true identity is a formidable act. Once we know who we are, and know that there are other real folk about us; once we understand that you and I are part of a community of souls—why, then it is possible to be fairly human, to live and die with dignity.

My eldest daughter, Monica, when she was less than three years old, suddenly said from her high-chair at the kitchen table to her mother and me, "I like myself!" My wife was not sure that she had understood the baby aright: "What did you say, Monica?" And the tiny girl answered, confidently, "I like myself: me, Monca."

Monica Rachel Kirk had discovered who she was. It is well to acquire a tolerable self-esteem at that age. The peril of many, arising not long later, is that one may acquire altogether too much self-esteem: one may become Kipling's orangutang, with "too much ego in his cosmos." As Arnold Toynbee remarks in *An Historian's Approach to Religion*, the human condition necessarily is tragic. For within every one of us two great conflicting impulses work. One of these is a yearning to make one's self the center of the universe; the other, a yearning for the love and communion of fellow-beings. And this contest ceases not until death. The person properly called "normal" is one who has maintained some tolerable tension between these impulses. The triumph of the first impulse may lead either to destruction or to a splendid misery; the triumph of the second impulse may bring on a feeble anonymity or a slavish running with the pack.

We cannot find our way in this world without images; for, as G. K. Chesterton tells us, all life is an allegory, and we can understand it only in parable. Nevertheless, the image often betrays. "Make unto yourself an image, and, in defiance of the Decalogue, worship it!" the young John Randolph of Roanoke wrote to a friend. No man of his time possessed a stronger self-image than did "Mad Jack" Randolph; yet in the fullness of time he learned that we all are made in the image of God, and breathe only because of that divine original. The saint is a human being who has put down his vanity: one who really does love his God with all his heart and soul, and his neighbor as himself. Still, it is not possible to know God unless one first knows himself; one proceeds from microcosm to macrocosm, from little human image to transcendent reality. Not knowing themselves well, most of the votaries of Transcendental Meditation, in the 'Seventies, could meditate only upon vacancy.

Because you and I are God's utopia, self-image is necessary: the old Hellenic truth, if you will, "Know thyself." Because you and I are God's utopia, also we endeavor to transcend the image of self and to glimpse the world beyond the world. My little daughter is strong in character because she knows and likes herself; but unless in the fullness of time she is able to see farther, to know and love something grander than herself, she will be—why, just an average sensual woman of our time.

Upon every American child of our era, there works the famous, or infamous, pressure of the "peer group"—that is, of juvenile mediocrity. In the typical household, children watch television before they can speak—indeed, before they can understand language; they are exposed to all the banality and crass commercialism of TV, and all of them watch the same stupid programs. In school, most of them study the same dreary basic readers. Superior achievement in school tends to be discouraged, sometimes even by physical menaces. School uniforms vanished years ago, but are supplanted by a fresh uniformity of bedraggled jeans and sweaters, the insignia of the proletarian Lonely Crowd. As they move toward high school, the boys are introduced to the imagination-ravaging blight of drugstore pornography; and perhaps the girls, too, are instructed by drive-in salacious films. There comes in time, for some, the affliction of narcotics, spreading outward from city to suburb to rural region. Thus the imagination first is neglected and then seared. The students of the 'Sixties and the 'Seventies were so prepared for college.

Such is the imagery which works upon the fancy of many of the rising generation. No previous generation had at its beck such instruments for corruption. Young people naturally look about for exemplars to emulate. Where do they find these nowadays? Why, possibly among television buffoons, racing-car drivers, perhaps eminent men of organized crime. School is detestable to many of the rising generation, understandably; as for the family—the parents' recreation commonly is the boob-tube, and every year more mothers are out at work. "Generation will not link with generation," in Burke's phrase, "and men will become as the flies of a summer." In such circumstances, when young people look for living models to pattern themselves upon, where will they find them? Why, they find one another: these are "other-directed" children, much of a sameness. Everywhere one hears boys and girls saying plaintively, "I don't want to be any different from anybody else." The image of the self is decayed to the image of the juvenile common denominator. Once upon a time, the saint and the knight, for most young people, were the exemplars; nowadays, little lonely dullness imitates little lonely dullness, at best; and parents are thankful for this small blessing, when the alternative is to take for mentors the racketeer and the tart. Upon these empty selves, in the 'Sixties and the 'Seventies, there burst the charismatic figures of the political charlatan and the religious charlatan.

When the images of reality have fallen to such grossness, why wonder that the notorious Identity Crisis afflicts every corner of society, fastening upon even the more promising natures? Who am I—only a cypher? Do I belong to anything enduring, or signify anything more than a perishable and precarious body? How do I fit into this sensual egalitarian world? Why wonder that some turn to the fantastic and perhaps fatal imagery of narcotics, for some moments' relief from the pain of being human?

In other ages, one found one's self in one's tight-knit family, one's tradition-governed close community, one's hopeful church, one's meaningful work. (Even following the plough confers identity of a sort.) For most people, that sort of identity sufficed. More inquiring minds and consciences, indeed, sought for loftier images; and these were found in religious art and music, in humane literature, in emulation of great and good men and women—living or dead. It is otherwise in our time, for most folk; and material gratifications do not compensate for the loss of self-confidence and the loss of membership in a community of souls. One may remark parenthetically that the material gratifications begin to diminish in their turn, once a society begins to suffer from failure of nerve; and the individuals in that decaying society cannot see themselves clearly.

In some ages—the period we call the Renaissance conspicuous among these—the overweening ego claims too much. In other ages—ours among them—the curse upon humankind is a listless uniformity, a submerging of the self in the herd. One parallel with our time is the age of Constantine, as described by Jacob Burckhardt. Life grows increasingly monotonous and impoverished; the old beliefs trickle away; even those in the seats of the mighty are coarse natures; the centralized state discourages and perhaps penalizes individual achievement; and increasingly the people ask themselves, "Is life worth living? Really, *is* it worth living? What are we doing here?"

One similarity between the age of Constantine and ours is the proliferation of curious cults, much of the populace whoring after strange gods. Within such a cult, grotesque though its tenets may be, not a few people diminish the problem of identity by immersing themselves in the cult's mysteries: Leviathan swallows them, and that is precisely what they desire, or think they desire. The cult's distorted images occupy the unbearable vacuum that had been left by the vanishing of the old images of the decaying traditional culture. No longer is there need for awareness of one's own identity, it seems: one has but to conform to, and obey unquestioningly, the new commandments of the Savage God—who may be either political or transcendental; or else submit to the absurd routine prescribed by some jelly-like set of abstractions.

In the year 1977, one mode for shedding the burden of selfhood was to submit to a pseudo-religious tyrant—any unctuous charlatan sufficed—and to spend one's days as a mendicant at airports, collecting alms for the greater glory of Simon Magus. The phenomenon that many air-travellers not merely submitted sheep-like to this infernal nuisance, but actually surrendered substantial hard cash to these young slaves, suggested that not a few airline credit-card holders didn't know who *they* were, either. In Aristotle's definition, a slave is a man who allows others to make his decisions for him. The person who has lost his own identity positively rushes to the slave-driver's shackles. I commend a sardonic English novel of nearly two decades ago, Nigel Dennis' *Cards of Identity*, which tells us how readily two or three clever and whimsical rogues can delude and enslave all sorts and conditions of people nowadays—supposing that their victims, representative enough of most modern folk, suffer from incertitudes as to their own identity. The man who does not know himself still retains a soul, but that soul is blind and deaf and dumb.

Yet, as I am fond of remarking, cheerfulness will keep breaking in. The very chaos of cults suggests that there has commenced a reaction against the purposelessness and facelessness of the Lonely-Crowd society. Without exemplars and images, few people can realize the self. The flicker of the television screen, the bustle of the standardized shopping-plaza, the consolations of the dirty magazine, the violent film, the "mind-expanding" drug—these do not answer the eternal question: "Who am I, and why am I here?" The flight from spiritual isolation into the craziness of certain cults is a form of incoherent protest against life without meaning and without self-knowledge. Once more mankind longs for signs and portents, for mystery and awe.

So we begin to discard the materialism and the mechanism of the past two centuries. Whether we throw away yesterday's nonsense to embrace tomorrow's nonsense, or whether we find our way out of superficiality into real meaning, must depend in part upon the images which we discover or shape. For the question "Who am I?" really means this: "Am I a spirit in prison? Am I made for eternity?" Such questions the American college and the American university were not prepared to answer in the 'Sixties and the 'Seventies.

A principal cause of the twentieth-century Identity Crisis has been the image of man imparted by a vulgarized scientism. I myself was reared, in no small measure, upon the facile scientism and the shallow historical notions of H. G. Wells, popularizer of mechanism and materialism. Popular opinions lag perhaps a century behind theories in the natural sciences, so that by 1977 the scientific doctrines of 1877 had trickled down, through vulgarizers and ideologues, to the mass of men and women. Thus the typical man or woman in the street forms an understanding of human nature upon confused and muddy representations of nineteenth-century thought, acquired from half-educated newspapermen, quarter-educated television personalities, and teachers whose interest in the realm of ideas ceased when they obtained their teaching certificates and their union cards.

Thus it is that when one of the national polling organizations, a few years ago, asked a representative sample of Americans whether they believed in personal immortality, the majority replied that they were not interested, one way or the other. Not interested? I suppose that such a reply really signified that most people nowadays entertain a notion that "Science says . . ." I mean this: whenever anyone tells you, "Science says . . ." you may be sure that he is about to tell you a whopper, perhaps for his own pecuniary advantage. True science does not speak with a single voice, nor pretend to explain simply everything in heaven and earth. But the average sensual man nowadays entertains a vague notion that Science says . . . why, that we're descended from apes, and that this life is the be-all and the end-all, and that keeping healthy is the main thing, and . . . well, anyway, we're not scientists, so we don't want to worry about stuff that doesn't get you anywhere financially.

Ultimate questions, for all that, keep intruding themselves, even into dull wits. Who am I? What am I doing here? If Holy Scientism will not answer these questions, Simon Magus will; certainly Simon says he knows. So we go seeking after strange gods. One after another, we embrace and then repel those strange gods. D. H. Lawrence's Dark God of sexuality begins to pall upon us; the multitudinous Eastern gods of the imported cults don't satisfy or deliver, despite the healthy fees we pay to be admitted to their presence; Marxism turns out to be the god that failed, in the Fabian phrase; perhaps next we will try Ares, the swaggering war-god. Give us a sign! Such were the bewildered pilgrimages of many students in the 'Sixties and 'Seventies; while others spent their time in Vanity Fair.

Although bored with mechanism and materialism, and frightened by loss of self-image, the rising generation will not get beyond Simon Magus—not unless doors are opened for them. The crowd perceives by means of images, true or false. But the discoverers or shapers of images are persons of extraordinary perceptions, not governed by the idols of the tribe or of the market-place. Some such already have spoken to us, in recent years; I believe that they will be heard increasingly, and that they may open our eyes to high mysteries once more, and that they may show us old-new images which are true images. Some of these perceptive people began to make themselves heard decades ago—as when Sir Arthur Eddington wrote, "The world is made up of mind-stuff." But they were little echoed in university or college during the 'Sixties and the 'Seventies.

I am suggesting that the natural sciences, for instance, may open windows through which you and I may look upon images of beauty and truth. What we call "science" necessarily speaks in symbols and images, abstractions and intellectual constructions. By way of fuller illustration, let me quote a great-souled woman who died young, Simone Weil.

"The true definition of science is this," Simone Weil wrote in *The Need for Roots*: "the study of the beauty of the world. (The motive of the scientist, if it is pure, must be the love of beauty.) The savant's true aim is the union of his own mind with the mysterious wisdom eternally inscribed in the universe. Scientific investigation is simply a form of religious contemplation."

Simone Weil compares the scientists of Hellas with the scientists of her own time—to the disadvantage of the latter—and then suggests (in her posthumous book *On Science, Necessity, and the Love of God*, published in 1968) that because modern science falters and seems to lose its way, modern folk think that no truth whatsoever remains:

"In the present crisis there is something compromised which is infinitely more precious than even science: it is the idea of truth, which had been very closely associated with science in the eighteenth century, and especially in the nineteenth. The association was erroneous, but the habit has persisted with us. The disappearance of scientific truth appears to our eyes as the disappearance of truth, thanks to our habit of mistaking the one for the other. So soon as truth disappears, utility at once takes its place, because man always directs his effort to some good or other. Thus utility becomes something which the intelligence is no longer entitled to define or judge, but only to serve. From being the arbiter, intelligence becomes the servant, and gets its orders from the desires. And, further, public opinion then replaces conscience as sovereign mistress of thoughts, because man always submits his thoughts to some higher control, which is superior either in value or else in power. That is where we are today."

Just so. Many of the students of the 'Sixties and the 'Seventies rejected utility as the good, and rightly so; but not having known truth before, they mistook ideology or strange gods for the good. Only a few professors at a few colleges and universities had pointed out to them visions of the truth; and objects, ends, aims, even the most ignorant must have.

Simone Weil could summon up images of the good, and unless we emulate her, we must sink into the condition of the prisoners in Plato's cave, mistaking shadow for substance, and so cribbed, cabined, confined for aye. As Simone Weil remarked, unless we perceive images, we will be ruled by force.

Images are representations of mysteries, necessarily; for mere words are tools that break in the hand, and it has not pleased God that man should be saved by logic, abstract reason, alone. Need we despair of recovering an awareness of mystery, and of regaining through our power of imagination those images which nurture the good?

One of the inquiring spirits of our time, Arthur Koestler, in recent years has written several books which argue that the sciences will, or should, take a new direction: that the sciences' hope lies in exploration of what is called parapsychology, the realm beyond the five senses. The grand question which parapsychology asks is this: "Who and what am I?"

According to the prevalent scientific speculation of our time, the newer science of our century, you and I are collections of electrical particles, so to speak, held in combination by forces and influences which we do not understand at all. Outwardly we seem to be material flesh and blood, but that is illusion: we are such stuff as dreams are made of, positive and negative electrical charges, as is all other matter. And yet within each of us some soundless voice inquires, "Who am I?"

This is the ghost in the machine, the immaterial impulse or mind-stuff which animates us. Our identity depends upon this directing power of which we are totally ignorant, and which we can delineate roughly only through images.

"We have heard a whole chorus of Nobel Laureates in physics informing us that matter is dead, causality is dead, determinism is dead," Koestler writes in his slim book *The Roots of Coincidence*. "If that is so, let us give them a decent burial, with a requiem of electronic music. It is time for us to draw the lessons from twentieth-century post-mechanistic science, and to get out of the strait-jacket which nineteenth-century materialism imposed on our philosophial outlook. Paradoxically, had that outlook kept abreast with modern science itself, instead of lagging a century behind it, we would have been liberated from that strait-jacket long ago."

The typical undergraduate of the quarter-century which has been described in this book was altogether ignorant of the post-mechanistic science of our century; his actions, so far as they were rational at all, were predicated upon vague vulgarized versions of nineteenth-century materialism and mechanism—for, what with cultural lag in the Grove of Academe, that typical undergraduate in the typical "survey of science" survey-course had been taught obsolete doctrine. He had been taught, at least by implication, that he was animal merely, producer-and-consumer merely, creature of appetite, circumstance, accident, environment merely. He had acquired his morals from *Playboy* and his taste from "The Price is Right." Had that typical undergraduate been offered, even so late as college, any inkling of a truth beyond the ordinary evidence of the senses—why, he might have made less of a fool of himself.

To discuss in detail the speculations of such thinkers as Weil and Koestler is beyond my compass in this chapter. I am suggesting here only that man's own image of himself in the last quarter of the twentieth century may be altered profoundly by new scientific discoveries and theories—or, rather, by the enlargement of theories which already have been enunciated. Once again, I suspect, the Academy will take notice of the soul and its images.

The image, I repeat, can raise us on high, as did Dante's high dream; also it can draw us down to the abyss. It is a matter of the truth or the falsity of images. If we study good images in religion, in literature, in music, in the visual arts—why, the spirit is uplifted, and in some sense liberated from the trammels of the flesh. But if we submit ourselves (which is easy to do nowadays) to evil images—why, we become what we admire. Within limits, the will is free.

It is imagery, rather than some narrowly deductive and inductive process, which gives us great poetry and scientific insights. When I write fiction, I do not commence with a well-concerted formal plot. Rather, there occur to my imagination certain images, little scenes, snatches of conversation, strong lines of prose. I patch together these fragments, retaining and embellishing the sound images, discarding the unsound, finding a continuity to join them. Presently I have a coherent narration, with some point to it. Unless one has this sort of pictorial imagery—Walter Scott had it in a high degree—he never will become a writer of good fiction, whatever may be said of expository prose.

And it is true of great philosophy, before Plato and since him, that the enduring philosopher sees things in images initially. I have dreamed only one metaphysical dream in all my life—only one, at least, that has lingered with me—but my little vision may serve to illustrate this point.

Only a few years ago, I dreamed a brief dream of order. In this vision, I found myself sitting in what appeared to be a London club, conversing with my chance neighbors on the questions which puzzled Milton's angels: fixed fate, free will, foreknowledge absolute. In particular we talked of whether God is just in saving some souls and consuming others. Of a sudden, the lot of us—chairs and all—were transported in the twinkling of an eye to outer space, where we hung suspended between heaven and earth, after the fashion of Mahomet's coffin.

The disputants and the chairs were the same, there among the stars, but the room had changed. It was eight-sided now, and there were eight tall windows, each hinged in the middle. Through those windows we could see the stars and the blackness of infinite space. And we sensed that we were in eternity; that never would we be returned to things terrestrial.

And we knew, without saying anything, that so long as we sat in our chairs, conversing, nothing would happen to us. Food and drink would appear at one's elbow, for the mere wishing. If we accepted these conditions, we were secure enough forever.

But some of our number were impatient of restraint, whatever the penalty for breaking the rules of this peculiar club. Those unquiet spirits hurried to the windows. Upon the slightest pressure, the hinged window-frames would swing outward, and those who leaned upon them were precipitated into the ghastly gulf of empty space, self-annihilated; wailing they went, and were lost to us forever.

As for me, I kept my chair, reflecting somewhat smugly, "My argument is vindicated. God does not damn anyone: those who destroy themselves do so from choice, refusing to accept the limitations of human existence."

I do not contend that this is a brilliant image, but it did teach me something. From sources unknown and perhaps unknowable, such true visions come to us—greater images to those imaginations which are greater than mine. The ancients said that true visions in sleep come from between the Gates of Horn, and false visions from between the Gates of Ivory. If we are uncertain of the origin of the images which occur to us—why, let us judge them by the images that have been given to us by men and women whose powers of perception exceed our own. A principal function of the higher learning used to be the transmitting of such high images to the rising generation.

What are you and I? In large part, we are what we imagine ourselves to be. William Butler Yeats advises us to clap masks to our faces and play our appropriate parts: the image becomes the reality. There is something, after all, in Randolph's bold admonition, "Make unto yourself an image, and, in defiance of the Decalogue, worship it." Randolph did not mean that we should cast a Calf of Gold; rather, he was saying that we grow into what we determine to make ourselves, God willing. We all suffer from limitations of mind and body and circumstance. Yet if we seek out images of the good, and apprehend them, and exert our wills, we will do something well—even if it is only to die well. We find our identity in the images we revere and in the work we undertake. If we seek out images of bravery (much neglected nowadays), we may grow brave; if we kneel before the images of cowardice, we must become cowards.

Similarly, if we neglect the claims of the imagination, we are punished terribly—by losing our identities. If you and I are not moral beings, then we are mere walking and talking machines composed of organic tissues. It is the moral imagination which fixes our identity. That lacking, men and nations come to the world's end—"not with a bang, but a whimper."

By 1977, interest in mystery, imagery, and imagination was stirring among the better minds of the Academy in these United States. Presumably that renewed interest, expressed in books and lectures over the years, would filter down gradually to the multitude of professors and instructors in the dark wood of America's many hundreds of colleges; it would even penetrate, later, to the secondary and elementary school-teachers. Later still, it would begin to produce changes of mind and heart among the abler undergraduates in the colleges, and they would convey some of that renewed perception of truth to the campus' Lonely Crowd. Meanwhile—why, what new body of illusions might intoxicate the Lonely Crowd for a few years?

Part Two

Conceivable Renewal

1

The Need for Reactionary Radicalism

C AN ANYTHING BE DONE?
    What we require is the recovery of objects in the higher
learning. The obstacles to any such restoration are formidable.
It will be recalled that at the beginning of this book, I listed four
principal afflictions of American university and college: purposelessness; intellectual disorder; gigantism in scale; the enfeeblement of
earlier schooling, so that college students come wretchedly unprepared for serious study. Also I named two principal fallacies which
have underlain the decadence of our higher learning: the misconception that the principal function of the higher learning is to promote
utilitarian efficiency; and the misconception that nearly everybody
ought to attend college. In the preceding twenty-five chapters, I have
touched upon many more ills of college and university. With all these
obstacles, what hope remains for the recovery of wisdom and virtue as
the ends of the higher learning?

Say not the struggle naught availeth. In the concluding portion of
this book, first I shall offer some general plans for recovering order
and integration of knowledge, and for renewing the moral imagination, in primary and secondary schools — particularly with a view to the
study of literature. Then I shall take up the question of what a sound
college should and can be. Third, I shall offer some examples of recent
renewal of the higher learning in existing colleges. Finally, I shall offer
some prognostications.

The reform of our higher learning must be radical: that is, it must go
to the roots of culture. Also the reform of our higher learning must be
reactionary: that is, it must react healthily against the intellectual diseases which have brought college and university to their present deca-

dence. My old friend the poet Roy Campbell used to say that a human body which cannot react is a corpse, and that so it is with social institutions. With T. S. Eliot and Allen Tate, I am perfectly willing to be called a reactionary. This book is a reaction—salutary, I hope—against misconceptions and corruption in the higher learning.

Here my notion of what we must do to restore the objects of the higher learning happens to coincide with the ideas of Dr. William Boyd, who became president of the University of Oregon in 1975. President Boyd calls himself a radical. He is a sagacious radical.

"The educational task before us is essentially a reactionary one—that of returning to a time when the purposes of a collegiate education were frankly moral as well as intellectual—useful but not utilitarian." So Dr. Boyd told the annual meeting, late in 1974, of the National Associations of State Universities and Land-Grant Colleges, a body unaccustomed to hearing such language.

President Boyd said that the American doctrine of Progress has gone glimmering, and that we stand in peril of embracing the doctrine of Misery instead. He saw before America an era of adversity and austerity, which might be stimulating or might be disastrous. "The question is whether the future will be dominated by a life-boat mentality, where the lucky passengers in the boat beat off those who are struggling to board, or by the snow-bound phenomenon, where sharing creates comradeship and turns a siege into a festival. Humans are capable of either response. Our problem is to educate in a way which will elicit the one rather than the other. The one thing of which we can be sure is that conditions of relative adversity are imminent."

We must divorce the idea of human happiness from dependence upon material prosperity: "Otherwise, the danger is real that, giving up on happiness, humans may decide to settle for pleasure instead. That short-fall of human aspirations could be the tragedy of our time."

Ours must be an epoch of retrenchment and reform in the higher learning, Dr. Boyd continued: we enter upon an age of no quantative growth. Student-driven models for the reformed university may be useful initially; but—"followed long, they will distort our universities, leading us away from our goal of a balanced, coherent, liberating education. That will be a consequence of student-driven models because students themselves are driven by anxieties, immediate needs, and bad advice from their elders. Under those conditions, if we reshape our universities according to their sense of present needs, we may decimate departments which are needed for those more distant future needs. The humanities, in particular, are going to be needed for the reconstruction of humane educational experiences."

The coming phase of reaction and reform, President Boyd declared, must be a "value-driven model", an educational design "with purpose and form guaranteed by requirements. . . . For a time we believed that requirements were an instrument of coercion, and we largely abandoned them; now requirements may re-emerge as an instrument of liberation—freeing universities from the tyranny of 'vogue' and 'relevance.' "

First of all, the university must cleanse itself morally. "Universities seem to be in at least as much of an ethical morass as legislative bodies and corporate structures. It just happened to be our luck to have escaped Nader's notice. The radical indictments of the late 'Sixties have never been quashed. The bullhorns are gone, but the charges remain—joined by new indictments laid down by a more conservative public."

Universities have lied often, Dr. Boyd said: to legislatures, to students. They have been corrupted by "grantsmanship." "The role of foundations, industry, and the federal government has become not merely dominant but domineering. The courtship between the researcher and the funder easily leads to an illicit affair. The legitimate slides into the illegitimate as getting grants becomes the object of the game. I have had colleagues teach plastic manners to airline stewardesses and teach manufacturers to make non-biodegradable plastic. The more successful and acclaimed on our faculties have learned to smell money, and tailor interests to those of the grantor. If they beckon, we sidle over. If they are hard to get, we hustle them. Our bad behavior covers a moral spectrum ranging from call-girl ethics to those of a hired gun."

Dr. Boyd had been vice-chancellor at Berkeley during some of the gravest troubles there, and had been president of Central Michigan University during the later phase of students' unrest and violence. In 1974, he was addressing an audience composed, in considerable part, of educational administrators guilty of just what he was denouncing.

The university had become a stronghold of hypocrisy, President Boyd went on. "We are indignant if public bodies submit to pressure, but we have thrown our senates open to mindless nihilists and capitulated to demand after demand. We prize openness, but are as secretive as if we held the H-bomb formula. We jealously keep our classrooms closed and are reluctant to say what we do with our time and other people's money. We believe in due process for others, but in the academic area we offer very little to our students. . . . The professor is the last stronghold of absolute authority in the western world. Even the Pope surrendered before he did."

American colleges and universities had been shamefully wasteful, Dr. Boyd emphasized. "We cry poverty, but we waste resources in a time of scarcity. The evidence is in that we are the capstone of an educational system which is repetitive to such a degree that even for an average student there is a year of waste encompassed in the brief span from grades eleven to thirteen. For the better students the wastage is probably nearer two years: years which must be multiplied by millions of students to state the cumulative impact on society. The notorious Pentagon over-runs are no more scandalous than that! The destruction of enthusiasm for learning is the unmeasured but even more significant part of that atrocity."

So, President Boyd concluded, "the essentially moral purposes of education must be restored. . . . I would hope that higher education can set a better pace and initiate its own orders—not waiting for direction from courts or an outraged public."

Thus William B. Boyd, a youngish president of one of the more pleasant state universities, stood up for wisdom and virtue as the objects of the higher learning. There are few more heartening symptoms of reactionary radicalism nowadays in the university than this address of his. He knew what needed to be done, and he spelled it out candidly to the members of an association which often had done its worst to barbarize American higher education. More men like William Boyd may come forward to renew our universities.

By the autumn of 1975, when President Boyd addressed the National Association of Universities and Land-Grant Colleges, enrollments throughout the country, with only local exceptions, were less than they had been in 1974. This signified, among other things, that the Academy had scraped the bottom of the barrel in its search for more warm bodies to entice or bully into the college classrooms. And this meant, too, that standards scarcely could fall lower than they had fallen already. Some college administrators even began to think of taking the opposite tack: attracting new students by offering *improved* standards—as a desperate last resort, of course.

From the end of the Second World War onward to 1975, all but a few universities and colleges had engaged in a ruinous competition to grow quantitatively, at whatever expense to quality of education. This folly had gone farthest at the public colleges of New York City, which had gone over to "open admissions" in the 'Sixties and 'Seventies—that is, any New York high school graduate, under the new policy, could enroll at a city college, paying no tuition, even if this student were virtually illiterate. Many would graduate from those city colleges (now loosely linked together to form a university) wondrously ignorant—for standards had been lowered to accommodate the stupidity, ignorance, or poor preparation of the newcomers. Of the several city colleges, only Queens College retained something resembling its old standards.

Until a few years earlier, it had been otherwise at New York's city colleges: most of the students had come from families of limited means, but they had been bright; academic standards had been strict, as had been standards for admission; and the graduates usually had succeeded in life, to the benefit of the public. There wrote to me in 1973 an elderly alumnus of City College, who had been graduated in 1908.

Then, he remarked, "It was necessary for a high-school graduate to have an average of ninety percent or better to matriculate in that free institution supported by New York's taxpayers. In the freshman and sophomore years all the subjects were required courses, no optionals. If a student flunked in three subjects he was automatically expelled."

In their sophomore year, this correspondent of mine and his fellow students read at sight the *Odes* of Horace. Nowadays, at City College, a good many sophomores would find it difficult to read at sight the verses of Ogden Nash, say. "In spite of the fact the our [arts] course emphasized the classics and humanities, we were required to take advanced physics, laboratory courses in chemistry and biology—and, amazingly, differential and integral calculus." All that had been swept away by 1973, to make room for "minorities."

To understand what had happened at City College, one profited in 1973 by reading a new book, *The Death of the American University*, by Dr. L. G. Heller; its subtitle ran *with Special Reference to the Collapse of City College of New York*. Dr. Heller was professor of classical languages and Hebrew at City College, and chairman of the College's committee on graduate studies.

Professor Heller had favored a policy of "open admissions" before it had been adopted—but on the assumption that, though anyone might enter City College, nevertheless such a policy would be accompanied by rigorous standards for academic performance, so that the unintelligent or indolent would be required to depart when it turned out that City College was not for them. Instead, City College had ceased to respect the works of the mind, once "open admissions" prevailed.

Dr. Heller described the terrible violence which broke out at City College—the burning of the splendid auditorium, the vicious crippling assaults upon female teachers and elderly people. He touched upon the cowardice and hypocrisy of City College administrators, and the weakness or political fanaticism of a good many professors. And he was candid about the "chain reaction" that had ended in the mass-production of incompetent graduates:

"Despite disclaimers to the contrary, by the new criteria for measurement, a class of nonreaders—many subliterate, some possibly even illiterate—were filling the seats. During the first such term, a conscientious teacher would be appalled, but would still carry on by the old measures of achievement. After a while, unfortunately, he would find himself unconsciously choosing 'simpler' vocabulary, giving shorter reading assignments, and generally pacing his presentation to the more limited capacities of his audience.

"It can be predicted that within a brief time any student who by previous measures would have been just an average student will be receiving straight As in his courses. The new average C student will be at a competence level that previously would not even have gained him admittance to the class."

And what would happen when such "students" were graduated with bachelor's degrees—as most of them might be? Why, Professor Heller wrote, "The most striking *reductio ad absurdum* of the process will be the consequences in the sciences. Who, for example, would care to undergo a kidney operation by someone who can barely tell the kidney from the liver? If that illustration is too extreme, consider driving an automobile over a bridge designed by someone who was weak in the computation of stress loads. Such a person would never have been licensed before. Tomorrow he will be a straight-A by virtue of the comparative ignorance of his classmates."

And so, by 1975, when Dr. Boyd addressed NASLUGC, it had come to pass. Even some of those in President Boyd's audience may have reflected that it might be better to graduate a class of one hundred intelligent bachelors of arts and sciences than to graduate a class of two thousand young persons with dubious degrees, of whom perhaps five per cent might be reasonably competent. By 1975, parents suspected that something was seriously wrong with college and university; so did members of state legislatures; the rising generation suspected it, and even liberal professors worried. So enrollments ceased to grow, or somewhat diminished. It seemed probably that, with a number of local and regional exceptions, there would come to pass no more massive growth of colleges and universities, ever, in the United States. Even the community-college movement had begun to encounter hard sledding.

The Department of Labor had begun to take note of the problem of "overqualified and underemployed" college graduates. Their statisticians estimated that during the decade between 1974 and 1985, some 13.1 million bachelors' degrees would be granted; yet only 12.2 million "job openings" for bachelors of something or other would occur during that same period. Thus nearly a million college graduates presumably would find themselves unemployable in the sort of posts and at the sort of salaries they had expected to obtain. As the construction-gangs departed from the campus, it seemed as if, at last, the academic community might have to settle for thought instead of "career training."

Yet what of the tremendous physical apparatus of higher education, with an outpost, it appeared, in nearly every county of every state in the Union? Would empty campuses be converted into old folks' homes, prisons, lunatic asylums, hospitals? What of the yet more tremendous snobbery that had helped to create these educational factories? Would not a large part of the rising generation continue to enroll in these institutions, intellectually and spiritually bankrupt though they had been demonstrated to be, for the sake of the empty snob-degree and the rather shoddy version of the old fun-and-games which lingered there? Was there any other way, indeed, to occupy the time of young people between the ages of seventeen and twenty-two than to lodge them in these quasi-custodial complexes?

What of the hundreds of thousands of professors and instructors, a vast salaried and tenured class, and what of the crowd of unemployed Ph.D.'s which the overblown graduate schools still turned out, annually? How would they be kept busy and happy—or happy and paid, anyway?

In short, a powerful entrenched interest, with lobbies in Washington and in every state capital, fearfully resists alteration of the existing inefficient and ineffectual apparatus of higher education. Although the decreasing birth-rate soon will affect colleges and universities as already it has caused the closing of a good many primary schools, and although it is virtually certain that America will lack the material resources for keeping up these educational institutions in the style to which they have become accustomed, still the people who run universities set their faces against retrenchment. William Boyd put this point well: "We academics are proud of our heightened moral sensibilities and disdain for materialism. Yet we clamour for carpeting when states are running deficits, custodial hospitals are snake pits, and humans are held captive under conditions worse than those of animals in the zoo."

So what with this entrenched resistance to radical-reactionary reform, and what with the desire for the snob-degree or the job-certification degree that still strongly moves a good many parents and young people, the alteration of the present structure will be slow. Some of the existing teachers' colleges—nearly all of them now styled universities—eventually will be abandoned because the demand for new teachers has been drastically reduced, and there are not enough potential students with other interests to fill the places of the vanishing education-majors. Even some state university campuses may be vacated: there has been talk in recent years of giving up the Riverside branch of the University of California, although when that campus was founded, in 1953, it was intellectually the most promising tentacle of the University of California octopus. Some community colleges, founded where the economic base was insufficient and there was no great population-density, are going to stand empty. Certain graduate schools, or departments thereof, will be abolished; already some of these have been reduced to accepting any candidates who turn up, and even so find only a handful of graduate students. (The University of California, prudently foreseeing this decline, years ago greatly reduced its graduate offerings.) Still more independent colleges, especially those which offer neither high academic standards nor any strong connection with a church, will be sold to anyone interested in acquiring their buildings.

This dismantling of the present structure, then, will be gradual and painful. As other public services insist upon being supported in a static or declining economy, the state and federal funds allocated to higher education will be reduced, at least proportionately—especially because both legislators and the general public have begun to doubt how much "higher" this education has been. Private benefaction also will be gravely affected both by rates of taxation and by the chastened American economy. A good many dormitories stand virtually empty already; others will be vacated, and perhaps utilized as inferior public housing. The ugliness and shoddiness of most campus construction since the Second World War considered, it will be no great pity if there occurs widespread demolition of superfluous campus buildings. Plant the trees again.

While this gradual attrition is in process, it is necessary to do what we can to restore objects and improve standards within the declining apparatus of higher instruction. If only from desire for survival, there may now occur competition in quality, by contrast with the competition in quantity which injured our higher learning from the end of the Second World War until very recently.

Also it is necessary to provide occupation for the Lonely Crowd between the ages of seventeen and twenty-two who gradually will filter out of the dormitories into the workaday world. Plenty of them will be needed to turn the great wheel of circulation, what with an aging

American population and an economy in which natural resources grow scarcer. The average college graduate had expected to live the life of a consumer; but young people in the 'Eighties must expect to live the life of producers. A college education will become once more what it was in nineteenth-century America, a privilege or a luxury, available only to the deserving or the wealthy. And why should it have been bestowed upon those who neither deserve it nor can pay for it? American society does not, on principle, give good-conduct medals to juvenile delinquents, or Cadillacs to welfare-clients. Higher education—the real thing, I mean—has to be paid for, as do all other costly goods and services; and sham "higher" education is becoming too much for America to bear. As to what the bulk of the rising generation will do to occupy themselves between the ages of seventeen and twenty-two, that is beyond the scope of this book. There exists plenty of work for them, if they find it necessary to undertake it. It always was foolish to maintain in comparative idleness millions of young people with no taste for the life of the mind.

And while the present inflated form of higher education is being reduced, it is necessary to provide alternative forms of the higher learning at once more genuine and less costly. Some of these alternatives will be suggested in the remaining chapters of this book; some of them already have begun to function.

I am not predicting or proposing a drastic reduction in the number of Americans to obtain a *true* higher education. On the contrary, we actually should be able to increase the number of genuinely educated men and women, despite economic difficulties. I mean that by the reform of educational methods, from kindergarten through graduate school; by relieving the educational apparatus, at its higher levels, of the immense burden imposed by the mob of unmotivated young people who ought to be somewhere else than in college; by returning to the objects of wisdom and virtue—why, we can waken the native intelligence of many now sunk into apathy and indifference, and we can insure that a bachelor's degree, or a master's, or a doctor's, shall come to signify achievement once more. Reactionary radicalism in the higher learning will improve, not subvert, the American democracy.

That reform must commence now, whether we relish it or not. Let me quote President Boyd once more:

"Had prosperity continued, I suspect that complacency would have, too. One of the virtues—and one of the vices—of affluence is that it permits the unexamined life. When all things are possible, few choices have to be made. When few things are possible, all things become vulnerable. We are now moving from the one situation to the other, and we are ill prepared. Our mind-set and all of our habits, born as they were of an earlier version of a bountiful America, now serve us poorly, and threaten betrayal to our students."

Nothing does more than adversity to summon up wisdom and virtue. Out of our present confusion and tribulation may arise an apprehension of the higher learning more salutary than we have known before in this country.

2

The Necessity for Dogmas in Schooling

T HE FIRST STEP that ought to be taken in the renewal of the higher learning is the restoration of the lower learning; also it is the hardest step to take. Illusion and incompetence are even more formidably entrenched in primary school and high school than in college and university; the public-school political lobby, or at least the teachers' lobby, is even stronger than the lobby of higher education; and social circumstances affecting the poor performance of the public schools are more difficult to alter than those affecting college and university.

Nevertheless, in this chapter and the two which follow I venture to offer some suggestions for the improvement of primary and secondary schooling. The performance of nearly all college students has been diminished by their inadequate preparation in the public-school apparatus. Their very ability to read, write, and understand mathematics has been unsatisfactory, this past quarter of a century and more, and the college has tried to enable them to compensate for their basic deficiencies—a task for which the college was not intended. In many other ways, elementary and secondary schooling have failed to prepare the rising generation for intelligent application to those abstractions which are the rightful concern of college and university. I shall confine myself, in these three chapters, to observations upon the neglect of moral instruction, of the social-studies disciplines, and of humane literature in the typical public school—with some recommendations as to what may be done by way of reform.

About 1953, the year when my chronicle of decadence commences in this book, a spate of sound books about primary and secondary education was pouring from the presses. About that time, too, there was founded the Council for Basic Education, dedicated to reform, and still courageously functioning. A quarter of a century later, one is depressed by what little impression the writings of Bernard Iddings Bell, Mortimer Smith, Arthur Bestor, Albert Lynd, James D. Koerner, and several others seem to have made upon the schools or the general public. Their books were widely and favorably reviewed, and sold well —so far as any serious books sell well in these United States. Yet according to all the indices, the performance of school pupils has been decaying for the last quarter of a century, and few of the reforms advocated by these intelligent writers have taken root. Functional illiteracy, for instance, appears to be even more widespread in 1978 than it was in 1953.

I am well aware that the public schools have labored under grave difficulties during this period. One of the major troubles has been the triumph of television: the average child spends far more time watching the boob-tube than he does in the classroom, let alone in homework. As great a trouble has been the confusion caused in schools by the perennial attempts at racial integration, provoking violence, lowering standards, diverting resources and the attention of school administrators and teachers, perennially altering school-district boundaries. Added to this have been the overflow of a general increase of violence and crime into the public schools, and the disruption of some schools by political passions and demonstrations imitated from the colleges. Unionizing of teachers during the same period did mischief in certain ways, of which strikes were only one. The decay of American cities—accelerated by misconceived "urban renewal" policies that actually created urban deserts and jungles—naturally was reflected in the classrooms. But there is no space here sufficient for a full litany of the schools' woes. The enormous subsidies granted to the public schools by the federal government during the past quarter of a century did little or nothing to check the decline of public instruction.

Yet all this conceded, still the public schools could have accomplished more toward preparing young people for higher education. Like colleges and universities, the schools had forgotten about wisdom and virtue—or had been frightened by certain Supreme Court decisions into avoiding any studies which might be interpreted as having a philosophical or an ethical bent. Nowadays the public schools are quieting down somewhat, and there is opportunity for something more than merely trying to secure pupils and teachers against physical assaults. Until the disciplines of the schools are restored, renewal of the higher learning for the average student must make headway only very slowly. The diminishing of school enrollments, and the present advantage of the schools in being able to pick and choose among the abundant candidates for teaching-posts, offer us some hope for attention to qualitative improvement.

Over the years, I have written a vast deal about primary and secondary schooling—materials for a later book, perhaps. In the present volume, I can address myself only to a few aspects of school learning that bear directly upon the decadence of college and university. The first of these is the question of dogmas.

All societies, in all times, have lived by dogmas. When dogmas are abandoned, the social bonds dissolve—swiftly or slowly; and the "open" society ceases to be a society at all, giving way to some new order. The successor-society may be imposed upon a people from without, or it may arise from within the decadent social order which had lost its principles of coherence. But the succeeding domination, whether it be harsh or gentle, supplants the old order precisely because the people of the new order believe in some body of truths, and the people of the failing order do not.

During the liberal era which now has sunk into decay nearly everywhere in the world, this word "dogmas" (or "dogmata") was a devil-term, conjuring up images of the Holy Office and a pile of faggots. "Dogmas" were held to be irrational, archaic, oppressive. Yet the attempt to sustain a society without dogmata is as vain as the attempt to make bricks without straw.

Actually, the word "dogmata" does not signify ignorant repression. "Dogma" is derived from a Greek root meaning "that which seems good." A dogma is a settled opinion: a principle, maxim, or tenet firmly established. It is a theory or doctrine received on authority—as opposed to one based on personal (or general short-run) experience or demonstration. When people forsake dogmas, they abandon the pursuit of real objects, as C. E. M. Joad noticed, and settle merely for the gratifications of "experience": the fundamental cause of decadence.

It is not foolish to accept on authority, or dogmatic statement, the commonly-accepted circumference of the earth: it would require infinite trouble to work out the earth's circumference for one's self, through mere experience, and most people are not capable of undertaking such voyages or calculations. If that particular scientific dogma ever is altered, the innovation will be worked by talented mathematicians and physicists and geographers—not through private experience or demonstration. And then the new calculation of the earth's circumference would itself become a kind of dogma.

Similarly, it is not foolish to accept on authority, or dogmatic statement, certain theological and moral and political dogmas. Life is short, personal experience is limited, and learning through demonstration may be both difficult and dangerous. We cannot all be prophets or philosophers. The theological dogma that God exists cannot be "demonstrated", in the sense that a simple experiment in chemistry may be demonstrated; and while that dogma conceivably may be reinforced by personal experience, the experience without the dogma ordinarily brings only wonder at best. The moral dogma that murder is evil indeed would be sustained by experience and demonstration; but meanwhile there would be slaughter. The political dogma that unchecked power is perilous to everybody doubtless would be vindicated through great suffering, were we to test it by submission to somebody like Idi Amin; but liberation from the resulting servitude would be slow and bloody.

When I was a soldier in a desert camp, some of my barracks-mates determined to get intoxicated on New Year's Eve. Having no whiskey, they drank denatured alcohol, of which we had plentiful supplies in the camp. They declined to accept the authoritative principle that wood alcohol is unfit for internal consumption; after all, none of them actually had tested that dogma. Some died, others were blinded, the fortunate ones were deathly sick. A society which ignores the principles of its coherence and vitality experiences similar consequences—a society that tries to subsist without dogmas.

Yet nowadays no word seems to frighten schoolteachers more than this word dogma. "We're not propagandists!" a representative teacher of the social sciences may exclaim indignantly, on hearing the suggestion that he ought to try to impart to his pupils some notions of moral worth and social obligation. Such teachers maintain that their responsibility is merely to "present the facts": children must make up their own minds upon questions of order in the soul and order in the commonwealth. Would you prefer to be the burglar, Johnny, or the burgled? Look at the "facts" and make up your mind; develop your own "value-preferences." One trouble with such a concept of "objectivity" is that, in the short run at least, it may seem distinctly more pleasant to burgle than to be burgled.

Nor is such a modern pedagogue's attitude one of moral neutrality merely: some teachers at every level consider it their duty to diminish old prejudices in the minds of the rising generation, that "open minds" may flourish. When I was an instructor at Michigan State College, an official committee of my colleagues developed a scheme for determining whether the Basic College, and the institution in general, were "achieving our mission." What was this mission? Why, to liberate the aspiring talents of youth by disabusing young men and women of the old fuddy-duddy opinions which they innocently had imbibed in family, church, local community, and earlier schooling.

To test the efficacy of this noble labor undertaken by the college, a lengthy set of questions was drawn up; this questionnaire was to be answered by all of the entering freshmen, in one year, and to be administered to them again, four years later, when they were about to be graduated. If the students' minds had been opened by the abandoning of dogmas, the college could take a just pride in its emancipating achievement.

The character of this questionnaire may be suggested by two of the inquiries put, sufficiently representative of the openmindedness of the scholars who set about this task of redemption. One question ran, "Do you believe that if you want a thing done well, you must do it yourself?" Another asked, "Do you believe it is wrong for brother and sister to have sexual intercourse?"

If the response to the first question was affirmative, clearly the freshman so stating was caught in the trammels of hoary platitude. Every enlightened professor knows through experience and demonstration that it is much better to have work done by committees. Don't we all recognize how beautifully and successfully academic committees function?

As for the second question, I do not suppose that my colleagues were zealous for incest on principle. Rather, they pleaded for toleration: for those who like that sort of thing, that is the sort of thing they like.

The freshmen submitted to the testing, and in the fullness of time the same young persons, as seniors, responded to the questionnaire all over again. To the hideous chagrin of my colleagues, few of those students had altered their opinions substantially. Alas, they had remained sunk in obscurantist attitudes, and the college had failed in its mission!

At an international conference in which I participated some years ago, Monk Gibbon, the Irish writer, remarked that the conference's resolutions were platitudes. Then he added that he had learned something about platitudes in the course of his life: the important thing about platitudes is that they are true. That is why they have become platitudes.

Platitudes are expressions of dogmatic belief. If teachers cannot live with platitudes, they ought to take up some other line of work. For, I repeat, the ends of education are wisdom and virtue. An apprehension of wisdom and virtue must commence with the acceptance of certain dogmata, often platitudinously expressed. Even if one aspires to challenge "conventional wisdom", one first must master that conventional wisdom: otherwise the skeptic's challenge is ignorant bluster.

In our time, there exists no danger that the mass of young people will be paralyzed by dull submission to ancient custom, convention, and deference. The motion of our age has been centrifugal, not centripetal; the tendency has been eccentric, not centric. Violence and fraud increase at every level of society; half the marriages end in divorce, and we slaughter myriads of unborn infants; the alienist is busier than a bee, and the cement of society disintegrates. The need is not for emancipating the young from fixed convictions, but rather for reminding them that there remain some convictions worth cherishing.

It is not the "center city" school merely that is tormented by assaults in its corridors, intimidation of teachers, addiction to narcotics, juvenile extortion: the rot spreads outward to suburbs and rural districts. It is not only the mass campus of Behemoth State U. that suffers from aimlessness and vandalism; the same ills trouble famous universities and colleges. (A phenomenon almost peculiar to our time torments not a few great universities—the proletariat of idle and sometimes criminal young non-students and "street people" who have settled after a fashion in Cambridge, New Haven, Berkeley, Ann Arbor, Austin, and even Princeton, on the fringes of the university, and who form a large element in "student" disorders, or live as predators.)

Despite all this, still we encounter in nearly every educational establishment oldfangled Liberal Era jargon about the holy task of secularizing everything; of instructing the young that "everything is relative" or "ambivalent"; and that everyone must decide for himself, out of his wonderful native powers of rationality, whether he should subject himself to "socially approved attitudes" which (a good many teachers imply) may be nothing better than "bourgeois morality" or regulations devised for the preservation of Vested Interests. Meanwhile the school itself slips into anarchy, and the society outside—well, nobody walks the streets o' nights.

True, now that the weak go to the wall on the school bus, and now that even the most naïve parent begins to perceive that college is an unlikely place for Ken and Barbie to acquire rectitude, a feeble disquiet results in seminars for "values clarification", "value-preference education", and the like. Some organizations make real money out of this pabulum.

But "teaching about values" cannot suffice. "Values" are private and frail reeds. One man's value is charitable work; another man's value is brothel-frequenting. Who can judge which is the preferable value—dogmata lacking? In our Father's house are many mansions, but they are not all on the same floor.

A dogma is not a value-preference. A dogma is a firm conviction, received on authority. No one but an ass would die that his value-preference might endure; while dogmatic belief sustains saints and heroes. In the Nazi concentration-camps, two classes of prisoners generally kept their sanity and tended to survive: Catholic priests and Communist agents. The dogmas of the Church will steel men and women; so, after their fashion, will the dogmas of the Savage God, Ideology. For a value-preference—do you prefer pushpin or poetry?—few persons will adventure much.

I repeat that any society lives by dogmata. For action, private or public, must be founded upon certainties. One thinks of a Sanskrit proverb: "If you forsake a certainty and depend upon an uncertainty, you will lose both the certainty and the uncertainty." Dogmas are formulated certainties, and one does not have to be forever reassessing his petty value-preferences in order to act—if he accepts long-beneficial dogmata. Life is for action, not for perpetual doubt, ambiguity, hesitation.

Against the Sanskrit proverb (or dogma), someone may quote the sentence of Francis Bacon: "If a man will begin with certainties, he shall end in doubts; but if he will be content to begin with doubts, he shall end in certainties." This may be true, in its fashion, for innovating men of science like Bacon or Einstein, say. But if applied to the circumstances of the average man or woman nowadays, this neat aphorism must work mischief. Practically, if the choice must be made, it is better to believe all things than to doubt all things: certainly the ingenuous man or woman is a pleasanter companion than the sour doubter and carper. If a bridegroom commences by doubting the fidelity of his bride, it is improbable that years of wise reflection may bring him to an opposite opinion, for if a woman has the name, she may as well have the game.

And if a professor begins by doubting whether history is anything but bunk, will decades of tenure convert him into an Augustine, a Bossuet? Or if a boy is instructed that the decision to steal or not to steal must be calculated according to his own best interests and value-preferences—why, will some years of practice as a lawyer secure the money and the reputation of his clients? My own value-preference is for wives, professors, and lawyers who do not begin dubiously—for dogmatic wives, professors, lawyers; for the commandments "Thou shalt not bear false witness" and "Thou shalt not steal." Bacon took bribes. I prefer proverbs to clever paradoxes.

Dogmas grow out of the ineluctable necessity for a core of common belief, in church, in state. Private judgment, unattached to dogmas, is insufficient for the moral order or the social order. As Burke tells us, "the individual is foolish, but the species is wise." Why not trust to one's experience? Because, as Benjamin Franklin's Poor Richard says, "Experience keeps a dear school, but fools will learn in no other."

Dogmata may be corrupted and may decay to virtual extinction. But when they do, soon they are supplanted by other dogmas—promulgated and enforced, commonly, with greater zeal and severity. Then the Savage God lays down his new commandments. Soviet Russia rejects the Christ, Communist China rejects Confucius; promptly, to supply motive for the civil social order, rigorous ideological dogmas are formulated, and conformity to them is exacted with a ferocity that makes the Spanish Inquisition seem the creation of ritualistic liberals. For lack of a transcendent sanction, secular dogmas necessarily are harsher far than religious dogma. If one thinks of dogmas as devilish—why, it is well to remember that it is safer to deal with the devil you know than with the devil you don't know.

Similarly, as the rising generation is left ignorant of our civilization's dogmas—or is encouraged to discard them—strange new dogmas rush in to fill the spiritual vacuum. Fraudulent cults, any god but God, enslave thousands of young Americans who wish to believe in something not altogether bound up with creature comforts. In the long run, life without faith and loyalty is unendurable. The old dogmas evaporated, some will choose Mao, others Simon Magus.

In our educational apparatus, dogmatic knowledge has been flouted for some decades; John Dewey and his disciples struck hard blows against it. In the schools, as in American life generally, ethical and cultural consensus have decayed. The vestiges of religious assumptions in public schools have been nearly eradicated by certain decisions of our omniscient Supreme Court—or by the interpretation placed upon those decisions by school administrators and school boards. Dogmatic instruction, in the larger sense of that phrase, has suffered also from a general loss of the order and integration of knowledge, extending from kindergarten to graduate school. The ethos of sociability in these United States is hostile toward the demands of dogma; while both vocationalism and the appeasement of the counter-culture folk have left little time for the imparting of truths not invented yesterday.

Yet all success in schooling depends upon the acceptance of necessary dogmas. We teach, or used to teach, in kindergarten the dogma that it is wrong for one child to kick another in the shins—and that if the aggressor persists in his value-preference, punishment must follow. Dogmas are first principles. Without first principles, nothing can be achieved intellectually or morally, even by brilliant teachers.

Am I advocating some especial form of "civil religion", that subject so much discussed in recent years? Not so. I am all against the fallacy advanced by Theodore Brameld, for instance, that we should abandon all old dogmas but should teach dogmatically, instead, "the religion of democracy." I recognize the difficulties, in this pluralistic society, of teaching in public schools the dogmas of a particular creed; that is one reason why we ought to be dismayed by the diminishing of church-related schools, or by their virtual absorption into the climate of opinion—or of non-opinion—which prevails in the public schools. And yet I believe, with Professor Philip Phenix of Teachers College, Columbia, that the whole curriculum of any school should be suffused with reverence—and that this remains possible in public schools.

Schools were founded so that young people might attain an ethical end through an intellectual means. Even in the most pluralistic societies, enduring ethical truths may be imparted through a variety of intellectual disciplines—literature, social studies, even the natural sciences: formal courses in religion and ethics, desirable though they may be, are not indispensable in this undertaking; for without sectarianism the principles of inner and outer order, the dogmata essential to a civilization, still may be woven into the general curriculum.

What I have in mind is best expressed by C. S. Lewis, in *The Abolition of Man*. In his appendix on the Tao, the Way, Lewis describes a "natural law" or body of beliefs, taught both by precept and by more subtle means, which may be found in every culture, because without these there can be no culture. These are ethical dogmata, if you will, expressed somewhat differently in this age or that land, yet at bottom a unity. Lewis distinguishes eight large laws of universal validity: the law of general beneficence; the law of special beneficence; duties to parents, elders, ancestors; duties to children and posterity; the law of justice; the law of good faith and veracity; the law of mercy; the law of magnanimity. Humane letters, as Lewis points out, have been a principal instrument for this teaching of ethical truth; yet in some degree this understanding of how we are to live with ourselves and with our neighbors used to run through every school discipline. What endured until not many years past may be raised up again, from painful necessity.

Would I go beyond this, all the way to political dogmata? Yes, I would —in moderation. I believe that there are social dogmas still vaguely recognized in America (though not wholly of American origin) well worth perpetuating. Among these are affirmation of the dignity of man; adherence to the benefits of representative government; knowledge that the tolerable society requires a tension between the claims of order and the claims of freedom; assertion that a humane and free economy is better than a servile economy. I would persuade teachers to believe in these first principles of the American Republic, and to pass them on. I find little benefit in vague discussions, in the classroom, of whether it would be better to have a leader like Mao or a leader like Carter, say. There exists a body of knowledge, sound and firm, about our political institutions; and the school ought to disseminate that knowledge, rather than asking "What do you think?" about grave matters concerning which a child has no basis for comparison.

Switzerland, we are told, has an "open society." Yet I understand that in Switzerland it remains an offense at law for a teacher to cast doubt upon the truth of the legend of Wilhelm Tell. The Swiss know that the survival of a state depends upon shared convictions—upon the dogmas which give motive to action, and upon the symbols which illuminate the dogmas.

Nowadays we are not living in any ossified ancient Egyptian or Peruvian society. We do not yield unquestioning obedience to doctrines suckled in a creed outworn. The question for us, instead, is whether we may maintain enough respect for revelation and reason to hold together the person and the republic. Dogmas lacking, order and justice and freedom do not long endure.

Freedom? Dare I couple the words "freedom" and "dogma"? I dare. It is dogmatic faith which makes possible personal and social freedom. Without some dogmata, the viewer is at the mercy of the seductions and the banalities of the boob-tube; without some dogmas, the student lies at the mercy of the silliest arrogant neoterist on the university's staff; without some dogmas, there is no reason why we should behave in community as spiritual brothers, or even as thirty-second cousins in spirit. Sound dogmata liberate us from enticement by fad and foible, from intellectual servility, from a society that is nothing better than a congeries of competing selfish interests.

Aye, I should like to hear less shallow talk about an "open mind"—if by that phrase is meant a mind exposed to every wind of doctrine, weather-beaten, a gale blowing in one ear and out the other. It was not the open mind that caused the founding of schools: it was the hope of a filled mind.

And I should like to hear less about the vaunted "market-place of ideas." School, college, and university are not commercial shopping-centers. "At the Devil's booth, all things are sold." Truth cannot be bought and sold. Does it never occur to the minds of the enthusiasts for the "intellectual market-place" that in a time of educational inflation, such as ours, Gresham's Law may operate in the Academy, bad money driving out good? The old-fashioned notion of a "temple of learning" at least is closer to the object of schooling than is the false image of the educational marketplace, offering its customers shoddy merchandise at exorbitant prices. If this be educational freedom, then give us again the credal regularity, but the actual liberty, of the medieval schools.

Rudyard Kipling makes my point for me, in "The Gods of the Copybook Headings":

"As I pass through my incarnations in every age and race,
"I make my proper prostrations to the Gods of the Market-Place.
"Peering through reverent fingers I watch them flourish and fall,
"And the Gods of the Copybook Headings, I notice, outlast them all."

Dogmas denied, the time comes when the Gods of the Market-Place fail us, and then "the Gods of the Copybook Headings with terror and slaughter return." I subscribe, however unfashionably, to the dogma that two and two make four, and to the dogma that the fear of God is the beginning of wisdom. In our time, the fear of dogma is the ruin of wisdom.

It should be understood that when I write of dogmatic instruction, I have in mind principally primary schooling; next, secondary schooling; and only incidentally the higher learning. If the lower learning has been thorough, it should be unnecessary and indeed imprudent to teach dogmatically at college and university. In the higher learning, there should be some testing of dogmas, and a fuller understanding of them as symbols of truth. But if no dogmas have been imparted in the first six grades of schooling, say, then no sure footing exists for the higher learning; the student gropes as if astray in the Grimpen Mire; he cannot even challenge first assumptions intelligently, for he does not know what the first assumptions are. This recovery of sound dogmata, in many fields, is the first labor of renewal in school learning.

3

Perishing for Want of Imagery

"IT IS IMAGINATION that governs the human race." No professor of literature wrote those words: that is an aphorism of the master of the big battalions, Napoleon Bonaparte.

In this chapter I discuss the renewal of the study of humane literature in the high schools. It is by literature, more than by any other discipline, that the moral imagination is nurtured. If imaginative literature is badly taught in high schools, the teaching of literature must be inadequate in colleges, because of the average student's lack of background and preparation. And a great many college students, specializing in some academic discipline or in some vocational curriculum almost from the first freshman term, may acquire in college no more literary culture than can be extracted from a survey-course in "communications skills", perhaps. First, therefore, I offer a rather lengthy example of bad literary instruction in high schools; then I proceed to suggest a sound literary program in secondary education.

In a time when we Americans ought to be entering upon an Augustan age, we seem enervated. A feeling of powerlessness oppresses many Americans. Even the President and the Congress, theoretically invested with immense authority, tremble and change color like so many chameleons on aspen leaves, whenever some wind of fantastic doctrine disturbs them. Something has trickled out of this society of ours—so many voices tell us.

But what has departed? The abortionist, the pathic, the female freak, and the psychopath strut upon the national stage; the mass of decent Americans grumble in bewilderment, almost leaderless, while order and justice and freedom are crushed in most of the world, while everything is engulfed by political power, while what we took to be the "permanent things" are eroded to skeletal remains. What genius has forsaken us?

Now and again I marvel at the näiveté of some of the people who cry *O tempora, O mores*. Too many folk fancy, for instance, that the decadence of the age is worked by economic fallacies. It is true enough that economic fallacies make mischief—especially the notion that we all can prosper somehow even if nobody works very hard. But economic error is only one aspect of larger blunders. Someone once told Irving Babbitt that the future would be concerned principally with economics; if so, Babbitt replied, the future would be superficial. We have it on the authority of Saint Ambrose that it is not God's will man should be saved by dialectic; still less will the world be saved by little tracts and pamphlets about economic theory. People who think our civilization mainly an exercise in economics, and so devote their energies and their money to theoretical defenses of an abstract "capitalism", actually are unconscious Marxists—embracing the postulates of an ideology which they profess to reject. It is freedom of spirit that produces a free economy, not the other way round.

Napoleon was right: the world is ruled not by money, not by force of arms, but by imagination. In the long run, it is poetry that governs the human race. Poetry, even bad verse, rouses the imagination and shapes our ends; without poetry, a civilization does not endure. I use the word "poetry" as Eliseo Vivas does in his book on D. H. Lawrence—that is, "as a short and convenient term to refer to the whole of imaginative literature, whether written in prose or verse." And there comes to my mind a passage in Vivas' introduction to his Lawrence book.

"The vision the poet offers us has order and splendor," Vivas writes, "whereas the objects of our vision are incomplete, opaque, vague. The first and most important step in arriving at knowledge of ourselves and of the world is to apprehend both immediately in their own terms as objects of the act of aesthesis. It is at this point that the work of the poet comes to its full non-residential utility: we do not see the world reflected in it, we see the world by means of it. And the difference between the alternatives is radical. It is in this special sense that the poet's world is normative."

Just so. My English friend Paul Roche, poet and translator of classical poets, argues that to every cabinet minister there ought to be attached a poet, and the politician ought to be compelled to listen to him. One such poet, Roche says, commanding the ear of a minister of transport, would have averted the ruinous folly of British highway-construction on the American model—a policy which the British government found it necessary to curtail after doing grave damage to the economy and the ecology. Similarly, a real poet breathing imagination into the federal Department of Housing and Urban Development might have averted the creation of America's urban deserts and jungles through miscalled "urban renewal." The poet perceives norms. When a blinkered utilitarianism suppresses poetry, those norms are forgotten, and the human condition descends by stages to its primitive circumstances, "poor, nasty, solitary, brutish, and short."

The modern practical statesman rarely thinks of sharpening his vision through poetry. Not long after Cambodia had fallen into the cauldron of the Indo-Chinese war, President Nixon invited me to the White House to talk with him privately about certain large questions. We did not discuss at all the matter of military operations. Mr. Nixon's concern was with questions of social decadence. Presently he asked me, "What one book should I read?" He was forever asking Henry Kissinger or D. P. Moynihan that question, he said, but they were given to recommending lists of a dozen books, and in his situation he had no time for reading a dozen books. "What one book should I read?"

I replied that he might take up T. S. Eliot's *Notes towards the Definition of Culture*. He asked why; and I remarked that among other things, Eliot discussed in that slim book the desirability of frequent exchange of views among men of public affairs and men of learning. I went on to say that the great poet of our time, perceiving the parlous condition of twentieth-century civilization, touched in this book upon the sources of order and culture—to know which religious and poetic insights are required. Later I sent President Nixon a copy of Eliot's essay in social criticism, and he thanked me for it; but I do not know whether he found opportunity to read it. A few months later, as in Eliot's poem "Difficulties of a Statesman," this cry was heard by the lately-triumphant chief of state, brooding in his retreat:

"We demand a committee, a representative committee, a committee
   of investigation

   RESIGN   RESIGN   RESIGN"

By imagery our minds are moved, our emotions are directed, our characters are formed; and if that imagery is base, a society degrades itself. By this word "imagery" I mean the formation of images by art; a type of general likeness; a descriptive representation; an exhibition of ideal images to the mind; figurative illustration. "Imagery" is mental representation. The lives of all of us are formed, willy-nilly, upon models we perceive and imitate. There is the emulation of the image of Christ, and there is the emulation of the image of Lucifer. Great poetry gives us mental images; the narcotic trance gives us mental images.

Though the Decalogue forbids molten images of divine beings, in another sense all of us make unto ourselves an image, and worship it. Were not that so, we would live merely as dogs do, from day to day.

Indulge me, then, in a digression here concerning the impoverishment of the creative imagination, of imagery, in America. For what has trickled out of our society, I believe, is moral imagination. We stray enervated and bewildered because we have ignored the poet's high vision.

America always was the least poetic of great nations. Until recent decades, nevertheless, we did not reject altogether what Michael Oakeshott calls "the voice of poetry in the conversation of mankind." But nowadays the voice of true poetry is nearly extinguished in our schools. Therefore—this among other causes—we fall away from the norms of order and justice and freedom, in the person and in the republic.

I venture to illustrate this point by examining a representative series of textbooks—subsidized by the federal government—in the discipline which used to be called humane letters. I take up a series of high-school anthologies, at three grade levels, called "Macmillan Gateway English: a Literature and Language Arts Program." This series is no worse than various others in its field. What with the limitations of space here, I confine my criticisms to Level Three of the Macmillan Gateway program—a set of four paperback anthologies, intended for high-school juniors or seniors. These four volumes are entitled *Rebels and Regulars*, *People in Poetry*, *Something Strange*, and *Ways of Justice*.

A product of the recent concentration of inner-city schooling, this Macmillan Gateway English series is meant to acquaint pupils with "relevant" literature. It was got up by the Project English Curriculum Center at Hunter College. As the Teacher's Manual puts it, " . . . the encouragement and the financial support out of which these units developed came from the U.S. Office of Education (Contract SAE OE-3-10-015) and from the Department of Education of Hunter College of the City University of New York"; so came to pass "the development of instructional materials which, it is hoped, will bring new understanding and heightened enjoyment by English to urban youth and their teachers." The editors were professors of education or high-school teachers; no professor of literature or man of letters had a hand in these volumes.

Certainly this recent "urban" and "relevant" look at English (actually, almost wholly American) literature contrasts strongly with the smugness and dullness of the typical high-school textbook of a few years ago. I commend a perceptive study by James J. Lynch and Bertrand Evans, *High School English Textbooks: a Critical Examination* (1963). Professors Lynch and Evans, in their recommendations concerning anthologies, listed nine principal vices of the typical textbook, the last of these "editorial tone." The following passages from Lynch and Evans suggest the foibles of yesteryear.

"Several of the anthologies stress the deliberate catering to the adolescent mind even to the point of embarrassment," they wrote in 1963. "Pieces are chosen because they lie within the narrow boundaries of the teen-age world, and their heroes and heroines are Dick and Jane just a few years older, now dating instead of playing, going to a dance instead of the local fire station, saying 'round, round, jump the rut, round, round, round, jump the rut, round, round, round—' instead of 'jump, Spot, jump,' but otherwise hardly different. The 'image' of the American Boy that emerges is a clean-cut, socially-poised extrovert, an incurious observer of life rather than a participant, a willing conformer, more eager to get than to give, a bit of a hypocrite but a rather dull companion—a well-adjusted youth not much above a moron. And the 'image' of the American Girl? She is one who likes the American Boy. The adolescent should read about adolescents, of course—but he can and will do so on his own. The constant restriction of the teen-ager's gaze to himself, his friends, his hobbies, his little world of which he is the center, is likely to produce nothing else so quickly as acute narcissism."

Too true; yet how all this was altered in a single decade! The more recent Macmillan Gateway English breathes nonconformity (sometimes for noncomformity's sake), relevance (meaning contemporaneity), social awareness, humanitarianism, pessimism, "minority" images, and novelty. Yet perhaps this is merely the other face of the coin: the Un-American Boy is no more charming than the American Boy. And there is little more genuine literature of the first rank in this new approach than there was in the old: the moral imagination of the rising generation is not refreshed.

These Hunter College educationists might break with the "values" of the smug anthology of yesteryear, but they retained—perhaps unconsciously—rather woolly humanitarian values of their own. One is reminded of C. S. Lewis' biting criticism of two British anthologists, in his slim book *The Abolition of Man* (1947). "Their scepticism about values is on the surface," Lewis wrote; "it is for use on other people's values; about the values current in their own set it is not nearly sceptical enough. And this phenomenon is very usual. A great many of those who 'debunk' traditional or (as they would say) 'sentimental' values have in the background values of their own which they believe to be immune from the debunking process. They claim to be cutting away the parasitic growth of emotion, the religious sanction, and inherited taboos, in order that 'real' or 'basic' values may emerge."

What values the Hunter College anthologists embraced may be suggested by certain sentences near the beginning of their Teacher's Manual. They were tempted to espouse dissent on principle:

"Adults who may have forgotten their own similar feelings, or who view the rebellion of today's youth as more fundamental, more overt, even more violent than their own, may be quick to condemn young people whenever they do not conform to adult expectations. Such condemnation contributes to the alienation young people feel toward the institutions and authority figures that are the gatekeepers of the adult world. . . . And if adolescent and young adult protest is more violent and more easily embittered today, adults must recognize the urgency of the problems—of war, racism, poverty—which the generation now coming of age must face."

Indeed? The problem of war is not more dismaying than it was in Shakespeare's time; the problem of 'racism' is not more complex than it was in Disraeli's age; the problem of poverty surely is less acute than it was in the day of Piers Plowman. (None of these writers, incidentally, finds a place in this Hunter-Macmillan series.) But for these new anthologists, the past scarcely exists; pupils must be exhorted to immerse themselves in activity and "becoming", not in reflection upon the permanent things.

Moods alter rapidly nowadays. I suspect that administrators and teachers in secondary schools are less eager to encourage activism among their charges in 1978 than they were when Macmillan Gateway was compiled, a decade ago; in that sense, Macmillan Gateway English itself has ceased to be 'relevant.' The editors of that series were concerned—perhaps overly concerned—for imparting "right attitudes." But what sort of character were they molding by *Rebels and Regulars*, the first volume of Level III?

They were not very fond of Regulars: far from commending conformity to the image of The American Boy, they presented pupils with a diversity of rebels against custom and convention. Almost the only cautionary voice tolerated in this anthology is that of John Dos Passos, writing about James Dean. Yet in general, these are not overtly violent rebels, the tone being set by Martin Luther King, whose "Letter from Birmingham Jail" is presented as a model of twentieth-century prose. Of the thirty-odd selections in *Rebels and Regulars*, only two are from authors (Hans Christian Andersen and Henry David Thoreau) of the nineteenth century; all the rest are twentieth-century pieces. If one hopes to form character through the study of literature, this policy confines students to a small compass in time and space; it is what T. S. Eliot called the error of contemporaneity.

"In our age," Eliot told the Virgil Society in 1945, "when men seem more than ever prone to confuse wisdom with knowledge, and knowledge with information, and try to solve problems of life in terms of engineering, there is coming into existence a new kind of provincialism which perhaps deserves a new name." Precisely that sort of provinciality is stamped upon *Rebels and Regulars*: so far as this anthology offers models for character, it presents those of one country and one century.

This is what Eliot called the provincialism of time—"one for which history is merely the chronicle of human devices which have served their turn and been scrapped, one for which the world is the property solely of the living, a property in which the dead hold no shares. The menace of this kind of provincialism is that we can all, all the peoples on the globe, be provincials together; and those who are not content to be provincials, can only become hermits. If this kind of provincialism led to greater tolerance, in the sense of forbearance, there might be something to be said for it; but it seems more likely to lead to our becoming indifferent, in matters where we ought to maintain a distinctive dogma or standard, and to our becoming intolerant, in matters which might be left to local or personal preference."

The editors of *Rebels and Regulars* commend tolerance and breadth of view; but they may be imparting something different—that is, a new conformity to a standardized "nonconformity" of amorphous humanitarianism. True, they devote considerable space to the grievances of Negroes, Puerto Ricans, Indians, and even Africans—whether or not the selections chosen for these topics possess literary worth. Yet one senses behind these diverse sketches a kind of doctrinaire egalitarianism, the notion that everybody belongs to everybody else, as in *Brave New World*. Everybody is protesting and rebelling—against what? It is hard to say what: for so little space is allowed in this collection for "Regulars" that protest itself is left without adversaries. Even a character of negation requires something to deny or reject; but *Rebels and Regulars* leaves its readers adrift—no splendor, no tragedy, no norms, no authority to flout, merely a pouting resentment. It leaves the rising generation, that is, bored and characterless. The small beer of the Un-American Boy is quite as flat as the small beer of the American Boy. What J. Frank Dobie wrote of the typical high-school anthology of ten years earlier is quite as true (with a few exceptions) of *Rebels and*

Regulars: "stuffed with banal tripe that would bore the brain of a hard-shelled terrapin."

After such prose (the selection from Thoreau, by the way, consisting of three sentences merely, as if the pupils' intellects would bear no longer passage of literate exposition), one turns for relief to *People in Poetry*, the second volume of Level Three. Most of the students who use this slim book will be seniors; for them, it will be their last formal approach to poetry, very possibly. And what do they get? More "relevance"; next to no beauty; for that matter, next to no rhyme. There is room for LeRoi Jones, but no space for the three most famous poets of the twentieth century—not one selection from William Butler Yeats, T. S. Eliot, or Robert Frost. (Frost's "Witch of Coos", however, is included in the following volume of the series.) One is given a surfeit of Carl Sandburg, true, because Sandburg is regarded as a poet of "democracy" and "protest."

Of the one hundred and nine poems—or items, rather—in this anthology of verse, only three are by well-known poets who wrote before the twentieth century. There are a few translations from other languages, also from twentieth-century poets. Nearly all the poets are Americans; some of them are obscure; some are wretched. All the poems are short, and of those by the better poets, the choice often is poor. One is interested to find that Bobbie Gentry, the singer, is a poet important enough to deserve the study of "urban" pupils; indeed, the second poem in the volume is her song "Ode to Billy Joe"—which owes whatever merits it may possess to its tune and to Miss Gentry's voice, not to her lyrics.

But why fret whether the verse is good or bad? It will fill up the kids' time, anyway; and, remember, this is an anthology entitled *People and Poetry*. So long as we have the people—John F. Kennedy, Harriet Tubman, and Martin Luther King, Jr.—why scan the verses? It seems to have been impossible to find tolerable verses about Dr. King, but the deficiency is supplied by a passage in prose entitled "A Drum Major for Justice and Peace" by that leader himself, in praise of himself. Doubtless it is better that young folk admire Martin Luther King than that they should admire Frank Sinatra, say; but I'd not print any "poems" by Sinatra, either.

In all this volume, there is not one great poem; nor are there many lyric or dramatic poems of the sort to catch a young person's imagination. One is tempted to apply to this anthology what T. S. Eliot said of the English Association's anthology *The Modern Muse*, in 1941: "brainless balderdash."

Something Strange is the third volume in this Third Level: a collection

of uncanny or fantastic tales and poems. When I took up this anthology, I was filled with hope: high-school students have been starved for
this genre. Two admirable storytellers, Ray Bradbury and Roald Dahl,
are represented; there are poems by Frost, Keats, Housman, William
Carlos Williams, and Archibald MacLeish.

The editor of this volume, in her preface, declares that we all are in
"a funhouse gone mad." Indeed it would be a relief to turn from the
fatuous jollity of a teen-age version of Dick, Jane, and Spot to the realm
of the fantastic. But after plodding out of one slough, the editors
plunge into another. These "strange" tales are the fantasy of despair,
of nihilism. In general, the vast outpourings of "science fiction" in
recent decades have been anti-utopian—to which characteristic I do
not object. Most of what has been chosen for this anthology, however,
reminds one of Ambrose Bierce's definition of suicide: "A door leading
out of the jail-house of life. It leads into the jail-yard." This really is a
"funhouse gone mad", deprived of norms and of hope.

A nasty vein of cruelty and despair runs through the textbook. At
least eight of the selections have to do with a predicted future that is
utterly ruined or dehumanized. One encounters next to no suggestions
that any sort of regeneration is possible. This terror without catharsis is
as bad, in its way, as stuffing young people with indigestible meliorism.
One is offered various glimpses of hell, but obtains no hint of divine
justice.

One might think that what students read in the newspapers, or
behold on television, or see at work in their own neighborhoods, might
insure that they would already have supped full on horrors. The world
of *Something Strange* is a world without mercy, faith, hope, charity,
justice, or purpose.

Justice? Why, that's provided in the final volume of this series, *Ways
of Justice*. "Justice" nowhere is defined by the editors; one gathers that it
is scarcely more than untutored sentiment, though praiseworthy.

The "justice" of this anthology is almost justice without judges. Two
selections might please Angela Davis. One of these is Carl Sandburg's
"What Is a Judge?", which instructs the reader that a judge is "a
snow-white crow . . . a featherless human biped having bowels, blad-
der, and intricate blood vessels of the brain. . . . Therefore should any
judge open his mouth and speak as though his words are an added light
and weight beyond the speech of one man?"

The other vial of scorn poured upon judges is Edgar Lee Masters'
"Judge Selah Lively"—who was a pillar of severity because he (being
five feet two) envied taller men. True, these comminations are balanced by some praise of particular judges. Louis Adamic eulogizes

Fiorello LaGuardia because he fined the spectators in his courtroom rather than fine an elderly thief; and Dr. Marjorie B. Smiley (senior editor in this Hunter program) prints a kind of poem of her own, lengthy but sufficiently represented by its concluding lines:

"A judge is a man
is where he's come from
is what he's done
is
where he aims to go."

This is "Mr. Justice Marshall"—Thurgood, that is, not John, the latter being unmentioned in this volume. For my part, I'd rather not be judged by a magistrate who "is where he aims to go"; I'd prefer one with knowledge of law.

Like its companion volumes, *Ways of Justice* makes much of injustice against "minorities"—in a fashion that may nurture resentments among some students and rouse reaction in others. The Establishment, this volume seems to suggest, is stupid and insensitive at best—frequently corrupt and evil. Is a different Establishment conceivable? If so, on what foundation? The editors do not inform their high-school readers.

Levels I and II of the Hunter-Macmillan program are no better than Level III. In general, Macmillan Gateway emphasizes the "generation gap"—without bridging that chasm by our patrimony of great humane literature, which joins dead and living and those yet unborn.

As Lynch and Evans wrote in 1963, "The conflict between youth and age is a natural condition of man older than Cicero and Bacon, and as necessary as it is natural; contempt enters the relationship when age pretends to be youth. And contempt can transfer itself from apparatus to selection, from selection to teacher, from teacher to subject, from subject to education, from education to the values by which civilized men live. Before the students can grow up, their textbooks must."

Macmillan Gateway English has not grown up. Except for a few cautionary selections—chiefly those in opposition to reckless drivers and junkies—the tendency of this program is to pander to the cult of youth and the fad of "relevance." Students' rebellion against the patronizing chumminess of yesteryear's English textbooks may be paralleled, already, by as strong a rebellion against the smug "rebel" chumminess of such a series as this. Neither type of textbook offers much for the reason or for the imagination; and youth abides anything except boredom.

So we return to *The Abolition of Man*. "Without the aid of trained emotions," Lewis wrote, "the intellect is powerless against the animal organism." Lewis found that the dryasdust school-anthologies he criticized were imprisoning young people in "contemporaneity" and in an arid pseudo-rationalism. Those manuals did not warm the heart; they did not adequately train emotions (or what Eliot called "sentiments"). It is so with the Macmillan-Hunter program.

"And all the time—such is the tragi-comedy of our situation—we continue to clamor for the very qualities we are rendering impossible," Lewis declared. "You can hardly open a periodical without coming across the statement that what our civilization needs is more 'drive', or dynamism, or self-sacrifice, or 'creativity.' In a sort of ghastly simplicity we remove the organ and demand the function. We make men without chests and expect of them virtue and enterprise. We laugh at honor and are shocked to find traitors in our midst. We castrate and bid the geldings be fruitful."

Macmillan Gateway English is a program well intended, no doubt, but in effect a program of gelding. What has been excised by the Hunter College crew? Why, great literature. The pupil is left with "approved attitudes"—which, even though disguised as "protest" and "being uniquely oneself", actually constitute a plodding humanitarian orthodoxy. In the main, these are anthologies of mediocre writing got up by mediocre professors and teachers. Shakespeare is excluded from this whole three-level program; perhaps the editors themselves cannot make head or tail of Shakespeare. (All the Xhosa children in the autonomous republic of the Transkei, in South Africa, study *Macbeth* and *Hamlet*, by the way; but that is too much to expect of New York children.) They leave their young charges adrift in a turbulent age—to be made tolerable, one takes it, merely through sympathizing with one's age-group peers and commiserating with one's self.

This is a program of "literature and language arts" deficient in power, aspiration, high thought, noble language, and norms. Though it is "moralizing" in the bad sense of that expression, this program has next to no true ethical character. One touch of Shakespeare, say, might have leavened this lump. But there is no yeast in the Project English Curriculum Center at Hunter College. The imagination of the students upon whom this program is imposed will be nourished by the sociology of Dr. Marjorie B. Smiley, professor of education, and the deathless lines of Bobbie Gentry, songstress of the Tallahachee Bridge.

Rising disheartened from my examination of this wearisome program, I went to some dusty shelves in my library on which I keep old textbooks. I found there the sixth-grade reader which I used at Starkweather School, in Plymouth, Michigan, in dear dead days beyond recall: *The Elson Readers*, Book Six, edited by William H. Elson and Christine M. Keck (1929). Also I encountered on those shelves my sister's copy of *Elson Basic Readers*, Book Five (1931). There had occurred a decay of standards in the Elson series even during those two intervening years. Nevertheless, my sister's fifth-grade reader was much superior, in content and in style, to the present Macmillan Gateway English intended for high-school students.

Now the Elson Readers, widely used during my school days, were not perfect. At Starkweather School we had a room where older basic manuals, no longer used in classes, were stored; and on two or three occasions I had the opportunity to browse in that storeroom. Even then, my half-developed critical sense informed me that the readers of a decade earlier distinctly had been more lively and more intelligent than those of 1929.

How marvellously superior my sixth-grade Elson was to any level of the secondary-school Macmillan-Hunter! "The foundation of the book must be the acknowledged masterpieces of American and British authors," the Elson editors wrote. My sixth-grade reader was divided into three parts: "Nature—Home and Country"; "Stories of Greece and Rome"; and "Great American Authors." In Part I we had admirable selections of some length about "The World of Nature" from Theodore Roosevelt, Samuel White Baker, Captain Mayne Reid, John James Audubon, Ralph Waldo Emerson, Bliss Carman, James Lane Allen, William Wordsworth, James Russell Lowell, and other worthies; and there was another section, "Home and Country", with essays or stories by Irving, Dickens, Tennyson, Lanier, Leigh Hunt, Ruskin ("The King of the Golden River"), Cardinal Mercier, Lincoln, Browning, and others.

Part II consisted of long extracts from the *Iliad*, the *Odyssey*, and the *Aeneid*, all in the prose of A. J. Church. Part III included several selections apiece from Benjamin Franklin, William Cullen Bryant, Henry Wadsworth Longfellow, Nathaniel Hawthorne, John Greenleaf Whittier, and Oliver Wendell Holmes.

I am not declaring that the discrimination of Elson and Keck was impeccable; it wasn't. Yet a great gulf is fixed between the Elson people, who did love literature, and the Hunter people, who did love "research" at the expense of the Office of Education.

It may be objected that television did the mischief to American literacy and taste for good literature. True, the boob-tube has diminished the imagination, the attention-span, and the functional literacy of many young people. Yet the decay of literary instruction in

American schools commenced years before most folk ever had heard of a television set. Certain publishers and too many teachers abandoned the ethical and aesthetic purposes of literary study, for the sake of "awareness" of, and "adjustment" to, contemporary life; often this dereliction of English-teaching made schooling smugly complacent.

Subtly unpleasant things happen to a people who cast off their literary patrimony as so much vexatious baggage. There subsists a close connection between the order of the soul and the order of the commonwealth, on the one hand, and the received insights of great men of letters, on the other hand. A people who have forgotten Homer and Plato and Virgil and Dante and Shakespeare and Cervantes and Johnson, and many more—who have forgotten their own Hawthorne and Melville—presently find themselves in personal and social difficulties: for their moral imagination is parched. Immersed in the ephemeral moment, and reading (if they read at all) at best the selections of the Book of the Month Club, such a people fail to apprehend adequately the human condition in the twentieth century, or in any other century.

It may be retorted that Russell Kirk must have attended an "elitist" school—whereas the Macmillan-Hunter program was intended especially for the "culturally deprived." Nay, not so. Starkweather School was built in the "Lower Town" of Plymouth, literally on the wrong side of the tracks; the neighborhood was a kind of railroad ghetto, near the great yards outside Detroit. My schoolmates and I came from families of limited and uncertain means. We had a sprinkling of "minority" children who didn't know that they were culturally disadvantaged. But all of us were offered a sound literary instruction, and with most of us it took root well enough.

One of the bookworms among us was Philip, a potato-faced Irish boy, who went truant at least a third of the time—running away from home in freight cars, carrying with him an armful of good books from the school library—which he dutifully returned after a week's peregrinations. Our favorite playground was a marshy triangle called "The Y" at the junction of the lines from Detroit and Toledo; there we played at being Knights of the Round Table. As for me, my parents and I lived in a creaky old house with no bathtub and an outside privy. Everybody took this existence for granted, and practically all the children liked the school, read competently, and chose good books. The school's admirable library was open all summer, and we used it. Our teachers of English literature and language knew their discipline and walked by its light.

Beyond simple skills of reading and writing, the object of studying literature—poetry, if you will—is to wake the imagination and to bring people to a fuller understanding of the human condition. Like many another textbook series of recent years, Macmillan Gateway English endeavors to substitute vague sentiments for reason and for the moral imagination of significant literature. If the teaching of literature is decadent, what wonder that young people had rather watch television? Perhaps many high-school students nowadays, not being able to read proficiently, can apprehend no prose more aspiring than what is contained in the Macmillan Gateway program. (Gateway to what?) But in some part, is not functional illiteracy to be laid at the doors of inadequate programs in "literature and language arts"? One doesn't have to be born to affluent suburban parents to profit from great poetry.

Talk of cultural deprivation! The Hunter College educationists are among the gentry who—doubtless with the kindliest of motives— contribute to the impoverishing of reason and imagination. Such a program condemns the teachers to the chore of mere adolescent-sitting (increasingly a career of danger and daring), and condemns the pupils to confinement in the crepuscular little corner of their moment in time. And the federal Office of Education subsidizes this deadly dullness.

When our minds are deprived of high poetic images, the vacancy will be filled by images of another origin and character. There are different types of imagination: the moral, the idyllic, the diabolic. The moral imagination is informed by the great ethical poets. The idyllic imagination responds to primitivistic fantasies—to the notions of Rousseau, for instance; it roused the radical emotions of young people in the 'Sixties, even though they knew Rousseau only at third hand, if at all. The diabolic imagination loves the violent and the perverse; one need not go so far as Sade to find it; it runs through D. H. Lawrence, for one.

So it is no mere coincidence that a time of literary decadence merges into a time of political disorder. When the images of Dante are rejected, the images of LeRoi Jones will be applauded. And, nature imitating art, presently a playwright may look from his window upon a howling revolutionary mob and murmur complacently, "There's my pageant passing!" But in the end, the mob will rend the dramatist too.

Michael Oakeshott remarks the poetic character of politics: "The assimilation of 'politics' to practical activity is characteristic (though not exclusively so) of the history of modern Europe, and during the last four centuries it has become increasingly complete. But in ancient Greece (particularly in Athens) 'politics' was understood as a 'poetic' activity in which speaking (not merely to persuade but chiefly to compose memorable verbal images) was pre-eminent and in which action was for the achievement of 'glory' and 'greatness'—a view of things which is reflected in the pages of Machiavelli."

The politics of Machiavelli, however imperfect, must be preferred above the politics of Hitler, of Mao, or of Idi Amin. Unpoetic politics must be politics without imagination—or, at best, illuminated only by the impractical idyllic imagination, to be followed by the grisly diabolic imagination. Imagery lacking, the commonwealth will not know glory or greatness. And the emasculated "literature and language arts" of our day, in this land, leave the rising generation ignorant of the poet's vision of order and splendor. Since somehow we must know the world through images, many of the rising generation, perishing for want of vision, find images of a sort—the pornographic film, the inanities of commercial television, and the "mind-expanding" drug. When all this decadence of imagery is sufficiently advanced, all coherence is lost — in the person, in the republic.

A silly high-school anthology is a symptom of a larger decay of imagination; also it is a contributory cause of that larger affliction. Were it not for the imagination, said Samuel Johnson, a man might be as happy in the arms of a chambermaid as in those of a duchess. Were it not for the imagination, the life of an ant would be as satisfying as the life of a man. Yet because we human beings are imaginative by nature, we cannot choose to live by the routine of the ant-hill. If deprived of the imagery of virtue, we will seek out the imagery of vice. The triumph of the diabolic imagination, however, soon terminates in personal and social extinction. Therefore, when the corrupting of imagination has proceeded to intolerable lengths, there emerges some grim new morality, very unlike the "New Morality" of license and irresponsibility so much talked about in recent years; and the punishments of the total state substitute, after a fashion, for that control over will and appetite previously exercised by the moral imagination.

That is one reason why I do not believe poetic images to be mere Corinthian ornaments of a culture. The conservators and the reformers of society ought to be men of poetic imagery, like Solon, if their labors are to endure. A principal object of the schools is the seeking of truth through images. (The memorizing of poems in school, something now almost wholly vanished, actually was no silly exercise, but rather a means of awakening children to the life of spirit.) It is not too late for us to restore, in elementary and secondary schools, the imagery of great literature—and so to make possible the recovery of the higher imagination in our higher learning.

*   *   *

So I suggest here, first, the *sort* of literature which ought to be taught; and then I will list, by way of concluding this chapter, certain works of imaginative letters—poetry, novels, plays, philosophical studies, and other branches of letters not embraced by the natural sciences or the social studies—especially commendable for this purpose. T. S. Eliot remarked that it is not so important what books we read as that we should read the same books. He meant that a principal purpose for studying literature is to give us all a common culture, ethical and intellectual, so that a people may share a general heritage and be united through the works of the mind. There exist a great many good books, Eliot knew; of these many commendable books, we need to select for general study a certain elevated few for particular patrimony. That is my purpose here—though I claim no sovereign authority, and stand ready to have other people substitute books of equal merit for some or many of the titles I suggest.

As mentioned in my discussion of the Macmillan-Hunter series, the usual anthology of literature, from the ninth grade through the twelfth, suffers from two chief afflictions. The first of these is a misplaced eagerness for "relevance." The second of these is a kind of sullen purposelessness—a notion that literature, if it has any end at all, is meant either to stir up discontents, or else merely to amuse.

Literature certainly ought to be relevant to something. But to what? Some anthologists and teachers fancy that humane letters ought to be relevant simply to questions of the hour—the latest political troubles, the fads and foibles of the era, the concerns of commercial television or the daily newspaper. Such shallow relevance to the trivial and the ephemeral must leave young people prisoners to what has been called the provinciality of time. (Incidentally, during the 'Sixties some of the students most violently insistent upon thrusting "relevance" into the curriculum also insisted upon spelling and pronouncing it "revelance.") Such training in literature is useless to its recipients, within a few years, and leaves them ignorant of enduring truths.

Genuine relevance in literature, on the contrary, is relatedness to the permanent things: to the splendor and tragedy of the human condition, to constant moral insights, to the spectacle of human history, to love of community and country, to the achievements of right reason. Such a literary relevance confers upon the rising generation a sense of what it is to be fully human, and a knowledge of what great men and women of imagination have imparted to our civilization over the centuries. Let us be relevant in our teaching of literature, by all means—but relevant to the genuine ends of the literary discipline, not relevant merely to what will be thoroughly irrelevant tomorrow.

As for the second affliction, purposelessness, the study of literature would not have been the principal tool of formal schooling for many centuries, had humane letters seemed to offer only a kind of safety-valve for personal discontents, or else merely a form of time-killing—the filling of idle hours. In every civilized land, literary studies were taken most seriously indeed, until recent decades. Literature and its related arts usually were called "rhetoric" in times past; and this word "rhetoric" means "the art of persuasion, beautiful and just." Literature, in short, was and is intended to persuade people of the truth of certain standards or norms. Literature has been regarded as the peer of theology and philosophy because literature's real purpose is quite as serious as the purposes of theology and philosophy. But literature's proper method differs from the methods of theology and philosophy. Unlike those disciplines, literature is supposed to wake us to truth through the imagination, rather than through the discursive reason. Humane letters rouse us to the beautiful and the just, through symbol, parable, image, simile, allegory, fantasy, and lively example. The purpose of literature is to develop the moral imagination. Or, to put it another way, the aim of humane letters, of our courses in "lit" or (hideous phrase) "communications skills", is to form the normative consciousness.

What I have written above ought to be commonplace. Yet these ideas seem to have been forgottten in many quarters. This normative endeavor ought to be the joint work of family and church and school. As the art of reading sometimes is better taught by parents than it can be taught in a large class at school, so a knowledge of good books comes from the home at least as much as from the classroom.

Whether one's reading-tastes are developed in the school, the public library, or the family, there are certain patterns of reading by which a normative consciousness is developed. These patterns or levels persist throughout one's education—whether that education is school-learning or self-instruction. We may call these patterns fantasy; narrative history and biography; imaginative creations in prose or verse; and philosophical writing (in which I include theology).

With these levels or patterns in mind, I set down below a sample program of reading for the concluding four years of secondary schooling. I list only works in the English language (or translations which have become part and parcel of English literature), because really "foreign" literature should be taught in classical languages, French, German, Spanish, and the like.

I repeat that I do not insist upon the particular books suggested below, although I think them excellent ones; all I am trying to do here is to suggest the general tone and quality of a good program in humane letters. I have included some old school favorites because their merit and importance have not diminished; on the other hand, I have excluded some old chestnuts (like George Eliot's *Silas Marner*) because actually they always were poor choices for high-school study.

Because wisdom and style did not expire with the nineteenth century, among my selections are a number of our better recent authors. Students between the ages of thirteen and eighteen ought to be treated as young adults, actually or potentially capable of serious thought; therefore this is not a list of "children's books." But neither is it an exercise in pop culture and contemporaneity.

These are books calculated to wake the imagination and challenge the reason. None ought to be too difficult for most young people to apprehend well enough—provided that they are functionally literate.

Ninth-Grade Level

For this year I emphasize fantasy, in the larger sense of that abused word. If young people are to begin to understand themselves, and to understand other people, and to know the laws which govern our nature, they ought to be encouraged to read allegory, fable, myth, and parable. All things begin and end in mystery. Out of tales of wonder come awe, and the beginning of philosophy. The images of fantasy move us life long. Sir Osbert Sitwell, when asked what lines of poetry had moved him most in all his life, replied candidly, "Froggie would a-wooing go, whether his mother would let him or no," the *hubris* and impending doom of this ominous first line having been impressed upon his little boy's mind. So here are my fantastic recommendations:

John Bunyan, *The Pilgrim's Progress*

William Shakespeare, *A Midsummer Night's Dream*

Nathaniel Hawthorne, *The House of Seven Gables* (or, perhaps preferably, *The Marble Faun*)

Robert Louis Stevenson, *Kidnapped* or one of his volumes of short stories

Ray Bradbury, *Something Wicked This Way Comes* or *Dandelion Wine*

Walter Scott, *Rob Roy* or *Old Mortality* (these being better romances than *Ivanhoe*, once commonly taught)

Select poems of Spenser, Burns, Coleridge, Wordsworth, Shelley, Tennyson, Whittier, Longfellow, Chesterton, Kipling, Masefield, Yeats, Frost, and others—selected with an eye to the marvellous and the mysterious

(It will be noted that in this grade, as in later ones, nearly all recommended books are available in inexpensive paperback editions—including paperback anthologies of poetry; it is unnecessary, except with incompetent teachers, to employ a fat and rather disheartening anthology.)

Tenth-Grade Level

Here our instrument for rousing the moral imagination is narrative history and biography of high literary merit. Reading of great lives does something to form decent lives. I draw for this branch of literature upon both "actual" and "imaginary" sources.

Daniel Defoe, *Robinson Crusoe*
William Shakespeare, *Macbeth* or *Julius Caesar*
Francis Parkman, *The Oregon Trail* or *The Conspiracy of Pontiac*
Mark Twain, *Huckleberry Finn* or *Life on the Mississippi*
Benjamin Franklin, *Autobiography*
William Makepeace Thackeray, *The Virginians* or *Henry Esmond*
Herman Melville, *Typee* or *Omoo*, or perhaps *Whitejacket*
Select poetry of a biographical or historical cast

Eleventh-Grade Level

Here, as "imaginative creations", I recommend for the third year of high school certain books which require serious interpretation and discussion.

John Milton, *Paradise Lost*
Jonathan Swift *Gulliver's Travels*—the original text, not a children's version
Charles Dickens, *Great Expectations* or *David Copperfield*
T. S. Eliot, *Murder in the Cathedral* (no drama being more relevant to the conflict of loyalties in the twentieth century)
George Orwell, *Animal Farm*
William Shakespeare, *As You Like It* or *The Merchant of Venice*
Select poems of a speculative cast

Twelfth-Grade Level

This is the year for developing a philosophic habit of mind through close attention to humane letters. "Scientific" truth, or what is taken popularly for scientific truth, alters from year to year—with accelerating speed in our time. But poetic and moral truths change little with the elapse of centuries; and the norms of politics are fairly constant.

> Select *Epistles* of St. Paul (King James version, taught as litera-
>   ture, which is quite constitutional even in public schools)
> Samuel Johnson, *Rasselas*
> Marcus Aurelius, *Meditations* (preferably in Long's translation)
> Edmund Burke, *Speech on Conciliation with the American Colonies*
> C. S. Lewis, *The Screwtape Letters* or *The Great Divorce*
> Christopher Marlowe, *Doctor Faustus*
> George Santayana, *The Last Puritan*
> Select short stories by Joseph Conrad
> Samuel Taylor Coleridge, *The Rime of the Ancient Mariner,* and
>   other poems
> Select poems of Frost, Robinson, Masters, Eliot, Santayana, Ches-
>   terton, and other twentieth-century poets

(It might be useful to to add to these a little book of reflections or essays—George Gissing's *Private Papers of Henry Ryecroft,* say, or Alexander Smith's *Dreamthorp,* or selections from Hawthorne's letters and journals, or Saint Augustine's *Confessions.*)

Tentative though the preceding recommendations are, I think them calculated to wake the interest of the average pupil, provided they are adequately taught. They are not so demanding as the parallel curriculum I studied in high school: I have omitted Chaucer's *Canterbury Tales*, for instance. I have had in mind here a program to which no serious objection could be raised in a public school, except that it is too intelligent. This program pays close attention to several of the greater poets, with three years' study of Shakespeare; it touches upon both the classical and the Christian sources of English humane letters; it introduces students to several important novels; and—unlike most existing programs in literature at the typical high school—it gives some place to history and biography.

Quite possibly these suggested lists may not please teachers who merely accept whatever they happen to find in anthologies, nor yet teachers who attempt to convert courses in literature into courses in current social problems. Certainly they will not please teachers who find thinking painful. I have a simple test of teacher-competence, and any instructor in high-school literature classes may apply it to himself or herself. It is this : can the teacher understand, and explain to a class, two very direct and memorable poems—Kipling's "The Gods of the

Copybook Headings" and Chesterton's *The Ballad of the White Horse?* If
he cannot, he has chosen the wrong vocation.

Certainly many of the folk who edit high-school anthologies have
chosen the wrong vocation. They think of classes in literature as a kind
of adolescent-sitting, or at best an opportunity to impart Approved
Social Attitudes. They despair of competing with Demon Television.
They seem strongly prejudiced against anything published before
1930. One way to escape from the clutches of this breed of "educator" is
to abjure anthologies altogether and turn instead to the original works
of literature, not to the anthology-snippets.,

How many favorites of my own have I omitted from this list! Where
are Ben Jonson, John Dryden, Alexander Pope, Lord Macaulay, John
Henry Newman, Benjamin Disraeli, John Ruskin, Washington Irving,
James Fenimore Cooper, William Morris, George Bernard Shaw, Sir
Thomas Browne, Roy Campbell, William Faulkner? I would not be
wounded if someone should substitute Trollope for Thackeray, or
Tolkien for Bradbury. What I am offering here is not a dogmatic
syllabus, but rather an approach to the study of humane letters by
young people—an approach meant to induce them to ask themselves
and one another and their teachers certain ultimate questions; also
meant to help them learn the difference between praiseworthy writing
and wretched writing.

Of course I do not mean that the books listed above, for these four
grades, are *the* Great Books, exclusively, of English letters. They are
some of the great books; all of them are important books; those who
read these books will be led to many other important books, in school or
out of it. We are embarrassed by the riches of English literature.

Readers of this inadequate chapter who are interested in fuller lists
of the books we ought to know would do well to take up Sir Arthur
Quiller-Couch's slim volume *The Art of Reading*, or more recent books
about great books by Montgomery Belgion, John Erskine, and others.
And for the teacher who seeks to learn how to make dead books come
alive, I suggest Gilbert Highet's *The Art of Teaching*.

The survival or the revival of the sound study of literature is bound
up with the survival of social order itself. Literary culture will endure
through these dark days if enough men and women become aware that
the purpose of literature is not simple amusement, nor sullen negation,
but instead the guarding and the advancement of the permanent
things, through the power of the word.

If literature has no object, it does not deserve to survive. Many
writers and publishers and reviewers clearly are of the opinion that
literature exists only to fill their pockets and tickle their vanity. Any

honest physical labor is more edifying than that. But perhaps we will begin to see a reaction against such decadence in letters, if only from mankind's primal instinct for the perpetuation of the species.

College freshmen who had studied literature in high school on some such plan as I have suggested above would be competent to enter upon the serious study of literature, in English or some other language, at an advanced level. Also they would have been taught how to think and to write by such a program, and thus generally prepared for an active part in the higher learning. Such preparation of their students lacking, even famous old colleges have become only glorified high schools.

The rejection of humane letters is an act of childish impatience and arrogance. The consequences of that rejection are not restricted to juvenile years, but may endure to the end of life. When the great books are forgotten or burnt—why, as George Orwell reminds us in *1984*, "Here comes a chopper to chop off your head."

4

Putting Life into Social Studies

HE CONCERN of humane letters is chiefly with the order of the soul; the concern of social studies is chiefly with the order of the commonwealth. The decay of the literary disciplines in elementary and secondary schools has been paralleled, or perhaps exceeded, by the decay of the social-studies disciplines. Until both are restored, especially in high schools, integration and ordering of knowledge in the colleges will be a hard row to hoe.

Educators of John Dewey's school, most of this century, have put forceful emphasis upon the primacy of "citizenship education", political socialization" through the public schools, and the like. Sometimes, indeed, it seemed as if the "Instrumentalist" or "Progressive" educationists were interested almost exclusively in training for democratic citizenship, to the exclusion of those disciplines which comfort the inner man—a point made by T. S. Eliot in his lectures on education. So the abject failure of social-science programs, after more than half a century of developing them and after expenditures which nobody has summed up, is astonishing.

For concrete evidence of how overwhelming a failure American secondary schooling in the social sciences has been, consider a careful study made in 1967 by Kenneth P. Langton and M. Kent Jennings, of the Survey Research Center of the Institute for Social Research, at the University of Michigan. (This study, subsidized by the Danforth Foundation, was published the next year in The *American Political Science Review*.) The survey was entitled "Political Socialization and the High School Civics Curriculum in the United States."

Some 1,669 high-school seniors, in ninety-seven secondary schools, were interviewed in the course of this survey; so was a parent of each student; so were many of these students' teachers. Langton and Jennings endeavored to ascertain how much political knowledge was obtained through courses in civics; how much political interest was aroused by these courses; "spectator politicization", or the degree to which civics courses stimulated attention to political content in the mass media; political discourse, or the frequency with which students came to discuss politics; political efficacy, or belief that the individual could influence political results; political cynicism, or mistrust of government (which civics courses are supposed to discourage); civic tolerance; and "participative orientation", or the inculcation of willingness to take a part in public affairs. On these eight heads, Langton and Jennings examined their random sample of students, parents, teachers, and school administrators. Under the general head of "civics", Langton and Jennings included courses in government, American politics, "problems of democracy", and the like.

To what degree, these researchers hoped to ascertain, did such studies in civics, during the junior and senior years of high school, result in increased knowledge, interest, and the rest? Might it be reasonable to suppose that those students interviewed by the Survey Research team, having studied civics in their junior and senior years, should be fifty per cent better off than their peers who did not study civics during the last two years of high school? Is fifty per cent too much to expect? Ten per cent advantage, perhaps? Would you believe five per cent?

If you would, you are too sanguine. For, this survey revealed, the typical student who had studied civics in his closing two years of high school *knew almost nothing more, and had almost no more interest in matters political*, than did his opposite number the typical student who had escaped enrollment in civics courses. The advantages of the student who had studied civics, in the phrase of the researchers, "border on the trivial. The highest positive eta coefficient is .06, and the highest partial beta is but .11 (for political knowledge)." To translate, Langton and Jennings discovered that enrollment in civics courses conferred only *one per cent* more knowledge upon students exposed to such studies, as compared with students who had abstained from the study of civics. On other heads than "political knowledge", the advantages reaped by such students of civics were less than one per cent. In fine, typical students gained next to nothing from these elaborate and expensive social-science programs in high schools.

Next to nothing? Why, that is to speak kindly. For one group of pupils did acquire a little knowledge of, and interest in, civics, government, and allied subjects: the Negro pupils. These black students did not gain a great deal from such courses, but they gained more than did the white students, doubtless in part because civil-rights controversies of that decade had made them attentive, relatively, to political discussion. Now if one were to have eliminated Negroes from the Langton-Jennings sample, it might have become clear that the average white student knew *less* about political concerns, and cared less, after taking advanced high-school courses in civics, than he would have known or cared if he never had been enrolled in such courses! It was not merely that our social-studies programs had accomplished nothing, at least in their upper levels; worse, it seemed possible that they had positively bored the pupils into political ignorance and apathy.

Now suppose that a survey of the teaching of physics, or of algebra, or of driver-training, had revealed that America's high schools not only imparted little or nothing of enduring knowledge in two years of advanced study of these subjects, but actually had been counterproductive of learning: what a tumult of protest and recrimination probably would have resulted! Yet the Langton-Jennings analysis attracted little general attention. It was as if school administrators, teachers, and the general public were resigned to failure in social studies; as if the social sciences were regarded, implicitly, as no better than a form of adolescent-sitting. Suppose, indeed, that professors of physical education had ascertained that at the end of two years of playing on school teams, young basketball players were no more accomplished in their sport than other boys who had not touched a basketball for two years: what howls of wrath would have been heard! But who minds social studies? Politicians can take care of themselves and us, you know.

Indeed, Langton and Jennings wrote, "the increments are so minuscule as to raise serious questions about the utility of investing in government courses in senior high school, at least as these courses are presently constituted. Furthermore, when we tested the impact of the history curriculum under the same control conditions it was as low as or lower than the civics curriculum."

These scholars suggested or implied some causes for this sorry state of social-science instruction: the fact that the most "advanced" civics courses were not advanced at all, but boringly repetitious of earlier courses; that they were got up without imagination or vigor; that the textbooks were dull and much of a sameness. Whatever the causes, it was clear enough in 1967 that one's son or daughter would have profited more from a course in camp cookery than from a course in problems of democracy—supposing us to be interested in improved political socialization.

Could it be that the educationist Dogma of Civics was dead wrong? Could it be that actually, all this time, the public schools had accomplished next to nothing by way of clearing the path for tomorrow's peaceful egalitarian society? Could "citizenship education" have been so ineffectual, ever since the Second World War, as it indubitably had been boring at the typical public school?

To Langton's and Jennings' suggested causes of the failure of civics-instruction, one might add a number of possibilities. For one thing, often the social-science teacher for the upper grades of high school was an athletics coach, at least in the smaller high schools, assigned to the painful task because "anybody can teach that civics stuff." For another, there existed the temptation, unreproved by school principals usually, for civics teachers to take out their high-school charges on desultory expeditions to the city hall, the police station, the municipal sewage works, for "culturally enriching experiences"—instead of actually teaching something about federal and state constitutions, say. Yet larger than these faults, it seems to me, there looms a deficiency in the usual social-science teaching which has been described by few writers on secondary education: the lamentable separation of "social science" from humane learning. The triumph of behaviorism in the universities and colleges has contributed to this dryness and dullness of social-science teaching, for the high-school teachers themselves, unless they are elderly, ordinarily have been taught behavioristic approaches to the social studies. Masses of social-science data, linked together by some civil-religion platitudes about the goodness of democracy, do not suffice to rouse the imagination and the affections of sixteen- and seventeen-year-old pupils.

It may be objected that I have been describing a survey ten years old. Have not methods and approaches improved since then? In some degree, yes, I think; but not nearly enough. Certainly the scholars who keep track of teaching in their respective disciplines are not cheered by improvements in secondary-school social-science instruction since 1967. Consider the teaching of history—which, as Langton and Jennings remarked, had results in 1967 quite as disheartening as the results in civics, or perhaps even worse. Let us examine the state of the teaching of history, ten years later.

At every level of schooling in America, the historical discipline has been declining since the Second World War. Not seldom it has been abandoned for the pursuit of studies in "special social problems." And of course television has made its inroads: who yearns for Thucydides when we have Fawcett-Majors? The professors of history, at least, recall the aphorism of Santayana that those who ignore history are condemned to repeat it.

Dr. Richard S. Kirkendall, executive secretary of the Organization of American Historians, made an interesting report late in 1975 on the decay of historical studies. The OAH, since then, has taken up the subject repeatedly in its *Newsletter*. *Time*, the Gallup Poll, the National Municipal League, and a considerable variety of newspapers, local school systems, and educational groups tested or questioned students and teachers, during 1976 and 1977, about historical knowledge and interest. All these surveys were discouraging, particularly when it is considered that they were conducted about the time of the Bicentennial Year of 1976, which must have revived at least some degree of interest in American history.

Professor Kirkendall's report, "The Status of History in the Schools" (*Journal of American History*, September, 1975), proved, "if proof is necessary, that history is at crisis and that history's crisis is not merely a part of the large difficulties of academic life at the present time." One of the chief causes for the decay of interest in history, Kirkendall and his colleagues found, was the notion that history "is not a practical subject." One thinks of Albert Jay Nock's essay "The Value of Useless Knowledge", in which Nock argued that though historical knowledge has no immediately practical application, nevertheless it is the most *valuable* of all intellectual disciplines. Professors of education, school-board members, and the typical teacher of the social sciences have not read Nock; nor have most college presidents.

"Signs of improvement are scarce," Dr. Kirkendall reported; and although the Organization of American Historians dredged up a few cheering symptoms of historical vitality here and there since 1975, in general the country is no better off in this discipline than it was two or three years past—perhaps slightly worse off. "Confidence and interest in history are not nearly as widespread and strong among students, educational administrators, and politicians as they were only a few years ago. Doubts about its usefulness for the individual and for society now exert a large influence on attitudes and decisions," Professor Kirkendall concludes. "It seems unlikely that historians can destroy the influence of presentism, but they can reduce the anti-historical consequences of it by demonstrating the value of historical perspective and historical comparisons and the importance of a sense of time and place."

Professor Kirkendall is a temperate historian. My own academic discipline, at three universities, was modern history; and I am tempted to be intemperate about the grim phenomenon of what amounts to deliberate neglect, or positive exclusion, of history from many elementary and secondary schools. This anti-historical attitude, found in many educationists, is another strong symptom of intellectual decadence.

Consider the results in St. Louis, in 1976, of testing a representative sample of one hundred and twenty-two high-school students on their knowledge of basic American history, government, and world affairs. The test, a sound if simple one, was prepared by the Gallup organization and the National Municipal League. The passing score was supposed to be seventy out of one hundred questions. But the average point-grade was 49.15. Only twenty-two students passed the St. Louis testing; one hundred failed. Most of these students were graduating seniors.

Or consider the *New York Times*' History Knowledge and Attitude Survey, conducted among 1,856 freshmen on one hundred and ninety-four colleges campuses in 1976. Forty-four questions were asked. The average student in the sample answered correctly only twenty-one of these questions; the highest score by any student was forty-one. Chairmen of history departments or social-science coordinators in six cities had been asked to evaluate this test. They had estimated that a typical college-bound high-school senior ought to be able to obtain a score of seventy per cent on the examination. Actually, only one college freshman in twelve scored so high.

One of the livelier historical writers of our century, Professor John Lukacs, has argued that we are entering upon an era when historical literature will supplant the novel and other forms of literary expression. Certainly the novel seems to be decaying as a form of art; but in general historical writing has not found a large public. The provinciality of time never more strongly afflicted the classes nominally educated.

"We learn from history that we learn nothing from history," Hegel wrote. After experience of adversity among us, perhaps that hard truth may revive our historical consciousness. I mean that when the gods of the copybook headings with terror and slaughter return, chastened men and women perceive afresh that they have paid heed to the record of achievement and failure which we call history.

If we cut off the rising generation from historical consciousness, we cut them off from knowledge generally, for the present is evanescent, the future unknowable. What can be done about this decay? Better historical writing and better teaching can help. I think of the advice of Benjamin Disraeli, in *Contarini Fleming*: "Read no history, only biography . . ." Disraeli meant that the historical solidity of biography captures the imagination more readily than does historical abstraction. This would be true especially in the teaching of history in primary and even secondary schools.

However that may be, the recent unhistorical, or a-historical, or anti-historical, attitude (most conspicuous in the public schools of New York state, in recent years) is unique in the history of civilized man. It seems to parallel a widespread disinterest, during the past few decades, in the question of the immortality of the soul. But interest in the latter subject has been reviving, these past few years; perhaps interest in history will be reinvigorated also. I suspect that people uninterested in their own souls may forfeit their own souls; and that a people uninterested in their own history presently will cease to have a history, though not in the sense implied by the phrase, "Happy the land that has no history." They may cease, indeed, to be a people.

From my wanderings over the face of the land, during the past quarter of a century, visting many universities and colleges and some high schools, I judge that schools at any level in this country accomplish little to form the opinions of the rising generation, where questions of public policy are concerned. My experience as president of one foundation concerned with higher education, and as consultant to another educational foundation, confirms this impression.

So far as the war in southeastern Asia was concerned, students were influenced by television, radio, newspapers, parental and church opinion, and—especially in the colleges—by the exhortations of student political organizations. Even though comment on Asiatic affairs was the topic of lectures or disputation in a good many classrooms (not always in classes relevant to foreign policy), the number of students persuaded to concur in the opinions of the teacher may have been equalled by the number of those students who, resenting indoctrination, reacted against a teacher's *obiter dicta*. What about the "teach-ins" of the 'Sixties? Why, those were not college classes at all, but political rallies harangued by ideologues. Teaching- and research-assistants indeed influenced the opinions of undergraduates concerning Vietnam, but not in their demi-professorial capacity—rather, in their capacity as upper-echelon students, usually as leaders of ideological student-groups.

This particular state of affairs woke no great discontent in me, for the classroom ought to be a place for the objective imparting of an intellectual discipline, not for the promulgation of the instructor's private judgments on prudential questions—particularly when those private opinions are of a partisan character. A class, at any level of schooling, ought not to be converted into a captive audience for factional rhetoric, no matter how well intended; and in college and university, especially, some toleration for differing opinions among the students is important. The scholar's primary responsibility is not toward faction (no matter how important a question of the hour may seem to be), but toward an intellectual inheritance and a body of knowledge: the professor ought not to convert himself into a political propagandist, and the student cannot be expected to accept passively a programmatic injunction concerning which there exist honest and serious differences of opinion.

Nor do I find it alarming that school and college had not communicated, until the Vietnamese war was upon us, much factual information about southeastern Asia. Time is limited; teachers and the authors of textbooks cannot accurately predict, or prepare themselves for, sudden changes in the affairs of nations; and until the war in Vietnam became a passionate issue, it was natural and right that whatever Oriental studies students might undertake should be centered upon China, Japan, and India.

So I was neither surprised nor displeased that secondary schools and colleges did not much affect the convictions of students concerning American measured in Asia, at least through classroom instruction. There was no single right view of these Asiatic complexities which should have been thrust upon students as if it had been a body of dogmas in international politics.

In a larger sense, nevertheless, school, college, and university have done too little to prepare their students for making considered judgments upon public affairs, foreign or domestic. At the school level— and even in a good many college textbooks and classes—political socialization too often amounts to little more than the imparting of a kind of ethos of sociability, with a faint *Animal Farm* aroma. The rising generation is assured, for instance, that there is only one tolerable form of government, anywhere, democracy (most vaguely defined or described); that practically anything ever done by "us Americans" has been wise and blameless, except for minor activities by isolated robber barons and ephemeral crypto-imperialists; that America's "problems" are mostly of a material sort, to be solved by positive legislation; that in foreign affairs, little is necessary but to trust in the omniscience of the United Nations. I find it small wonder that students are bored and resentful at this bland intellectual diet, and that neither their political principles nor their attitudes toward social questions of the hour are directly affected by such instruction.

Although I am not sorry that John Dewey's hopes for democratic socialization through the schools have gone glimmering, still school and college necessarily bear considerable responsibility for the maintenance of a just social order. Among a population lacking deference toward any class or restricted body of informed opinion (with reference here to Walter Bagehot's of description of the deferential democratic English of Victorian times), political apathy or ignorance must result eventually in the making of public decisions by demagogues, special-interest groups, or ideological cliques. And decisions must be made in this age which will be irrevocable; in a time when the fountains of the great deep are broken up, smug inculcation of approved democratic attitudes in an American society allegedly secure—why, that will not suffice. The very small percentage of American adults positively active in politics—to the extent of merely of attending a political gathering, contributing a dollar to a political party, or urging somebody else to vote—is said to be at its highest in California; and even there only some five per cent of the voting public is thus active. This is an evidence, in part, of the failure of schools and colleges to rouse interest in public concerns or to convey much useful political knowledge. An even more striking piece of evidence in this matter is the very low turn-out of college students as voters, now that they can vote when eighteen years old; on some campuses, only five per cent of the eligible students vote in public elections—even national elections.

Worse still, perhaps, the dearth of imagination among leaders of both political parties, and the necessity which those leaders feel for reliance upon sloganizing, suggest that our formal education in politics amounts to little more than an amorphous description of existing institutions. In a fit of absence of mind, collectively we slide toward the mass-age, as if things were in the saddle, riding mankind; few Americans take long views, and fewer suggest alternative public courses. We are awakened only by violence to the disintegration of urban life and the growth of an American proletariat, or to the consequences of an erratic foreign policy.

Of many reformatory programs which might be commenced, I think it especially important to reunite the ethical understanding with the study of politics. Economics moves upward into politics, politics upward into ethics. A political structure without discernible ethical foundation will attract little interest or loyalty from young people; students in both college and high school are starved for first principles today—

and many of them know it. It will not do to talk windily of "the essential rightness of democracy" or of "the religion of democracy" as a simplistic substitute for political theory.

It does not follow that an introduction to political theory and precept need be abstract. The ethical imagination may be moved, particularly early in life, through the tool of biography—by which I do not mean simple panegyric. Young people need models, exemplars; and often political institutions and historical processes are better discerned through biographical examination of great men than through abstract or chronological analysis. This approach has been much neglected for the past thirty years and more. Andrew Jackson, for instance, is interesting to high-school freshmen; the Bank and the tariffs aren't really. But one can learn much about the Bank and the tariffs through a lively study of Jackson.

One promising reform might be the introduction of a course in the history of ideas and institutions, the sort of thing now postponed until college, and done badly there. I can imagine, for instance, such a course that would commence with revelation and social order—the Hebraic and Jewish origins; which would touch upon the glory that was Greece, as seem in Sophocles, Thucydides, and Plato (though not, for heaven's sake, labelling Plato as some sort of modern ideologue); which would proceed to the grandeur that was Rome, discussing the high old Roman virtue, and the minds of Virgil and Cicero; which would not blandly ignore Christianity, but would have to do with St. Paul and St. Augustine; which would trace the growth of European order, from Gregory the Great to Dante, and touch on the dignity of man, and confront Luther and Calvin, and tell of European thought in the century of genius; which would describe English freedom and justice, and the growth of constitutions and the common law; which would tell something of the age of Edmund Burke and Adam Smith; would examine the foundations of American society, the generation of Revolution and Constitution, through thought and background; which would analyze enduring standards in the twentieth century, emphasizing authority and freedom, the inner order of the soul and the outer order of the commonwealth, the complementary character of permanence and change.

This would be a far cry from the pabulum fed to young people nowadays: it would be a study of moral philosophy, if you will, as related to social institutions. But I believe that even the mediocre student would find it more satisfying than the dull and repetitious courses to which he is subjected today. It offers something for the parched imagination. And American society cannot be properly understood, or preserved, or improved, without an apprehending of its sources.

A few years ago I attemped myself something of this sort: I wrote a fat book called *The Roots of American Order*. The people who persuaded me to write that book had been confident that it would be widely adopted as a textbook in schools, and there work much improvement. I wrote the book as directly and simply as was in me, but not a single secondary school has made use of it, so far as I know: it was found too difficult. A few colleges assigned the book to classes, but even at that level most instructors fear to venture beyond the conventional dryas-dust textbook. My book did sell well—but to the general adult public, the old "common reader." Most high-school teachers and even college instructors now seem to take it for granted that their students are indolent dull tools, with limited vocabularies and more limited interests.

So I confess that we are poorly prepared for such a reinvigoration as I have suggested above. Among political scientists and sociologists and even professors of history in university and college, the dominant modes of thought have been behavioristic and institutional; this intellectual climate of opinion has overshadowed teachers' colleges and secondary schools, too. Little place is left for theory, and for the moral imagination. Even should we commence a vigorous improvement of social studies today, the results would not be apparent in colleges for some years, and no sooner in high schools; certainly this reinvigoration would not occur in time to affect the present drift of American policy in Africa, say. But there always will be wars and rumors of wars, and the high decisions which the American republic must make will not diminish with the passing of time.

We must much improve the training of teachers of social studies, for primary and intermediate and secondary schools. We must have fewer course in educational technique, and more and better courses in genuine history, genuine politics, and genuine philosophy. There must be less reliance upon the crib, by teacher and by student. A system or hierarchy of social studies should commence in the first grade, proceeding right up to the college level; at present, most schools have only an erratic omnium-gatherum doing duty for the regular social disciplines.

In this last particular, cheerfulness breaks in. The Educational Research Council of America already has produced a complete program of social studies, all the way from kindergarten through the twelfth grade, including history, government, geography, economics, ethics, and related disciplines; and this complete program has been made generally available through a textbook-publishing firm. It is the best program of the sort ever to have been devised in this country, despite concessions which any educational foundation or publisher is compelled to make nowadays to various pressure-groups. Other publishers are emulating or imitating the ERC approach—so that, directly or indirectly, the Educational Research Council's long labors now are beginning to influence a large proportion of American school pupils. Gradually teachers are won over to the intelligent methods of the Council, for all their reluctance to abandon the dull manuals and methods to which they have been accustomed. It is worth remarking that the ERC program never attracted any support from the federal Office of Education.

When the ERC program and any similar programs have turned out high-school graduates in some numbers, there will occur a marked improvement of college instruction in the social disciplines. An ethical understanding of the civil social order runs through the Educational Research Council's undertaking—this the contribution, in large part, of Dr. Raymond English, the program's director.

Politics is the application of ethics to the concerns of the commonwealth. Politics cannot be apprehended properly without reference to biographical and historical models for order, justice, and freedom; nor without reference to theory, which is not at all the same thing as ideology. Any community, great or small, is knit together by belief in certain enduring norms or principles. When knowledge of those norms dwindles, the fabric of society wears thin. Lacking a knowledge of the permanent things, a people become interested chiefly in immediate self-advantage or pleasure. Then things fall apart. And good-natured, unambitious men, as George Bernard Shaw put it, "stand by in helpless horror."

I do not pretend that the study of the social sciences in college would be reformed automatically by a raising of the standards of high-school teaching in those subjects. Much college instruction in politics, sociology, psychology, and related studies is independently bad. Some old colleges of high reputation turn out graduates whose knowledge of history and politics would have discredited an eight-grade student in the 'Twenties. There is fixed in my memory a classroom scene at one such college. A distinguished visiting professor of American studies had addressed, as guest lecturer, a class of sophomores; his discourse had been witty and provocative. He called for questions. No student could think of anything to say; neither, apparently, could the regular instructor for the class, who had taught political science at this college ever since the Second World War.

At last one student inquired, in rather a whining tone, "Why didn't Congress impeach Nixon for firing Hickel?" (This reference to the resignation of President Nixon's first secretary of the interior was quite irrelevant to the visiting professor's lecture.) Everyone in the class, the regular instructor included, seemed to consider this an intelligent inquiry, not being aware that members of the cabinet serve at a President's pleasure.

My friend the visiting professor apparently took this question as facetious merely; he called for other questions. None was forthcoming. He then proceeded to put his own questions to the class: what did they think of the soundness of a recent Supreme Court decision? No one present had an opinion. At length the regular instructor volunteered, "The Constitution is so vaguely written that no one knows what it means."

The improvement of the social-science curriculum in high schools would not remove such pseudo-professors from college, but such improvement might raise up freshmen and sophomores competent to challenge entrenched professorial ignorance. We have to begin somewhere.

Much more ought to be said about the reform of elementary and secondary schooling. But there have been many good books on that subject published already, and I have confined myself in this chapter and the preceding chapter to academic disciplines which I have taught myself, although at college or university levels. We pass, then, in the next chapter, to an attempt at describing what a real college ought to be—presuming that even nowadays enough competent freshmen could be found to enroll in a few such colleges, and praying that many more such competent freshmen may emerge from reformed high schools, before the end of this century.

5

The Revitalized College: a Model

PERHAPS FIFTEEN YEARS ago, a graduate of a university in New York brought suit against his *alma mater*. He had been enticed to enter those academic halls (so ran his brief) by the promise that through collegiate studies he would obtain wisdom. But after being graduated, he found himself ignorant as before; so he demanded his money back, and compensation for the loss of his time. I am sorry that the courts of New York did not find in his favor: had they done so, some reform of the higher learning in America might have commenced then.

The Liberty Fund, an Indianapolis foundation, once asked a number of persons, including myself, to present models for a good college of arts and sciences, regardless of whether there should be any remote possibility of such an institution being founded or renewed, and without concern for its prospects of survival, should it be founded. Being no Gnostic or Utopian, however, I then ventured to outline a reasonably practical scheme for such an institution: a model of a college which *could* be brought into being and *could* endure under favorable circumstances. There exist historical, and indeed some extant, examples of what should be done; in an eclectic manner, I blended some of the virtues of those examples into my model. Change being the means of our preservation, I suggested various adaptations or improvements calculated to make the traditional American college relevant to the modern age. That model, somewhat polished, I present again in this chapter.

The chief practical obstacle to the success of such a college as I have in mind (and it should be understood that I am describing a college of arts and sciences, not a university with graduate faculties and large facilities for research) is the low estate to which the American high school has fallen. Albert Jay Nock, in an exercise similar to mine, suggested once that before a really good college could commence its work, a sound high school—nay, primary and intermediate schools, too—must be founded, so that the students intending to enroll in the college might obtain adequate preparation, then as now available in very few schools anywhere. Surely that would be a mighty advantage for such a new college. Failing that, however, it might not be impossible to attract first-year college students of tolerably decent preparation by active seeking of them up and down the land; for as Nock (after Isaiah and Matthew Arnold) himself remarked in a different essay, there exists always a Remnant, more numerous than any prophet thinks possible, who will hearken to a clear call and promise. A portion of that educational Remnant, aged seventeen or eighteen years, would suffice to form a hopeful first-year class, for the number ought to be kept small.

First of all, let me suggest the chief objects or ends of such a model college (bearing in mind that I am describing an independent or "private" college, probably church-related, as distinguished from an "honors" college within a state university, to be outlined in a later chapter). Then let us consider the chief approaches to those ends; next discuss the failings, and the hopes for regeneration, within existing independent colleges; finally, offer certain concrete proposals for the general frame and conduct of this model college.

We begin with first principles, which always sound platitudinous. What are the principal objects of a college of arts and sciences? I defined them early in this book: they are the imparting of some measure of wisdom and virtue to the rising generation. A college, at least in the American understanding of that word, generally is intended for the transmitting of an existing body of knowledge to young people; it is distinguished thus from a university, which possesses advanced schools, less strongly emphasizes the function of teaching, and may have facilities and opportunities for more creative work and research.

The object of a college education is not success, pleasure, or sociability, but the acquiring of wisdom and virtue. (Success, pleasure, and sociability are all very well for a college, so long as they do not interfere seriously with the college's primary objects.) Wisdom and virtue are not the same as facts, or utility, or training, or even knowledge. No college can confer wisdom and virtue automatically, but a good college can help its members to find the means for pursuing wisdom and pursuing virtue. Wisdom means apprehension of enduring reality; virtue means the development of strong moral principles and habits. (I refer here to Aristotle's "intellectual virtue"—the kind of virtue which may be taught, as distinguished from the kind of moral virtue derived from inheritance and custom.)

I do not say that these objects have been forgotten altogether in the typical college of our day, but surely they have been obscured. If the college can recover relevance to these objects, we may move toward a more tolerable private order and a more just and secure public order.

The true college is an academic community, on a humane scale, in which a body of senior scholars (the professors) and a body of junior scholars (the students) are united in seeking after truth. Once upon a time, whether at English and Scottish university colleges or at American independent colleges, the members of such an academic community were joined also in a common religious profession. Common belief about the nature of the human condition, and common worship, remain desirable in a true college—though today most college chapels have been reduced to assembly-halls, if that. I endeavor to present to readers of this book a model college that might help to make the acquisition of wisdom and virtue less difficult than it is at present; a college conducted by learned men, some of whose graduates might be philosophers (lovers of wisdom), and all of whose graduates might know something of virtue, and be people of right reason, humane inclinations, and sound taste.

There have been such colleges in this country. One such was St. Stephen's College—now called Bard College—at Annandale-on-Hudson, when Dr. Bernard Iddings Bell was president there. (He told me once that he gave up the presidency when strong objection was raised to his rule that the students should dress decently and rise when professors entered a room.) There are a few still which approximate to my model.

For a literary model of such a college we do well to turn to the writings of John Henry Newman. The best-known of these is Newman's *The Idea of a University*; the most moving, his discourse "What Is a University?" in *The Office and Work of Universities*. Newman was describing a university with several faculties, not a liberal college merely; but most of what he wrote may be applied to our present concern. His university never took on flesh: the Ireland of his day was not ready for it, and Ireland seems less ready now.

Newman emphasized that the aim of the formal higher learning was cultivation of the intellect for the intellect's own sake. (In his Irish circumstances at that time, it was necessary that he emphasize the claims of the intellect; for the Irish bishops, fearing the modern mind, were all too ready to settle for faith and morals, looking upon the proposed university mainly as an enlarged seminary.) Yet if we examine Newman's work in general, we come to understand that by "intellect" or "knowledge" he meant no narrow Rationalism. He knew that the fear of God is the beginning of wisdom; he knew, too, that a primary function of the higher learning is to develop the moral imagination; he understood that the arrogant reason may be baneful unless it is disciplined and directed to ethical purposes.

Deriving my principles from Newman in part, I hold that the higher learning is an intellectual means to an ethical end; that the college is meant to join knowledge with virtue, so helping to develop persons who enjoy some wisdom because they subordinate private rationality to what Eliot called "the permanent things." The means must be strictly and rigorously intellectual; the end must be ethical, in that right reason is employed to attain moral worth.

I recommend, then, a restoration of genuinely liberal education, within which the natural sciences, in their philosophical sense, are comprehended. By a liberal discipline, says Newman in the fifth discourse of *The Idea of a University*, "A habit of mind is formed which lasts throughout life, of which the attributes are, freedom, equitableness, calmness, moderation, and wisdom; or what in a former discourse I have ventured to call the philosophical habit." We should not claim too much for such a discipline: "Its direct business is not to steel the soul against temptation or to console it in its affliction, any more than to set the loom in motion, or to direct the steam carriage; be it ever so much the means or the condition of both material and moral advancement, still, taken by and large, it as little mends our hearts as it improves our temporal circumstances." It cannot directly instill virtue: "Quarry the granite rock with razors, or moor the vessel with a thread of silk; then you may hope with such keen and delicate instruments as human knowledge and human reason to contend against those giants, the passion and the pride of man."

Not learning or acquirement, but thought or reason exercised upon knowledge, is the end of intellectual training. What we seek through formal education, Newman declares, is "the clear, calm, accurate vision and comprehension of all things, as far as the finite mind can embrace them, each in its place, and with its own characteristics upon it."

What higher education can accomplish is limited. But if it can confer, or help to confer, this wise vision, it will have done much to enable a man to order his own soul and thereby come to a condition of moral worth. By doing that, it will have contributed mightily toward order in the commonwealth.

I think that the peculiar conditions of our time and our society demand, more than before, a reinvigoration of truly liberal learning. This hour, in some ways, is favorable to the restoration or the establishment of colleges with principle. Most colleges today, nevertheless, seem terrified of commitment to principle; indeed, they seem opposed to principles on principle. At too many colleges, trustees and presidents and professors tend to think of doubt as good in itself, of "ambivalence" as identical with the liberal understanding, and of faith as bigotry. Thus such colleges are left with merely quantitative standards or (at best) a vague aestheticism. What a rudder in a sea of troubles! The better students, or perhaps most students, at these institutions have become aware of the lack of ethical character—and do not rejoice in it, whatever their private lives may be; they are attracted to any professor who seems to believe strongly in something or other, even if his belief has devastating consequences.

It is the college which can boast justifiably of its commitment to principle, and of its high standards, and of its humane scale, that will attract the better senior scholars, the better junior scholars, and the benefactions of private patrons, foundations, and business. The college can survive and prosper not by imitating the mass-schooling methods of Behemoth University, or the educational shams of Brummagem University, but by offering a discipline of intellect, ethical in aim, which mass-education and sham-education neglect. So before I proceed to some regenerative recommendations, I touch again upon ways in which the American college has gone astray.

The aim of the oldfangled college was ethical, I repeat—the development of moral understanding and of humane leadership; but the method was intellectual, the enlargement of mind and conscience through well-defined literary disciplines. A college was an establishment for the study of great literature: it was nearly that simple.

Through the study of great literature, young people prepared themselves for teaching, for the ministry, for the law, for politics, for public leadership. This was what Sir Thomas Elyot had called "the education of governors." Whatever the deficiencies of this mode of higher education, it produced a body of sound-principled and literate men to be the leaders of the American democracy. They learned to govern themselves and to serve the republic through close attention to wise books: the poetry, the philosophy, and the history of Greece and Rome; the Bible, and the history of the Jews; something of modern thought and languages; and something of the literature of mathematics and science.

The subjects of study were few, and the course of study was uniform.

The intention of the college was not to confer a vague smattering of every branch of knowledge upon its students, but to teach students the fundamental disciplines of logical thought, provide them with a taste and a critical faculty for independent reading and reflection, and then send them into the world with a cast of character fitted for ethical and intellectual leadership. If these young persons remembered no more from college than something of Biblical history and precepts from Cicero and episodes from Plutarch (though some young men learned and retained a great deal besides), still that knowledge prepared them better for life—the life of their time, or of ours—than does the cafeteria-curriculum of many universities and colleges nowadays, whose graduates may not open a single important book after they have snatched their diplomas.

Most surviving American liberal-arts colleges fail to achieve this fairly modest goal because they try to be all things to all men. They promise what they cannot perform, and never could perform. They promise to teach adjustment to the group, social polish, sociability, trades, salesmanship, business acumen, and the art of worldly wisdom—or what you will. They ape the functions of large universities or of technical schools. With murmured apology and shamefacedness, they consign to a dusty corner of the curriculum their old disciplines—when, that is, they do not abolish altogether the classics, humane letters, languages, moral philosophy, and speculative science. Those arts which teach us what it is to be fully human are thrust aside by business science, communications skills, journalism, premedicine, rudimentary sociology, and even "pop culture." Most of the colleges have abandoned their ethical object and forgotten their intellectual means. The wonder is not that the colleges are in difficulties, but that they survive at all. For when function ceases, form atrophies.

Certain things a college can do very well. It can give the student the tools for educating himself throughout his life. It can present to him certain general principles for the governance of personality and community. It can help him to see what makes life worth living. It can teach him basic disciplines which will be of infinite value in professional specialization at a graduate school or in his subsequent apprenticeship to any commercial or industrial occupation.

And certain things no honest college can pretend to do at all. It cannot teach the student directly to win friends and influence people. It cannot make him a successful captain of industry, an accomplished engineer, or a specialized scientist. It cannot guarantee him worldly prosperity. It cannot enroll him in a survey-course in "world culture" and pour the milk of learning into him.

Now it is quite possible that a person who has been immersed in the pseudo-schooling and the vocational shams of a corrupted college may enjoy a considerable measure of practical success and, at the same time, be an intelligent and honest man. Two friends of mine, who attended the college that I did, there majored in journalism. One can no more really learn the craft of journalism in college than one really can learn the craft of whaling from reading *Moby Dick*. One may acquire in college, indeed, a knowledge of something about the modern age from the study of history, geography, and politics, or some aptitude for writing from steady practice at preparing papers for various courses. But "majoring in journalism" does not make one a newspaperman. My two friends, despite their academic curriculum, came to read good books and to fill responsible positions: one a chief project engineer at an automobile factory, the other chief underwriter for an insurance firm. They redeemed themselves from the weaknesses of their formal education, and, for that matter, learned much in their college years— but not from the vocational training they fondly had embraced. The "useful" knowledge, the "practical" instruction, is obsolete almost before the student enters the busy world. A college wastes its resources and its students' time when it pretends to teach what can be taught only in workaday life, in the trade school, or in the graduate school.

What the college actually ought to do, and can do, was better expressed by Irving Babbitt than I could put it: "The best of the small colleges," Babbitt wrote in *Literature and the American College*, "will render a service to American education if they decide to make a sturdy defense of the humane tradition instead of trying to rival the great universities in displaying a full line of educational novelties. In the latter case, they may become third-rate and badly equipped scientific schools, and so reenact the fable of the frog that tried to swell itself to the size of an ox. . . . Even though the whole world seems bent upon living the quantitative life, the college should remember that its business is to make of its graduates men of quality in the real and not the conventional meaning of the term. In this way it will do its share toward creating that aristocracy of character and intelligence which is needed in a community like ours to take the place of an aristocracy of birth, and to counteract the tendency toward an aristocracy of money."

For the past seven decades, the average American college has disregarded Babbitt's admonition, pleading that the college must give the public what the public seems to desire. But now the time is upon us when the college must heed the principles which Babbitt himself so well exemplified. Behemoth U. and Brummagem U. have so totally yielded to the presumed "public demand" for vocationalism, specialization, and intellectual egalitarianism that even the most complaisant college of arts and sciences no longer can compete successfully with its enormous tax-supported rivals for the favor of those students who desire, or think they desire, a shallow veneer of "culture", a trade-school training with a college diploma, and four years of idleness. If the independent college competes with the state-supported institutions along those lines, the college will succeed in enrolling only those students who fail to meet even the relaxed academic requirements of the state-supported institution—plus a sprinkling, perhaps, of students who are attracted by a college's relationship to a Christian denomination, supposing that the college has bothered to retain anything of that sort. And few will be passionately interested in keeping alive a college that has become not much better than an intellectual bargain-basement stuffed with rejects from the upper floors.

So I set down here, tentatively, some general principles by which colleges might begin to resume their old functions—and perhaps to improve upon their old performance. To clothe these principles with flesh would require some courage of the people responsible for a college's policies. But the American college cannot afford to drift much longer with the current of events. Out of urgent necessity, if from no higher motive, the college policy-makers may begin to re-examine the ends and means of a college education.

I. The college should reaffirm that the objects of the higher learning are wisdom and virtue, and that it seeks to attain an ethical purpose through intellectual means.

II. The college should make it clear that this ethical end is sought through disciplines of the mind, exacting in character, which regard "useless knowledge" as more valuable than simple utilitarian skills.

III. The college should return to a concise curriculum emphasizing religious knowledge, moral philosophy, humane letters, rhetoric, languages, history, logic, and the theoretical sciences.

IV. The college should set its face against amorphous "survey courses" and similar substitutes for intellectual disciplines. Such a smattering produces only that little learning which is a dangerous thing.

V. The college should turn away from vocationalism, resigning to trade schools and industrial "in-service training" what the college never was founded to undertake.

VI. The college should abandon its attempt to encroach upon the specialized and professional studies which are the proper province of the graduate schools.

VII. The college should say less about "socialization" and "personality building" and more about the improvement of the human reason, for the reason's own sake. The development of sound character will follow from that.

VIII. The college should give up as lost endeavor its aspiration to attract those students who desire the "extra-curricular benefits" of Behemoth State University, and should offer instead its own natural advantages of personal relationships, smallness of scale, and respect for individuality.

IX. The college should not content itself with enrolling those students who cannot obtain entrance to a large university or state college. On the contrary, it should begin to set its standards higher than those of Behemoth University.

X. The college should endeavor deliberately to keep its student body within reasonable limits, its humane scale being one of its principal virtues.

XI. The college should emancipate itself from quasi-commercialized programs of athletics, an expensive and often anti-intellectual pastime in which it cannot compete successfully with Behemoth University.

XII. The college should reduce to a minimum the elective features of its curriculum, for one of the college's principal strengths, formerly, was its recognition of order and hierarchy in the higher learning, and the undergraduate ordinarily is not yet capable of judging with discretion what his course of studies ought to be.

XIII. The college should bear in mind that its "service to the community" consists in truly educating some young people who will leaven the lump of society with their reason and their moral worth; that otherwise the college is not a "service institution."

XIV. The college should inculcate in its students a sentiment of gratitude toward the generations which have preceded us in time and a sense of obligation toward the generations yet to be born. It should remind the rising generation that we are part of a long continuity and essence, a community of souls transcending time; and that we moderns are only dwarfs standing upon the shoulders of giants. This consciousness lies at the heart of a liberal education.

Canon Bernard Iddings Bell once showed a visitor from England about the environs of Chicago. They drove past a handsome Gothic building of stone. "Is that a school?" inquired the visitor.

"Yes—a new one, 'distressed' to appear old," Dr. Bell replied.

"Indeed! Who is the headmaster?"

"There is no headmaster."

"Curious! A kind of soviet of teachers, I suppose."

"There are no masters at all."

"Really? Do the boys teach one another?"

"As yet, there are no students. Here in the United States, we proceed educationally in a way to which you are unaccustomed," Canon Bell told his friend. "First we erect a building; then we obtain pupils; next we recruit teachers; then we find a headmaster; and at last we determine what is to be taught. You begin at the other end in England."

Let it be otherwise with our model college. The first matter to determine is the program of study, some outlines of which I already have sketched, but which will bear more detailed examination. After that, we turn to the staff, then to the students, and finally to the "plant."

The Curriculum. The program of studies ought to be designed to develop right reason and wake the moral imagination: to impart an apprehension of reality through disciplines which concern the nature of man and the condition in which we find ourselves in this world, it being understood that human beings are moral beings, in whose existence splendor and misery are blended. These studies should be thorough branches of knowledge, not "surveys" or "rap sessions" or courses of ideological exhortation. It will be recalled that in our model college we assume the presence of undergraduates capable of some serious intellectual endeavor, they having obtained a tolerable schooling before they enroll in our model college.

There should be only a few subjects taught, but those should be taught thoroughly and well. It would be best to have no one enroll in more than three courses each term. The college year should consist of six months only, after the Scottish fashion; in the month-long vacations at Christmas and Easter, and during summer, the students would have opportunity—and perhaps necessity—for independent reading, discussion among themselves, and travel.

The primary disciplines ought to be moral philosophy (not the fashonable logical positivism), humane letters (to develop critical power, not mere "appreciation"), rhetoric (perhaps united with humane letters), history (philosophically considered), political economy (not the amorphous rudimentary "sociology" or "social science" which afflicts most colleges nowadays), physics and higher mathematics (these being most important for developing the philosophical cast of mind), biological science (also with a view to theory), classical and modern languages and literatures, and perhaps music and the visual arts (these latter being critical and historical studies, not crafts). Other chairs or subjects might be added, depending upon resources, but they ought not to be added if that would reduce attention to the primary disciplines.

I do not insist that the curriculum suggested above is the only tolerable program of study; I would be willing to accept some amendments, and in later chapters I will give some account of curricula at innovating or restoring colleges which are both sound and interesting. But in general, the subjects I name above are the subjects which should be emphasized in a good college of arts and sciences.

Within these several fields, proliferation of course-offerings and intensive specialization should be discouraged. There ought to be taught methods of approach to a scholarly discipline, rather than masses of information. Specialization might be arranged *within* a general course, according to the talents and interests of professor and student, with "honors" credit for such individual work, perhaps.

Whether there should be a department of theology or religion is a matter for dispute; of course I am outlining a college here, not a seminary. I should not like to see, at the college level, theology separated from philosophy, or religion treated as if it somehow stood outside the province of regular intellectual disciplines. The whole curriculum should be suffused with reverence, in the phrase of Philip Phenix.

A bachelor's degree should be awarded at the end of three years, not four: much time is wasted on courses virtually worthless, at most existing colleges. Perhaps an additional year of study, more specialized, would bring an honors degree. Tests and examinations should be reduced to a minimum, perhaps only at the end of an academic year, but then thorough and severe. Those failing might be permitted to take a similar examination before the commencement of the autumn term of the next academic year; those still failing at this second opportunity would be dismissed from the college.

Instruction ordinarily should be by formal lecture, well prepared. The students would be expected to read thoroughly, far beyond the crib called a textbook. Any professor or instructors whose lectures might be merely the equivalent of a standard textbook would be summarily dismissed. A tutorial system should be adopted, if possible, permitting frequent conferences and programs of reading and paper-writing. This is expensive; but we are discussing the *model* college.

The Staff. Professors and instructors should be appointed upon the basis of learning and liveliness, regardless of degrees. Experience of the world, or personal achievement in a particular field, often might be given preference over a doctoral degree, or over a list of specialized publications.

Every member of the staff should enjoy a degree of freedom in his own approach to instruction, it being understood that he is to teach an intellectual discipline, not some private *doxa*. In a first-year course in history, for example, he might employ the lecture-period for an examination of a particular historical period or problem, thus teaching the historical method and leaving historical narrative to the investigation of the students, a great number of books being available to them.

Management of the college's academic affairs should be in the hands of a college senate, in large part, composed of senior members of the staff. Deans might be chosen by that senate from among their own number, to serve for only a year or two, more or less in rotation. The president might be chosen by the regents or trustees from a number of persons placed in nomination by the senate, ordinarily. New appointments and promotions should lie in the hands of the president and the deans, though to be ratified by the board of regents or trustees. This, like other matters touched upon here, takes it for granted that professors and instructors will be temperate and prudent people chosen only after deliberation. Soundness of character should be a factor in appointment and advancement; for a professor teaches as much by what he is as by what he professes.

The Students. Undergraduates should be admitted upon the basis of real intellectual interests and tolerable preparation; they should understand that they are partners in an academic community, though junior partners. Serious educational deficiencies would be a bar to admittance to this college, but it is unnecessary—nay, undesirable—that all students should be sobersidely and self-consciously intellectual, some diversity in character being commendable. Nor would students need to place high on standard admissions-tests, necessarily, have been in the very first rank at secondary schools, or be required to furnish evidence of possessing some astonishing intelligence-quotient. What matters most is intellectual liveliness, application to studies, and literary competence.

To assure that students' interests are adequately represented, it might be well for them to elect, at intervals of two or three years, a rector—after the pattern of the Scottish universities. This official should be a gentleman and a scholar of mature years, chosen from outside the college, and willing to serve actively; he would have the powers of a tribune.

Numerous scholarships, awarded without regard to students' individual means, should be available. Tuition and fees ought to be kept low, in part through endowments, in part through economy in the expenditure of the college's resources: through the elimination of costly competitive athletic programs, abstinence from grandiose educational schemes, elimination of unnecessary course-offerings, and prejudice against bricks-and-mortar expansion. Also it would be well to encourage, and perhaps to arrange, programs for long-term loans to students, through which they could repay to the college or to a bank, some years after being graduated, the equivalent of their direct cost of instruction.

The Plant. If adequate funds are available for our model college, and a new campus is to be created, the college's buildings should be conspicuously handsome and permanent, but not luxurious. The administration building should be as small and uncomfortable as possible, to discourage educational bureaucracy.

There exist alternatives to the construction of a campus. One of the more obvious is to acquire the premises of a defunct or dying college, supposing its buildings to be pleasant and not altogether too commodious. (Many of the college buildings erected since the Second World War are ugly and shoddy—no bargain at any price.) Another possibility is to buy a large building in the center of a city, adapt and restore it, and lodge the whole college within: the finest example of this is Roosevelt University, Chicago, established in the splendid Romanesque opera house. A community college in Dallas has successfully adapted a large office-building. Sometimes such a purchase will secure better architecture and greater convenience than could the building of a new campus, the costs and options of present-day construction considered.

The model college should avoid, if possible, entering upon the housing business, the feeding business, and the bookshop business; also it should apply the doctrine of *in loco parentis* sparingly. Unless the college is isolated, students should be expected to find their own lodgings and their own meals—though a dining-commons (not a clattering cafeteria) is desirable as a center for conversation, supposing its management is not a burden upon the college.

The first building to be erected (supposing that a college must be built, rather than reformed or acquired by reformers) should be the faculty commons or club, to promote the development of community among the senior scholars. Around that center the college could develop, intellectually and physically. (After more than a century of existence, many American universities and colleges have no adequate gathering-place for professors.)

The second building to be erected should be the library, which need not be vast, but which should contain a careful collection of books, under the charge of a scholar-librarian, not a library technician. There should be easy access at all reasonable hours, and the place should not be overheated; and there must be adequate provision of serious periodicals.

The third building to be erected should be a chapel (whether or not the college is sponsored by a church); I put this third only because the faculty commons or the library might be used for worship until the college has a body of undergraduates.

The fourth building to be erected should be one of lecture-halls and laboratories. There need not be extravagant provision for classrooms, because on most American campuses, through inefficient scheduling, there occurs much waste of classroom space; and there would be fewer class-sessions held at this model college than at the typical American college.

Other buildings would be added. The campus should be compact, the buildings harmonious, and the whole should seem self-contained, almost cloistered. It is of the first importance *not* to employ an architect accustomed to designing public schools. There should be a number of pleasant, quiet gathering-places or study-retreats out of doors.

General Considerations. This should be a college segregated—by sex. There might be a model college for men and a model college for women, perhaps not far distant from each other. But one thing to avoid is the dating-and-mating pattern which obsesses the typical American campus. Wine and beer should be available on the campus, according to Housman's and Chesterton's principle that beer does more than Milton can to justify God's ways to man; besides, such availability of drink takes the lure of the forbidden out of drink, and discourages, rather than invites, heavy drinking. The students would be assumed to be mature persons, not children, so that recurrent disorderly conduct would not be tolerated. Students with serious psychiatric problems should be transferred to another sort of institution: despite its recognition of moral worth, this model college should be engaged in the improvement of intellects, not the curing of psychoses.

Here I have offered merely the bare bones of a model; others may clothe this skeleton with flesh, or with draperies from the wardrobe of a moral imagination. I do not expect that this college would supplant Behemoth University or Brummagem University, even though those institutions are far gone in decadence. This model has no mission to the masses whose parents desire snob-degrees and sham-degrees for their progeny; nor is it to be a halfway-house on the road from adolescence to bread-winning. For those intelligent students now discontented with the pabulum they are fed, this model college might be a vision come true; for those senior scholars who still earnestly stand by the works of the mind, this model college might be the crown of life. A college of this sort, governed by the traditions of reverence, learning, and civility, goes against the grain of present-day American education. But I attest the rising generation.

Have I indulged in a mere amusing exercise? Not wholly: after all, some colleges resembling my model have been founded in recent years, and I shall touch upon them presently; also some long-established colleges still exist which, with no tremendous effort, could resume the character I have described. Yet I am quite aware that no trumpet of mine will bring down the walls of Behemoth University or Brummagem University, overnight. The overgrown and corrupted institution of "higher" learning will continue to school the large majority of American young people, for the foreseeable future. What may be done to restore some learning and some sense of community within the sprawling mass-education centers? That is my topic for the next chapter.

6

Palliatives and Partial Remedies

ALTHOUGH FROM NECESSITY there will come large changes in the swollen apparatus of America's higher education, as President Boyd of the University of Oregon suggests, still presumably another quarter of a century will elapse before a new general pattern for the higher learning is discernible. Meanwhile, what can be done to instill some purpose and coherence, for at least the abler students, into Behemoth U. and Brummagem U.—or to provide alternatives to spending four years on either of those campuses?

It would be wearisome to reiterate all the fallacies and blunders which have brought about the decadence of university and college. Yet indulge me here in my brief summary of what has happened to the higher learning since the Second World War, so that palliatives and partial remedies appropriate to the disease may be suggested.

Fundamentally, the trouble is this: neglecting its ends of wisdom and virture, the institution of higher learning has identified itself with the market-place—with Vanity Fair. Therefore it has ceased to be a true academic community, and has sunk to the condition of an academic collectively conferring adulterated degrees.

I am aware that there are exceptions to this impeachment, and I have mentioned some of those exceptions in earlier chapters. The University of Chicago, for instance, maintained its high intellectual standards throughout the period I have described. That pleasant big place Louisiana State University was little affected by the disorders of the 'Sixties. Despite some changes, colleges like Davidson in North Carolina, or Hampden-Sydney in Virginia, or Calvinist colleges like Hope and Calvin in Michigan, or Grove City in Pennsylvania, or Dartmouth, or two score more I might name—some old and famous, some little-known but deserving—have preserved their old character. At even the institutions worst affected by the lowering of standards or the violence of the 'Sixties, some good professors and some good students could be found throughout, and can be found today. It remains possible to recommend to young people that they might do well to study, as undergraduates or as graduate students, at Drew, Vanderbilt, the University of Dallas, Duke, Georgetown, and a fair number of other independent universities. Some state universities, particularly those which have not expanded overmuch, still are good places; and some state colleges are sensible and quiet enough. Not all is lost.

Yet on the whole—to express myself mildly—the higher learning in America is a disgrace. By obsession with quantity, the typical university or college has surrendered its campus to the Lonely Crowd. And because this Lonely Crowd of young people, bewildered and bored and purposeless, cannot meet the old qualitative standards of the higher learning, those standards and purposes have been reduced to accommodate nearly anybody who can pay the fees, or have his fees paid by his parents or by some agency of government.

Providing places for the new mobs of students, the educational apparatus sacrificed nearly everything to the goal of magnitude. Under these circumstances, pressures of social conformity and certification thrust into college many who would have preferred to be somewhere else. As the high-school diploma earlier had become an inflexible requirement for vocational advancement, so now the college degree is demanded of anyone who means to rise in governmental services, business, or industry—even if apprenticeship or its equivalent would be better preparation. Bachelors' degrees becoming so common, students who hoped to rise above mediocre situations found that they must spend more years in graduate schools; the master's degree, too, had been cheapened by its commonness; now it must be the doctorate, if one meant to get anywhere. A not inconsiderable portion of the rising generation found themselves kept in the classroom uninterruptedly for twenty-two years or more—from kindergarten to doctoral commencement. It became difficult *not* to go to college.

Whether from lack of aptitude, lack of interest, or lack of preparation, then, a large part of the typical student body is purposeless. This disheartens a college's staff, and wastes their time. It oppresses and defrauds the more intellectually active students, through a drastic lowering of aims and methods, a dulling and darkening of the academic atmosphere. It makes academic community a snare and a delusion.

Of this bewildered crowd of "students" who study nothing of importance, many should be engaged in practical training of a sort for which the American college is not suited, in apprenticeship, or in ordinary gainful work. Some may develop intellectual interests later; therefore they should enroll in college not now, but later. Others would be better satisfied, and more useful, if they engaged in volunteer service, abroad or in the United States. They ought to be emancipated from the classroom, for their sake and the sake of the higher learning.

Because this purposeless crowd of young people injures the whole tone of an educational institution, many students who potentially are competent enough nevertheless sink into mediocrity and indifference, conforming to the dullness about them. And of those students who really are interested in what college and university have to offer, many grow angry and frustrated at being held captive in a whited sepulchre of Academe. Given some more years of this neglect of mind and conscience in the very places which are supposed to develop aspiring talents, America will be starved for leadership, or even ordinary integrity, or even the skills that maintain our civilization.

Despite this prospect, it remains public policy to crowd as many young people as possible into college and university, out of sentimental egalitarianism. During the academic year 1977-78, some nine hundred and fifty million dollars from the federal treasury were appropriated for "student aid"—the National Direct Student Loan, the College Work-Study, and the Supplemental Educational Opportunity Grant. All these programs were intended to persuade the "needy" to obtain college degrees—although actually much of the money, through subterfuges, goes to the children of well-to-do parents. Some 2,615 colleges and institutions of post-secondary education were entitled to receive NDSL money; CWS funds went to 3,197 universities, colleges, and vocational institutes; SEOG money to about 3,600 institutions. The powerful educationist lobby at Washington pushed these appropriations through Congress, despite the miserable academic performance of many of the young beneficiaries of these grants in previous years—and despite massive defaulting on students loans. To nearly a billion dollars, in one year, of federal funds must be added state appropriations for similar purposes—in the state of New York, especially generous and especially ill-spent. The public goal seemed to be a snob-degree or a certification-degree for every young person not confined in public institutions of another sort—with nobody left to do the nation's work.

A considerable class of perpetual students had arisen out of this situation—"students" who married and lived well upon renewed grants and loans, bought or plagiarized term papers, presented ghost-written theses and dissertations, occasionally appeared in the classroom, and often lamented the lack of social justice in a ruthless capitalist society with no concern for intellectuals. Education became a good thing, in more ways than one.

What of the professors and instructors? Most of them had been expensively and lengthily schooled—perhaps in too specialized a fashion, the doctoral discipline having little relevance to the sort of activity now dominant on the average campus. Many of them now suspect that they are living a lie, as are the perpetual students. I commend a candid book, *Confessions of an American Scholar,* by a professor who uses the pseudonym of Simon O'Toole. "I now think that truth is a lie and universities are places for liars and cheats to lie cleverly, and I believe that the free pursuit of truth encourages spinelessness as much as tyranny ever did," O'Toole writes. He refers to the university's pretense that it still imparts an objective "truth", when in reality it supplies only "facts"—and those in haphazard fashion.

Going through the motions of teaching a reputable intellectual discipline, when actually an instructor confronts the bored Lonely Crowd, does not refresh the soul. This being so, many professors isolate themselves from students and colleagues, escaping into "research" if they can, even though their talents as scholars or writers may be small. Too many, especially young instructors and graduate assistants, find consolation in the arms of ideology, dealing with a class as if it were a captive audience, inflicting their political views of the moment upon students, preferring the captive mind to the critical faculty.

As for the administrators of Behemoth U. and Brummagem U., some are caught in the degradation unwillingly, and others enjoy it and profit by it. Practically every quondam technical institute or normal school now is entitled by act of legislature to style itself "university." (One of the best places left to study, incidentally, is the College of William and Mary—which, actually, is the second oldest university in the United States, but retains a certain dignity and modesty, and almost certainly never will desire to inflict upon itself a title so discredited as "university" has become.) The prosperity of the academic administrators depends, at Behemoth and Brummagem, upon perpetuation of intellectual decadence.

On the mass campus, with its perennial disorder of "registration", the college catalogue's empty profusion of proffered courses leads to an "education" that is no better than a random assortment of subjects, almost totally unrelated one to another, irrelevant to either wisdom or virtue. If administrators and professors have no more respect for the works of the mind than to enlarge "diversity" of this sort, why should undergraduates be expected to try to create some intellectual order out of this academic chaos?

"Open admissions" and "open curriculum" put an end to any meaningful pattern of learning, on many campuses. Students study, or do not study, whatever attracts them at the moment. At one independent university in Long Island, a few years ago, all requirements for historical studies were abolished; enrollments in the department of history promptly fell from two thousand students to five hundred. Did those fifteen hundred previously required to study history then enroll in some stiffer or more specialized discipline? No: courses in "pop culture", folk music, expressionism through daubing, and sociological pabulum filled the vacuum. If college is only an adolescent-sitting enterprise anyway, a boring or occasionally diverting interim before one is admitted to real life, why not pass through that interval with minimum intellectual effort? Only credits count for certification; and to make credits still more easily attainable, on some campuses grading was abolished.

So today's college has something for everybody—except for those students who still sense that the higher learning ought to be concerned with wisdom and virtue, and for those professors who obdurately profess, despite the intellectual promiscuity of the time, their belief in some coherent body of knowledge. Funds and energies are squandered upon those students (or inmates, rather) and those programs which show the most slender promise. In our time, we have seen the speedy degeneration of the higher learning into aimless sociability on the one hand, and into anti-intellectual ideology on the other. What of the person and the republic?

Because the state of the Academy scarcely could grow worse, it may grow better. In the remaining sections of this chapter, I touch upon some aspects of possible reform. First I take up endeavors to alter the monolithic structure of the university; second, alternatives to spending much time on a campus; third, a model for an "honors college" within a university's structure; finally, the hard knocks which one honors program has endured. First, then, I offer some remarks on the excessive centralization of universities and large colleges, the "multiversity" blunder, and what has been or might be done about this condition, which was a principal cause of the activist students' loud lament, "We are oppressed!"

The state universities and colleges generally, and most of the larger independent institutions, suffer from concentration of authority, academic bureaucracy, lack of a sense of community, stultifying uniformity of methods and approaches within the institutional complex, and the afflictions of excessive bigness generally. They seem like miniatures of the totalist state—like Kafka's Castle. The political form of democracy is not suitable for the conduct of a university, but neither is the form of tyranny, or of oligarchy. Probably the proper governance of a university most nearly resembles the political form of an aristocratic republic; we have instead, at best, benevolent despotism. I understood well enough what the radical students meant by "oppression"—even if those students themselves, politically ignorant, would have substituted anarchy for authoritarianism. The American university was not deliberately designed to be an academic collectivism instead of an academic community; but what with the inordinate increase of student enrollments and the size of staffs and the proliferation of schools and departments, it has worked out that way. Can academic community and diversity be restored at all? Are there extant models of community and diversity? Why do we have educational monoliths in what we still fancy to be a pluralistic, democratic American society?

There exist historical causes for this academic centralization and standardization. The original American institutions of higher learning were unitary little colleges which later developed into universities like Harvard, Yale, Princeton, and Columbia; they grew almost in a fit of absence of mind; and only tardily, after most of the growth had taken place, did some of them perceive the need for academic communities smaller than the university itself, and so make some gestures—generally not very satisfactory ones—toward devolution of powers. The pattern of state universities tended to be set by the University of Virginia, where Jefferson's eagerness to secure "Republican" views among professors and students, and his Deism that made him suspicious of church influence upon education, led him to establish a unitary rather than a collegiate structure. (Later he did write that he had expected Christian denominations to establish their own seminaries on the University's fringe; but even had they done so, which they did not, those church-related colleges would have had no voice in the University's affairs.) While universities' enrollments remained small, this unitary character did little mischief; one sees the old pattern still at the University of the South, which was intended to have a distinct college for each southern state, but after the Civil War never developed beyond the one existing college.

When the prestige of the German universities affected American higher education in the last quarter of the nineteenth century, the newer American universities, beginning with Johns Hopkins, adopted Germanic structures. Thus the Oxford and Cambridge pattern of independent colleges loosely associated in a university—the pattern of Paris and some other Continental universities also, of course—was nearly forgotten in the United States. (The Scottish universities, too, originally had a collegiate structure like that of the English, but for the most part lost it because of their poverty.) So few people with influence in the American higher learning thought seriously about really autonomous colleges within a university—as distinguished from professional schools and administrative divisions—until the immense growth of enrollments after the Second World War made the problem of academic scale a grave one. The violent protests of "multiversity" students in the 'Sixties against the anonymity and "lostness" of the typical big campus induced university administrators to think tardily about alternatives or palliatives to the Leviathan character of their institutions, and here and there actually to try to do something about the decay of academic community into academic collectivism.

The chief example of genuine collegiate structure in a state university is the University of California at Santa Cruz, founded in 1965, at the height of students' unrest in California's complex edifice of public higher education. This vast embryo campus was designed to accommodate eventually some twenty-seven thousand students; but its plan was radically different from that of the Berkeley and Los Angeles campuses of the University of California. The models for Santa Cruz were Oxford and Cambridge.

At Santa Cruz, the university acquired the spreading old Cowell Ranch, the historic buildings of which were preserved. More than a score of separate colleges were scheduled to be built there—the first of them, Cowell, opening its doors in the autumn of 1965. Two distinguished scholars were chosen as the chancellor and the provost of Cowell. Even before the new first college was erected, highly individualistic students were coming down from Berkeley on their motorbikes, hoping to transfer to the new campus, and informing Chancellor Dean McHenry and Provost Page Smith that Santa Cruz was the remedy for "The Machine" against which they had demonstrated. Although the administrators at Santa Cruz had little appetite for establishing a kind of sanctuary for academic *Frondeurs,* they did aspire to a complex in which the person would have primacy.

The Santa Cruz colleges receive from two hundred and fifty to one thousand students each. Every college leans toward some particular branch of study—humane letters, the arts, the natural sciences, and the like—although remaining a foundation of liberal learning in general. Most students reside in their own colleges, as do some of the professors and instructors. Every provost is in residence. The colleges have their own dining-halls and small libraries. The expense of all this in the long run, according to the original estimates, should not exceed that of the mammoth structure of a centralized campus. The rolling acres and old trees of the Cowell ranch diminish that oppressive sense of being "built in" which has been one subtle cause of discontent on the typical new mass campus.

Professional and graduate schools have been, or are being, developed at Santa Cruz, too. It will be a long while before these colleges acquire, through continuity of experience and growth of tradition, the deep-rooted academic community of their Oxbridge prototypes. But the Santa Cruz plan is heartening. Enrollments have not grown so rapidly, by any means, as was expected in 1965: Santa Cruz has few more than six thousand students now—which is all to the good. As yet it has not been emulated by state systems of higher education: the next vast campus of the University of California to be created, Irvine, resumed the centralized pattern, with colossal buildings.

In California, too, is America's only thriving example of an independent university on the Oxbridge collegiate scheme—and it does not call itself a university. This is Claremont College, or the Claremont Colleges, in the very pleasant and shaded town of Claremont—now, alas, at the edge of the Greater Los Angeles smog-zone. At Claremont, five autonomous colleges, plus a common venture, make up one of the most satisfactory centers of learning in the United States. They are Pomona, Scripps, Claremont Men's, Harvey Mudd, and Pitzer—respectively, a co-educational liberal-arts college, a women's liberal-arts college, a college specializing in preparation for leadership in government and business, an engineering college, and a college emphasizing social studies. (The federal Affirmative Action misconception, by the way, now makes it difficult to specify colleges as "men's" or "women's".) All five enjoy admirable reputations. The density of population in southern California makes this concentration possible. They join, after a fashion, to form a kind of holding company, Claremont College, which manages Claremont Graduate School and the common library of the colleges.

So, in substance, Claremont is a little university—as big as some British universities. By a loose confederation, the constituent colleges can afford a very good library, a highly-praised graduate school, and a variety of special curricula. Wide differences of opinion and method exist among the colleges, a healthy diversity. Retaining the humane scale, they escape from the curse of the colossal. Should there be need for expansion, they can admit a new college, with its own staff and residence-halls, rather than crowding their present facilities. But Claremont, like Santa Cruz, has not been emulated substantially, and the time when private benefaction could create whole complexes of independent colleges seems to be gone by. Nevertheless, independent colleges situated in the same city or district often would do well to form a consortium comparable to Claremont's so far as possible, and there have been some recent instances of that.

The University of the Pacific, an independent institution at Stockton, California, has developed a collegiate structure on its one campus, one college specializing in languages, another in Asiatic studies, and the like. There are a few other examples of recent hopeful undertakings of this type. But the pattern of nearly all universities and colleges is restricted by their existing "plant." What with enforced economies and prospects of diminished enrollments, they cannot afford to demolish many of the monstrous buildings now standing and to build residential colleges on a humane scale—even had they imagination sufficient to work that reform.

Therefore other alternatives are being sought. One alternative, with various forms to it, is for students to spend as little time as possible upon a conventional campus, seeking academic community, or at least academic leisure, far from the shadow of the Ivory Tower. Two principal "de-campusing" concepts are proposed, and I discuss those next.

One form of this emancipation from the campus is the proposal for the "external degree"—as yet in embryo only. The other form is the "free college" without a campus—which has been tried a good deal, usually in vain, but which still may make some headway.

Nowadays many Americans understand the truth of T. S. Eliot's remark that there should be many different kinds of education for many different kinds of people. Campus collegiate studies are only one form of higher education—and not the best form for many young people. The "external degree" is one decent alternative to campus residence.

Long known in Britain, Canada, and some other countries, but unfamiliar in the United States, the external degree is awarded for study—often over a considerable number of years—in connection with a college or university; but study performed, for the most part, elsewhere than on the campus. (Sometimes a residence of one or two years is required, but the rest of the work can be done elsewhere.) Certain types of intellectual experience sometimes count toward the attaining of an external degree; otherwise, this study is undertaken through correspondence, consultation, and examination, without classroom attendance. Some of the abler university administrators of my acquaintance advocate the granting of external degrees to a large proportion of the men and women who at present, whether or not they profit from conventional methods, are compelled to live on or near a campus.

As I mentioned in an earlier chapter, instruments for this sort of off-campus study are at our disposal. Closed-circuit television, ready availability of "quality" paperbacked books, tape-recorded lectures, and similar developments and devices of recent origin now make it possible to decentralize the process of higher education. Students could live and study at home, for two or three of their college years, if not for the whole period; they could combine remunerative employment with home study. Thus they would not be alienated from society at large, they would not lose their roots in social community, and they might develop character rather than flocking with the campus Lonely Crowd for four years. They might even read some good books on their own time, a custom now rare at Brummagem U.

Studying on their own, or in small groups, most American undergraduates might acquire more respect for the ways of the mind, and might be freed from compulsions to share in the latest diversions and passions of the mass campus. This external-degree method would be far less costly than the present system, for the student and for the public treasury. More important still, it would diminish infatuation with college graduation, old style, as a form of social snobbery.

"Why spend thousands of dollars to send your children off to a wild, undisciplined campus," a Chevy Chase woman writes to me, "where it is impossible to study in the dormitories?" One reason why the community colleges have grown apace is this often-expressed disgust with the foolishness, sometimes baneful, of many campuses; should the external-degree program be developed by a number of reputable colleges, it might spread swiftly. This approach to the higher learning has its disadvantages, among them the lack of communication between student and professor; but at Behemoth U. and Brummagem U., no mere student ever talks with a professor, anyway.

As for the "free college", it was much tried during the 'Sixties, and nearly all of those attempts at loosely-structured approaches to the higher learning have failed since then—because of bad management, insufficient funding, ignorance on the part of the would-be teachers, and eccentricity on the part of the would-be students. The "free college" extreme of freedom undid itself. One thinks of a sign posted near the trenches of the Catalonian Anarchist soldiers during the Spanish civil war: "What Catalonian Anarchists need is better organization."

Still, a "free college" emancipated from the heavy costs of maintaining a campus, dispensing with most administrators, tenured professors with large salaries, IBM computers and the rigamarole of credits, and all that, remains an attractive possibility—if those who direct it are sound, practical, intelligent people. One such institution exists and is achieving success—International College, with offices in Los Angeles, which I will describe in the next chapter.

In general, the "free college" or "free university" signifies a kind of cooperative, low-cost college, perhaps meeting in old buildings in the heart of a city, with close relationships between instructors and students; the students may pay their instructors directly. This is meant to strip away all the fringes and trappings of the typical campus. In the 'Sixties, the studies pursued at such experimental centers were so eccentric and amorphous, and often fanatically ideological, that few people seriously interested in the higher learning can be greatly pained by the collapse of these undertakings. Yet considerable possibilities lie latent here.

The principal inspirer of the "free college" movement was the late Paul Goodman, who styled himself a conservative anarchist, and had many crochets, among them a preoccupation with what he called "sexual servitude", allegedly suffered by the young of America all the way from kindergarten to graduate school. Goodman made strong points, nevertheless, in his book *The Community of Scholars* (1962).

He commended the idea of the college which was a reality in the ages of faith, arguing that the medieval college was a true community of learned men and earnest students. And he saw the modern American college, with a few honorable exceptions, as sham and failure.

Of all American colleges, he wrote, "One could not name ten that strongly stand for anything peculiar to themselves, peculiarly wise, radical, experimental, or even peculiarly dangerous, stupid, or licentious. It is astounding that there should be so many self-governing communities, yet so much conformity to the national norm." Weighed down often by Philistine and aggrandizing administrators, engaged in training rather than in education, inordinately expensive for the results they produce, boring to many of the better potential students, American colleges of 1962 were detestable to Paul Goodman; and his vitriolic denunciation was applauded by a good many students.

The medieval university, which accomplished something, was small, Goodman emphasized, having from a few hundred students to a thousand—or, in some instances, less than a hundred. One of its

principal virtues was the close relationship between the man of learning and the student. But contemptuous of the humane scale, we
Americans rejoice in the mass-campus, which produces the mass-mind.

"Most of our colleges being what they are," Goodman declared, "I
fear that many of the best youth would get a better, though very
imperfect, education if they followed their impulse and quit; and
certainly many teachers ought to be more manly even if they risk being
fired."

Teaching machines, Dr. James Bryant Conant, and even John
Dewey received some imaginative criticism in Goodman's pages. De-
molishing Conant's notion of the higher learning as directed to "national goals" of a utilitarian character, Goodman sought instead to
restore the community of scholars; to offer something for the mind,
with genuine freedom for scholar and student. American colleges, he
insisted, were doing neither one thing nor the other:

"Rather, they are great, and greatly expanding, images of Education, no different from the other role-playing organizations of the
modern world. Fortified in their departments and tenure . . . the
senior scholars are not much disturbed by either the students or by one
another or by the administration. And society is satisfied by the symbolic proof that a lot of education is going on, fat syllabi, hundreds of
thousands of diplomas, bales of published research. . . . The administrators engage in a tooth-and-nail competition to aggrandize their
institutions and produce these very condition. . . . We do not hear that
they have gotten together to decide on a judicious policy for distributing the different kinds of goods of education. . . . Instead they behave
like department stores opening new departments and sometimes
branches, and increasing efficiency by standardizing the merchandise
and the sales force."

The remedy which Goodman proposed was a small secession from
the present universities and colleges. He would have vigorous professors—a handful of them, here and there—take some of their students
and form unorthodox little communities of scholars, with a few rooms
in which to hold classes (ten to fifteen students in each class)—and little
else. They could use public libraries, and could support themselves by
charging tuition well below that of present good (and endowed)
liberal-arts colleges. "I am proposing simply to take teaching-and-
learning on its own terms, for the students and teachers to associate in
the traditional way and according to their existing interest, *but entirely
dispensing with the external control, administration, bureaucratic machinery,
and other excrescences that have swamped our community of scholars.*"

Goodman was somewhat naïve in thinking that it was possible to escape altogether from academic administration. Some adventurous souls embraced Goodman's proposals, had a go—and sank out of sight. Yet at heart Goodman's notions are fruitful. As Goodman suggested, nowadays, for many inquisitive members of the rising generation, the only way to learn something—especially if one can't pay high tuition—is to become a beatnik and curl up with a paperback. But, as Goodman added, those too perish.

The external-degree proposal lies little developed; the "free college", too rashly charging the troops of academic error, lies a trophy to its enemies. But there remains one large practical reform which still can be worked, even within Behemoth U. and Brummagem U.: the establishment of an *honors* college, inside every big university or every overgrown "college." Perhaps there should be more than one honors college within an institution, divided possibly into the disciplines of the arts and the disciplines of the sciences. To such an honors college should be admitted only the ten per cent, or five per cent, or one per cent, of the student body that seem genuinely interested in wisdom and virture, and reasonably competent to pursue such objects. A degree awarded by such an honors college would have meaning, and the better students would be liberated from their present servitude to mediocrity and frivolity.

At some big institutions, I am aware, honors colleges were established years ago. In general, however, these experiments do not constitute any grand change from the academic program for most students, except that a more or less select body of undergraduates is admitted, and that fewer "survey" courses are inflicted upon these elect. Already, on various campuses where nominal "honors colleges" or "honors programs" have been adopted, the degradation of the democratic dogma operates: that is, students of poor performance and dull aptitudes are admitted to such honors courses if they desire it. The practical effect of such feebleness is to reduce the honors programs to the general level of mediocrity, in fairly short order—a development distinctly unjust to the more earnest students.

What I recommend is no half-way measure. The standards of such an honors college should be high, and its curriculum should vary conspicuously from that pursued—or ignored—by the mass of students. But if such standards and curricula are honestly established, the intellectual freedom and even the academic leisure of students within the honors college ought to be enlarged.

Models for such an honors college already exist, in some degree; I will describe one of them in the concluding section of this chapter. A number of old liberal-arts colleges which have not adulterated their standards and programs would have much to teach the founders of the honors college within a mass institution. And one can turn for guidance to certain aspects of the older British universities. Diversity of approach is to be tolerated and even encouraged. I suggest here, therefore, only the general tentative outlines of such a collegiate reform.

First, I venture to say that it would be well to have separate honors colleges for the arts and for the sciences. This step would require that those admitted be reasonably well schooled in a general way before entering the honors college, so that arts students would not be altogether ignorant of the sciences, or science students of the arts: that division has worked well enough in the Scottish universities, without the disastrous consequences rather shallowly predicted by Lord Snow in his little book *The Two Cultures*. "If we would know anything," John Henry Newman wrote, "we must remain ignorant of much." It simply is not possible, nowadays, to school everybody in everything, and yet to achieve a tolerable discipline in any particular realm of understanding.

With really well-prepared freshmen or sophomores, it might be possible to go yet farther, and to establish honors colleges in political economy (liberally interpreted), say, or in natural sciences, or in humane letters, or in some other broad discipline or grouping. The more an honors college can appeal to the definite intellectual interests of its students, the better its chance for success. Ordinarily, however, a choice of either arts or sciences would be the first step in extricating students and instructors from the morass of "general" and mediocre education.

Second, given adequate funds, the model honors college could be at once residential and non-residential, as are Oxford and Cambridge colleges today: that is, some students could reside in the college buildings, and others who prefer private lodgings or for whom there might not be space could reside elsewhere. It is especially important that a number of professors and instructors, like English dons or fellows, either reside in the college or be closely attached to it, so that there be a humane relationship between teacher and student. If possible, the college should have its own intimate library and a dining commons. There should be a certain ceremony and formal participation in such a college—borrowing in part from the better aspect of American fraternities.

Third, the course of study would extend over three years only, at the end of which the bachelor's degree would be conferred; for an additional year of study, more specialized, an "honors" degree of B.A. or M.A. might be granted. Already a good many universities and colleges discuss the possibility of shortening the period of undergraduate residence from four years to three, by reducing the number of course credits required and eliminating peripheral courses. This would be especially desirable and practicable in the proposed honors college, since its students presumably would be diligent, and its program of instruction would strike out the shallow and time-wasting courses, of doubtful value for any purpose, that were increased in number (as if they had not been more than sufficient already) by the demands of rebellious student groups in the 'Sixties.

Fourth, the program of study would be either "liberal" or "scientific" in an exacting sense, but genuinely integrated and not compartmentalized into a multitude of unrelated branches. Below, what with limitations of space and of personal knowledge, I sketch simply a possible program for an honors program in arts; those interested in establishing an honors college of sciences might do well to turn to the ideas of such scientific scholars as Professor Michael Polanyi, who combine thorough scientific methods with broad philosophical views.

In an arts college, the primary disciplines should be the literary and the philosophical. Some years ago I discussed with Dr. Max Lerner the essential foundations of college study; we came to agree that the basic disciplines are literary, philosophical, and mathematical—and that other conventional disciplines should be subsumed under these. (Although I would leave a thorough training in higher mathematics to an honors college of sciences, certainly I would not ignore such knowledge in a college of arts—subsuming quantum mechanics, say, under philosophy, for the purposes of an arts college.)

Literature would include the study of classical and modern languages, both as bodies of humane knowledge and as rhetoric. The emphasis would be upon the philosophical and ethical *meaning* of literature—not merely *belles lettres* for the sake of *belles lettres*. This discipline would be humane, or humanistic, in the original signification of that abused word. In considerable part, history would be subsumed under literature.

Philosophy would include metaphysics, ethics, politics, and perhaps aesthetics, with considerable attention to physical and mathematical foundations. Sociology and psychology would be dealt with simply as aspects of philosophy; Dr. Lerner and I agreed that both these disciplines, if taken in the abstract, are unsuitable as undergraduate specialties. (Sociological knowledge, for example, is the crown of social studies, not the footing.) As in the case of literature, the study of philosophy would be the pursuit of meaning, not of pedantic distinctions.

All lesser branches of learning, then, would be related to these two basic disciplines. Economics would be regarded both in the literature of the great economists and in the theories of political economy; it would not be shut off by itself. Biology, a legitimate concern of an arts college, would be related to the literature of that study and, more conspicuously, to the philosophical understanding of organic life; more detailed examination would be the province of an honors college of the sciences.

Although literature relating to the audio-visual arts would not be neglected, and those arts would be studied philosophically as aesthetics, no attempt would be made in the model honors college to teach *skills* in painting, sculpture, music, and such aspects of the arts; technique is more properly left to specialized non-collegiate institutes, or to the private pursuit of undergraduates. Similarly, or more emphatically, no vocational instruction would be offered: the arts college would teach politics, but not political administration; the science college would teach the principles of mechanics, but not technical engineering. Such practical studies are best left either to graduate schools (more quickly entered when the undergraduate curriculum should be reduced to three years) or to in-service training. Although study in the arts college should be an admirable preparation for study of the law, it would not offer a "pre-law curriculum"; although the graduate of such a college would make a good teacher, there would be no distinct department of education.

It will be asked, naturally, how the well-educated graduates of such honors colleges, or of the model independent college which I outlined in the previous chapter, are to obtain employment. The answer is simple enough: if the most intelligent and diligent students out of the whole body at Behemoth U. are the graduates of the honors colleges, employers in many fields will prefer them eagerly over the mediocrity of the ordinary Behemoth degree. With quickened minds and sharpened perceptions, the honors-college graduates will be able to apply their schooled talents efficiently to any occupation or profession. We would develop, that is, a body of educated young people prepared for a considerable range of occupations and public offices—prepared not by premature and dull specialization or vocationalism, but by the cultivation of intellect and conscience; by having pursued wisdom and virture. And still more important, we would wake these students to the fullness of the human condition, and cultivate in and through them that moral imagination essential to order in the soul and order in the republic.

Can this thing be done? Yes, given fortitude and sound sense. The better students are eager for such a liberating reform; the better professors and educational administrators know how urgent the cause of educational improvement has become. Entrenched dullness and entrenched self-interest are the adversaries of qualitative improvement; but dullness and self-interest are not invincible. A professor-friend said to Irving Babbitt once, "Intelligence will tell in the long run, even in a university." Babbitt's friend nevertheless left Harvard and took up another line of work, lest a host of blockheads tread him down. Most serious students, being unfree in present circumstances to depart altogether from the Academy, would find it a goodly work to commence now. And in present circumstances, those in the seats of the mighty are rather more willing to listen to students than they were before the troubles of the 'Sixties—especially when the projects of reform involve no pulling down.

Such an honors college as I have sketched would be far more free than the most extravagant form of the "elective" system—because the whole program would be relevant to the students' central interests, and none of them would be there under compulsion. Within the honors program, a wide-ranging diversity of personal specialization would be possible, under the supervision of competent senior scholars. Individual talents would be given scope and encouragement; but those talents would be developed within the framework of a genuine ordering of knowledge.

Once such honors colleges should begin to make their mark, the whole tone of a university in general might begin to improve. Students now apathetic, though of some native intelligence, would be stimulated to emulation and would seek participation in an honors college. The better professors would be challenged to keep intellectually lively and sanguine. And the public might discover that nothing is more practical, in the long run, than pure learning.

These suggestions of mine are seeds cast upon the wind, and some will fall among tares, or in a parched educational wasteland. Yet I believe that mere quantitative expansion already lies under a heavy cloud—indeed, it is becoming impossible—and that qualitative renewal of the higher learning is desired today by more people than the educational establishment recognizes.

*   *   *

The honors college is meant to be an enclave of culture in the midst of academic barbarism. The best which we can expect of Behemoth U. and Brummagem U., so far as internal improvement is concerned, must be the creating of honors colleges which use existing classroom buildings and laboratories, and have their students lodged in conventional dormitories or in private digs—but which offer superior programs of study and attract keen students of similar interests.

Even so limited and relatively inexpensive a reform has hard sledding. Strong opposition to the very idea of honors colleges is manifest within American universities; and on several campuses, such colleges were abolished within a few years of their creation. One reason for this hostility is the American university's proclivity to centralization and uniformity, already discussed in this chapter. Although of course most universities have professional schools which more or less manage their own business, and also have "colleges" of arts, sciences, engineering, business, education, and the like at the undergraduate level, actually these latter "colleges" ordinarily are mere divisions or enlarged departments, subject in nearly all important particulars to the general (and often arbitrary) authority of the university, and not constituting real communities or "little platoons" of senior scholars and junior scholars. Now the honors college is an irregularity, an anomaly, a Corinthian ornament upon a concrete-block erection; it contrasts with the featureless mediocrity that pervades the rest of Behemoth State U.; it worries some administrators and professors. Why do these "honors" people have to be different? Why can't they take the normal courses and conform to the normal pattern of campus life? An unbecoming protruberance, an excrescence—that is how the honors college seems to President Boomer, perhaps, or Professor Dryasdust. Why can't everybody be just like everybody else on this campus?

Besides, we must not forget the power of envy on the campus, as in every other human institution and walk of life. Instructors who have to teach composition or elementary mathematics to lacklustre run-of-the-mill freshmen may resent the advantages of professors who conduct honors courses. Why should they get all the plums? "Why shouldst thou sit, and I stand?" says Envy, in *Doctor Faustus*. And then there are the sentimental egalitarians on the faculty. These influences place obstacles in the way of honors programs; more, they obstruct any deviation from the standard mediocre curriculum.

Consider, at the University of Kansas, the successes and tribulations of the Integrated Humanities Program, formerly called Pearson College. This is not, strictly speaking, an "honors" program, for all interested students are admitted; but in aims and standards, it rises far above the usual course of studies at that university. Founded in 1970-71, this IHP is one of the more encouraging college innovations anywhere in America. Once it was Pearson College, but in 1976 "colleges within the College" were abolished on that campus, and this venture survives as "a special course for freshmen and sophomores."

The three professors who make up the whole faculty of the program call it "an experiment in tradition." They remark that their convictions were well expressed by Mark Van Doren in his book *Liberal Education*. They impart to students, in this two-year program, what may be called "the perennial philosophy" or "the great tradition."

During the first semester of the first year, the course includes reading in Homer, Plato's *Republic*, Aesop, Herodotus, Thucydides, and Aeschylus' *Oresteia*; during the second semester, Virgil, Caesar, selections from Plutarch, Lucretius, Cicero *On Duty*, and selections from the Old Testament. For the second year, the first semester's readings are the New Testament, St. Augustine's *Confessions*, *Memoirs of the Crusades*, *Two Lives of Charlemagne*, *Sir Gawain and the Green Knight*, Boethius, St. Francis' *Little Flowers*, and the *Canterbury Tales*; for the second semester, the first part of *Don Quixote*, Cellini's *Autobiography*, *Hamlet* and *Henry IV*, Descartes' *Meditations*, a portion of Gibbon, Scott's *Ivanhoe*, Burke's *Reflections on the Revolution in France*, Parkman's *Oregon Trail*, selections from Newman and Huxley on education, and Dostoyevsky's *Crime and Punishment*.

This program varies somewhat from year to year. Also there are an optional (but strongly recommended) Latin sequence, the memorizing of great poetry, studies in rhetoric, teaching of calligraphy—Italic script, anyway—and even expeditions to Italy or Ireland in summer. All this means hard work for the staff of three, who prepare regular formal lectures.

Those three confess to professing a common view of life and education which "may be called 'traditional' or 'perennial' in so far as it follows the common understanding of reality which is handed down from Plato and the Old Testament, through Virgil and the New Testament, through the Christian Middle Ages and the Renaissance into our own times." They consider the intellectual challenges to this perennial philosophy.

Students who have been graduated from this two-year program praise IHP to the skies. They, with the three professors, form a distinct academic community in the midst of a huge impersonal university. The program has its ceremonies and its community celebrations. So satisfactory an association of senior and junior scholars is found on very few campuses.

Yet I mentioned "opponents." Who wouldn't be delighted by such a program, so admirably executed? Why, the majority of the faculty of the University's College of Liberal Arts and Science seem not to be delighted. At one time, they deprived Pearson, or IHP, of having its work accepted as fulfilling university requirements for credit in the humanities. Since then, a whole series of impediments has been thrust into the path of IHP, so that enrollment in the program, which once reached nearly two hundred, recently sank to fifty students. (The total enrollment at the University of Kansas is nearly twenty-four thousand students; it does not seem excessive to have leavened this lump by tolerating less than two hundred freshmen and sophomores who enjoy studying great books.)

Many people on the staff of the University of Kansas would like to force even the remaining fifty students of IHP back within the confines of the University's standard "humanities" curriculum. What would they lose if they were so compulsorily enrolled? Why, here is the College of Arts and Sciences regimen, as reported to me by a friend of Pearson—IHP:

"Three English composition and literature courses, where one gets a watery diet of graduate-student instructors and the usual miscellany of books; an elementary speech course, also taught by the graduate students and with much 'interpersonal' groupiness; and a 'Western Civilization Program,' this taught almost exclusively by graduate students. For years this program has been held in contempt by nearly all students. The readings are mostly bits and pieces, ninety per cent drawn from post-sixteenth-century authors, with heavy emphasis on political theory. Students have learned that the comprehensive examination can be passed without reading the texts, by studying a set of notes which has all but official endorsement."

In fine, the alternative to IHP is dullness and mediocrity, of a sort familiar enough at every big center of mass education. What charges have the adversaries of Pearson—IHP brought against its championship of the perennial philosophy? Many: but chiefly, it appears, that "only one point of view" is represented. One wonders whether these critics, when they teach theories of biological evolution, devote equal time to "fundamentalist" views; whether, in astronomy or geography, they give full impartial attention to the doctrine that the earth is flat; or whether they balance an hour's discussion of the poems of John Milton with an hour's discussion of the poems of Edgar A. Guest.

The unstated charge against IHP is that the program is subversive. True, IHP's three professors are men of conservative mind, and all happen to be Catholics; but they are subversive because they are undermining the established boredom and vacuity of a big state university.

If IHP should make headway, the imagination of some students might be waked, and then there'd be heaven to pay. For what would happen to all the tenured mediocrity of institutions like the College of A&S, if IHP should survive? In such entrenched "humanities" curricula as the standard program at the University of Kansas, the pseudo-professor (or teaching assistant, rather) professes nothing but a dim ideology of liberal secularism—which saves him the pain of thinking. If IHP should triumph, the pseudo-professor might find it necessary actually to read some of the great books at which he now sneers for presenting "only one point of view."

IHP's adversaries have prodded a congeries of agencies and people into harassing the program's three professors. IHP was prevented from making its offerings known to entering freshmen. It was investigated for alleged Title IX sex-discrimination (perhaps on the theory that a staff of three persons should include one and one-half female scholars)—but acquitted. American Civil Liberties Unionists have talked about action at law against IHP, on the ground that one student in the program ceased to be a Unitarian, like his parents, and became not merely a Catholic, but a novice in a French monastery—a fate worse than death, of course, involving that famous Wall of Separation between church and state. (I know it sounds as if I were inventing all these absurdities, but actually such is the state of the higher learning at Lawrence, Kansas.)

Yet, as Babbitt's friend said, intelligence will tell in the long run, even in a university. Some few fortunate students at the University of Kansas probably will continue to enjoy the rare privilege of being permitted to read great books. I have digressed at this length to suggest that the greater obstacles to reform in the higher learning are found within, not without, the Academy. Say not the struggle naught availeth.

7

Innovative Reactions

OW TO OBTAIN a thorough education within the cunning passages, the contrived corridors and issues, of our tremendous unimaginative establishment of the higher learning in America—that is the question. As I suggested in the preceding chapter, even honors colleges and honors programs, given much lip-service in college and university, suffer repulses when they presumptuously venture to storm the ramparts of the fortified waist-high culture of the typical campus.

During 1977, the federal government alone spent nearly eight billion, one hundred million dollars in aid of higher education. That was only supplementary funding, of course: the larger share by far of the funds to support the higher learning came from state treasuries, private benefactions, foundation grants, endowment-income, and students' tuition. In a single year, America spends more upon higher education than all the people of the world, throughout history, had spent upon the higher learning down to the time of the Second World War. What generosity, how indiscriminate, how ineffectual! Profligacy can do more damage to learning than can parsimony. The epoch of profligate expenditure for educational extravagances may be coming to an end, but meanwhile we make no provision for the future of true learning.

Praiseworthy universities and colleges survive, although handicapped by the poor preparation of many of their students, by excessive governmental regulation, by illusion and doubt within their walls, by the materialistic and utilitarian climate of opinion within which they subsist. It remains easy enough to obtain admirable technological instruction in America; competent doctors and dentists are turned out;

and there seems to be no conceivable course of study, however strange, that is not offered by some institution or other. Yet to learn of wisdom and virtue—aye, there's the rub. I do not mean that no students seek or obtain those ends of education; some do. But are there enough such to sustain the order of the soul and the order of the republic?

Against the educational follies of the time, some intelligent reaction may be observed. Because we have been so involved in educational process as to forget educational ends, occasionally this reaction seems daringly innovative. The purpose of the reactionary innovators, nevertheless, is restoration, not revolution. In this chapter, I offer a few select examples of fresh—or revived—approaches to education that are succeeding. I am writing about very small, if very important, undertakings in the higher learning; how far their contagion may spread, it is too early to say; certainly there are educationists who will consider their influence pestilential, because subversive of the empire of dullness and triviality. The mountain of the educational establishment labors, and brings forth a mouse, or perhaps a rat; these little reactionary innovations in education possibly may father giants.

Time was when the rising generation acquired higher learning by following some sage or philosopher: Confucius in Lu, Socrates in Athens, Abelard in Paris, George Wythe in Williamsburg. A student obtained what wisdom and virtue he could from discipleship to a master, and built upon that over the years. There existed no academic bureaucracy, so learning thrived.

Something of that sort has been undertaken, since 1970, by International College (with offices, but no campus, in Los Angeles), "a viable alternative to traditional higher education." This college is primarily an international guild of tutors, nearly a hundred of them, living in several countries. International College has no classrooms and virtually no staff; nor has it accreditation, since it does not fit at all into the inflexible pattern of American university and college. It has no endowment and little help from public funds. Its only assets are imagination and intelligence. International College does confer the degrees of bachelor, master, and doctor, and slightly more than two hundred students are enrolled, at latest count. They have such an opportunity to gain a true education, through independent study, supposing them capable of it, as I never knew.

A student who enrolls with International College spends a four-month term, or a year, or perhaps two years, in association with some well-known scholar, writer, artist, musician, or professional person.

That student can obtain his degree either from International College or (through an arranged International "honors program") through some conventional college or university where he has completed most of his study. Usually undergraduates are required to have been enrolled at some regular institution for two years before entering upon study with an International College tutor.

Study with the guild of tutors does not involve formal lectures, regular examinations, or letter grades. But it does require a capacity for asking the right questions, reading the right books or pursuing the right disciplines, and thinking for one's self. These students ordinarily live near the tutor during their period of study, and in a few cases in the tutor's house. They are expected to produce some really good work during "internship", and they cannot succeed without some strength of character.

The tutor may be a famous humane professor, or a distinguished scientist, or a great architect, or an influential writer or painter or sculptor, or a creative musician, or even a public official. The members of this teaching guild (most of whom never see one another) are scattered over the face of the civilized world.

Sir George Catlin, in London, accepts students in international relations.

Buckminster Fuller, in Philadelphia, accepts students in "comprehensive anticipatory design science."

Milton Mayer, in Carmel (who is International College's dean of faculty), accepts students in the writing of non-fiction.

Frank Willett, curator of the Hunterian Museum, Glasgow, accepts students in African art.

Richard Ellman, in Oxford, accepts students in the writings of Joyce and Yeats.

Bertrand de Jouvenel, in Paris, accepts students in futuristics.

Ravi Shankar, in Los Angeles, accepts students in the music of India.

Lawrence Durrell, at Sommieres, in France, accepts students of the novel and the poetry of France and England.

Ivan Illich, at Cuernavaca, in Mexico, accepts students in intercultural studies.

Yehudi Menuhin, in London, accepts students in violin performance.

James Farmer, in Washington, accepts students in public policy training.

Arne Naess, in Oslo, accepts students in philosophy or in the study of ecology.

Johan Galtung, in Dubrovnik, accepts students in interdisciplinary studies.

Kenneth Rexroth, in Santa Barbara, accepts students in poetry.

The most popular of the tutors was the late Anaïs Nin, novelist and diarist. Through International College, one may study with a Viennese director of theater; with environmentalists and educationists; with a leading figure in international banking; with mathematicians, Swedish sociologists, and Jewish scholars of Zen. International College has no curriculum whatsoever, no ideological prejudices, no library, no placement-office. All that International College does is to arrange for a distinguished tutor to accept a promising pupil—and, on the completion of studies, to grant or refuse a degree, the decision being made by external examiners. The guarantee of International College's probity and judgment is the high reputation of the tutors, for the names of many of them may be conjured with. Many of those tutors are very busy people of long-established reputation and ample means. Presumably they contribute their time to the work of International College because they are painfully aware of the need for leavening the lump of today's higher education.

The sort of student for whom International College is intended is one who believes that the unexamined life is not worth living, and that high achievement requires painstaking self-education. Such students never have been numerous. Yet perhaps there are more of them, at least potentially, in the United States than ever there were before.

The best advantage of International College's program is direct intellectual or artistic discourse with a man or woman of sound achievement in some discipline: mind speaking to mind, conscience to conscience. Nothing of that sort is possible for undergraduates, and rarely for graduate students, on the big campuses. But one International College student may be the only undergraduate whom a particular tutor will accept for the whole year: that learning, that talent, that personality are focused upon just one junior scholar.

The second-best advantage of International College is that the student concentrates upon what truly interests him. (Ordinarily he is required to study with at least two tutors in order to obtain a degree, so the student has at least some variety of educational experience.) He is not bored by graduation-requirements which seem irrelevant to his own cast of mind and abilities. Of course there exists another side to this educational coin—the danger that such an education might become narrowly specialized and eccentric. That is one reason why International requires, for undergraduates, two years of study in a more broad and conventional academic program.

The third-best advantage of the International program is that it de-campuses students who do not relish the average American campus. International College students rent their own rooms, find their own friends, buy the books they like, and talk with the tutor over coffee-cups. They have been liberated from the all-conquering academic collectivism of Behemoth State U.

Discourse with a learned, if severe, tutor was the chief benefit of residence at Oxford and Cambridge in the great years of those universities. The International College people quote Sir Eric Ashby on Clare College in 1326:

"Much of the teaching was a private contract between Fellow and pupil. . . . In this simple society was to be found the secret of excellence in universities. . . . It was an environment for the continuous polishing of one mind by another. Its basic formula was very simple. The essential ingredients were a reflective, disciplined, learned man willing to learn; and a balance of numbers between teacher and student so that the relation between them was intimate and personal."

In the twentieth century, unlike the fourteenth century, such a discipline and such a relationship in the realm of learning are most difficult to establish: such is the progress of our civilization.

International College is for a Remnant—for those remaining students who genuinely seek what, in the beginning, college and university were all about. Most people who graduate with a degree from International College, or who have participated in the International honors program, will succeed in life. They will succeed externally because they actually have learned something solid about something important. They will succeed internally because, if they persist, they will have acquired discipline of mind and habit.

Except for some tuition-scholarships and loans, no public funds from Washington or Sacramento will nurture the International College program. Public funds are for accredited conventional institutions—not for the support of individualistic young scholars who play the violin with Yehudi Menuhin, or study design with Buckminster Fuller, or politics with Sir George Catlin, or the novel with Lawrence Durrell.

Nor is it to be expected that the Lonely Crowd at Behemoth State will see the light and rush to enroll at International College. There would not be tutors enough to accept them, if they did abruptly hunger and thirst for wisdom and virtue. Yet even a handful of men and women whose minds have been formed by discourse with persons of real intellects and real talents—a few hundred such people, a few thousand—could do much to improve thought and action in this land.

*　*　*

I have set down too little in this book concerning many aspects of the higher learning. The merits and demerits of graduate schools I have touched upon only glancingly, for lack of space, and I can merely advise those interested to read the observations of Jacques Barzun and other shrewd critics of higher education. Also, thus far, I have neglected Great Books curricula—except in connection with the Integrated Humanities Program at the University of Kansas—and I have said little about colleges committed to Christian doctrine. These latter omissions I atone for, as best I can, in the following section of this chapter. Thomas Aquinas College, in California, a recent foundation for innovative reactions, combines the Great Books method of education with the Catholic mind, and has made itself probably the best college in the United States for obtaining a systematic traditional discipline, united to the Christian understanding of the human condition.

The Great Books approach is borrowed by Thomas Aquinas College chiefly from St. John's College, with its campuses at Annapolis and Santa Fe. To any really able prospective college student, for the past quarter of a century, who might ask me where he could go to obtain a really demanding education, I have answered, "St. John's College." I have met a number of graduates of St. John's, and they all are well-educated people. There are not many alumni, for St. John's always has been small and particular—and exacting of its students. St. John's insistence upon the mastery of classical and modern languages would suffice to deter any young man or woman not ready to spend full time at books. For providing an old-school literary and philosophical discipline, St. John's is unexcelled in this country.

It is not that I am an enthusiast for the Great Books curriculum, St. John's famous method. Devoting four years to the systematic examination of certain really important works of literature, in various fields, is a very good approach to the higher learning. But it is not the only very good approach, and I prefer a curriculum organized about a few subjects, as suggested in my models for independent college and honors college, in earlier chapters. For one thing, it seems to me that the Great Books method tends to neglect historical continuity somewhat; also that it does not include quite enough imaginative literature. Moreover, despite the claim of Mortimer Adler and Robert Hutchins that their well-known list of the Great Books was scientifically and impartially drawn up, still the unconscious prejudices of Adler and Hutchins are revealed by the conspicuous omissions from their list: no Cicero, no Burke, no Newman, but instead a good many writers inferior in power and influence to those. I am not wholly easy with other people's lists of Great Books.

Still, the Great Books method is one sound method, and St. John's College has employed it well, if sometimes a trifle pedantically. It would be pleasant to give more attention to St. John's here. But in this chapter I have to deal with new innovating colleges; and St. John's, having been founded in 1696, does not fall neatly into that category.

St. John's approach was emulated by St. Mary's, a Catholic college in northern California; and St. Mary's, in turn, helped to transmit the St. John's "Great Books" pattern to Thomas Aquinas College. Turmoil in the Catholic Church, during the 'Sixties and 'Seventies, caused the founding of three or four new Catholic colleges adhering to venerable doctrines; Thomas Aquinas is the most successful of these.

Lodged temporarily in the buildings of a disused seminary at a handsome old estate in Calabasas, California, Thomas Aquinas cannot accept many more than a hundred students, for lack of dormitory-rooms. By accident or providence divided almost equally between young men and young women, the student body at Aquinas has been said to consist of ninety-nine Catholics and a Buddhist. Its Scholastic curriculum smacks somewhat of the seminary, with strong emphasis on the *Summa* of the college's patron. For the rest, the curriculum partici-pates in the virtues and the vices of St. John's Great Books method, except that the sort of Adler-Hutchins omissions I mentioned earlier have been repaired. It begins to sound as if I am describing a satisfac-tory but rather dull college. That is not my intention: for I think that Thomas Aquinas College would be the best place in America for my four daughters to study, when they come to that time of life and if they seem so inclined and capable of profiting by college years. I think it the best college for anyone in America to choose, provided that he is willing to work very hard at his books, and entertains no strong prejudice against Papist dogma and doctrine.

Dr. Ronald McArthur, president of Thomas Aquinas College and its principal founder, knew what was wrong with most Catholic colleges in America when he set about establishing a new one, and he said so candidly. "Religious courses were isolated," he wrote, "and in no way performed a sapiential function with respect to the rest of the curricu-lum, contenting themselves with passing on some of the truths of Catholicism and the richness of the Catholic heritage—all the while claiming to be the most important part of Catholic education. The Catholic college was, therefore, a house divided against itself, which asked its students either to retreat into the narrow confines of a Chris-tian philosophy unable to cope with the modern world, or to abandon in the name of that world the Christianity which was their valuable possession. It is not suprising, therefore that under constant pressure, the fatal flaw would become manifest even to the educators who proposed it in the first place, and that it would lead the Catholic college to question its own existence and its own relevance for the students and the community it sought to serve.

"Added to this weakness is the general debility of all the American colleges, which long ago abandoned any genuine liberal education, substituting for it a random collection of courses to serve the multifarious demands of the students and to train them for the professions by satisfying the demands of the graduate and professional schools."

So Dr. McArthur and his colleagues dedicated their new college—an independent Catholic college, not diocesan nor sponsored by an order, its board of governors and its faculty made up almost wholly of laymen—to the essential truths of Christian learning, "giving order and purpose even to the teaching and learning of the secular disciplines." Its curriculum is confined to theology, philosophy, languages, mathematics, speculative science; it rejects all vocationalism, socialization, veneer-of-culture surveys, and obsession with "current awareness."

The students of Thomas Aquinas, despite the warmth of the rustic valley where their college stands, study intensively the Scriptures, the dialogues of Plato, the works of Aristotle, selected treatises of St. Augustine and St. Thomas Aquinas; there is time, too, for seminars centering about the thought of other men of genius. An understanding of natural science is attained through study and discussion of Euclid, Ptolemy, Galileo, Einstein, and a few other philosophical scientists. There is no fragmentation of the curriculum into narrow departments.

As President McArthur puts it, "Liberal education . . . begins in wonder and aims at wisdom. . . . In keeping with the immeasurable value of its end, and the discouraging remoteness of that end, it does not disdain the study of those humbler disciplines that are the first steps on a long road. Thus it begins with the liberal arts, proceeds to the particular philosophical disciplines, and terminates in wisdom."

Dr. McArthur is a professor of philosophy, Scholastic variety. For my taste, the curriculum of this new college is more abstract than I might wish it to be : not enough of history and humane letters, rather a surfeit of metaphysics. For all that, Thomas Aquinas College is the most close-knit community of scholars—senior and junior—in this country, and therefore a stimulating, cordial, cheerful place to be. Aquinas College knows freedom under dogmas, which is no paradox. It is a circle of friends, everyone knowing his companions, all bent upon the objects of wisdom and virtue, all sharing a common faith. And it is a highly intellectual community, in the better sense of "intellectual": the Thomas Aquinas tutors could talk rings around the sentimental liberals or the carping radicals on the faculty of Behemoth State U.

In the tiled hacienda-house at Calabasas, one grasps what the early medieval colleges were like—thirsty for the truth, joined in charity and a common quest. Eight or ten tutors and other members of the staff, some pleasant buildings of yesteryear, very little money, a fair number of books, a common dining-hall, inquiring intellects, good consciences: these are all that a college requires for success, and a tolerable university is not much more than a collection of colleges, with certain facilities added. Harvard, and William and Mary, and Yale, and King's College, and the College of New Jersey, must have been very like this in colonial times; indeed, the shape of such things still is visible at William and Mary. The fear of God, which might end in the love of God, was a moving force at those little colonial colleges. So it is now at Thomas Aquinas College. Both the fear and the love of God were quite lacking from my own undergraduate schooling.

Other sound curricula for vigorous Christian colleges are possible, of course. Another Catholic college opened its doors in the autumn of 1977: Cardinal Newman College, in St. Louis. This new college is an endeavor to renew in the American consciousness the Christian humanism of Newman. It is not a seminary, and it is not a trade-school. Newman College's fundamental approach, by contrast with that of Aquinas College, is the historical method. The core curriculum emphasizes the history of culture. All freshmen study the classical and Hebraic age in their first semester, the Hellenistic age in their second semester. All sophomores study early Christianity in their first semester, the Gothic age in their second semester. All juniors study Renaissance and Reformation in their first semester, and the early modern world in their second. All seniors study the modern world in their first semester, the contemporary world in their second.

Both these colleges seem radically innovating, because they draw upon traditions of learning which twentieth-century America had forgotten. One thinks of a passage in George Santayana's little essay "Americanism":

"Modern civilization has an immense momentum, not only physically irresistible but morally and socially dominant in the press, politics, and literature of the liberal classes; yet the voice of a dispossessed and forlorn orthodoxy, prophesying evil, cannot be silenced, and what renders that voice the more disquieting is that it can no longer be understood. When the prophets or apologists of the modern world attempt to refute those vaticinations, they altogether miss fire, because of their incapacity to conceive what they attack; and even in the exposition of their own case they are terribly confused and divided. It is seldom indeed that their conscience or their thoughts have passed over entirely to the side of their action."

At Behemoth U. and Brummagem U., the voices of Thomas Aquinas College and Cardinal Newman College cannot be understood, and therefore are somewhat frightening, when heard at all. Yet I suspect that by the end of this century, despite all the troubles of Christian colleges, the part of the mass-campus in the conversation of mankind will have diminished, and the part of Aquinas and Newman will have increased. The Christian college can speak of things transcendent, but the state university cannot; and in times of prolonged tribulation, humankind once more seeks beyond the senses.

I wish I could parallel the descriptions of the new Aquinas and Newman colleges with accounts of strong new Protestant colleges. Yet *new* Protestant colleges with intellectual power worth remarking have not arisen recently, so far as I am aware. There remain intellectually vigorous Protestant colleges—Gordon College, in Massachusetts, is one of my favorites—some of which continue to subscribe to the Apostles' Creed, and we should be badly off if they should disappear. Many Protestant denominations now do little to keep alive the colleges which earlier members of their church founded; Protestants, for a variety of reasons, often are more easily absorbed into the secular universities and colleges than are Catholics. By the end of this century, conceivably, the only independent colleges with church-connections remaining may be Catholic colleges, or those few Catholic colleges, like Thomas Aquinas College, which give only to God the things that are God's.

In Canada, with no restrictions upon their religious doctrines, practices, and symbols, church-related colleges form constituent colleges of provincial universities—St. Michael's at the University of Toronto, for instance, and the College of St. Thomas More at the University of Saskatchewan, and parallel Protestant colleges. Here in the United States, for all our praise of religious toleration, no state university permits such an association. The effect of public policies, whether or not intentional, may be to extinguish all church colleges, eventually, and to confer monopoly of higher education upon an arrogant secularism.

A principal trouble with the state university is that it cannot clearly define the objects of the higher learning, except in a utilitarian fashion; while a university or college founded upon religious doctrines can define those objects, and develop standards from them. I discovered this truth late, but now I know that it bears upon the whole problem of educational decadence.

Are these examples of independent study through tutors and of tiny Christian colleges all that I have to offer by way of alternatives to Behemoth State University's misconceptions and maleducation? Can I possibly believe that Behemoth silently will steal away, and that these innovative reactions will occupy Behemoth's place?

No, I do not believe that. There will be large changes at Behemoth U. and Brummagem U. before the end of this century, but those institutions will not evaporate. What I have been suggesting in this chapter is not a total supplanting of the present educational establishment, but rather some ways in which the minority of people seriously interested in obtaining a genuine higher education may find what they seek. It may be that sham schooling will continue to be supplied, at vast public expense and considerable personal and social damage, through the decadent establishment we know. If so, still it will be necessary that some people acquire a real education; and such alternatives as I have described would help to provide for that. Also the intellectual successes of such innovative reactions gradually may work, by force of example, upon Behemoth U. and Brummagem U.—acting as yeast to give us some edible bread.

Colophon: Augustan Learning?

T HE AMERICAN PUBLIC, by and large, has forgotten—or else never knew—that the the ends of education are wisdom and virtue. The average American has looked upon education as a means to material ends: the way of practical success, social advancement and general jollity. Although these may be desirable aspirations, they are not the true objects of the higher learning. They may be achieved through *training* (as distinguished from *education*), through personal endeavor of a kind not scholastic, and through a state of mind like that of Democritus, the laughing philosopher. But these goals are not the primary concerns of real colleges and universities.

The Americans, Tocqueville says, tend to neglect the general for the particular: that is, to shy away from theory. A pragmatic attitude dominated the United States before the term 'pragmatism" was coined among us. When a people achieve great power and corresponding responsibilities, nevertheless, there occurs urgent need for reference to first principles. That time is upon us. No longer do all Americans take for a sign of health the impulse for compelling young people to "adjust" to modern society, without reflection. If the time is out of joint, conformity to vulgar errors is sin and shame.

Any society depends for the mere mechanics of its functioning, as for much else, upon the maintenance of a high level of imagination and integrity among the people who make decisions, small or great. And any society depends for the foundation and scaffolding of its intellectual life, as for much else, upon the accumulated wisdom of our intellectual and moral patrimony. The decay of the higher learning among us has diminished that imagination and our understanding of that patrimony.

Perhaps a grand act of will—or rather, a series of such acts, preceded by serious reflection on the part of many of us—may yet redeem higher education in this country. Some people suggest that we may have to abandon established "Education", as a kind of ideological infatuation or mass-production business offering next to nothing for mind and conscience. Let the usurpers have it, these critics say. The awakening of imagination, by the discipline of the intellect, may have to be undertaken by new independent associations, in defiance of the educationist establishment.

That may be so; yet possibly there remains to us hope for the reformation of college and university. Decadence is not inevitable, so long as a tolerable number of men and women retain the elements of reason and the will to survive. Has the higher education in America been a democratic triumph or an egalitarian disaster? Neither, as yet—although in recent decades we have been sliding toward the latter consummation. If the choice had to be made, Eliot wrote once, it would be better to educate well comparatively few people than to school everybody shoddily; for in the former circumstance, at least we should possess some competent leadership. An egalitarian disaster has not yet occurred in this country only because in fact we have not yet wholly abandoned the older understanding of education as an intellectual means to an ethical end. No democracy can endure if it rests upon intellectual apathy and indifference.

We have succeeded in sending a great many people to college and university; we have not succeeded in educating most of them. We have fallen into grave error by attempting to convert college and university into cauldrons for brewing equality of condition. We have not developed so effective a system of popular instruction as Switzerland has, nor yet so admirable a system of higher education as Britain used to have. The typical product of our colleges and universities is mediocre in mind and spirit—no triumph, as yet no disaster.

But the times demand more than mediocrity. Our failure to quicken fallow minds accounts for many of our national difficulties, now formidable. Our public men tend to lack moral imagination and strength of will; our cities turn ugly and violent because vision and courage are lacking. Mediocrity in a pattern of education may not be ruinous in itself, and yet it may contribute gradually to private and public decadence. Mediocre appeals for excellence will not suffice, in the absence of sincere and vigorous educational reform.

Despite our prodigious expenditure of energy and money upon schooling, we have accomplished little toward clearing the way for the human potential in America; nay, we have obstructed that way in our higher learning. In this argument I am reinforced by W. T. Couch's serious book *The Human Potential* (Duke University Press, 1974)—a study ignored by most of the book-review media. Couch describes our present precarious—and complacent—state:

"There is a functional relation between universities and the societies in which they exist that neither the societies nor the universities can safely ignore. Once the great institutions of society begin making caricatures of their functions, or even give the public the impression that in crucial ways they are failing, they and their society are in grave danger. . . . The time has come in human history when the cultivation of the human potential in ways that serve both the best interests of the individual and the general welfare is necessary if the level of human life is to be raised rather than lowered. There is no possibility that the present level will cease to move; and it can go down as well as up."

Amen to that. W. T. Couch would endeavor to improve general education in the United States through "new institutions": first, a special independent institute for general education in a free society; second, a new encyclopedia of ordered and integrated knowledge, capable of being a real instrument for the dissemination of learning. (The institute, among other endeavors, would develop the encyclopedia—which might become as influential as the eighteenth-century French Encyclopedia, though by no means framed on identical intellectual principles.)

Short of the new institutions which Couch outlines—and as yet nobody has done anything to bring them into existence—we must make what we can of present establishments. Who at Behemoth State University aspires to any such abstract ends as wisdom and virtue? Yet if those with power in the educational establishment remain unconcerned for wisdom and virtue, the ethos of sociability and material aggrandizement must evaporate, perhaps quite swiftly—leaving a vacuum to be filled, conceivably, by force and a master.

Livy, a great historian in a decadent time, once was much read in America. "Of late years," Livy wrote of the perishing Roman Republic, "wealth has made us greedy, and self-indulgence has brought us, through every form of sensual excess, to be—if I may put it so—in love with death, both individual and collective."

Close parallels may be drawn with our age, and sometimes the death-wish seems to be operating in the American higher education. Yet even as Livy wrote that sentence, the Augustan age of renewal was taking form about him, and would carry on the civilizing mission of Rome for some centuries.

So it may come to pass with us in America. From causes in part explicable, in part mysterious, sometimes civilizations are reinvigorated. We Americans possess the resources for such a fullness of the higher learning as bloomed in the age of Augustus, and for more than that. Either we will become Augustans in the dawning age, I suspect, or we will take the road to Avernus.

It may be that Americans are not addressed to vanity, but instead are meant to strive imaginatively toward the human potential. If, pulling down our vanity, we are to make ourselves Augustans—why, an urgent necessity, not to be denied, is the recovery of the higher learning.

Index